RAND

INTERNET ADDICTION

INTERNET ADDICTION

A Handbook and Guide to Evaluation and Treatment

Edited by
Kimberly S. Young
Cristiano Nabuco de Abreu

WILEY

John Wiley & Sons, Inc.

Library of Congress Cataloging-in-Publication Data:

Internet addiction: a handbook and guide to evaluation and treatment / edited by
  Kimberly S. Young and Cristiano Nabuco de Abreu.
      p. ; cm.
    Includes bibliographical references and index. ISBN 978-0-470-55116-5 (cloth : alk. paper);
  ISBN 978-0-470-89224-4 (ebk); ISBN 978-0-470-89225-1 (ebk); 978-0-470-89226-8 (ebk)
    1. Internet addiction.   2. Internet addiction–Treatment.   I. Young, Kimberly S.
  II. Abreu, Cristiano Nabuco de.
    [DNLM: 1. Behavior, Addictive–psychology. 2. Internet–utilization.
  3. Behavior, Addictive–diagnosis. 4. Behavior, Addictive–therapy. WM 176 I615 2010]
  RC569.5.I54I53 2010
  616.85′84–dc22   2010018071

Contents

PART II PSYCHOTHERAPY, TREATMENT, AND PREVENTION

Foreword

ELIAS ABOUJAOUDE, MD
*Director, Impulse Control Disorders Clinic, Stanford University
School of Medicine*

T HE INTERNET has exploded to become a daily part of our lives. For the majority of individuals, the Internet represents an incredible information tool and unquestionable opportunity for social connectedness, self-education, economic betterment, and freedom from shyness and paralyzing inhibitions. For them, the Internet enhances their well-being and quality of life. For others, however, it can lead to a state that appears to meet the *DSM* definition of a mental disorder described as "a clinically significant behavioral or psychological syndrome associated with present distress or with a significantly increased risk of suffering death, pain, disability, or an important loss of freedom" (American Psychiatric Association, 2000).

Dr. Kimberly Young, co-editor of this volume, was the first to bring clinical attention to this issue when she published a 1996 case report of problematic Internet use (Young, 1996). Her patient was a non–technologically oriented 43-year-old homemaker with a content home life and no prior addiction or psychiatric history, who within three months of discovering chat rooms was spending up to 60 hours per week online. The patient reported feeling excited in front of the computer and dysphoric and irritable when she would log off. She described having an addiction to the medium like one would to alcohol.

Since that report, a sizable and informative body of data originating in the East and West has accumulated over the past decade. Taken as a whole, the data tell a cautionary tale of the Internet's real potential to cause psychological harm. Research studies have documented a variety of subtypes of Internet-related problems such as online sexual compulsivity, Internet gambling, MySpace addiction, and video game addiction, which the American Medical Association estimates five million children suffer from and once considered calling gaming overuse an addiction in its revised diagnostic manual.

The problem of Internet addiction is still relatively new, and while research has documented what has become a growing health care problem, no current books pull this body of literature together. *Internet Addiction: A Handbook and Guide to Evaluation and Treatment* offers the first empirically based book to address this emergent field. This book summarizes the research conducted to date and proposes clinical, societal, and public health interventions that target the general population as well as adolescents—a group deemed at higher risk for developing the problems discussed. This book will enable practitioners to learn about the contemporary and current clinical implications, assessment methods, and treatment approaches in screening and working with clients who suffer from this new addictive disorder.

For a medium that has so radically and irreversibly changed the way we conduct our lives, the Internet's effects on our psychological health remain understudied, talked about more by sensationalism-driven reporters than practicing clinicians or expert researchers. And even as our understanding of basic Internet psychology lags, symptoms are changing as the technology evolves—from traditional browsers to smart phones that combine Internet capability with talking, texting, and video games. Simply stating that similar fears have been raised with every new technology misses the point: The immersive and interactive qualities of the virtual medium, combined with its sheer penetration into every aspect of life, make it different from all media forms that preceded it, and more prone to overuse or misuse. As our dependency on technology grows, this book adds to the clinical legitimacy and raises public and professional awareness of the problem that will enable future research in this evolving field to be conducted. This field is rapidly developing with new areas of scientific exploration, which is why research-driven books that educate us about the problems inherent in the virtual world are such a necessity.

REFERENCES

American Psychiatric Association. (2000). *Diagnostic and statistical manual of mental disorders* (4th ed., text rev.). Washington, DC: Author.

Young, K. S. (1996). Addictive use of the Internet: A case that breaks the stereotype. Psychology of computer use: XL. *Psychological Reports, 79,* 899–902.

Acknowledgments

S OME SAY that the knowledge we'll accumulate over the next five years will be greater than that collected throughout the history of mankind up until now. Surely a little more than a decade ago we would doubt this statement—imagining it was the result of exaggeration and faulty perspective. We were still using fax machines and watching movies on videocassette tapes, and the computer still was an object of both wonder and suspicion. But if we consider that the cell phones we carry reflect more sophisticated technology than the one in the Apollo 12 spacecraft, it may be that the outrageous-sounding prediction was correct.

We are at the epicenter of a major change in the history of science. We can be eyewitnesses to a great revolution in the field of knowledge and human behavior. There are many implications stemming from these changes, among them the consequences of this technology's effects on everyday life. Reliance on the Internet has emerged as one of the issues challenging society, families, clinicians, and researchers. This book can shed some light on this subject, even though very little is yet known about the long-term implications of this new communication system. We hope this book helps professionals who work to relieve the suffering that the improper use of the Internet has brought to millions of people. This book is dedicated to those sufferers.

We would also like to thank Patricia Rossi and Fiona Brown at John Wiley & Sons and our agent, Carol Mann at the Carol Mann Literary Agency. They supported us and believed in our project.

KIMBERLY S. YOUNG, PhD
CRISTIANO NABUCO DE ABREU, PhD

About the Editors

D R. KIMBERLY S. YOUNG is an internationally known expert on Internet addiction and online behavior. Founded in 1995, she serves as the clinical director of the Center for Internet Addiction Recovery and travels nationally conducting seminars on the impact of the Internet. She is the author of *Caught in the Net*, the first book to address Internet addiction, translated in six languages, *Tangled in the Web* and her most recent, *Breaking Free of the Web: Catholics and Internet addiction*. She is a professor at St. Bonaventure University and has published over 40 articles on the impact of online abuse.

Her work has been featured in *The New York Times*, *The London Times*, *USA Today*, *Newsweek*, *Time*, *CBS News*, *Fox News*, *Good Morning America*, and ABC's *World News Tonight*. She has been an invited lecturer at dozens of universities and conferences including the European Union of Health and Medicine in Norway and the First International Congress on Internet Addiction in Zurich. She serves on theeditorial board of CyberPsychology & Behavior and the International Journal of Cyber Crime and Criminal Justice. In 2001 and 2004, she received the Psychology in the Media Award from the Pennsylvania Psychological Association and in 2000 she received the Alumni Ambassador of the Year Award for Outstanding Achievement from Indiana University at Pennsylvania.

D R. CRISTIANO NABUCO DE ABREU is a psychologist who has a PhD in Clinical Psychology from the University of Minho (UM) in Portugal with a Postdoctoral Fellow in the Department of Psychiatry, Hospital das Clinicas, Faculty of Medicine, University of São Paulo (USP). He has experience in Cognitive Therapy and Internet addiction, and coordinates the Internet Addicts Program of the Impulse Disorders Clinic (AMITI) of the Institute of Psychiatry, Faculty of Medicine, University of São Paulo. With a pioneering work method in Brazil and Latin America, the unit has offered therapy sessions and counseling to adults, adolescents, and their family members since 2005. Dr. Nabuco de Abreu has also published numerous articles in Portuguese for various journals.

He is the ex-president of the Brazilian Society of Cognitive Therapies (SBTC) and is a member of the Advisory Board of the Society for Constructivism in Human Science (USA). He is the author of numerous scientific articles and seven books on Mental Health, Psychotherapy, and Psychology, including, *Cognitive Therapy and Cognitive Behavior Therapy*, *Psychiatric Disorders: Diagnostic and Interview for Health Professionals*, and *Clinical Handbook for Impulse Control Disorders*, among others.

List of Contributors

Keith W. Beard
Department of Psychology
Associate Professor
Marshall University
Huntington, West Virginia

Ed Betzelberger
Illinois Institute for Addiction
  Recovery
Proctor Hospital
Illinois

Libby Bier
Illinois Institute for Addiction
  Recovery
Proctor Hospital
Illinois

Lukas Blinka
Institute for Research
  on Children
Youth and Family
Faculty of Social Studies
Masaryk University
Czech Republic

Tonya Camacho
Illinois Institute for Addiction
  Recovery
Proctor Hospital
Illinois

Scott E. Caplan
Department of Communication
University of Delaware
Newark, Delaware

Shannon Chrismore
Illinois Institute for Addiction
  Recovery
Proctor Hospital
Illinois

David L. Delmonico
Department of Counseling
Psychology & Special Education
Associate Professor
Duquesne University
Pittsburgh, Pennsylvania

Franz Eidenbenz
Professional Psychologist for
  Psychotherapy
Director of the Escape Center
Zurich, Switzerland

Dora Sampaio Góes
Impulse Disorders Outpatient
  Unit
University of São Paulo
Institute of Psychiatry
Brazil

David Greenfield
The Center for Internet and
  Technology Addiction
West Hartford, Connecticut

Elizabeth J. Griffin
Internet Behavior Consulting
Minneapolis, Minnesota

Mark Griffiths
Professor of Gambling Studies
International Gaming Research
  Unit
Nottingham Trent University
UK

Andrew C. High
Department of Communication
  Arts & Sciences
The Pennsylvania State University
University Park, Pennsylvania

Jung-Hye Kwon
Department of Psychology
Korea University
Seoul, Korea

Robert LaRose
Department of Telecommunications
  Information Studies, and Media
Michigan State University
East Lansing, Michigan

David Smahel
Institute for Research on Children
  Youth and Family
Faculty of Social Studies
Masaryk University
Czech Republic

Monica T. Whitty
Reader in Psychology
Nottingham Trent University
UK

Li Ying
Institute of Chinese Youth
  Association for Internet
  Development
China

Xiao Dong Yue
Department of Applied Social
  Studies
City University of Hong Kong
Hong Kong

Introduction

O VER THE past decade, the concept of Internet addiction has grown in terms of its acceptance as a legitimate clinical disorder often requiring treatment (Young, 2007). Hospitals and clinics have emerged with outpatient treatment services for Internet addiction, addiction rehabilitation centers have admitted new cases of Internet addicts, and college campuses have started support groups to help students who are addicted. Most recently, the American Psychiatric Association has decided to include the diagnosis of Internet addiction in the Appendix in the *DSM-V* as further studies are conducted.

Internet Addiction: A Handbook and Guide to Evaluation and Treatment focuses on the current research in the field intended for academic and clinical audiences. The first study on Internet addiction occurred in 1996 by Dr. Kimberly Young when she presented her findings on 600 subjects who met a modified version of the *DSM* criteria for pathological gambling. The paper, "Internet Addiction: The Emergence of a New Disorder," was presented at the American Psychological Association's annual conference held in Toronto. While controversial at first, with academics debating the existence of the problem, since then empirical research on Internet addiction has grown substantially.

New studies across cultures and across academic disciplines have focused on understanding this new clinical and social phenomenon. New studies have furthered our understanding of Internet behavior and how adolescents and adults have come to use this new technology. New clinical studies have attempted to understand diagnosis, psychosocial risk factors, symptom management, and treatment of this new disorder. Internet addiction has been identified as a national problem not only in the United States but also in countries such as China, South Korea, and Taiwan, and government intervention has grown to battle Internet addiction and what has become a serious public health concern.

It is difficult to determine how widespread the problem is. One national study that originated from a team at the Impulse Control Disorders Clinic at Stanford University School of Medicine estimated that one in eight Americans suffers from at least one indicator of problematic Internet use. In other countries such as China, South Korea, and Taiwan, media reports suggest that Internet addiction has reached epidemic proportions.

During the late 1990s, research on Internet addiction grew. Health care professionals started seeing cases of people who suffered from Internet-related clinical problems. Pioneer treatment centers specializing in Internet addiction recovery emerged at McLean Hospital in the Boston area (a Harvard Medical School affiliate) and at the Illinois Institute for Addiction Recovery at Proctor Hospital in Peoria, Illinois. Inpatient addiction rehabilitation centers such as the Betty Ford Clinic, Sierra Tucson, and The Meadows started to include Internet-related compulsivity as one of the subspecialties they treated. Globally, the first inpatient treatment center opened in Beijing, China, in 2006, and today, it is estimated that South Korea has more than 140 Internet addiction treatment recovery centers.

Research has also studied subtypes of Internet-related problems such as online sexual compulsivity, Internet gambling, MySpace addiction, and video game addiction. Video game addiction had become such a concern that in 2008 the American Medical Association estimated that five million children suffered from an addiction to games and considered calling gaming overuse an addiction in its revised diagnostic manual.

While much attention has been paid to Internet addiction in the academic and clinical fields, developing universal standards of care and assessment have been difficult because the field is culturally diverse and terminology in the academic literature has varied from Internet addiction to problematic Internet use, pathological Internet use, and pathological computer use, in the same way that different inventories are used for their assessment. With our reliance on technology, trying to define Internet addiction is even more difficult as we blur the boundaries between needing and wanting to use the Internet. We need to use the technology, so the question is: When is it an addiction?

The problem of Internet addiction is relatively new, and while research has documented what has become a growing health care problem, scientific understanding of the problem is evolving. *Internet Addiction: A Handbook and Guide to Evaluation and Treatment* is the first comprehensive compilation of the current research to address this emergent field. The book is inclusive of both online and computer-related compulsions, making it relevant to a wide audience. Scholars searching for specific information on the latest research on Internet addiction and current trends in the field will find this book useful. Practitioners from a variety of fields, including social work, addiction counseling, psychology, psychiatry, and nursing in search of empirically based assessment and treatment methods will also find this book useful regarding evidence-based approaches.

The first part of the book provides a theoretical framework to understand how to define and conceptualize compulsive use of the Internet from a clinical perspective. The book includes various theoretical models from the psychiatric, psychological, communication, and sociological fields. Leading researchers from various countries explore the global and cultural impact of Internet addiction and combine these fields to conceptualize diagnosis of

Internet addiction and its prevalence. To further help therapists diagnose Internet addiction, this book examines the epidemiology and subtypes of Internet addiction such as online pornography, Internet gambling, and online games. The book also examines the impact of Internet use on children, individuals, and families, as well as risk factors that have been associated with the development of the disorder.

The second part of the book examines assessment and treatment of Internet addiction. As computers are relied upon with great frequency, health care professionals may be confronted with new cases of problem computer users. Yet, given the popularity of computer use, detecting the disorder may be difficult. Signs of a problem may easily be masked by legitimate use of the Internet, and clinicians may overlook signs because it is still a relatively new condition. Therefore, the book outlines assessment strategies to screen for and evaluate the presence of addictive use of the Internet, including clinical interview questions to ask, and describes the Internet Addiction Test, the first psychometrically validated measure of problematic Internet use (Widyanto & McMurren, 2004). Also, utilizing treatment outcome data, the book explores evidenced-based treatment approaches from a variety of clinical perspectives, including child and adult interventions, group therapy, 12-step recovery, and inpatient rehabilitation.

Finally, the implications of including the diagnosis of Internet addiction in the *DSM-V* are many. Its inclusion in the Appendix of the *DSM-V* would raise clinical legitimacy of the disorder to a higher level and would allow further scientific understanding of the nature of Internet addiction to be studied. The concluding chapter explores these implications and how greater public awareness and recognition of Internet addiction would bring new opportunities for future research funding on treatment and training. The concluding chapter also explores further areas for research such as long-term treatment outcomes and systematic comparisons of various treatment modalities to determine their therapeutic efficacy. We hope as the field continues to grow and evolve that this book opens an important dialogue for practitioners and scholars alike. We hope this book will enable practitioners to learn about the contemporary and current treatment approaches in screening and working with clients who suffer from this condition. We also hope this book serves as a resource guidebook for clinics, hospitals, inpatient rehabilitation centers, and outpatient treatment settings. Last, we hope it offers academics pursuing further research in the area of Internet addiction and online behavior a compendium of resources relevant to the contemporary literature in the field.

REFERENCES

Widyanto, L., & McMurren, M. (2004). The psychometric properties of the Internet Addiction Test. *CyberPsychology & Behavior, 7*(4),445-453.

Young, K. S. (2007). Cognitive-behavioral therapy with Internet addicts: Treatment outcomes and implications. *CyberPsychology & Behavior, 10*(5), 671–679.

PART I

Understanding Internet Behavior and Addiction

CHAPTER 1

Prevalence Estimates and Etiologic Models of Internet Addiction

KIMBERLY S. YOUNG, XIAO DONG YUE, and LI YING

INTERNET ADDICTION was first researched in 1996, and findings were presented at the American Psychological Association. The study reviewed over 600 cases of heavy Internet users who exhibited clinical signs of addiction as measured through an adapted version of the *DSM-IV* criteria for pathological gambling (Young, 1996). Since then, subsequent studies over the past decade have examined various aspects of the disorder. Early studies attempted to define Internet addiction and examined behavior patterns that differentiated compulsive from normal Internet usage. More recent studies examined the prevalence of Internet addiction and investigated the etiologic factors or causes associated with the disorder. Much of this examined the impact of computer-mediated communication on the way people will adapt to interactive features of the Internet, and initial studies from the United States spread into the United Kingdom and countries such as Russia, China, and Taiwan. As the problem has become more widespread, little is still understood as to the reasons why people become addicted to the Internet. This chapter presents the data associated with prevalence of Internet addiction, as available in various countries, to gather a sense of the scope of the problem. The chapter also provides the theoretical frameworks to understand the etiologic models or causal factors associated with the development of Internet addiction. From the academic perspective, this chapter helps identify future areas of research as new studies in the field continue to emerge. From the mental health perspective, the chapter will assist clinicians in developing more empirically sound methods to assess and potentially treat Internet-addicted clients.

PREVALENCE ACROSS CULTURES

Early research has investigated the prevalence of addictive use of the Internet. In one of the first studies, Greenfield (1999) partnered with ABCNews.com to survey Internet users. From 17,000 responses, the study estimated that 6% of Internet users fit the profile of Internet addiction. While this study relied on self-reported data, it did include a cross-sectional population and was considered one of the largest psychological surveys conducted solely on the Internet. Another well-known U.S. study, conducted by a team of researchers at Stanford University Medical Center, found that one in eight Americans suffered from one or more signs of Internet addiction (Aboujaoude, Koran, Gamel, Large, & Serpe, 2006).

Studies among college populations showed slightly higher prevalence rates than found in the general population of Internet users. Using various versions of the *DSM*-based criteria, at the University of Texas, Scherer (1997) found 13% of 531 campus students surveyed exhibited signs of Internet dependency. Morahan-Martin and Schumacher (1999) found that 14% of students at Bryant College in Rhode Island met the criteria, and Yang (2001) estimated that 10% of students met the criteria at the University of Taiwan. Conclusions suggested that college students had easier access to the Internet and it was more encouraged, contributing to the higher prevalence of addictive use on campuses.

Among adolescents, a study in Finland investigated the prevalence of Internet addiction among 12- to 18-year-olds. Findings suggested that 4.7% among girls met the definition of Internet addiction as assessed by Young's Internet Addiction Diagnostic Questionnaire (1998), and of boys 4.6% met the definition. Studies related to the prevalence of specific types of Internet abuse also emerged by the late 1990s. Studies on online sexual activities were the most prevalent, and estimates based on survey data showed that 9% of users fit signs of addiction related to sexually explicit material on the Internet (Cooper, 2002).

In 2001, Bai, Lin, and Chen reported the results of a survey to determine the prevalence of Internet addiction disorder among visitors to a virtual mental health clinic where 100 volunteer mental health professionals provide, at no charge, online answers to visitors' questions about mental problems. During the study period all visitors to the virtual clinic completed Young's eight-item Internet Addiction Diagnostic Questionnaire. Among the 251 clients, 38 clients or 15% met criteria for Internet addiction disorder. Clients who met the criteria did not differ significantly from those who did not in age, gender, education, marital status, occupation, or impending diagnosis. However, the rate of comorbid substance use disorder was significantly higher among clients who met the criteria for Internet addiction disorder than among those who did not.

In 2003, Whang, Lee, and Chang investigated the prevalence of Internet overuse in Korea. They used a modified version of Young's Internet Addiction

Scale, and 13,588 users (7,878 males, 5,710 females), out of 20 million from a major portal site in Korea, participated in this study. Among the sample, 3.5% had been diagnosed as Internet addicts (IAs), while 18.4% of them were classified as possible Internet addicts (PAs).

A study, I-Cube 2006, conducted by the Internet & Mobile Association of India, covering 65,000 individuals by household survey in 26 cities in India, says that about 38% of Internet users in that country have shown signs of heavy usage (about 8.2 hours per week). Young males, especially college students, form the major chunk of Internet user base. Indians go online for a number of activities, including e-mail and instant messaging (98%), job search (51%), banking (32%), bill payment (18%), stock trading (15%), and matrimonial search (15%).

There are limited numbers of studies estimating how common the issue of Internet addiction is in India. Kanwal Nalwa, PhD, and Archana Preet Anand, PhD, of the department of psychology, Punjabi University in India, conducted a study for preliminary investigation of the extent of Internet addiction in schoolchildren 16 to 18 years old in India (Nalwa & Anand, 2003). They identified two groups, dependents and nondependents. Dependents were found to delay other work to spend time online, lose sleep due to late-night logons, and feel life would be boring without the Internet. Not surprisingly, dependents spent more time online and scored higher on loneliness measures than the nondependents.

The understanding that Internet use can be a disorder is still in its initial stages in India. Since 2007, certain educational institutions, such as the Indian Institutes of Technology (IITs), a group of leading engineering universities, have been restricting campus Internet use during night hours because of reports of some suicides being linked to the presumed antisocial behavior that excessive Internet use promotes (Swaminath, 2008).

According to the most recent Statistical Report on Internet Addictions in China (Cui, Zhao, Wu, & Xu, 2006) by the China Youth Association for Internet Development, adolescent Internet addicts in China make up about 9.72% to 11.06% of the total number worldwide of adolescent Internet users. Specifically, of 162 million Internet users in China, those users who are younger than 24 years old occupy approximately 63% of the total number of Internet users, which amounts to about 100 million. Of these 100 million young users, about 9.72% to 11.06% are serious addicts, amounting to about 10 million young people.

Prevalence statistics vary widely across cultures and societies. In part, researchers are utilizing various instruments to define Internet addiction, making it harder to have consistency across studies. Further, these studies are confounded by various methodologies, some using online survey data posted to the World Wide Web using cross sections of populations, and some only targeting a specific campus or university. Generally, we can say that it seems that the prevalence of Internet addiction is the lowest among adolescents, with ranges of 4.6 to 4.7%. That number goes up among the general population of Internet users, with ranges of 6 to 15% of the general population fitting the signs of addiction; and it goes up to 13 to 18.4% among college students, who appear to be the most at risk. These numbers estimate the scope of the problem and suggest that a significant proportion of online users may suffer one or more signs of Internet addiction.

ETIOLOGIC FACTORS

Addictions are defined as the habitual compulsion to engage in a certain activity or utilize a substance, notwithstanding the devastating consequences on the individual's physical, social, spiritual, mental, and financial well-being. Instead of addressing life's obstacles, tackling daily stress, and/or confronting past or present trauma, the addict responds maladaptively by resorting to a pseudo coping mechanism. Typically, addiction manifests both psychological and physical characteristics. Physical dependence occurs when an individual's body develops a dependence on a certain substance and experiences withdrawal symptoms upon discontinuing the consumption, such as drugs or alcohol. While initially an addictive substance induces pleasure to the user, his or her continued consumption is driven more by a need to eliminate the anxiety brought about by its absence, thus leading the individual to compulsive behavior. Psychological dependency becomes evident when the addict experiences withdrawal symptoms such as depression, cravings, insomnia, and irritability. Both behavioral addiction and substance addiction usually give rise to psychological dependence. The following outlines various models proposed to explain Internet addiction related to the psychological dependency. As a behavioral addiction, the focus on psychological issues that increase consumption of the Internet is helpful to aid in clinical understanding of why people overuse.

COGNITIVE-BEHAVIORAL MODEL

Caplan (2002) viewed technological addictions as a subset of behavioral addictions; Internet addiction featured the core components of addiction (i.e., salience, mood modification, tolerance, withdrawal, conflict, and relapse). From this perspective, Internet addicts displayed a salience for the activity, often experiencing cravings and feeling preoccupied with the Internet when offline. He also suggested that using the Internet as a way to escape troubling feelings, developing a tolerance for the Internet to achieve satisfaction, experiencing withdrawal when reducing Internet use, suffering from increased conflicts with others because of the activity, and relapsing back to the Internet were also signs of addiction. This model has been applied to behaviors such as sex, running, food consumption, and gambling (Peele, 1985; Vaillant, 1995) and is useful to examine pathological or addictive Internet use.

Davis (2001) introduced a cognitive-behavioral theory of pathological Internet use (PIU) that attempts to model the etiology, development, and outcomes associated with PIU. Davis characterizes PIU as more than a behavioral addiction; instead he conceptualizes PIU as a distinct pattern of Internet-related cognitions and behaviors that result in negative life outcomes. Davis proposes that there are two distinct forms of PIU: specific and generalized. Specific PIU involves overuse or abuse of content-specific functions of the Internet (e.g., gambling, stock trading, viewing pornography). Moreover, Davis argues that such stimuli-specific behavioral disorders would likely be manifested in some alternative way if the individual were unable to access the Internet. Generalized PIU is conceptualized as a multidimensional overuse of the Internet itself that results in negative personal and professional consequences. Symptoms of generalized PIU include maladaptive cognitions and behaviors related to Internet use that are not linked to any specific content. Rather, generalized PIU occurs when an individual develops problems due to the unique communication context of the Internet. In other words, the person is drawn to the experience of being online in and of itself, and demonstrates a preference for virtual, rather than face-to-face, interpersonal communication.

Within this context, researchers have suggested that moderated and controlled use of the Internet is most appropriate to treat Internet addiction (Greenfield, 2001; Orzack, 1999). Specifically, cognitive behavioral therapy (CBT) has been suggested as the preferred mode of therapy treatment for compulsive Internet use (Young, 2007). CBT is a familiar treatment based on the premise that thoughts determine feelings. In one study of 114 patients, CBT was used to teach patients to monitor their thoughts and identify those that trigger addictive feelings and actions while they learn new coping skills and ways to prevent a relapse. CBT required three months of treatment or approximately 12 weekly one-hour sessions. The early stage of therapy is behavioral, focusing on specific behaviors and situations where the impulse-control disorder causes the greatest difficulty. As therapy progresses, there is more of a focus on the cognitive assumptions and distortions that have developed and the effects of the compulsive behavior.

Specifically, research suggests that the focus of recovery should examine both computer behavior and noncomputer behavior (Hall & Parsons, 2001). Computer behavior deals with actual online usage with a primary goal of abstinence from problematic applications while retaining controlled use of the computer for legitimate purposes. For example, a lawyer addicted to Internet pornography would need to learn to abstain from adult web sites, while still being able to access the Internet to conduct legal research and to e-mail clients. Noncomputer behavior focuses on helping clients develop positive lifestyle changes for life without the Internet. Life activities that do not involve the computer, such as offline hobbies, social gatherings, and family activities, are encouraged. Similarly to food addiction, where recovery can be objectively measured through caloric intake and weight loss, online addicts can objectively measure success through maintaining abstinence from problematic online applications and increasing meaningful offline activities. Once a baseline has been established, behavioral therapy is used to relearn how to use the Internet to achieve specific outcomes, such as moderated online usage and more specifically abstinence from problematic online applications and controlled use for legitimate purposes. Behavior management for both computer usage and adaptive noncomputer behavior focuses on current online behavior.

From a cognitive perspective, addictive thinkers will for no logical reason feel apprehensive when anticipating disaster (Hall & Parsons, 2001). While addicts are not the only people who worry and anticipate negative happenings, they tend to do this more often than other people. Young (1998) first suggested that this type of catastrophic thinking might contribute to compulsive Internet use in providing a psychological escape mechanism to avoid real or perceived problems. Subsequent studies hypothesized that other maladaptive cognitions such as overgeneralizing or catastrophizing and negative core beliefs also contribute to compulsive use of the Internet (Caplan, 2002; Caplan & High, 2007; Davis, 2001; LaRose, Mastro, & Eastin, 2001). Those who suffer from negative thinking often suffer from low self-esteem and maintain pessimistic attitudes. They may be the ones drawn the most to the anonymous interactive capabilities of the Internet in order to overcome these perceived inadequacies. Early treatment outcome studies show that CBT can be used to address these negative thoughts to overcome their personal feelings of low esteem and worth (Young, 2007). The cognitive model helps to explain why Internet users develop a habit or compulsive use and how negative self-thoughts maintain patterns of compulsive behavior.

NEUROPSYCHOLOGICAL MODEL

Scholars from mainland China have paid increasing attention to the problem of Internet addiction in Chinese society. In its 2005 report, the China Youth Association for Network Development (CYAND) puts forward, for the first time, a standard to judge the Internet addiction as having one prerequisite and three conditions (CYAND, 2005). The prerequisite is that the Internet addiction must severely jeopardize a young person's social functioning and interpersonal communication. An individual would be classified as an Internet addict as long as he or she meets any one of the following three conditions: (1) one would feel that it is easier to achieve self-actualization online than in real life, (2) one would experience dysphoria or depression whenever access to the Internet is broken or ceases to function; (3) one would try to hide his or her true usage time from family members. Ying, director of the Institute of Psychological Development for the CYAND, has proposed a neuropsychological chain model to account for the Internet-addictive behavior (Tao, Ying, Yue & Hao, 2007) (see Figure 1.1 and Table 1.1).

When examining the primitive drive associated with addiction, much of research stems from brain behavior related to chemical dependency. The pharmacological activation of brain reward systems is largely responsible for producing a drug's potent addictive properties. Personality, social, and genetic

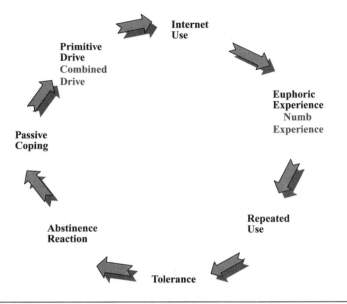

Figure 1.1   Neuropsychological chain model of Internet addiction

Table 1.1
Explanation of the Neuropsychological Link of Internet Addiction

Main Concept	Specific Explanation
Primitive drive	The instinct of an individual to pursue pleasure and avoid pain, which is representative of various motives and impulses to use the Internet.
Euphoric experience	The Internet activities stimulate the central nervous system of the individual, who will feel happy and satisfied. The feeling will drive the individual to continuously use the Internet and extend euphoria. Once addiction is formed, the euphoric experience will soon be transformed into a habit and numbness state.
Tolerance	Because of repeated use of the Internet, the sensory threshold of the individual increases; in order to achieve the same happy experience, the user must increase time and passion. High-level tolerance is the springboard for Internet addiction and the result of reinforcement of euphoric experience concerning the Internet.
Abstinence reaction	The physical and psychological syndromes happen once the individual stops or after decreased Internet use, mainly including dysphoria, insomnia, emotional instability, irritability, and so on.
Passive coping	Passive behaviors accommodating to the environment form once the individual is confronted with frustration or receives outside harmful effects, which include passive behaviors such as adverse event imputation, cognition falsification, and the formed suppression, escape, and aggression.
Avalanche effect	The avalanche effect includes passive experience consisting of tolerance and abstinence reaction, and combined drive consisting of individual passive coping styles on the basis of the primitive drive of the individual.

factors may also be important, but the drug's effects on the central nervous system (CNS) remain the primary determinants of drug addiction. Nonpharmacological factors are likely to be important in influencing initial drug use and in determining how rapidly an addiction develops. For some substances, nonpharmacological factors may interact with the drug's pharmacological action to produce compulsive substance use. In these cases, addictive behavior may involve use of substances that are generally not considered addictive.

Dopamine is one of a number of neurotransmitters found in the central nervous system. Dopamine has received special attention from psychopharmacologists because of its apparent role in the regulation of mood and affect and because of its role in motivation and reward processes. Although there are several dopamine systems in the brain, the mesolimbic dopamine system appears to be the most important for motivational processes. Some addictive drugs produce their potent effects on behavior by enhancing mesolimbic dopamine activity (Di Chiara, 2000). The neurochemical connection to behavioral addictions such as gambling or food have yet to be made, but early studies have suggested that neurochemical processes play a role in all addiction, whether to substances or to behaviors (Di Chiara, 2000).

The proposed model of brain reward circuitry in addiction involves the increase of dopamine when certain areas of the brain are stimulated. The brain has specialized pathways that mediate reward and motivation. Direct electrical stimulation of the medial forebrain bundle (MFB) produces intensely rewarding effects. Psychomotor stimulants and opiates can also activate this reward system by their pharmacological actions in the nucleus accumbens and ventral tegmental area, respectively. The ventral tegmental action of opiates probably involves an endogenous opioid peptide system (ENK), but the anatomical location of that system has not yet been identified. Natural rewards (e.g., food, sex) and other substances (e.g., caffeine, ethanol, nicotine) may also activate this brain reward system (Di Chiara, 2000).

As we discover new areas of neurochemical processes in addictive behavior, it is essential to understand the physical and psychological effects. Researchers have long associated addiction with changes in neurotransmitters in the brain, and some theorists have argued that all addiction, independent of type (sex, food, alcohol, the Internet), can be triggered by similar changes in the brain. To this end, new studies have been conducted on pharmacological treatments of Internet addiction. At Mount Sinai School of Medicine in New York, researchers tested the use of the antidepressant escitalopram (Lexapro, from Forest Pharmaceuticals) in 19 adult subjects who had impulsive-compulsive Internet usage disorder, defined as time-consuming and uncontrollable, or distressing Internet usage resulting in social, occupational, or financial difficulties (Dell'Osso et al., 2008). Study participants took escitalopram in an open-label phase for 10 weeks, and then those who responded were randomized in a double-blind, placebo-controlled nine-week phase to continue with this drug or switch to a placebo. During the open-label phase, addicts had a very healthy response to the drug; on average, the number of hours spent online went from 36 hours to 16 hours. While this study is one of the first, and further research in larger trials is needed to investigate drug efficacy for addressing Internet addiction, it is important to identify the impact of drug treatment with this disorder and other associated pharmacological treatments in compulsive disorders.

COMPENSATION THEORY

The Institute of Psychology of the Chinese Academy of Sciences proposed a "compensation theory" to account for the causes of young people's Internet addiction in China. Specifically, Tao (2005) argues that the "single assessment system" for academic excellence has led many young people to look for "spiritual compensation" from the online activities. In addition, by engaging in Internet activities, the young people also look for compensation for self-identity, self-esteem, and social networking. For the past 20 years, Chinese young people have used poetry, the guitar, and sports to express their needs and feelings, whereas now they tend to use electronic games and other Web-based tools.

Previous research has also examined the notion of adults as well as children using the Internet as a means to compensate or cope with deficits in self-esteem, identity, and relationships. Using the UCLA Loneliness Scale (Russell, Peplau, & Cutrona, 1980), one early study found higher levels of loneliness among students who were considered pathological or addicted users of the Internet (Morahan-Martin & Schumacher, 2003). In general, Internet addicts have difficulty forming intimate relationships with others and hide behind the anonymity of cyberspace to connect with others in a nonthreatening way. Online, a person can create a social network of new relationships. With routine visits to a particular group (i.e., a specific chat area, online game, or Facebook), a person can establish a high degree of familiarity with other group members, thus creating a sense of community. Like all communities, the cyberspace culture has its own set of values, standards, language, signs, and artifacts. Individual users adapt to the current norms of the group. Existing solely online, the group often disregards normal conventions about privacy (e.g., by posting personal messages to public bulletin boards or chat rooms); it exists in a parallel time and space and is kept alive only by users connecting with one another via the computer.

Once membership in a particular group has been established, Internet addicts rely on the conversation exchange for companionship, advice, understanding, and even romance. The ability to create a virtual community leaves the physical world behind to the degree that well-known, fixed, and visual people no longer exist, and anonymous online users form a meeting of the minds living in a purely text-based society. Through the exchange of online messages, users compensate for what they may lack in real life (Caplan & High, 2007). They may be able to use chat, instant messaging, or social networking to find psychological meaning and connection, quickly form intimate bonds, and feel emotionally close to others. The formation of such virtual arenas creates a group dynamic of social support to answer a deep and compelling need in people whose real lives are interpersonally impoverished and devoid of intimacy. Some life circumstances, such as being a homebound caretaker, disabled person, retired individual, or homemaker, can limit a person's access to others. In these cases, individuals are more likely to use the Internet as an alternative means to develop the social foundations that are lacking in their immediate environments. In other cases, those who feel socially awkward or who have difficulty developing healthy relationships in real life find that they are able to express themselves more freely and find the companionship and acceptance missing in their lives.

In the now-famous Home Net Study, Krant et al. (1997) also found that social isolation and depression were correlated with Internet usage. The researchers at Carnegie Mellon University conducted one of the few longitudinal studies on the psychological impact of Internet use. Researchers there randomly selected families with no prior computer experience and gave them computers and instructions on Internet use. After one to two years, increased use of the Internet was associated with decreased family communication and reduced size of the local social circle. The researchers' findings showed that even within small amounts of Internet use, participants experienced increased loneliness and depression. Increases in loneliness and decreases in social support were particularly pronounced for the youth. Researchers have found that the more Internet-addicted users were, the more likely they used the Internet to escape (Young & Rogers, 1997). When they got stressed out by work or were just depressed, Internet addicts showed a high tendency to access the Internet and reported higher degrees of loneliness, depressed mood, and compulsivity compared to the other groups. Depression has been linked to Internet overuse in general. It has not been shown whether depression causes the addiction or if being addicted causes depression, but studies have shown the two syndromes are highly correlated, reinforcing one other.

As researchers continue to understand the dynamics associated with Internet addiction, it is important for clinicians to understand how users may compensate for what is missing in their lives through their Internet use. Internet use can become highly reinforcing to overcome low self-esteem, social awkwardness, loneliness, and depression. Those who suffer from these problems may be more at risk and vulnerable to developing the disorder. Treatment models with this in mind need to examine other comorbid factors the client may be dealing with. That is, is the client using Facebook to fulfill missing social needs? Is the client using online relationships to make friends because of social phobia? Is the client using online games to feel powerful when suffering from low self-esteem? Is the client using the Internet to cope with clinical depression? Helping the client to understand how he or she uses the Internet to compensate for missing social or psychological needs will be a useful first step toward recovery.

SITUATIONAL FACTORS

Situational factors play a role in the development of Internet addiction. Individuals who feel overwhelmed or who experience personal problems or who experience life-changing events such as a recent divorce, relocation, or a death can absorb themselves in a virtual world full of fantasy and intrigue (Young, 2007). The Internet can become a psychological escape that distracts a user from a real-life problem or difficult situation. For instance, someone going through a painful divorce can turn to online friends to help cope with the situation. For someone who has recently been relocated by a new job or within the came company, starting over can be lonely. As a means to cope with the loneliness experienced by the new surroundings, a user can turn to the Internet to fill the void of those lonely evenings. The user may also suffer from a history of alcohol or drug dependency, only to find in compulsive use of the Internet a physically safe alternative to their addictive tendency. They believe that being addicted to the Internet is medically safer than being addicted to drugs or alcohol, yet the compulsive behavior still avoids the unpleasant situation underlying addiction.

Users who suffer from multiple addictions are at the greatest risk to suffer from Internet addiction. People who have addictive personalities may be more likely to use alcohol, cigarettes, drugs, food, or sex as a way of dealing with problems. They have learned to cope with situational difficulties through addictive behavior, and the Internet seems a convenient, legal, and physically safe distraction from those same real-life problems. In cases where an Internet addict also suffers from a sexual or gambling addiction, the Internet serves as a new outlet to engage in sexual or gambling behavior. Sexual compulsives discover a new source for sexual gratification through online pornography and anonymous sex chat. The Internet allows them a way to continue in the sexual behavior without the physical need of visiting strip clubs or prostitutes, and provides a new and socially acceptable way to cope. Those with a history of gambling addiction can visit virtual casinos and poker sites to gamble.

In China, there is one cultural factor not present in U.S. studies. Some have argued that the Chinese educational system constitutes the major situational factor for teenagers' Internet addictive behaviors (Tao, 2005; Tao et al., 2007). Dr. Ran Tao, director of the Center for Youth and Adolescent Development of the Beijing General Military Hospital, explains that as Chinese parents all hope their children have a bright future, and passing the college entrance examination has been a "gold index" for personal success, this has contributed significantly to children's pressure for learning and stress at school at the cost of their fun-seeking after school (Lin & Yan, 2001; Lin, 2002).

We see that situational stress, whether divorce, bereavement, recent loss of a job, or striving for academic success, can drive someone to utilize the Internet with greater intensity. Those individuals who use the Internet as a momentary escape or means of coping with situational stress may not initially be addicted to the Internet. Their behavior may be temporary and even fade over time. However, in cases where the behavior becomes persistent and continuous, online activities can become all-consuming. Behavior progressively revolves around Internet use. Behavior adapts to more of a focus on applications that may have initially been required for work use, such as a BlackBerry device, or may have been an activity that the user did for recreation, such as a chat room or game. As behavior escalates, online use becomes more chronic and more ingrained and develops into a compulsive obsession. At this stage, life becomes unmanageable for the addict, as relationships or careers are jeopardized because of the compulsive behavior.

A person is vulnerable to addiction when that person feels a lack of satisfaction in life, an absence of intimacy or strong connections to other people, a lack of self-confidence or compelling interests, or a loss of hope (Peele, 1985, p. 42). In a similar manner, individuals who are dissatisfied or upset by a particular area or multiple areas of their lives have an increased likelihood of developing Internet addiction because they don't understand another way of coping (Young, 1998). For example, instead of making positive choices that will seek out fulfillment, alcoholics typically drink, which dulls the pain, avoids the problem, and keeps them in a status quo. However, as they become sober, they realize that their difficulties have not changed. Nothing is altered by drinking, yet it appears easier to drink than to deal with the issues head-on. Paralleling the alcoholics' behaviors, addictive users access the Internet to dull the pain, avoid the real problem, and keep things in status quo. However, once offline, they realize that nothing has changed. Such substitution for missing needs often allows the addict to temporarily escape the problem, but the substitute behaviors are not the means to solve any problems. Therefore, it is important for the therapist or treating practitioner to assess a client's current situation in order to determine if he or she is using the Internet as a security blanket to avoid an unhappy situation such as marital or job dissatisfaction, medical illness, unemployment, or academic instability.

IMPLICATIONS

Over the past decade a great deal has been published regarding Internet addiction and compulsive use of the Internet. While preliminary in nature, this research suggests that addictive use of the Internet has created a significant psychological and social problem. Of all the ways of measuring Internet addiction, *DSM*-based criteria appear to be the most accepted way to define the disorder. Recently, the American Psychiatric Association has considered including Internet addiction in the *DSM-V* (Block, 2008) and decided to include it in the appendix.

From the mental health perspective, Internet users who become addicted fear that the field has been slow to respond, as a limited number of recovery centers have dedicated services related to Internet addiction. To pursue such effective recovery programs, continued research is needed to better understand the underlying motivations of Internet addiction. Future research should focus on how a psychiatric illness such as depression or obsessive-compulsive disorder plays a role in the development of compulsive Internet use. Longitudinal studies may reveal how personality traits, family dynamics, or interpersonal skills influence the way people utilize the Internet. Last, further outcome studies are needed to determine the efficacy of specialized therapy approaches to treat Internet addiction and compare these outcomes against traditional recovery modalities. From the technical perspective, new software designed to prevent Internet misuse and overuse has emerged as monitoring software for companies such as WebSense or Spy Monkey for personal use to manage online time.

Studies to specifically examine the use of 12-step programs have not been documented. The field appears too young to have achieved relevant data on the potential effectiveness of support groups as part of the treatment protocol with Internet-addicted clients. It has been discussed in the literature that research on Internet addiction has been problematic. Several studies lack the empirical robustness of experimental design, relying more on survey data and self-reported data from self-selected populations. The research also lacks proper use of control groups, and in some cases it utilizes a small number of anecdotal case studies and questionnaires to draw conclusions. While methodological problems remain, studies have replicated results in various parts of the world, and certain trends can be drawn from numerous viewpoints presented in the field.

REFERENCES

Aboujaoude, E., Koran, L. M., Gamel, N., Large, M. D., & Serpe, R. T. (2006). Potential markers for problematic Internet use: A telephone survey of 2,513 adults. *CNS Spectrum, The Journal of Neuropsychiatric Medicine, 11*(10), 750–755.

Bai, Y.-M., Lin, C.-C., & Chen, J.-Y. (2001). The characteristic differences between clients of virtual and real psychiatric clinics. *American Journal of Psychiatry, 158,* 1160–1161.

Block, J. J. (2008). Issues for DSM-V: Internet addiction. *American Journal of Psychiatry, 165,* 306–307.

Caplan, S. E. (2002). Problematic Internet use and psychosocial well-being: Development of a theory-based cognitive-behavioral measurement instrument. *Computers in Human Behavior, 18,* 553–575.

Caplan, S. E., & High, A. C. (2007). Beyond excessive use: The interaction between cognitive and behavioral symptoms of problematic Internet use. *Communication Research Reports, 23,* 265–271.

China Youth Association for Network Development (CYAND). (2005). Report of China teenagers' Internet addiction information 2005 (Beijing, China).

Cooper, A. (2002). *Sex & the Internet: A guidebook for clinicians.* New York: Brunner-Routledge.

Cui, L. J., Zhao, X., Wu, Z. M., & Xu, A. H. (2006). A research on the effects of Internet addiction on adolescents' social development. *Psychological Science, 1*, 34–36.

Davis, R. A. (2001). A cognitive behavioral model of pathological Internet use. *Computers in Human Behavior, 17*, 187–195.

Dell'Osso, B., Hadley, S., Allen, A., Baker, B., Chaplin, W. F., & Hollander, E. (2008). Ecitalopram in the treatment of impulsive-compulsive Internet usage disorder: An open-label trial followed by a double-blind discontinuation phase. *Journal of Clinical Psychiatry, 69*(3), 452–456.

Di Chiara, G. (2000). Role of dopamine in the behavioural actions of nicotine related to addiction. *European Journal of Pharmacology, 393*(1–2), 295–314.

Greenfield, D. N. (1999). Psychological characteristics of compulsive Internet use: A preliminary analysis. *CyberPsychology & Behavior, 2*, 403–412.

Greenfield, D. N. (2001). Sexuality and the Internet, *Counselor, 2*, 62-63.

Hall, A. S., & Parsons, J. (2001). Internet addiction: College students case study using best practices in behavior therapy. *Journal of Mental Health Counseling, 23*, 312–322.

Krant, R., Patterson, M., Lundmark, V., Kiesler, S., Mukopadhyay, T., & Scherlis, W. (1997). Internet paradox: A social technology that reduces social involvement and psychological well-being? *American Psychologist, 53*, 1017–1031.

LaRose, R., Mastro, D., & Eastin, M. S. (2001). Understanding Internet usage: A social-cognitive approach to uses and gratifications. *Social Science Computer Review, 19*(4), 395–413.

Lin, X. H. (2002). A brief introduction to Internet addiction disorder. *Chinese Journal of Clinical Psychology, 1*, 74–76.

Lin, X. H., & Yan, G. G. (2001). Internet addiction disorder, online behavior and personality. *Chinese Mental Health Journal, 4*, 281–283.

Morahan-Martin, J., & Schumacher, P. (1999). Incidence and correlates of pathological Internet use among college students. *Computers in Human Behavior 16*, 1–17.

Morahan-Martin, J., & Schumacher, P. (2003). Loneliness and social uses of the Internet. *Computers in Human Behavior, 19*, 659–671.

Nalwa, K., & Anand, A. (2003). Internet addiction in students: A cause of concern. *CyberPsychology & Behavior, 6*(6), 653–656.

Orzack, M. H. (1999). Computer addiction: Is it real or is it virtual? *Harvard Mental Health Letter, 15*(7), 8.

Peele, S. (1985). The concept of addiction. In S. Peele, *The meaning of addiction: Compulsive experience and its interpretation.* Lanham, MD: Lexington Books.

Russell, D., Peplau, L. A., & Cutrona, C. E. (1980). The revised UCLA Loneliness Scale: Concurrent and discriminant validity evidence. *Journal of Personality and Social Psychology, 39*, 472–480.

Scherer, K. (1997). College life online: Healthy and unhealthy Internet use. *Journal of College Development, 38*, 655–665.

Swaminath, G. (2008). Internet addiction disorder: Fact or fad? Nosing into nosology. *Indian Journal of Psychiatry [serial online], 50*, 158–160. Available from http://www.indianjpsychiatry.org/text.asp?2008/50/3/158/43622.

Tao, H. K. (2005). Teenagers' Internet addiction and the quality-oriented education. *Journal of Higher Correspondence Education (Philosophy and Social Sciences), 3*, 70–73.

Tao, R., Ying, L., Yue, X. D., & Hao, X. (2007). *Internet addiction: Exploration and intervention.* [In Chinese]. Shanghai, China: Shanghai People's Press, 12.

Vaillant, G. E. (1995). *The natural history of alcoholism revisited.* Cambridge, MA: Harvard University Press.

Whang, L., Lee, K., & Chang, G. (2003). Internet over-users' psychological profiles: A behavior sampling analysis on Internet addiction. *CyberPsychology & Behavior, 6*(2), 143–150.

Yang, S. (2001). Sociopsychiatric characteristics of adolescents who use computers to excess. *Acta Psychiatrica Scandinavica, 104*(3), 217–222.

Young, K. S. (1996). Internet addiction: The emergence of a new clinical disorder. Poster presented at the 104th Annual Convention of the American Psychological Association in Toronto, Canada, August 16, 1996.

Young, K. S. (1998). *Caught in the Net: How to recognize the signs of Internet addiction and a winning strategy for recovery.* New York: John Wiley & Sons.

Young, K. S. (2007). Cognitive-behavioral therapy with Internet addicts: Treatment outcomes and implications, *CyberPsychology & Behavior, 10*(5), 671–679.

Young, K. S., & Rogers, R. (1997). The relationship between depression and Internet addiction. *CyberPsychology & Behavior, 1*(1), 25–28.

CHAPTER 2

Clinical Assessment of Internet-Addicted Clients

KIMBERLY S. YOUNG

D IAGNOSIS OF Internet addiction is often complex. Unlike chemical de- pendency, the Internet offers several direct benefits as a technological advancement in our society and not a device to be criticized as addic- tive. Individuals can conduct research, perform business transactions, access libraries, communicate, and make vacation plans. Books have been written outlining the psychological as well as functional benefits of the Internet in our lives. By comparison, alcohol or drugs are not an integral or necessary part of our personal and professional lives, nor do they offer any direct benefit. With so many practical uses of the Internet, signs of addiction can easily be masked or justified. Further, clinical assessments are often very comprehensive and cover relevant disorders for psychiatric conditions and addictive disorders. However, given its newness, symptoms of Internet addiction may not always be revealed in an initial clinical interview. While self-referrals for Internet addiction are becoming more common, often the client does not present with complaints of computer addiction. People may initially present with signs of clinical depression, bipolar disorder, anxiety, or obsessive-compulsive ten- dencies, only for the treating professional to later discover signs of Inter- net abuse upon further examination (Shapiro, Goldsmith, Keck, Khosla, & McElroy, 2000).

Therefore, diagnosing Internet addiction upon clinical interview can be challenging. It is consequently important that treating professionals screen for the presence of compulsive use of the Internet. This chapter reviews ways to evaluate possible Internet addiction. It reviews the evolution of Internet addiction and current conceptualizations of pathological computer use as outlined for the *DSM-V*. As part of the assessment process, this chapter also presents the first validated measure of Internet addiction, which is an especially useful tool to measure the severity of symptoms once diagnosed. Finally, the chapter outlines specific clinical interview questions and treatment issues that clients present with in the early stages of recovery. These include a client's motivation for treatment, underlying social problems, and multiple addictions.

CONCEPTUALIZATION

According to Dr. Maressa Hecht Orzack, the director of Computer Addiction Services at McLean Hospital, a Harvard Medical School affiliate, and a pioneer in the study of Internet addiction, Internet addicts demonstrate a loss of impulse control where life has become unmanageable for the online user, yet despite these problems, the addict cannot give up the Internet. The computer becomes the primary relationship in the addict's life (Orzack, 1999).

Although time is not a direct function in diagnosing Internet addiction, early studies suggested that those classified as dependent online users were generally excessive about their online usage, spending anywhere from 40 to 80 hours per week, with sessions that could last up to 20 hours (Greenfield, 1999; Young, 1998a). Sleep patterns were disrupted due to late-night log-ins, and addicts generally stayed up surfing despite the reality of having to wake up early the next morning for work or school. In extreme cases, caffeine pills are used to facilitate longer Internet sessions. Such sleep deprivation caused excessive fatigue, impairing academic or occupational performance and increasing the risk of poor diet and exercise.

Given the popularity of the Internet, detecting and diagnosing Internet addiction is often difficult, as its legitimate business and personal use often masks addictive behavior. The best method to clinically detect compulsive use of the Internet is to compare it against criteria for other established addictions. Researchers have likened Internet addiction to addictive syndromes similar to impulse-control disorders on the Axis I Scale in the *DSM* (American Psychiatric Association, 1994) and have utilized various forms of *DSM-IV*-based criteria to define Internet addiction. Of all the references in the *DSM*, Pathological Gambling was viewed as most akin to this phenomenon. The Internet Addiction Diagnostic Questionnaire (IADQ) was the first screening measure developed for diagnosis (Young, 1998b). The following questionnaire conceptualized the eight criteria for the disorder:

1. Do you feel preoccupied with the Internet (think about previous online activity or anticipate next online session)?
2. Do you feel the need to use the Internet with increasing amounts of time in order to achieve satisfaction?
3. Have you repeatedly made unsuccessful efforts to control, cut back, or stop Internet use?
4. Do you feel restless, moody, depressed, or irritable when attempting to cut down or stop Internet use?

5. Do you stay online longer than originally intended?
6. Have you jeopardized or risked the loss of a significant relationship, job, or educational or career opportunity because of the Internet?
7. Have you lied to family members, therapists, or others to conceal the extent of involvement with the Internet?
8. Do you use the Internet as a way of escaping from problems or of relieving a dysphoric mood (e.g., feelings of helplessness, guilt, anxiety, depression)?

Answers evaluated nonessential computer/Internet usage, such as use that was not business or academically related. Subjects were considered dependent when answering by endorsing five or more of the questions over a six-month period. Associated features also included ordinarily excessive Internet use, neglect of routine duties or life responsibilities, social isolation, and being secretive about online activities or a sudden demand for privacy when online. While the IADQ provides a means to conceptualize pathological or addictive use of the Internet, these warning signs can often be masked by cultural norms that encourage and reinforce online use. Even if a client meets all the criteria, signs of abuse can be rationalized (e.g., "I need this for my job" or "It's just a machine") when in reality the Internet is causing significant problems in a user's life.

Beard and Wolf (2001) further modified the IADQ, recommending that all of the first five criteria be required for diagnosis of Internet addiction, since these criteria could be met without any impairment in the person's daily functioning. It was also recommended that at least one of the last three criteria (e.g., criteria 6, 7, and 8) be required in diagnosing Internet addiction. The reason the last three were separated from the others is the fact that these criteria impact the pathological Internet user's ability to cope and function (e.g., depressed, anxious, escaping problems), and also impact interaction with others (e.g., significant relationship, job, being dishonest with others). New studies that empirically tested the IADQ found that using three or four criteria was just as robust in diagnosing Internet addiction as using five or more and suggested that the cutoff score of five criteria might be overly stringent (Dowling & Quirk, 2009). Finally, Shapiro et al. (2003) put forth an approach to diagnosing Internet addiction under the general style of impulse-control disorders per the *DSM-IV-TR* (American Psychiatric Association, 2000) that further broadened the diagnostic criteria for problematic Internet use. This included a maladaptive preoccupation with Internet use, as indicated by either an irresistible preoccupation with the Internet or excessive use of the Internet for periods of time longer than planned. Also, use of the Internet or preoccupation with its use caused clinically significant distress or impairment in social, occupational, or other important areas of functioning. Finally, the excessive Internet use did not occur during periods of hypomania or mania and was not better accounted for by other Axis I disorders.

Most recently, the American Psychiatric Association has considered including the diagnosis of pathological computer use in the upcoming revision of the *DSM-V* (Block, 2008). Conceptually, the diagnosis is a compulsive-impulsive spectrum disorder that involves online and/or offline computer usage (Dell'Osso, Altamura, Allen, Marazziti, & Hollander, 2006) and consists of at least three subtypes: excessive gaming, sexual preoccupations, and e-mail/text messaging (Block, 2007). All of the variants share the following four components: (1) *excessive use*, often associated with a loss of sense of time or a neglect of basic drives; (2) *withdrawal*, including feelings of anger, tension, and/or depression when the computer is inaccessible; (3) *tolerance*, including the need for better computer equipment, more software, or more hours of use; and (4) *negative repercussions*, including arguments, lying, poor achievement, social isolation, and fatigue (Beard & Wolf, 2001; Block, 2008). This later set of criteria pulls together the previous forms of classification defining Internet addiction in a comprehensive manner to include the major components associated with the compulsive behavior.

THE INTERNET ADDICTION TEST (IAT)

The Internet Addiction Test (IAT) is the first validated instrument to assess Internet addiction (Widyanto & McMurren, 2004). Studies have found that the IAT is a reliable measure that covers the key characteristics of pathological online use. The test measures the extent of a client's involvement with the computer and classifies the addictive behavior in terms of mild, moderate, and severe impairment. The IAT can be utilized in outpatient and inpatient settings and adapted accordingly to fit the needs of the clinical setting. Furthermore, beyond validation in English, the IAT has also been validated in Italy (Ferraro, Caci, D'Amico, & Di Blasi, 2007) and France (Khazaal et al., 2008), making it the first global psychometric measure.

ADMINISTRATION

Simply instruct the client to answer the 20-item questionnaire based on the following five-point Likert scale. Clients should consider only the time spent online for nonacademic or nonjob purposes when answering. That is, they should consider only recreational use.

To assess the level of addiction, clients should answer the following questions using this scale:

0 = Not Applicable
1 = Rarely
2 = Occasionally
3 = Frequently
4 = Often
5 = Always

1. How often do you find that you stay online longer than you intended?
2. How often do you neglect household chores to spend more time online?
3. How often do you prefer the excitement of the Internet to intimacy with your partner?
4. How often do you form new relationships with fellow online users?
5. How often do others in your life complain to you about the amount of time you spend online?
6. How often do your grades or schoolwork suffer because of the amount of time you spend online?
7. How often do you check your e-mail before something else that you need to do?
8. How often does your job performance or productivity suffer because of the Internet?
9. How often do you become defensive or secretive when anyone asks you what you do online?
10. How often do you block out disturbing thoughts about your life with soothing thoughts of the Internet?
11. How often do you find yourself anticipating when you will go online again?
12. How often do you fear that life without the Internet would be boring, empty, and joyless?
13. How often do you snap, yell, or act annoyed if someone bothers you while you are online?
14. How often do you lose sleep due to late-night log-ins?
15. How often do you feel preoccupied with the Internet when offline, or fantasize about being online?
16. How often do you find yourself saying "Just a few more minutes" when online?
17. How often do you try to cut down the amount of time you spend online and fail?
18. How often do you try to hide how long you've been online?
19. How often do you choose to spend more time online over going out with others?
20. How often do you feel depressed, moody, or nervous when you are offline, which goes away once you are back online?

After all the questions have been answered, add the numbers for each response to obtain a final score. The higher the score range, the greater the level of addiction, as follows:

Normal Range: 0–30 points
Mild: 31–49 points
Moderate: 50–79 points
Severe: 80–100 points

Once the total score for the client has been calculated and the category is selected, to enhance the utility of the instrument, evaluate those questions for which the client scored a 4 or 5. This type of item analysis is useful to review with the client to identify and pinpoint specific problem areas related to Internet abuse. For example, if the client answered 4 (often) to Question 12 regarding feeling life would be empty and boring without the Internet, did he or she realize this dependency and the associated fear with regard to any consideration for giving up the Internet? Perhaps the client answered 5 (always) to Question 14 about lost sleep because of Internet usage. Probing further might reveal that the client stays up excessively late every evening, which has made it difficult to function at work or attend classes for school or to perform routine chores around the house, and has taken a toll on the client's overall health. These are important areas to further investigate with clients, as these are both symptoms and consequences created by Internet addiction. Overall, the IAT provides a framework for assessment of specific situations or problems that have been caused by computer overuse to use in subsequent treatment planning.

MODERATION AND CONTROLLED USE

Use of the Internet is legitimate in business and home practice such as in electronic correspondence to vendors or electronic banking. Therefore, traditional abstinence models are not practical interventions when they prescribe banned Internet use in most cases. The focus of treatment should consist of moderated Internet use overall. While moderated Internet use is the primary goal, abstinence of problematic applications is often necessary. For example, within the intake evaluation, it is often discovered that a specific application such as a chat room, an interactive game, or a certain set of adult web sites will trigger Internet binges. Moderation of the trigger application may fail, however, because of its inherent allure and clients will need to stop all activity surrounding that application. It is essential to help the client target and abstain from the problematic application(s) while retaining controlled use over legitimate Internet usage.

Treatment includes a variety of inventions and a mix of psychotherapy theories to treat the behavior and address underlying psychosocial issues that often coexist with this addiction (e.g., social phobia, mood disorders, sleep disorders, marital dissatisfaction, or job burnout). To help clients abstain from problematic online applications, recovery interventions apply structured, measurable, and systematic techniques. Using outcome data, cognitive-behavioral therapy (CBT) has been found to be an effective approach with this population (Young, 2007).

MOTIVATION FOR TREATMENT

In the early stages of recovery, clients will typically deny or minimize their habitual use of the Internet and the consequences their behavior may have on their lives. Often, a loved one, a friend, a spouse, or a parent has pushed the individual into seeking help. The client may feel resentful and deny the extent that use of the Internet is a problem. To break this pattern, after diagnosis, the therapist should use motivational interviewing techniques that encourage the client to commit to treatment as an integral aspect of recovery (Greenfield, 1999; Orzack, 1999).

The concept of motivational interviewing evolved from experience in the treatment of problem drinkers, and was first described by Miller (1983). These fundamental concepts and approaches were later elaborated by Miller and Rollnick (1991) in a more detailed description of clinical procedures. Motivational interviewing is a goal-directed style of counseling for eliciting behavior change by helping clients to explore and resolve ambivalence. Motivational interviewing involves asking open-ended questions, giving affirmations, and reflective listening.

Motivational interviewing is intended to confront the client in a constructive manner to evoke change, or to use external contingencies such as the potential loss of a job or relationship to mobilize a client's values and goals to stimulate behavior change. Clients dealing with addiction or substance-abuse problems often feel ambivalent about quitting, even after they admit they have a problem. They fear the loss of the Internet; they fear what life might be like if they were unable to chat with online friends, engage in online activities, and use the Internet as a form of psychological escape. Motivational interview helps clients confront their ambivalence.

Questions can be asked such as:

- When did you first begin to use the Internet?
- How many hours per week do you currently spend online (for nonessential use)?
- What applications do you use on the Internet (specific sites/groups/games visited)?
- How many hours per week do you spend using each application?
- How would you rank order each application from most to least important? (1 = first, 2 = second, 3 = third, etc.)?
- What do you like most about each application? What do you like least?
- How has the Internet changed your life?
- How do you feel when you log offline?
- What problems or consequences have stemmed from your Internet use? (If these are difficult for the client to describe, have the client keep a log near the computer in order to document such behaviors for the next week's session.)
- Have others complained about how much time you spend online?
- Have you sought treatment for this condition before? If so, when? Have you had any success?

The answers to these questions create a clearer clinical profile of the client. The therapist can determine the types of applications that are most problematic for the client (chat rooms, online gaming, online pornography, etc.). The length of Internet use, the consequences of the behavior, a history of prior treatment attempts, and outcomes for any treatment attempts are also assessed. This helps clients begin the process of examining how the Internet impacts their lives. It is helpful for the client to gain a sense of responsibility for his or her behavior. Allowing clients to resolve their ambivalence in a manner that gently pushes them helps them to be more inclined to acknowledge the consequences of their excessive online use and engage in treatment. Generally, the style is quiet and eliciting rather than aggressive, confrontational, or argumentative. For therapists accustomed to confronting and giving advice, motivational interviewing can appear to be a hopelessly slow and passive process. The proof is in the outcome. More aggressive strategies, sometimes guided by a desire to "confront client denial," easily slip into pushing clients to make changes for which they are not ready.

Helping the client explore how he or she feels just before going online will help pinpoint the types of emotions being covered by the behavior (or how the client is using the Internet to cope or escape from problems). Answers may include issues such as a fight with a spouse, depressed mood, stress at a job, or a poor grade in school. Motivational interviewing should explore how these feelings diminish when online, looking for how the client rationalizes or justifies using the Internet (e.g., "Chatting makes me forget about the fight with my husband"; "Looking at online porn makes me feel less depressed"; "Gambling online makes me feel less stressed at work"; "Killing other players in an online game makes me feel better about my poor grade at school"). Motivational interviewing is also meant to help the client recognize consequences stemming from excessive or compulsive use. Problems may consist of issues like "My spouse becomes angrier"; "My feelings return when I turn off the computer"; "My job still stinks"; "I will lose my scholarship if I don't get my grades up." The therapeutic relationship is more like a partnership or companionship than expert/recipient roles to examine and resolve ambivalence. The operational assumption in motivational interviewing is that ambivalence is the principal obstacle to be overcome in triggering change. Overall, the specific strategies are designed to elicit, clarify, and resolve ambivalence in a client-centered and respectful therapeutic manner.

MULTIPLE ADDICTIONS

Once ambivalence toward treatment has been resolved, the next issue is to examine how a client experiences addiction. Is this the first time the client has been addicted to something? Or does the client have a long-standing history of addiction? Often, Internet addicts suffer from multiple addictions. Clients with a prior history of alcohol or drug dependency often find their compulsive use of the Internet to be a physically safe alternative to their addictive tendency. They believe that being addicted to the Internet is medically safer than being addicted to drugs or alcohol, yet the compulsive behavior still avoids the unpleasant situation underlying addiction.

Clients who suffer from multiple addictions (to the Internet as well as to alcohol, cigarettes, drugs, food, sex, etc.) are at the greatest risk to relapse. This is especially true when it comes to the Internet. Often, addicts will need to use the computer for work or school, so the temptation to return to the problematic behavior feels constant because the computer is always available. Multiple addictions in a client also suggest that the person suffers from an addictive personality and has compulsive tendencies, making relapse more likely.

"I always think about cybersex when I feel stressed and overwhelmed on the job," admitted one client after being addicted to sex chat rooms for three years. "I always promise to only do it for a half an hour or an hour but time just slips by. Each time I log offline I promise that I will never do it again. I hate myself for all the wasted time I spend online. I go a few weeks and then the pressure builds inside. I play mind games, telling myself just a little won't hurt. No one will know what I am doing. Sometimes I actually believe that I am in control. I wear myself down and the whole process starts all over again. I feel defeated that I will never get rid of these feelings."

This describes what has been defined as the Stop-Start Relapse Cycle (Young, 2001, pp. 65–66). Many Internet addicts engage in a self-destructive internal dialogue of rationalizations that serve to bring about relapse. The pattern begins with rationalizing the behavior is okay or harmless, followed by a period of regret. The regret is followed by promises to stop the behavior, then temporary abstinence. Abstinence may last days, weeks, or months. Emotional pressure builds until these rationalizations creep back into the addict's mind, triggering relapse. The Stop-Start Relapse Cycle falls into four distinct but interdependent stages:

Stage 1: Rationalization. The addict rationalizes that the Internet serves as a treat after a long, hard day of work, often making a statement such as "I work hard; I deserve it"; "Just a few minutes won't hurt"; "I can control my Internet use"; "The computer relaxes me"; or "With the stress I've been under, I deserve this." The addict justifies the need to look at a few adult sites or chat for a few minutes with an online lover or game with friends, only to discover that the behavior is not so easily contained.

Stage 2: Regret. After the Internet experience, the addict experiences a period of deep regret. Turning off the computer, the addict realizes that work is piling up and feels guilty for the behavior, making statements such as "I know this is hurting my job"; "I can't believe I wasted all this time"; or "I am a horrible person for what I just did."

Stage 3: Abstinence. The addict views the behavior as a personal failure of willpower and promises never to do it again, so a period of abstinence follows. During this time, he or she engages in healthy patterns of behavior, works diligently, resumes interests in old hobbies, spends more time with his or her family, exercises, and gets enough rest.

Stage 4: Relapse. The addict craves the online high or experience as temptations to return to the Internet emerge during stressful or emotionally charged moments. The addict recalls the self-medicating effects of being online and its associated relaxation and excitement. The addict remembers how good it felt to be online and forgets how bad it felt afterward. The rationalization period starts again, and the availability of the computer easily starts the cycle anew.

Addicts use several rationalizations to minimize the impact of the Internet in their lives, such as "Just one more time won't hurt"; "I can't get addicted to a computer"; "It's better to be addicted to the Internet than to drugs and drinking"; or "I'm not as bad as other people I see." These rationalizations feed the addictive behavior. Addicts will rationalize that spending 8, 10, or 15 hours a day online is normal. They use poor judgment and compare themselves to someone they know who is worse than they are—"I'm not as bad as so-and-so." They rationalize that their online use isn't a problem and ignore the consequences created by their behavior.

The rationalizations are the origin of the cycle, and in order to stop the cycle it is important for the client to examine his or her preoccupations and cravings related to online use.

Assessment questions to help clients evaluate cravings or signs of withdrawal include:

- Do you feel preoccupied with the Internet?
- What attempts have you made to control, cut back, or stop computer use?
- How often do you think about going online?
- How often do you talk about going online?
- How often do you plan ways to use the Internet?
- How often do you forgo other responsibilities or duties to go online?
- Have you ever used the Internet to escape from feelings of depression, anxiety, guilt, loneliness, or sadness?
- What is your longest period of abstinence from the Internet?

The answers show how much clients think about being online or feel preoccupied with the Internet. The answers also show patterns of abstinence and relapse if the client has been trying to quit for weeks, months, or years. In addition, the answers show the types of feelings clients are escaping from by using the Internet and how they feel when they are forced to go without it.

These rationalizations utilized by the client are important for the therapist to understand as they begin the recovery process. From a cognitive perspective, these serve as cravings or signs of withdrawal that trigger problem Internet use (Beck, Wright, Newman, & Liese, 2001).

Such maladaptive cognitions result in problematic computer use (Caplan, 2002; Davis, 2001). Therapists need to identify and eventually attack the cognitive assumptions and distortions that have developed and the effects of these on behavior. This may involve cognitive approaches such as problem solving, cognitive restructuring, and keeping thought journals.

Clients must not be permitted to minimize their addiction to the Internet as less harmful than an addiction to drugs, alcohol, gambling, or sex. Clients who become addicted to the Internet may suffer from a number of emotional and personal problems. They see the Internet as a safe place to absorb themselves mentally to reduce their tension, sadness, or stress (Young, 2007). Individuals who may feel overwhelmed or may be experiencing job burnout or money problems or life-changing events such as a recent divorce, relocation, or death in the family can absorb themselves in a virtual world inside the computer. They can lose themselves in anything from online pornography to Internet gambling and online gaming. Once online, the difficulties in their lives fade into the background as their attention becomes completely focused on the computer.

Addressing all unhealthy or compulsive behaviors early on the evaluation process will aid the client. Working within the motivational interviewing context, clients can see how they use the computer as a new way of escaping without really dealing with the underlying problems in their lives. They will also learn that an addiction to the Internet can be as harmful as other addictions they may have by continuing to avoid problems without ever resolving them.

UNDERLYING SOCIAL PROBLEMS

Excessive or problematic Internet use often stems from interpersonal difficulties such as introversion or social problems (Ferris, 2001). Many Internet addicts fail to communicate well in face-to-face situations (Leung, 2007). This is part of why they use the Internet in the first place. Communicating online seems safer and easier for them. Poor communication skills can also cause poor self-esteem and feelings of isolation, and can create additional problems in life, such as trouble working in groups, making presentations, or going to social engagements. Therapy needs to address how they communicate offline. Encouraging affect, communication analysis, modeling, and role-playing are helpful interventions to apply to establish new ways of interacting and social functioning (Hall & Parsons, 2001). Others may have limited social support systems in place, which is in part why they turn to virtual relationships as a substitute for the missing social connection in their lives. They turn to others on the Internet when feeling lonely or in need of someone to talk to. What is worse, online affairs are occurring at an alarming rate (Whitty, 2005). An online affair is a romantic or sexual relationship initiated via online contact and maintained predominantly through electronic conversations that occur through e-mail, chat rooms, or online communities (Atwood & Schwartz, 2002). The problem has grown, and according to a study conducted by the American Academy of Matrimonial Lawyers, 63% of attorneys said that online affairs were the leading cause of divorce cases (Dedmon, 2003).

Due to their addiction, clients often damage or lose significant real-life relationships, such as with a spouse, a parent, or a close friend (Young, 2007). Often, these were individuals who provided the addict with support, love, and acceptance before the Internet, and their absence only makes the addict feel worthless and reinforces past notions of being unlovable. The addict must make amends and reestablish these broken relationships to achieve recovery and find the support necessary to fight the addiction. Rebuilding relationships and providing new ways to relate to others allows for amends to be made. Involving loved ones in recovery can be a rich source of nurturing and sponsorship to help a client maintain sobriety and abstinence. Couples or family therapy may be necessary to help educate loved ones about the addiction process and engage them more fully in helping the client maintain boundaries established with the computer.

When evaluating social problems, it is important to investigate how the client has been using the Internet. If in interactive environments such as chat rooms, instant messaging, or social networking sites, then the therapist should evaluate aspects of online use such as: Does the person make up a persona? What kind of screen name does the person use? Does the Internet and its use disrupt current social relationships? How so? These factors are important to evaluate in terms of understanding the social dynamics underlying online usage and how relationships formed on the Internet may be substituting for or replacing real-life relationships. Possible questions to consider are:

- Have you been honest about your Internet habit with your friends and family?
- Have you ever created an online persona?
- Did you develop an identity or persona online?
- Have there been online activities that you kept secret or thought others would not approve of?
- Have online friends disrupted real-life relationships?
- If so, who (husband, wife, parent, friend) and how were they impacted?
- Does Internet use disrupt your social or work relationships? If so, how?
- In what other ways has Internet use impacted your life?

Questions like these help structure the clinical interview to provide more detailed information on how the Internet has impacted relationships in the client's life. Many times, clients create online personas and the answers provide specific information on the characteristics and nature of these online personas. Therapists can understand the psychological motives, the ways online personas develop, and how they may be used to fulfill missing or unmet social needs. Once this type of critical examination takes place, the therapist can work with the client to develop new social relationships or reestablish former social connections that will sustain the client's motivation for continued treatment.

FUTURE TRENDS

Studies on Internet addiction originated in the United States. Most recently, studies have documented Internet addiction in a growing number of countries, such as Italy (Ferraro et al., 2007); Pakistan (Suhail & Bargees, 2006); and the Czech Republic (Simkova & Cincera, 2004). Reports also indicate that Internet addiction has become a serious public health concern in China (BBC News, 2005), Korea (Hur, 2006), and Taiwan (Lee, 2007). About 10 percent of China's more than 30 million Internet gamers were said to be addicted. To battle what has been called an epidemic by some reports, Chinese authorities regularly shut down Internet cafes, many illegally operated, in crackdowns that also include huge fines for their operators. The Chinese government has also instituted laws to reduce the number of hours adolescents can play online and opened the first inpatient treatment center for Internet addiction in Beijing.

It is difficult to estimate how widespread the problem is. A nationwide study conducted by a team from Stanford University's School of Medicine had estimated that nearly one in eight Americans exhibited at least one possible sign of problematic Internet use (Aboujaoude, Koran, Gamel, Large, & Serpe, 2006).

Independent of culture, race, or gender, Internet addiction seems to be a growing problem. College counselors have argued that students are the most at-risk population to develop an addiction to the Internet because of the encouraged use of computers, wired dorms, and mobile Internet devices (Young, 2004). Away from home and their parents' watchful eyes, college students long have exercised their new freedom by engaging in pranks, talking to friends at all hours of the night, sleeping with their boyfriends and girlfriends, and eating and drinking things parents would not approve of. They utilize that freedom by hanging out in chat rooms or sending messages to friends on Facebook or MySpace with no parent to complain about their refusal to get off the computer.

For companies, Internet addiction has been shown to be both a legal liability as well as a productivity problem. As corporations rely on management information systems to run almost every facet of their business, employee Internet abuse and its potential for addiction has become a possible business epidemic. Studies show that employees abuse the Internet during work hours, resulting in billions of dollars of lost productivity. Media reports show that companies such as Xerox, Dow Chemical, and Merck have terminated employees for incidents of abuse. IBM has been sued for $5 million for wrongful termination (Holahan, 2006); a former employee who used chat rooms during work hours is suing the firm under the Americans with Disabilities Act for terminating him rather than providing rehabilitation. More wrongful termination lawsuits at smaller companies may follow. The issue becomes that the company has supplied the so-called digital drug, and companies may be liable for providing treatment and prevention programs on Internet addiction as a means to reduce their legal ramifications.

A good diagnostic evaluation should include a complete history of symptoms, whether the symptoms were treated, and if so what treatment was given. The therapist should ask about alcohol and drug use, and questions about a family history of addiction. The proper evaluation of Internet addiction is important for both clinical and legal implications. Clinically, therapists need to properly diagnose the problem and understand the dynamics associated with the condition. This includes things about Internet use that may not be readily available. A therapist may ask about only the number of hours one spends online, but that is just one aspect of the complete clinical profile. Therapists need to understand the ambivalence clients often feel about treatment, especially in cases of addiction, and encourage them to moderate and control their use of the Internet. They also need to understand the dynamics of what clients do online; creating personas, romantic relationships, and gaming can take on a variety of forms. Finally, accurate diagnosis is important from a legal perspective. Corporations face increasing legal liability as computers and the Internet become a recognized addiction warranting treatment. Other social laws may follow, such as divorce cases involving the Internet or criminal cases such as online pedophilia that involve accurate assessment for rehabilitation.

Overall, as Internet addiction becomes a more common and recognized condition, the need for accurate and thorough clinical evaluation becomes more important in a variety of fields and for a variety of reasons.

REFERENCES

Aboujaoude, E., Koran, L. M., Gamel, N., Large, M. D., & Serpe, R. T. (2006). Potential markers for problematic Internet use: A telephone survey of 2,513 adults. CNS Spectrum, *The Journal of Neuropsychiatric Medicine*, 11(10), 750–755.

American Psychiatric Association. (1994). *Diagnostic and statistical manual of mental disorders (DSM)* (4th ed.). Washington, DC: Author.

American Psychiatric Association. (2000). *Diagnostic and statistical manual of mental disorders (DSM)* (4th ed., text rev.). Washington, DC: Author.

Atwood, J. D., & Schwartz, L. (2002). Cyber-sex: The new affair treatment considerations. *Journal of Couple & Relationship Therapy*, 1(3), 37–56.

BBC News. (2005). China imposes online gaming curbs. Retrieved August 7, 2007, from http://news.bbc.co.uk/1/hi/technology/4183340.stm

Beard, K. W., & Wolf, E. M. (2001). Modification in the proposed diagnostic criteria for Internet addiction. *CyberPsychology & Behavior*, 4, 377–383.

Beck, A. T., Wright, F. D., Newman, C. F., & Liese, B. S. (2001). *Cognitive therapy of substance abuse*. New York: Guilford Press.

Block, J. J. (2007). *Pathological computer use in the USA. In 2007 international symposium on the counseling and treatment of youth Internet addiction* (p. 433). Seoul, Korea: National Youth Commission.

Block, J. J. (2008). Issues for DSM-V: Internet addiction. *American Journal of Psychiatry*, 165, 306–307.

Caplan, S. E. (2002). Problematic Internet use and psychosocial well-being: Development of a theory-based cognitive-behavioral measurement instrument. *Computers in Human Behavior, 18*, 553–575.

Davis, R. A. (2001). A cognitive behavioral model of pathological Internet use. *Computers in Human Behavior, 17*, 187–195.

Dedmon, J. (2003). *Is the Internet bad for your marriage? Study by the American Academy of Matrimonial Lawyers*, Chicago, IL. [News release]. Retrieved January 28, 2008, from http://www.expertclick.com/NewsReleaseWire/default.cfm?Action=ReleaseDetail&ID=3051

Dell'Osso, B., Altamura, A. C., Allen, A., Marazziti, D., & Hollander, E. (2006). Epidemiologic and clinical updates on impulse control disorders: A critical review. *Clinical Neuroscience, 256*, 464–475.

Dowling, N. A., & Quirk, K. L. (2009). Screening for Internet dependence: Do the proposed diagnostic criteria differentiate normal from dependent Internet use? *CyberPsychology & Behavior, 12*(1), 21–27.

Ferraro, G., Caci, B., D'Amico, A., & Di Blasi, M. (2007). Internet addiction disorder: An Italian study. *CyberPsychology & Behavior, 10*(2), 170–175.

Ferris, J. (2001). Social ramifications of excessive Internet use among college-age males. *Journal of Technology and Culture, 20*(1), 44–53.

Greenfield, D. (1999). *Virtual addiction: Help for Netheads, cyberfreaks, and those who love them*. Oakland, CA: New Harbinger Publication.

Hall, A. S., & Parsons, J. (2001). Internet addiction: College students case study using best practices in behavior therapy. *Journal of Mental Health Counseling, 23*, 312–322.

Holahan, C. (2006). *Employee sues IBM over Internet addiction*. Retrieved November 15, 2007, from http://www.businessweek.com/print/technology/content/dec2006/tc20061214_422859.htm

Hur, M. H. (2006). Internet addiction in Korean teenagers. *CyberPsychology & Behavior, 9*(5), 514–525.

Khazaal, Y., Billieux, J., Thorens, G., Khan, R., Louati, Y., Scarlatti, E., et al. (2008). French validation of the Internet Addiction Test. *CyberPsychology & Behavior, 11*(6), 703–706.

Lee, M. (2007). *China to limit teens' online gaming for exercise*. Retrieved August 7, 2007, from http://www.msnbc.msn.com/id/19812989/

Leung, L. (2007). Stressful life events, motives for Internet use, and social support among digital kids. *CyberPsychology & Behavior, 10*(2), 204–214.

Miller, W. R. (1983). Motivational interviewing with problem drinkers. *Behavioural Psychotherapy, 11*, 147–172.

Miller, W. R., & Rollnick, S. (1991). *Motivational interviewing: Preparing people to change addictive behavior*. New York: Guilford Press.

Orzack, M. H. (1999). Computer addiction: Is it real or is it virtual? *Harvard Mental Health Letter, 15*(7), 8.

Shapiro, N. A., Goldsmith, T. D., Keck, P. E., Jr., Khosla, U. M., & McElroy, S. L. (2000). Psychiatric evaluation of individuals with problematic Internet use. *Journal of Affect Disorders, 57*, 267–272.

Shapiro, N. A., Lessig, M. C., Goldsmith, T. D., Szabo, S. T., Lazoritz, M., Gold, M. S., & Stein, D. J. (2003). Problematic Internet use: Proposed classification and diagnostic criteria. *Depression and Anxiety, 17,* 207–216.

Simkova, B., & Cincera, J. (2004). Internet addiction disorder and chatting in the Czech Republic. *CyberPsychology & Behavior, 7*(5), 536–539.

Suhail, K., & Bargees, Z. (2006). Effects of excessive Internet use on undergraduate students in Pakistan. *CyberPsychology & Behavior, 9*(3), 297–307.

Whitty, M. (2005). The realness of cybercheating. *Social Science Computer Review, 23*(1), 57–67.

Widyanto, L., & McMurren, M. (2004). The psychometric properties of the Internet Addiction Test. *CyberPsychology & Behavior, 7*(4), 445–453.

Young, K. S. (1998a). *Caught in the Net: How to recognize the signs of Internet addiction and a winning strategy for recovery.* New York: John Wiley & Sons.

Young, K. S. (1998b). Internet addiction: The emergence of a new clinical disorder. *CyberPsychology & Behavior, 1,* 237–244.

Young K. S. (2001). *Tangled in the Web: Understanding cybersex from fantasy to addiction.* Bloomington, IN: Authorhouse.

Young, K. S. (2004). Internet addiction: The consequences of a new clinical phenomenon. In K. Doyle (Ed.), *American behavioral scientist: Psychology and the new media* (Vol. 1, pp. 1–14). Thousand Oaks, CA: Sage.

Young, K. S. (2007). Cognitive-behavioral therapy with Internet addicts: Treatment outcomes and implications, *CyberPsychology & Behavior, 10*(5), 671–679.

CHAPTER 3

Online Social Interaction, Psychosocial Well-Being, and Problematic Internet Use

SCOTT E. CAPLAN and ANDREW C. HIGH

RESEARCHERS FROM a variety of different disciplines have sought to better understand online social interaction and its relationship to both problematic Internet use (PIU) and psychosocial well-being. In this chapter, PIU refers to a constellation of thoughts, behaviors, and outcomes, rather than to a disease or addiction. Specifically, this chapter employs PIU to describe a syndrome of cognitive and behavioral symptoms that result in negative social, academic, and professional consequences (Caplan, 2002; see also Davis, 2001; Davis, Flett, and Besser 2002; Morahan-Martin & Schumacher, 2003). Rather than limiting its scope to problems rising to the level of addiction or clinical disorder, this chapter conceptualizes PIU as a broader form of deficient self-regulation that results in negative outcomes (LaRose, 2001; LaRose, Eastin, & Gregg, 2001; LaRose, Lin, & Eastin, 2003; LaRose, Mastro, & Eastin, 2001). Throughout the chapter, the terms *Internet abuse* (Morahan-Martin, 2008); *Internet addiction* (Young, 1998; Young & Rogers, 1998); *pathological Internet use* (Morahan-Martin & Schumacher, 2000); *excessive Internet use* (Wallace, 1999); *compulsive Internet use* (van den Eijnden, Meerkerk, Vermulst, Spijkerman, & Engels, 2008); and *Internet dependence* (Scherer, 1997; Young, 1996) are viewed as more extreme examples of the broader concept of PIU.

This chapter examines the relationship between PIU and the interpersonal functions of the Internet. Online social interaction differs from ordinary face-to-face (FtF) conversations in important ways that may be especially appealing to people who exhibit PIU (Caplan, 2003; McKenna & Bargh, 2000; Morahan-Martin & Schumacher, 2000). As this chapter explains, compared to FtF contexts, computer-mediated interpersonal communication affords greater anonymity, more time creating and editing verbal messages, and more control over self-presentation and impression management (Walther, 1996). It is not surprising, then, that research indicates a positive association both between PIU and online social behavior and between PIU and interpersonal problems such as social skill deficiency, loneliness, and social anxiety (Caplan, 2005, 2007; Morahan-Martin & Schumacher, 2000, 2003). Valkenburg and Peter (2007) asserted that "if the Internet is to influence well-being it will be through its potential to alter the nature of communication and social interaction" (p. 44). In one review of the literature, Morahan-Martin (2007) observed that "there is a growing consensus that the unique social interactions made possible by the Internet play a major role in the development of Internet abuse" (p. 335). This chapter seeks to present a theoretical account of the relationship between interpersonal Internet use and PIU and to propose directions for future studies to explore. The following sections examine research supporting the claim that interpersonal Internet use is associated with psychosocial well-being and PIU. Later sections articulate a detailed cognitive behavioral model of *how* and *why* online social interaction, psychosocial well-being, and problematic Internet use are related to one another.

ONLINE SOCIAL INTERACTION, PIU, AND WELL-BEING

This section reviews research indicating relationships among mental and social well-being, online interpersonal behavior, and PIU. In this particular literature, there are three important points relevant to the current chapter. First, studies show a link between interpersonal uses of the Internet and problematic outcomes of Internet use. Next, the literature also suggests that people who experience psychological problems are particularly drawn to the interpersonal features of online behavior. And, finally, a number of reports illustrate an association between interpersonal difficulties and levels of PIU. Taken together, the studies reviewed here provide substantial evidence of an association among well-being, online social behavior, and PIU.

ONLINE SOCIAL INTERACTION AND PIU

People who report negative outcomes associated with their Internet use are especially drawn to the interpersonal functions of the Internet (Caplan, 2002, 2003, 2005, 2007; Chak & Leung, 2004; Davis, Flett, & Besser, 2002; McKenna & Bargh, 2000; Morahan-Martin, 1999, 2008; Ngai, 2007; Young, 1996, 1998; Young & Rogers, 1998). In one recent review of this literature, Morahan-Martin (2008) noted that "research consistently has supported that the unique social interactions made possible by the Internet are important in the development of both generalized and specific IA [internet abuse]" (p. 51). Morahan-Martin (2007) explained that those who report negative outcomes due to their

Internet use are more likely to use the Internet for interpersonal activities and to go online to meet people, form relationships, and seek emotional support. Similarly, Wallace (1999) observed "synchronous spaces are not the only compelling Internet environments, but they do seem to be chief culprits in excessive Internet use" (p. 182).

According to one early study, whereas nondependent Internet users spent most of their time online using e-mail and surfing web sites, dependent users spent most of their time online using synchronous interpersonal communication applications (Young, 1996). In another study, Scherer (1997) reported that Internet-dependent college students were 26% more likely than other students to go online in order to meet new people. Scherer observed that Internet-dependent students had different motives for using the Internet than did the other students. Specifically, the dependent students were attracted to the opportunities for unique social experiences available online. Similarly, Morahan-Martin and Schumacher (2000, 2003) found that people who exhibited PIU were more likely than others to go online to meet new people, talk to others with similar interests, seek emotional support, and use interpersonal functions such as chat rooms, forums, and interactive games. A study by Kubey, Lavin, and Barrows (2001) revealed a similar pattern of results. The researchers surveyed 572 college students, measuring Internet usage (type and frequency), study habits, academic performance, and personality variables. The results of Kubey et al.'s research revealed that Internet-dependent students used synchronous chat applications significantly more frequently than did nondependent students.

A more recent study (van den Eijnden et al., 2008) employed a longitudinal design to test the hypothesis that "online communication, more than other Internet applications, is related to increases in compulsive use" (p. 658). During the first wave of the study, researchers measured adolescents' frequency of use of a variety of different Internet functions, including downloading, gaming, e-mailing, instant messaging, chat rooms, information seeking, pornography, and surfing. At a six-month follow-up, the same participants completed a measure of compulsive Internet use. The results revealed that, compared with the noninterpersonal Internet functions, instant messaging and chat room participation were the strongest predictors of adolescents' future levels of compulsive Internet use (there was no effect for e-mail). The authors concluded that "only real time communication functions, that is, instant messaging and chatting, had higher incidences of compulsive Internet use 6 months later" (p. 662).

In another recent study of 4,000 massively multiplayer online (MMO) game players, Caplan, Williams, and Yee (2009) reported significant positive correlations between PIU and instant messaging use, using the Internet to meet new people, and using the Internet to visit forums. Whereas the same study revealed a positive association between PIU and deriving a sense of community from people met online, a negative association emerged between PIU and deriving a sense of community from FtF relationships. In other words, the more players derived a sense of community from online relationships rather than face-to-face interaction, the greater their level of PIU. These results are similar to those obtained by Kim and Davis (2009), who reported that "for those participants who used the Internet to communicate with family and friends, heavy usage had little negative implications for PIU. In contrast, those who used the net to make new friends were much more likely to have high PIU scores" (p. 496). Taken together, the studies reviewed here suggest that those who report PIU seem to be particularly drawn to interpersonal Internet functions.

Although the literature just reviewed clearly indicates a relationship between online social behavior and PIU, a closer look reveals that this relationship may apply to only some groups of people—namely, those with psychosocial difficulties. The argument in this chapter is that psychosocial difficulties predispose some people to develop a preference for online social interaction (POSI) over face-to-face conversation, which, in turn, leads to deficient self-regulation of Internet use and negative outcomes (Caplan, 2003, 2005, 2010).

ONLINE SOCIAL INTERACTION AND WELL-BEING

Studies suggest that people with psychological problems and social difficulties appear to be drawn to online social interaction. With regard to depression, for example, a national survey of adolescents found that adolescents who reported depressive symptoms were more likely than their nondepressed counterparts to talk with strangers online, use the Internet most frequently for interpersonal communication, and be more self-disclosive online (Ybarra, Alexander, & Mitchell, 2005). The study by van den Eijnden et al. (2008), mentioned earlier, also found that instant messaging use among adolescents predicted increased depression, but lower loneliness, six months later.

Prior research also indicates relationships between severe psychological problems and online social interaction. For example, Mitchell and Ybarra (2007) examined data from the Second Youth Internet Safety Survey where 1,500 adolescents were asked about self-harming behaviors and online activities. The results indicated that, compared to youths who did not engage in self-harm, self-harming youths were twice as likely to use Internet chat rooms. In addition, the self-harming youths were significantly more likely to have a close relationship with someone they met online. However, the youths were equally likely to have mediated conversations with people they knew in person. Researchers have also identified associations between online social activity and serious personality disorder. A study by Mittal, Tessner, and Walker (2007) examined the online social behavior of adolescents with schizotypal personality disorder (SPD). The results revealed that people with SPD "reported significantly less social interaction with 'real-life' friends, but used the Internet for social interaction significantly more frequently than controls" (p. 50). More specifically, both SPD severity and depressive symptoms were positively correlated with the amount of time people spent in chat rooms and on Internet gaming. The study also found a negative correlation between participants' number of real-life friends and time spent in Internet chat. Taken together, these studies suggest that for some people, online interpersonal behavior is related to serious psychological difficulties.

Other research links online interpersonal activity to self-esteem, another indicator of psychosocial well-being. For example, one study found a negative relationship between using social network sites and self-esteem. Valkenburg, Peter, and Schouten (2006) found that frequent use of social networking was indirectly associated with adolescents' self-esteem and overall well-being. Moreover, the relationship was moderated by whether the users received positive or negative feedback on their profiles. Negative feedback predicted lower self-esteem and well-being whereas positive feedback predicted healthier outcomes. Thus, the valence of feedback was related to psychological well-being.

INTERPERSONAL DIFFICULTIES AND PIU

Researchers have also documented a correlation between interpersonal difficulties (i.e., loneliness, social anxiety, low social skill, and introversion) and PIU. In a recent review, Morahan-Martin (2008) observed that "those who are chronically lonely and those who are socially anxious share many characteristics, which may predispose them to develop IA [Internet abuse]" (p. 52). Indeed, several studies have reported positive associations between loneliness and PIU (Amichai-Hamburger & Ben-Artzi, 2003; Caplan, 2002; Morahan-Martin & Schumacher, 2003). Similarly, research indicates that social anxiety is positively correlated with PIU (Caplan, 2007). Erwin and colleagues (2004) explain that "in the case of introverted or socially anxious individuals, Internet use may serve as a way to avoid being alone and may intensify disconnection from face-to-face relationships" and that "introverted individuals using Internet communication as a substitute for face-to-face relationships seem unlikely to succeed in getting their interpersonal needs met" (Erwin, Turk, Heimberg, Fresco, & Hantula, 2004, p. 631). Similarly, other researchers report that highly troubled adolescents are more likely to form close online relationships than those who have healthy familial relationships (Wolak, Mitchell, & Finkelhor, 2003). With regard to social skill, Caplan (2005) found that college students' levels of self-presentational social skill were significant negative predictors of their preference for online social interaction.

Additionally, there is evidence that social anxiety is positively correlated with PIU (Caplan, 2007). Erwin and colleagues (2004) explain that "in the case of introverted or socially anxious individuals, Internet use may serve as a way to avoid being alone and may intensify disconnection from face-to-face relationships" and that "introverted individuals using Internet communication as a substitute for face-to-face relationships seem unlikely to succeed in getting their interpersonal needs met" (p. 631). In their study Erwin and colleagues found that people with more severe social anxiety indicated that the

Internet made it easier for them to avoid regular FtF interactions. These authors concluded that "individuals with the most severe social anxiety disorder may gain comfort with cyberspace interactions, particularly if they spend greater amounts of time doing so. However, these gains may prove to be elusive, belying greater isolation, anxiety, and impairment associated with non-cyberspace interactions, and greater misinformation and entrenchment of maladaptive beliefs" (p. 643). In sum, the studies just reviewed lend support to the claim that people with psychological and and interpersonal difficulties are drawn to online interaction.Thus far, this chapter has reviewed research indicating a significant positive association among PIU, online social interaction, and psychosocial difficulties. What the literature is less clear about, however, is *how* and *why* these associations occur. The remainder of this chapter presents a theoretical model that explains these relationships and suggests directions for future research.

ONLINE SOCIAL BEHAVIOR AND THE COGNITIVE BEHAVIORAL MODEL

Davis (2001; Davis et al., 2002) introduced a cognitive-behavioral theory of PIU that attempts to model the etiology, development, and outcomes associated with PIU. Since its introduction, this model has been useful in developing a better understanding of PIU and interpersonal Internet use. The cognitive-behavioral model asserts that Internet-related cognitions and behaviors that lead to negative outcomes are *consequences*, rather than *causes*, of broader psychosocial problems (e.g., depression, social anxiety, loneliness, social skill deficit). In other words, this perspective asserts that psychosocial problems predispose individuals to develop maladaptive cognitions that lead to deficient self-regulation, ultimately resulting in negative outcomes associated with Internet use (Davis, 2001; Caplan, 2005, 2010).

Researchers have suggested that one cognitive symptom of PIU is a preference for online social interaction (POSI) over FtF social interaction (Caplan, 2003; Davis, 2001; Morahan-Martin & Schumacher, 2000; for a review see Morahan-Martin, 2008). POSI is "a cognitive individual-difference construct characterized by beliefs that one is safer, more efficacious, more confident, and more comfortable with online interpersonal interactions and relationships than with traditional FtF social activities" (Caplan, 2003, p. 629). Individuals who prefer online social interaction also believe they possess interpersonal advantages online. Research indicates that POSI is associated with both psychosocial well-being and behavioral elements of PIU (i.e, compulsive use). For example, Morahan-Martin and Schumacher (2000) found that college students who engaged in Internet abuse were more likely than other students to say they preferred online social interaction over FtF exchanges:

> Social aspects of Internet use consistently differentiated those with more Internet use problems from others. Pathological users were more likely to use

the Internet for meeting new people, emotional support, talking to others sharing the same interests, and playing socially interactive games.... [Pathological users] are friendlier, more open, and more themselves and they report it is easier to make friends when online. They have more fun with people online than non-pathological users and are more likely to share intimate secrets online as well ... for them, the Internet can be socially liberating, the Prozac of social communication. (Morahan-Martin & Schumacher, 2000, p. 26)

A study by Caplan (2003) found that, consistent with the cognitive-behavioral model, POSI mediated the relationship between psychosocial problems and negative outcomes of Internet use. More specifically, Caplan (2003) found that participants' self-reported levels of loneliness predicted their levels of POSI, which in turn predicted the extent to which they reported experiencing negative outcomes due to their Internet use. In another study on impression-management skill, Caplan (2005) found that POSI mediated the negative association between social skills and compulsive Internet use. This particular study examined college students' self-presentational skill, which Riggio (1989) defined as one's ability to be "adept, tactful, and self-confident in social situations" and to "fit in comfortably in just about any type of social situation" (p. 3). Caplan (2005) hypothesized that "in order to increase their perceived self-presentational ability and to decrease social risk, people with [self-presentational] skill deficits are likely to seek out communicative channels (such as CMC [computer-mediated communication]) that minimize potential costs and enhance their limited abilities" (p. 724). The results revealed that college students' level of self-presentational skill was inversely related to their levels of POSI, compulsive Internet use, and levels of negative outcomes due to Internet use. That is, the lower one's self-presentational skill, the greater one's level of POSI and compulsive Internet use and the more one experienced negative outcomes for online activity. In that study, POSI mediated the association between social skill deficit and negative outcomes of Internet use.

Additionally, there is also empirical evidence that social anxiety is associated with POSI (Caplan, 2007; Erwin et al., 2004; Morahan-Martin, 2008). In a review of this literature, Morahan-Martin (2008, pp. 5253) observed that "the preference for online over [FtF] interaction may be a key factor in the relationship between [Internet abuse] and both loneliness and social anxiety. Those who are chronically lonely and those who are socially anxious share many characteristics which predispose them to develop IA. Both are apprehensive in approaching others, fearing negative evaluations and rejection. They tend to be self-preoccupied with their perceived social deficiencies, which leads them to be inhibited, reticent, and withdrawn in interpersonal situations and avoid social interactions."

A study by Erwin et al. (2004), mentioned earlier, examined Internet use among people with social anxiety disorder. Participants with social anxiety disorder reported that they use the Internet because they experience greater comfort interacting on the Internet than face-to-face. The participants' social anxiety levels were positively correlated with "endorsement of most aspects of using the Internet that may enable avoidance of face-to-face interactions" (p. 640). Highly anxious individuals actually felt it was easier for them to interact in CMC than in FtF situations. Even more, socially anxious individuals spent most of their time passively observing online social interactions, rather than actively engaging in these activities. Thus, there appears to be a specific relationship among social anxiety, POSI, and PIU.

In sum, the literature presented in this section demonstrates that, as hypothesized by the cognitive-behavioral model, well-being is correlated with a preference for online social interaction. There is a clear and consistent pattern in the literature indicating that POSI is associated with loneliness, depression, social anxiety, and low social skill. In order to understand why people with psychosocial difficulties might be attracted to online social interaction, the next section reviews the major theories that have shaped our understanding of how CMC and FtF interaction are similar and how they are different.

HOW IS CMC DIFFERENT FROM FTF COMMUNICATION?

As the Internet has changed over the past decades, so have theories seeking to explain the important differences between FtF and computer-mediated conversation (for a review see Walther, 2006). Describing consistent channel differences between CMC and FtF contexts is a difficult task as technologies evolve and people become more skilled users of technology. As such, the literature reveals numerous contradictory findings about channel differences between CMC and FtF contexts.

A number of theories describe ways in which interpersonal processes in CMC applications are distinct from FtF interaction (for more extensive reviews see Hancock & Dunham, 2001; Ramirez, Walther, Burgoon, & Sunnafrank, 2002; Walther, 2006; Walther & Parks, 2002). In general, most theories that recognize differences between FtF and CMC contexts fall into either of two theoretical paradigms. Early CMC theories reflect the *cues filtered out paradigm*, which emphasizes channel limitations and asserts that CMC limits the information people obtain from nonverbal cues. Due to the diminished nonverbal cues online, scholars argued that online interaction does not possess adequate resources for effective relational interaction (Culnan & Markus, 1987; Daft, Lengel, & Trevino, 1987; Kiesler, 1986; Kiesler, Siegel, & McGuire, 1984; Rice & Case, 1983; Short, Williams, & Christie, 1976). Cues-filtered-out theorists contend that CMC's lack of nonverbal cues universally constrains the medium such that it can never match the efficacy of FtF channels.

In contrast, the more modern *cues filtered in* theories contend that CMC is an especially effective channel for interpersonal communication (Postmes, Spears, & Lea, 1998; Postmes, Spears, Lea, & Reicher, 2000; Walther, 1992, 1996, 2006, 2007). Cues-filtered-in theories embrace CMC's diminished nonverbal cues and argue that the limited information transmitted online is actually an interpersonal advantage for some people. In fact, some theorists assert that CMC's unique properties allow online interactants to achieve more social success online than in FtF interactions (Walther, 1996, 2006). For the purposes of this chapter, cues-filtered-in theories offer the cognitive-behavioral model of PIU a theoretical account of why people with psychosocial problems might be drawn to online social interaction.

Cues-filtered-in theories argue that CMC's features facilitate relational development and help people to achieve meaningful relationships with positive interpersonal outcomes online. For example, *social information processing* (SIP) theory explicitly rejects the assumption that CMC's lack of nonverbal cues limits communicators' capabilities (Walther, 1992). Instead, SIP theory posits that people adapt to the lack of nonverbal information online by putting more weight on the content, style, and timing of verbal messages (Walther, 1992, 1996). From this perspective, the cues that are available online carry information normally transmitted via a host of nonverbal cues in FtF exchanges.

According to SIP theory, the key difference between relational information exchanged online and information exchanged in FtF interaction "has to do not with the *amount* of social information exchanged but with the *rate* of social information exchange" (Walther, 1996, p. 10). Thus, the relative lack of nonverbal information in CMC does not necessarily limit the amount of information users can transmit; however, it does slow the rate of information transmission. SIP theory posits that relational communication takes longer to emerge in CMC than in FtF conversations (Walther, 1992; Walther & Parks, 2002). Yet, the theory argues that, after sufficient time passes and users exchange numerous messages, levels of relational development in CMC will begin to equal those experienced in FtF interactions (Walther, 1993). One important question for PIU researchers to ask is whether SIP's hypothesis that intimacy development in CMC requires more time than in FtF conversations might help explain why POSI may lead to negative outcomes from Internet use. That is, people may need to invest more time in order to manage their online relationships, which would lead them to spend greater amounts of time online.

The *social identity model of deindividuation effects (SIDE)* is another cues-filtered-in theory, which proposes that people adapt to the lack of nonverbal cues online (Postmes et al., 1998; Postmes et al., 2000). Rather than assuming people are constrained by fewer nonverbal cues online, SIDE posits that in cue-limited online interactions, people focus their attention on contextual cues and information related to the social status of interactants (Lea & Spears, 1992; Spears & Lea, 1992). The theory hypothesizes that the anonymous or deindividuated conditions of CMC promote a social identity and strong group-based bonds. In the absence of personally identifying information, SIDE theory contends that people downplay their personal identities and emphasize the social identity they share with their fellow CMC conversants. Accordingly, people might emphasize identities related to shared group memberships or typographical styles. Rather than being an impersonal environment filled with superficial impressions, SIDE frames CMC as a socially rich environment in which group-based cues are overattributed in the absence of individuating information (Spears & Lea, 1992).

Finally, and perhaps most importantly for the current chapter, the *hyperpersonal perspective* is a cues-filtered-in theory that counters the cues-filtered-out paradigm by arguing that online interaction may be superior to FtF exchanges. Hyperpersonal theory asserts that the relative lack of nonverbals online enhances interpersonal communication such that social goals can be more effectively pursued online than in FtF conversations. As Walther (1996, p. 17) described, hyperpersonal communication is "CMC that is more socially desirable than we tend to experience in parallel FtF interaction." According to the hyperpersonal perspective, mediated interaction affords actors the opportunity to adapt to and exploit the diminished nonverbal cues in CMC in ways that enhance their ability to attain interpersonal goals (Dunthler, 2006; Walther, 1996, 2006). For example, the verbal content that dominates CMC exchanges is easier to control and strategically manipulate than nonverbal behaviors (Ekman & Friesen, 1969). Specifically, CMC requires people to type their responses before sending them; a communicator is able to revise or abandon unfavorable messages more easily than in FtF conversations (Walther, 1996, 2006).

The hyperpersonal perspective also hypothesizes that a positive feedback loop exists in CMC whereby interactants positively reflect upon a partner's selectively presented information and then treat them consistently with these reflections (Walther, 1996). In other words, mediated selective self-presentation may lead partners to form more favorable impressions than in FtF settings, which, in turn, leads to continued positive behavior by the sender. According to Walther (1996), "this may explain how such surprisingly intimate, sometimes intense, and hyperpersonal interactions take place in CMC. CMC provides an intensification loop" (p. 27).

The hyperpersonal perspective offers a useful explanation for why people may prefer online social exchanges, suggesting that CMC enables people to express identity-important characteristics that they are unable to express in parallel FtF situations (Bargh, McKenna, & Fitzsimmons, 2002). Online, interactants can mask or edit undesirable and uncontrollable cues while magnifying preferred cues (Walther, 1996, 1997). According to the hyperpersonal perspective, CMC enables conversational actors to "engage in selective self-presentation and partner idealization, enacting exchanges more intimate than those of FtF counterparts" (Tidwell & Walther, 2002, p. 319). By reducing the nonverbal cues that sometimes contradict verbal messages, partners in CMC are particularly likely to base their impressions of one another on the selectively presented information they exchange online (Walther, 1996). In fact, hyperpersonal theory speculates that receivers often overattribute the selectively presented social information transmitted via CMC (Walther, 1997; Walther, Slovacek, & Tidwell, 2001). These overattributions then result in idealized perceptions of relational partners (Walther, 1996, 1997). From this perspective, people engaging in online social interaction are likely to form idealized impressions based on limited but strategically filtered personal information. Walther (2006) suggests that hyperpersonal communication may foster higher levels of relational immediacy and affection than normal FtF interactions. Along these lines, scholars have documented that relational intimacy develops faster and reaches higher levels online than FtF (Hian, Chuan, Trevor, & Detenber, 2004). Thus, the hyperpersonal perspective posits several interpersonal benefits to online communication.

The hyperpersonal perspective is especially useful for explaining why people with pre-existing psychosocial problems, such as social anxiety, prefer online social interaction (High & Caplan, 2009). These individuals may be drawn to hyperpersonal communication online because they perceive it to be safer, easier, and more effective than ordinary face-to-face conversation (Caplan, 2007; Erwin et al., 2004; Morahan-Martin & Schumacher, 2003). Morahan-Martin and Schumacher (2003) asserted that "online, social presence and intimacy levels can be controlled; users can remain invisible as they observe others' interactions, and can control the amount and timing of their interactions. Anonymity and lack of face-to-face communication online may decrease self-consciousness and social anxiety" (p. 659). In one study, O'Sullivan (2000) examined preference for different interpersonal communication channels (CMC, FtF, telephone) and found that people's preferences varied depending on how much self-presentational risk they appraised the situation to have. O'Sullivan's participants preferred mediated interpersonal channels when their self-presentation was threatened. As Davis et al. (2002) proposed, "for some individuals, the Internet becomes a buffer for threatening social interactions" (p. 332).

Additionally, the hyperpersonal perspective argues that the lack of nonverbal cues in CMC should enable communicators to free more cognitive resources to devote to message production, reception, and exchange processes (Walther, 1996, 1997). In other words, from this perspective, the cognitive demands associated with social anxiety or interpersonal difficulties might be alleviated in an online context where people feel more socially confident and efficacious. Thus, another reason why people with psychosocial problems might prefer online social interaction is that CMC enables people to devote increased cognitive resources to positive self-presentation and advancement of interpersonal goals. In sum, the perceived ease, effectiveness, and safety of CMC theorized in the hyperpersonal perspective may draw individuals with psychosocial problems to mediated interaction.

Research supports the hyperpersonal perspective and suggests that hyperpersonal communication is common in online social interaction (Chester & Gwynne, 1998; Gibbs, Ellison, & Heino, 2006; Henderson & Gilding, 2004). For example, Dunthler (2006) found that in CMC contexts, communicators had more time to produce messages, were better able to organize their thoughts, and were able to better manage how they presented themselves. Henderson and Gilding (2004) observed that respondents took special care to strategically construct messages in CMC. Researchers have also observed that synchronous

CMC channels appear to be particularly conducive to hyperpersonal communication. In these channels, users benefit from relaxed temporal commitments and can compose their messages when they feel comfortable doing so. More precisely, scholars have noted that asynchronous communication allows people to organize, plan, edit, and develop their thoughts more mindfully and deliberatively than they can in temporally immediate media (Dunthler, 2006; Hiemstra, 1982). Walther (1996) contends, "Asynchronous interaction may thus have the capacity to be more socially desirable and effective as composers are able to concentrate on message construction to satisfy multiple or single concerns at their own pace" (p. 26). Accordingly, people are able to produce more polite messages via asynchronous, text-based CMC than they can in synchronous channels (Dunthler, 2006). Asynchronicity allows people to spread the cognitive load of message construction across a longer time period than exists in synchronous contexts. Thus, asynchronicity is likely to be attractive to individuals who find FtF interactions difficult or who experience a high cognitive or emotional demand when managing FtF situations.

Thus far, this chapter has (1) presented research indicating that people with various psychosocial problems prefer online social interaction and (2) argued that the hyperpersonal perspective offers a useful theoretical account of why this may occur. The remainder of the current chapter explores how and why POSI might facilitate the development of other symptoms of PIU. In general, Caplan (2010) proposes that individuals who prefer online social interaction develop a reliance on online social interaction that may result in other symptoms of PIU—going online to alter moods, cognitive preoccupation, compulsive use, and negative outcomes.

Two important cognitive symptoms of PIU are motivation to use the Internet for mood regulation and a cognitive preoccupation with the online world (Caplan, 2003, 2005, 2010; Davis et al., 2002). Mood regulation refers to using the Internet to alleviate a dysphoric affective state such as anxiety, loneliness, or depression. Cognitive preoccupation refers to obsessive thought patterns involving the Internet use (i.e., "I can't stop thinking about going online" or "When I am offline, I can't stop wondering what is happening online"). Caplan (2005, 2010) argues that when individuals exhibit a substantial POSI, they are likely to use computer-mediated communication to regulate their mood. For example, people with high POSI may seek to mitigate the social anxiety they experience in FtF situations by using CMC to meet their interpersonal needs.

Additionally, individuals who have a high POSI may be especially likely to seek out computer-mediated sources of social support to alleviate affective distress. In other words, POSI may lead individuals to use the Internet rather than traditional FtF contexts, when they seek comforting and companionship from members of their support network. A study by Caplan (2010) revealed that POSI positively predicted use of the Internet for mood regulation and that both POSI and using the Internet for mood regulation predicted cognitive preoccupation with the Internet and compulsive Internet use. In other words, these results suggest that POSI and using the Internet for mood regulation are associated with greater levels of deficient self-regulation of Internet use.

The cognitive-behavioral theory argues that, if the cognitive symptoms of PIU are salient enough, they lead to behavioral symptoms that ultimately result in negative outcomes. For the most part, however, scholars have recognized that excessive use in and of itself is not necessarily problematic (Caplan, 2003; Caplan & High, 2007; Kim & Davis, 2009). In terms of specifying particular online behaviors that give rise to generalized PIU, Davis (2001) argues that "there is not a specific time limit or behavioral benchmark" for identifying Internet use as problematic; instead, the cognitive-behavioral model of PIU "posits a continuum of functioning" (p. 193).

From this perspective, then, the primary behavioral symptom of PIU is *compulsive Internet use*—an inability to control, or regulate, one's online behavior. Indeed, in a review of research on PIU, Shapira and colleagues (2003) concluded that, "based on the current limited empirical evidence, problematic Internet use may best be classified as an impulse control disorder" (p. 207). Caplan (2003) compared the extent to which excessive Internet use and compulsive Internet use predicted negative outcomes associated with PIU. Excessive and compulsive Internet use were both significant predictors of negative outcomes associated with Internet use; however, "excessive use was one of the weakest predictors of negative outcomes, whereas preference for online social interaction, compulsive use, and [cognitive preoccupation] were among the strongest" (pp. 637–638). In another study, Caplan and High (2007) found that the relationship between excessive Internet use and its negative outcomes was moderated by cognitive preoccupation with the Internet.

The cognitive-behavioral model advanced here predicts that deficient self-regulation of Internet use will result in negative outcomes. Studies support this hypothesis as well. Caplan (2010) found that POSI and using the Internet for mood alteration both were significant predictors of deficient self-regulation (i.e., compulsive use and cognitive preoccupation). The results also revealed that the deficient self-regulation was a significant predictor of negative outcomes. The findings indicated that POSI and mood regulation predicted negative outcomes *indirectly* via their association with deficient regulation. In other words, deficient self-regulation mediated the association both between POSI and negative outcomes and between mood regulation and negative outcomes. Together, the cognitive and behavioral symptoms (POSI, mood regulation, and deficient self-regulation) accounted for 61% of the explained variance in participants' negative outcome scores. These results support the hypothesis that POSI and mood regulation facilitate deficient self-regulation and, ultimately, negative outcomes from Internet use.

CONCLUSION

To summarize, this chapter sought to explain the association between online social interaction, psychosocial well-being, and PIU. Research reviewed at the beginning of the chapter demonstrated an association between interpersonal Internet use and both psychosocial difficulties and PIU. In an effort to explain how and why these associations happen, the remainder of the chapter presented a cognitive-behavioral model suggesting that people's psychosocial problems may predispose them to prefer online social interaction and, in turn, lead to mood regulation, deficient self-regulation, and negative outcomes. Overall, the literature reviewed in this chapter supports the claim that interpersonal uses of the Internet are associated with PIU because POSI plays a major role in the etiology of problematic use.

As research on interpersonal Internet use and PIU continues to evolve, there are a number of questions that researchers have yet to answer. The cognitive-behavioral model would benefit from further detail explicating how and why POSI is related to using the Internet for mood regulation (what are the mechanisms at work in this relationship?). Along a similar line, although we know that POSI predicts compulsive use indirectly via mood regulation, studies indicate there is also a direct association between POSI and deficient self-regulation (Caplan, 2010). Here, researchers need to try to better understand the other ways that POSI predicts deficient self-regulation. Future research might also improve the model by considering whether different types of interpersonal Internet use (i.e., instant messaging, chat rooms, e-mail) are more or less strongly associated with POSI, mood regulation, deficient self-regulation, and negative outcomes. And, finally, researchers need to examine why using the Internet for mood regulation predicts deficient self-regulation and negative outcomes. Indeed, we can also identify situations where using CMC for mood alteration might predict more positive outcomes (e.g., online support groups and online therapy) (for a review see Wright, 2009). Why might using online interaction for mood alteration help some and hinder others?

In sum, although the Internet has done much to enhance our ability to engage in interpersonal communication across time and distance, the research presented in this chapter indicates that such interactions may create problems for some people. It is important to emphasize that the literature reviewed here does not suggest that online social behavior per se is dangerous or risky; rather, the literature indicates that people with psychosocial problems are likely to prefer online social interaction and may be particularly vulnerable to using the Internet to manage their moods and to experiencing difficulty controlling their use.

REFERENCES

Amichai-Hamburger, Y., & Ben-Artzi, E. (2003). Loneliness and Internet use. *Computers in Human Behavior*, *19*, 71–80.

Bargh, J. A., McKenna, K. Y. A., & Fitzsimmons, G. M. (2002). Can you see the real me? Activation and expression of the "true self" on the Internet. *Journal of Social Issues*, *58*, 33–48.

Caplan, S. E. (2002). Problematic Internet use and psychosocial well-being: Development of a theory-based cognitive-behavioral measurement instrument. *Computers in Human Behavior, 18,* 553–575.

Caplan, S. E. (2003). Preference for online social interaction: A theory of problematic Internet use and psychosocial well-being. *Communication Research, 30,* 625–648.

Caplan, S. E. (2005). A social skill account of problematic Internet use. *Journal of Communication, 55,* 721–736.

Caplan, S. E. (2007). Relations among loneliness, social anxiety, and problematic Internet use. *CyberPsychology & Behavior, 10,* 234–241.

Caplan, S. E. (2010). Theory and measurement of generalized problematic Internet use: A two-step approach. *Computers in Human Behavior, 26,* 1089–1097.

Caplan, S. E., & High, A. C. (2007). Beyond excessive use: The interaction between cognitive and behavioral symptoms of problematic Internet use. *Communication Research Reports, 23,* 265-271.

Caplan, S. E., Williams, D., & Yee, N. (2009). Problematic Internet use and psychosocial well-being among MMO players. *Computers in Human Behavior, 25,* 1312–1319.

Chak, K., & Leung, L. (2004). Shyness and locus of control as predictors of Internet addiction and Internet use. *CyberPsychology & Behavior, 7,* 559–570.

Chester, A., & Gwynne, G. (1998). Online teaching: Encouraging collaboration through anonymity. *Journal of Computer-Mediated Communication, 4.* Retrieved from http://jcmc.indiana.edu/vol4/issue2/chester.html

Culnan, M. J., & Markus, M. L. (1987). Information technologies. In F. M. Jablin, L. L. Putnam, K. H. Roberts, & L. W. Porter (Eds.), *Handbook of organizational communication: An interdisciplinary perspective* (pp. 420–443). Newbury Park, CA: Sage.

Daft, R. L., Lengel, R. H., & Trevino, L. K. (1987). Message equivocality, media selection, and manager performance: Implications for information systems. *MIS Quarterly, 11,* 355–366.

Davis, R. A. (2001). A cognitive-behavioral model of pathological Internet use. *Computers in Human Behavior, 17,* 187–195.

Davis, R. A., Flett, G. L., & Besser, A. (2002). Validation of a new scale for measuring problematic Internet use: Implications for pre-employment screening [Special issue: Internet and the workplace]. *CyberPsychology & Behavior, 5,* 331–345.

Dunthler, K. W. (2006). The politeness of requests made via email and voicemail: Support for the hyperpersonal model. *Journal of Computer-Mediated Communication,* 500–521.

Ekman, P., & Friesen, W. V. (1969). Nonverbal leakage and cues to deception. *Psychiatry, 32,* 88–105.

Erwin, B. A., Turk, C. L., Heimberg, R. G., Fresco, D. M., & Hantula, D. A. (2004). The Internet: Home to a severe population of individuals with social anxiety disorder? *Anxiety Disorders, 18,* 629-646.

Gibbs, J. L., Ellison, N. B., & Heino, R. D. (2006). Self-presentation in online personals: The role of anticipated future interaction, self-disclosure, and perceived success in Internet dating. *Communication Research, 33,* 1–26.

Hancock, J. T., & Dunham, P. J. (2001). Impression formation in computer-mediated communication revisited: An analysis of the breadth and intensity of impressions. *Communication Research, 28*, 325–347.

Henderson, S., & Gilding, M. (2004). "I've never clicked this much with anyone in my life": Trust and hyperpersonal communication in online friendships. *New Media & Society, 6*, 487–506.

Hian, L. B., Chuan, S. L., Trevor, T. M. K., & Detenber, B. H. (2004). Getting to know you: Exploring the development of relational intimacy in computer-mediated communication. *Journal of Computer-Mediated Communication, 9.* Retrieved from http://jcmc.indiana.edu/vol9/issue3/detenber.html

Hiemstra, G. (1982). Teleconferencing, concern for face, and organizational culture. In M. Burgoon (Ed.), *Communication yearbook 6* (pp. 874–904). Beverly Hills, CA: Sage.

High, A., & Caplan, S. E. (2009). Social anxiety and computer-mediated communication during initial interactions: Implications for the hyperpersonal perspective. *Computers in Human Behavior, 25*, 475-482.

Kiesler, S. (1986). The hidden messages in computer networks. *Harvard Business Review, 64*, 46–54.

Kiesler, S., Siegel, J., & McGuire, T. W. (1984). Social psychological aspects of computer-mediated communication. *American Psychologist, 39*, 1123–1134.

Kim, H., & Davis, K. E. (2009). Toward a comprehensive theory of problematic Internet use: Evaluating the role of self-esteem, anxiety, flow, and the self-rated importance of Internet activities. *Computers in Human Behavior, 25*, 490–500.

Kubey, R. W., Lavin, M. J., & Barrows, J. R. (2001). Internet use and collegiate academic performance decrements: Early findings. *Journal of Communication, 51*, 366–382.

LaRose, R. (2001). On the negative effects of e-commerce: A sociocognitive exploration of unregulated on-line buying. *Journal of Computer-Mediated Communication, 6.* from http://jcmc.indiana.edu/vol6/issue3/larose.html

LaRose, R., Eastin, M. S., & Gregg, J. (2001). Reformulating the Internet paradox: Social cognitive explanations of Internet use and depression. *Journal of Online Behavior, 1*(2). Retrieved from http://www.behavior.net/JOB/v1n2/paradox.html

LaRose, R., Lin, C. A., & Eastin, M. S. (2003). Unregulated Internet usage: Addiction, habit, or deficient self-regulation? *Media Psychology, 5*, 225–253.

LaRose, R., Mastro, D., & Eastin, M. S. (2001). Understanding Internet usage: A social-cognitive approach to uses and gratifications. *Social Science Computer Review, 19*, 395–413.

Lea, M., & Spears, R. (1992). Paralanguage and social perceptions in computer-mediated communication. *Journal of Organizational Computing, 2*, 321–341.

McKenna, K. Y. A., & Bargh, J. A. (2000). Plan 9 from cyberspace: The implications of the Internet for personality and social psychology. *Journal of Personality and Social Psychology, 75*, 681–694.

Mitchell, K. J., & Ybarra, M. L. (2007). Online behavior of youth who engage in self-harm provides clues for preventive intervention. *Preventive Medicine, 45*, 392–396.

Mittal, V. A., Tessner, K. D., & Walker, E. F. (2007). Elevated social Internet use and schizotypal personality disorder in adolescents. *Schizophrenia Research, 94,* 50–57.

Morahan-Martin, J. (1999). The relationship between loneliness and Internet use and abuse. *CyberPsychology & Behavior, 2,* 431–440.

Morahan-Martin, J. (2007). Internet use and abuse and psychological problems. In J. Joinson, K. McKenna, T. Postmes, & U. Reips, *Oxford handbook of Internet psychology* (pp. 331–345). Oxford, UK: Oxford University Press.

Morahan-Martin, J. (2008). Internet abuse: Emerging trends and lingering questions. In A. Barak (Ed.), *Psychological aspects of cyberspace: Theory, research and applications* (pp. 32–69). Cambridge, UK: Cambridge University Press.

Morahan-Martin, J., & Schumacher, P. (2000). Incidence and correlates of pathological Internet use among college students. *Computers in Human Behavior, 16*(1), 13–29.

Morahan-Martin, J., & Schumacher, P. (2003). Loneliness and social uses of the Internet. *Computers in Human Behavior 19,* 659–671.

Ngai, S. S. (2007). Exploring the validity of the Internet Addiction Test for students in grades 5–9 in Hong Kong. *Journal of Adolescence and Youth, 13,* 221–237.

O'Sullivan, P. B. (2000). What you don't know won't hurt me: Impression management functions of communication channels in relationships. *Human Communication Research, 26,* 403–431.

Postmes, T., Spears, R., & Lea, M. (1998). Breaching or building social boundaries? SIDE-effects of computer-mediated communication. *Communication Research, 25,* 689–715.

Postmes, T., Spears, R., Lea, M., & Reicher, S. D. (2000). *SIDE issues centre stage: Recent developments in studies of deindividuation in groups.* Amsterdam: Royal Netherlands Academy of Arts and Sciences.

Ramirez, A., Jr., Walther, J. B., Burgoon, J. K., & Sunnafrank, M. (2002). Information-seeking strategies, uncertainty, and computer-mediated communication: Toward a conceptual model. *Human Communication Research, 28,* 213–228.

Rice, R. E., & Case, D. (1983). Electronic messages systems in the university: A description of use and utility. *Journal of Communication, 33,* 131–152.

Riggio, R. (1989). *The social skills inventory manual: Research edition.* Palo Alto, CA: Consulting Psychologists Press.

Scherer, K. (1997). College life on-line: Healthy and unhealthy Internet use. *Journal of College Student Development, 38,* 655–665.

Shapira, N. A., Lessig, M. C., Goldsmith, T. D., Szabo, S. T., Lazoritz, M., & Gold, M. S., et al. (2003). Problematic Internet use: Proposed classification and diagnostic criteria. *Depression & Anxiety, 17*(4), 207–216.

Short, J., Williams, E., & Christie, B. (1976). *The social psychology of telecommunications.* London: John Wiley & Sons.

Spears, R., & Lea, M. (1992). Social influence and the influence of the "social" in computer-mediated communication. In M. Lea (Ed.), *Contexts of computer-mediated communication* (pp. 30–65). Hertfordshire, England: Harvester Wheatsheaf.

Tidwell, L. C., & Walther, J. B. (2002). Computer-mediated communication effects on disclosure, impressions, and interpersonal evaluations: Getting to know one another a bit at a time. *Human Communication Research, 28,* 317–348.

Valkenburg, P. M., & Peter, J. (2007). Internet communication and its relationship to well-being: Identifying some underlying mechanisms. *Media Psychology, 9,* 43–58.

Valkenburg, P. M., Peter, J. & Schouten, A. (2006). Friend networking sites and their relationship to adolescents' well-being and social self-esteem. *CyberPsychology & Behavior, 9,* 584–590.

van den Eijnden, R. J. J. M., Meerkerk, G., Vermulst, A. A., Spijkerman, R., & Engels, R. C. M. E. (2008). Online communication, compulsive Internet use, and psychosocial well-being among adolescents: A longitudinal study. *Developmental Psychology, 44,* 655–665.

Wallace, P. M. (1999). *The psychology of the Internet.* New York: Cambridge University Press.

Walther, J. B. (1992). Interpersonal effects in computer-mediated interaction: A relational perspective. *Communication Research, 19,* 52–89.

Walther, J. B. (1993). Impression development in computer-mediated interaction. *Western Journal of Communication, 57,* 381–398.

Walther, J. B. (1996). Computer-mediated communication: Impersonal, interpersonal, and hyperpersonal interaction. *Communication Research 23,* 3-43.

Walther, J. B. (1997). Group and interpersonal effects in international computer-mediated collaboration. *Human Communication Research, 23,* 342–369.

Walther, J. B. (2006). Nonverbal dynamics in computer-mediated communication, or :(and the Net :('s with you, :) and you :) alone. In V. Manusov & M. L. Patterson (Eds.), *Handbook of nonverbal communication* (pp. 461–480). Thousand Oaks, CA: Sage.

Walther, J. B. (2007). Selective self-presentation in computer-mediated communication: Hyperpersonal dimensions of technology, language, and cognition. *Computers in Human Behavior, 23,* 2538–2557.

Walther, J. B., & Parks, M. R. (2002). Cues filtered out, cues filtered in: Computer-mediated communication and relationships. In M. L. Knapp, J. A. Daly, & G. R. Miller (Eds.), *The handbook of interpersonal communication* (3rd ed., pp. 529–559). Thousand Oaks, CA: Sage.

Walther, J. B., Slovacek, C. L., & Tidwell, L. C. (2001). Is a picture worth a thousand words? Photographic images in long-term and short-term computer-mediated communication. *Communication Research, 28,* 105–134.

Wolak, J., Mitchell, K. J., & Finkelhor, D. (2003). Escaping or connecting? Characteristics of youth who form close online relationships. *Journal of Adolescence, 26,* 105–119.

Wright, K. B. (2009). Increasing computer-mediated social support. In J. C. Parker & E. Thorson (Eds.), *Health communication in the new media landscape* (pp. 243–265). New York: Springer Publishing.

Ybarra, M. L., Alexander, C., & Mitchell, K. J. (2005). Depressive symptomatology, youth Internet use, and online interactions: A national survey. *Journal of Adolescent Health, 36,* 9–18.

Young, K. S. (1996). Psychology of computer use XI: Addictive use of the Internet; A case study that breaks the stereotype. *Psychological Reports, 79*, 899–902.

Young, K. S. (1998). Internet addiction: The emergence of a new clinical disorder. *CyberPsychology & Behavior, 1*, 237–244.

Young, K. S., & Rogers, R. C. (1998). The relationship between depression and Internet addiction. *CyberPsychology & Behavior, 1*, 25–28.

CHAPTER 4

Uses and Gratifications of Internet Addiction

ROBERT LAROSE

H OW DO online activities that begin as fleeting diversions evolve into favorite activities and pleasurable habits but sometimes progress to problematic forms of excessive Internet use? And, given the ready availability of so many different enjoyable online pastimes, how is it that problematic forms of use are not even more prevalent? This chapter examines the development of Internet habits from the perspective of communication research that focuses on the uses and gratifications (UGs) that individuals seek online. It develops a model of Internet usage among normal populations that combines both conscious and nonconscious mental processes to account for the initial stages of the progression from normal Internet use to more problematic forms. The self-regulatory mechanisms that moderate excessive Internet use are discussed along with prevention strategies for controlling the growth of potentially harmful Internet habits.

USES AND GRATIFICATIONS OF INTERNET ADDICTION

In order for therapists to assess clients who suffer from Internet addiction, it is important to consider what makes the Internet so appealing. The following outlines several theories on uses and gratifications of Internet addiction. Among addicts, their use of the Internet goes beyond using technology as a functional information tool. Among addicts, something much deeper and richer is occurring. It is important for therapists assessing a client who suffers from Internet addiction to understand the underlying reasons contributing to the behavior. What is often called media habits, each client uses the Internet with specific intentions. These intentions can take on multiple forms from general pleasure-seeking behavior, to using it as a form of entertainment, to using it as a means to fulfill social needs. The reasons vary but throughout these models each is explained so that therapists can examine what needs Internet use is fulfilling among clients. This will enable them to develop individualized treatment plans that should sustain recovery.

GOOD INTERNET HABITS AND BAD ONES

How do ordinary Internet activities initially attract their users, develop into diverting favorite activities, and then sometimes become fulfilling pastimes but at other times turn into potentially harmful or even pathological habits that disrupt the lives of their users? Also, given the wide range of appealing online activities tailored to seemingly every conceivable need and available 24/7, how do so many Internet users avoid becoming hooked on a favorite pastime and descending into a downward spiral of mounting use, withdrawal from vital life activities, and rising isolation and despair? In the context of the present volume, the goal is to help clinicians, educators, and parents understand and encourage healthy, normal use as well as uncover the processes that may lead to excessive use that threatens psychological well-being.

The present investigation explores these issues from the perspective of the uses and gratifications (UGs) paradigm of communication research that seeks to explain media use among normal, nonclinical populations. Long considered a dominant paradigm accounting for the use of so-called old media modalities such as television and newspapers, the UGs paradigm has enjoyed something of a renaissance through its application to the Internet (e.g., by Papacharissi & Rubin, 2000; Song, LaRose, Lin, & Eastin, 2004), where its explanatory power has been enriched by the conceptualization of new mechanisms that help to explain the initiation of pleasurable pastimes and the development of media habits (e.g., LaRose, 2009; LaRose & Eastin, 2004; LaRose, Lin, & Eastin, 2003).

The chapter begins by recounting the basic elements of UGs. Next, it reviews applications of the paradigm to Internet use and recent refinements that explain new media use. Then the processes by which normal Internet use may progress to problematic habits are explained. Finally, the chapter considers the implications of UGs for the prevention of problematic forms of Internet use.

THE USES AND GRATIFICATIONS PARADIGM

The uses and gratifications (UGs) paradigm originated in the efforts of the communication researchers of the 1940s to identify the functions of the mass media (Ruggerio, 2000). Elihu Katz, a noted media sociologist and student of Karl Lazarsfeld's, and his colleagues are often credited as the originators of the UGs paradigm as it is known today. The basic premises of UGs are that media users are active in their selection of media content and make deliberate choices among the media alternatives available to them based on their needs. Simply put, UGs are the reasons people give for using various media. Katz, Gurevitch, and Haas (1973) is a frequently cited seminal study that differentiated media based on the needs they fulfilled for their audiences. For example, television was associated with entertainment needs whereas newspapers were associated with information needs, offering support for the basic premise that media selections fulfill distinct audience needs.

Gratifications are assessed through responses to verbal statements about respondents' reasons for media consumption (e.g. enjoyment, social interaction), typically assessed on a multipoint rating scale. For example, Rubin (1984) used a five-point agree-disagree scale ranging from "strongly disagree" to "strongly agree," whereas Papacharissi and Rubin (2000) asked how much respondents' reasons were like the stated reasons on a scale ranging from "exactly" to "not at all." An early refinement was to distinguish gratifications sought from the media from gratifications obtained and to examine the match between the two in order to obtain superior predictions of media consumption behavior. The difference between gratifications sought and gratifications obtained is in the time frame of the assessment—that is, whether respondents are asked about the gratifications they will seek from future media use or about the gratifications they experienced from past media use. If the same person is asked about both past and future use, the arithmetic difference between the two can be computed, a measure of how well expectations were met. However, gratifications sought produced the best empirical predictions of media consumption compared to gratifications obtained or to the arithmetic difference between the two, so gratifications sought became prevalent in the research that followed. These are posed in the present tense (e.g., "I use the Internet . . . to help others," Papacharissi & Rubin, 2000) to convey the sense that the statements are continuing motivations for media use.

Thus, to assess whether an individual is using the Internet as a form of entertainment, the statements in Table 4.1 under the heading "entertainment gratifications" would be presented to the individual and they would be asked to indicate how much each statement was like their own reason for using the Internet, on a scale of one to five, where 1 is not at all like their own reason and five is exactly like their reason. The total score across the three questions provides an indication of the degree to which entertainment is a motivation for Internet use. The scores may then be compared between gratification dimensions to determine the primary motivation for each individual. As will be explained below, high scores on the "pass time" dimension are of particular interest since that is the one most associated with the development of problematic Internet use. A complex model of interactions among gratifications, psychological (e.g., needs, habits), and sociological constructs (e.g., media systems, social norms) was also proposed at that time (Palmgreen, Wenner, & Rosengren, 1985). However, in practice, UGs researchers focused on delineating the gratifications sought from various media channels (e.g., television, VCRs, face-to-face communication) and types of content (e.g., soap operas, sports, prime-time entertainment), often starting from lists of gratifications adapted from an early study of television (Rubin, 1983). The gratifications are assessed by media consumers on multipoint rating scales and subjected to exploratory factor analysis, yielding the UGs dimensions associated with the medium or type of content in question. The factors that emerge typically number at least four gratifications: entertainment; information seeking; to pass time (e.g., to relieve boredom); and for social reasons (e.g., to have something to talk about with friends). Media can then be described in terms of the most salient uses and gratifications associated with them and through correlations with measures of consumption, consumer demographics, or other psychosocial variables of interest. However, the ability of UGs to explain media consumption behavior is rather limited, usually accounting for no more than 10% of the variance in media usage (Palmgreen et al., 1985) and the same range of results has been found for Internet use (Papacharissi & Rubin, 2000).

Although media habits were present in early conceptualizations of UGs (e.g., Palmgreen et al., 1985, p. 17), they were not thought to have a direct effect on behavior. Rather, their effect was through beliefs about the media and gratifications sought—that is, by active media selection processes. At the operational level, gratification statements from Rubin (1983) implying the presence of habits (e.g., "Because it's a habit, just something to do"; "Just because it's there") were often included in later UGs studies. Based on a factor analysis of viewing motivations, Rubin (1984) made a conceptual distinction between an instrumental media orientation, marked by goal-directed information seeking through selection of media content, and a ritual orientation, "the more or less habitualized use of a medium to gratify diversionary needs or motives" (Rubin, 1984, p. 69). However, Rubin's own data did not strongly support this distinction. His habit measure had only a moderate loading (.59) on a factor that also included "pass time" and companionship motivations, identified with ritualistic uses. The habit item used in that study was also significantly correlated with convenience, economic, communication, and behavioral guidance gratifications, motivations associated with the instrumental orientation. Thus, active gratification seeking and habits remained more or less confounded, both conceptually and empirically.

Later researchers often drew upon Rubin's motivations, including the habit-related items. However, lacking the minimum number of three items required to identify a statistically reliable separate variable, habits were either dropped from the analyses or confounded with other gratifications dimensions, usually with entertainment or "pass time" factors (LaRose, 2010). As a result, the influence of habit was not fully appreciated by UGs researchers for many years or, in the words of one team of researchers who attempted to revive the concept, habit was left "lurking in the literature" (Stone & Stone, 1990) as a fringe issue even as accounts of media addictions began to emerge (McIlwraith, Jacobvitz, Kubey, & Alexander, 1991).

USES AND GRATIFICATIONS OF THE INTERNET

The advent of the Internet posed both opportunities and challenges to UGs. On the one hand, the interactive capabilities of the new medium were clearly an "active audience" experience that might amplify the power of UGs to explain media consumption (Ruggerio, 2000). On the other hand, researchers realized that the gratifications articulated by television viewers (from Rubin, 1983) that were the basis of many old media UGs studies would not necessarily fit the new interactive medium.

New types of gratifications emerged from Internet-related studies. The most ambitious of these started over with qualitative research that asked participants to identify the uses of the Internet (Charney & Greenberg, 2001; Korgaonkar & Wolin, 1999) without reference to UGs found in previous old media studies. Some of the gratification dimensions that resulted paralleled those long recognized for conventional media, including entertainment, information seeking, social interaction, and "pass time" gratifications. Others were perhaps relevant to both new and old media but had been overlooked by the mass media researchers, such as novel sights and sounds (Charney & Greenberg, 2001). Yet others reflected unique aspects of the new online world. For example, Papacharissi and Rubin (2000) proposed adding interpersonal communication gratifications to the standard list used in mass communication research, recognizing the widespread use of applications like e-mail and chat. Other new gratification dimensions have included problem solving, persuading others, relationship maintenance, status seeking, coolness, career, and search, as well as interactivity and economic control (Korgaonkar & Wolin, 1999); personal insight (Flanagin & Metzger, 2001); virtual community (Song et al., 2004); peer identity (Charney & Greenberg, 2001); and cognitive gratifications (Stafford & Stafford, 2001). Table 4.1 reproduces the Internet gratifications from one such study that has been widely cited in the communication literature.

A SOCIAL COGNITIVE MODEL OF UGS

The advent of the Internet also reopened the question of whether other variables besides gratifications sought might explain media attendance. My colleagues and I (Eastin & LaRose, 2000; LaRose & Eastin, 2004; LaRose, Mastro, & Eastin, 2001) proposed additions to the UGs paradigm drawn from Bandura's (1986) Social Cognitive Theory (SCT). Recognizing that the Internet was a new and, in the beginning at least, a rather challenging medium to master, we added Internet self-efficacy, or belief in one's ability to successfully perform behaviors in pursuit of valued attainments (Eastin & LaRose, 2000).

We also reconsidered the meaning of gratifications sought, noting that there were important distinctions between them and outcome expectations, or the subjective probability that a particular outcome will be obtained for future

Table 4.1
Internet Uses and Gratifications

Interpersonal Utility Gratifications
I use the Internet . . . To help others, To participate in discussions, To show others
   encouragement, To belong to a group, Because I enjoy answering questions, To
   express myself freely, To give my input, To get more points of view, To tell others what
   to do, Because I wonder what other people said, To meet new people, Because I
   want someone to do something for me.

Pass Time Gratifications
Because it passes time when bored, When I have nothing better to do, To occupy my
   time.

Information Seeking Gratifications
Because it is a new way to do research, Because it is easier, To get information for free,
   To look for information, To see what is out there.

Convenience Gratifications
To communicate with friends and family, Because it is cheaper, Because it is easier to
   e-mail than tell people, Because people don't have to be there to receive e-mail.

Entertainment Gratifications
Because it is entertaining, Because I just like to use it, Because it is enjoyable.

Note: Response options ranged from exactly (5) to not at all (1) like my own reason for using the Internet.
Source: Papacharissi and Rubin (2000).

behavior. That is, behavior is better determined by what individuals expect its consequences to be for themselves (i.e., expected outcomes) rather than by the outcomes they presently seek but may not actually expect going forward (i.e., gratifications sought). For example, someone may say that they use the Internet because it is entertaining, to use a common UGs formulation, but might be thinking of past occurrences rather than what they expect of future use. Also, commonly used frames of reference used to pose gratification-sought statements such as the one on the previous sentence do not allow for the possibility that different gratifications may be expected in the future. SCT also offered a priori dimensions of expected outcomes and gratifications: novel stimuli, monetary, enjoyable activity, social, status, and self-reactive outcomes (Bandura, 1986, p. 232ff). An analysis of Internet UGs studies (LaRose, Mastro, & Eastin, 2001) suggested that status and monetary outcomes had been overlooked in previous research, perhaps owing to the limited ability of conventional mass media to deliver them. Following this argument, an "entertainment" gratification statement could be rephrased thusly: "Using the Internet how likely is it that you will feel entertained," assessed on a seven-point scale ranging from "very likely" (scored as 7) to "very unlikely" (scored as 1; see LaRose & Eastin, 2004).

In the current context the most important addition to the UGs model was the self-regulatory mechanism of SCT. That mechanism can explain how deficiencies in self-regulation lead to habitual behavior that is not under the control of active self-instruction. Self-regulation has three subprocesses: self-observation, judgmental process, and self-reaction (Bandura, 1991). Self-observation entails paying attention to the relationship between behavior and its outcomes and the regularity of the rewards for behavior. In the judgmental process self-observations of behavior are compared to personal, social, and collective norms. Self-reactive influence may be applied when behaviors are observed and found to fall short of standards of conduct or fail to maintain compliance with norms. For example, individuals may observe that they are spending too much time on the Internet relative to their own standards for efficient time utilization. Or they may realize that they are failing to conform to norms for participation in family activities due to their online activities. In response, individuals may resort to a variety of self-control methods in an attempt to bring their behavior under control. For example, they may reward themselves for cutting back on the number of hours they spend playing online games, or may punish themselves by indulging feelings of guilt or engaging in self-criticism:"I am becoming such a mouse potato that I can't stand myself!"

Empirically, deficient self-regulation breaks down into two dimensions: deficient self-observation and deficient self-reaction (LaRose, Kim, & Peng, 2010). The former indicates lack of awareness and attention to behavior (e.g., "It is part of my regular routine") while the latter reflects a failure of self-control (e.g., "I feel my Internet use is out of control"). While habits involve deficient self-regulation, not all forms of deficient self-regulation are habits. For example, impulsive behaviors that occur at the first opportunity to perform them also reflect deficient self-regulation but are not habits since no repeated behavior is involved. However, the focus of the research reported here has been on habitual forms of deficient self-regulation.

The addition of self-efficacy and self-regulation mechanisms substantially improved the predictive power of UGs to explain between 30% and 40% of the variance in Internet consumption behavior. In this model (see Figure 4.1), expected outcomes, self-efficacy, deficient self-observation,[1] and deficient self-reaction[2] are direct predictors of Internet use. Self-efficacy is also a predictor of outcome expectations, deficient self-observation, and deficient self-reaction. That is because an individual's perceived ability to use the Internet is a logical precursor to experiencing its outcomes and to trying out behaviors that later become habits and even later may become uncontrollable ones. However, these relationships are likely reciprocal in nature. The achievement of expected outcomes bolsters self-efficacy as users progressively master more complex online tasks. The repetition of behavior initiates habits but also provides practice that enhances self-efficacy as well. Finally, prior experience with the Internet is a precursor of both Internet self-efficacy and expected outcomes. These latter links reflect the enactive learning mechanism of socio-cognitive theory in which expected outcomes are shaped by direct experience.

---

[1]Habit strength in the original version.
[2]Deficient self-regulation in the original.

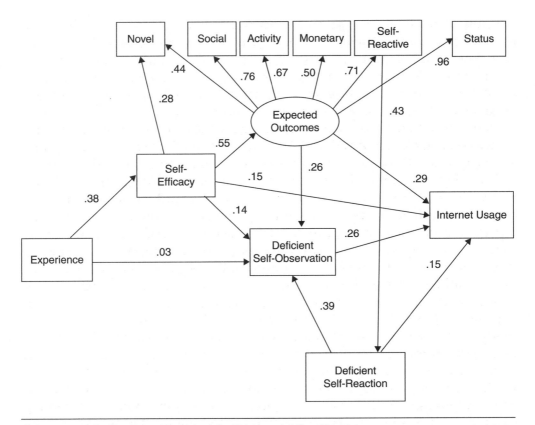

Figure 4.1   Socio-Cognitive Model of Uses and Gratifications

Source: Adapted from LaRose and Eastin (2004).

Observational learning from the experiences of others can also affect expected outcomes but is not illustrated in the diagram.

FROM USES AND GRATIFICATIONS TO NONCONSCIOUS HABITS

The relationships among expected outcomes, deficient self-observation, deficient self-reaction, and behavior hold the key to understanding how normal media use becomes habitual. With repetition, media consumption may become automatic and no longer be controlled by conscious thinking about immediate outcome expectations. That means that media selections are no longer active in the sense proposed by UGs (LaRose, 2010). Automatic behaviors are characterized by a lack of awareness, attention, intentionality, and/or controllability. Deficient self-observation encompasses the first three of these dimensions, while deficient self-reaction is identified with the fourth, lack of controllability. Thus, when examining repeated behavior as opposed to novel or impulsive behavior, deficient self-observation and deficient self-reaction are two dimensions of habit.

Habitual behaviors may be prompted by internal or external cues that were present in the context in which the habit was initially established. While active selections based on gratifications sought guide the initial selection of media, control is transferred to nonconscious processes with repeated selections of the same media. Thus, UGs initially cause habits to form through the repetition of behaviors that are initially under conscious control.

Habit formation is hastened by repeating the behavior under stable circumstances (Verplanken & Wood, 2006). Then, after habits are formed, behaviors are cued under those same circumstances and may be performed automatically. "*May be* performed automatically" is an important qualifying phrase to bear in mind since all habits, even deeply ingrained ones, are subject to cortical control. For example, a normally irresistible urge to respond to an incoming tweet might be suppressed if the user is engaged in an online game.

A wide variety of stimuli have been suggested as components of the stable circumstances thought to be required for the establishment of habits (i.e., in Verplanken & Wood, 2006). These include time, location, the presence of others or selected objects, preceding behaviors, goals, and mood states. But recognizing that habits are cognitive structures, it is possible that any related thought process could provide the necessary stable circumstance. So an online gaming habit might be triggered by the arrival of daily game time, the sight of one's computer or a familiar play partner, the goal of relaxing after a day's work, or an encroaching feeling of boredom. However, any game-related image or cognition might serve as a trigger. For example, an online gambling habit might be evoked by seeing a magazine ad for a Las Vegas casino. Also, media habits seem to be less context-dependent than habits in other domains (LaRose, 2010). This may be a function of the ubiquity of the media and their images across locations and times and their increasing platform independence. Moreover, habits are continually undergoing reorganization in the quest for greater cognitive efficiency and may be prompted by a changing array of cues that may not have been present initially. This is especially likely to be the case for Internet habits due to the wide variety of contexts and unlimited moments of time in which they may be accessed. For example, an Internet gaming habit originally tied to the computer in the gambler's bedroom might subsequently be prompted by the sight of a workstation in the place of employment.

As habits gain in strength, control by active selection processes diminishes, even to the point that conscious intentions no longer have a significant impact on online behavior in the presence of strong habits (Limayem, Hirt, & Cheung, 2007). Evidence of the progression of habitual control over online behavior is found by comparing UGs studies reflecting differing points in the process of habit formation. Lin (1999) explained nearly 50% of the variance in the intended use of the Internet, an unprecedented degree of success in the annals of UGs research, among a sample of adults who had not yet adopted the Internet, for whom habit formation was impossible. LaRose and Eastin (2004) found that the deficient self-observation dimension of habit was an equally important predictor of general Internet usage as expected outcomes or gratifications. Another study (LaRose, Kim, & Peng, 2010) found that both deficient self-observation and deficient self-reaction were equal in strength to gratifications when a favorite Internet activity for which habitual use patterns had presumably been established (e.g., social networking, downloading, gaming), as opposed to general Internet use, was the criterion variable.

After habits are established, UGs may still determine behavior to some degree, such as when an entertaining favorite activity consistently ceases to amuse, activating conscious selection processes anew. However, it is also possible that when asked about media behaviors that have become habits, individuals may endorse gratifications that they no longer actively seek. Not wishing to appear to be mindless so-called mouse potatoes, they may do so to rationalize media consumption to themselves or to manipulate the impressions they make on the researcher. In that sense, habits may to some degree cause gratifications (Newell, 2003). Another possibility is that when researchers ask about gratifications sought for habitual behaviors, individuals summon memories of the active selection processes that originally guided their behavior. For example, they may dimly recall that they initially went online to access e-mail (fulfilling a social gratification such as "I use the Internet to keep up with friends") even though their current uses revolve around multiplayer games.

Recent findings in brain physiology and social psychology (reviewed in LaRose, 2010) support the contention that behavioral control passes from active consideration of the outcomes associated with media consumption centered in the brain's cortex to automatic association with contextual stimuli that trigger behavior, governed by structures in the cerebrum called the basal ganglia. This mechanism is necessary to maintain daily functioning in a complex environment. Were it not possible to assign certain behaviors to automatic control, individuals would be unable to process the information necessary to make the myriad of decisions that face them each day. In other words, automatic thinking conserves scarce attentional resources. After some number of repetitions (the exact number is unknown), media behavior is controlled by nonconscious, automated processes although still subject to override by the cortex. Individuals no longer need to attend closely to the behaviors they perform nor to the outcomes they expect as a result, entering a state of deficient self-observation in present terms.

LOSING CONTROL

Deficient self-reaction has been proposed to explain how gratifying Internet activities turn into habits and sometimes into potentially harmful ones that disrupt the lives of individuals (LaRose, Lin, & Eastin, 2003). Deficiencies in self-reactive influence indicate a behavior that is out of control. The operational measures of the variable (e.g., "I have tried unsuccessfully to cut down on the amount of time I spend online") indicate that individuals have tried to moderate their behavior without success. Still, that is not necessarily an indication of pathology since they may have been responding to routine reminders to budget their time more effectively, such as repeated reminders to arrive at dinner on time, rather than to relationship- or job-imperiling threats.

Earlier, habits were defined as a form of automatic behavior lacking in awareness, attention, intentionality, and/or controllability. However, these four dimensions are independent (Saling & Phillips, 2007). So individuals may be painfully aware of an excessive online behavior and even intend to discontinue it but still be said to have a habit by virtue of the behavior's lack of controllability, or deficient self-reaction in present terms. Likewise, individuals may lack awareness, attention, or intentionality (i.e., deficient self-observation) but still feel in control of a media behavior, or at least have not as yet failed to control it.

Deficient self-reaction has proven to be a consistent predictor of Internet usage in studies conducted by my colleagues and me (LaRose & Eastin, 2004; LaRose, Kim, & Peng, 2010; LaRose, Lin, & Eastin, 2003; LaRose, Mastro, & Eastin, 2001). The same relationship is found in research using variables with different names but that convey the same sense of failed self-control. For example, the Compulsive Internet Use Scale ("How often have you tried unsuccessfully to spend less time on the Internet?" "How often do you find it difficult to stop using the Internet when you are online?") was correlated .42 with Internet usage (Meerkerk, van den Eijnden, Vermulst, & Garretsen, 2009). Leung (2004) found that respondents with five or more symptoms of Internet addiction (e.g., "Have you made unsuccessful attempts to cut down how much time you spend online?") averaged 35 hours a week online, compared to 27 hours for those with fewer symptoms. However, the latter variables also include indicators of the consequences of use, such as missing social engagements or getting into trouble at work or school, which might be better regarded as expected (negative) outcomes of Internet use in the present model.

The presentation of correlations between measures of compulsive/ problematic/pathological Internet use and the amount of time spent on the Internet as evidence of the validity of the former raises the question of how much Internet use is "excessive" or "problematic." But that is perhaps the wrong question. For example, millions of adults in the United States function normally even while consuming over 30 hours of television per week. Why would 30 hours of leisure Internet use necessarily be problematic? Total media consumption averages 50 hours a week, and more and more of those media are accessed online, so why would 50 hours a week necessarily cause problems? Even 60 hours a week leaves plenty of time for work and sleep. Multitasking media use while eating, housecleaning, and commuting expands the boundaries of "excessive" even further. However, only a few hours a week could be problematic if other life activities in a busy schedule are forsaken or if those few hours are being spent running up ruinous online

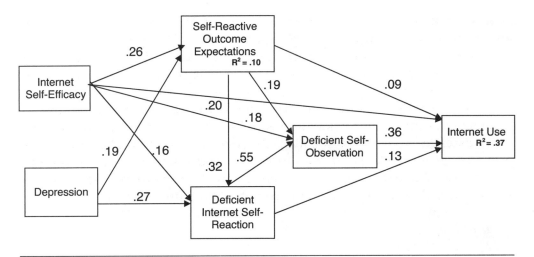

Figure 4.2 Internet Addiction Model

Source: Adapted from LaRose, Lin, and Eastin (2003).

gambling debts, making unaffordable online purchases, or carrying on an extramarital affair online.

It is the function of the usage rather than its amount that can make the Internet use excessive and problematic. The linkage between self-reactive outcome expectations and deficient self-reaction shown in Figure 4.1 may hold the key. That relationship suggests the possibility that when the Internet is being used as a form of primary mood adjustment for dysphoric moods, it overwhelms rational self-control. Behavioral addictions may result (Marlatt, Baer, Donovan, & Kivlahan, 1988); that is, those expecting the Internet to cheer them up or relieve boredom are likely to also be deficient in self-reaction.

A pattern of mounting use resulting in the neglect of relationships and important life activities may also trigger a downward spiral as the consequences of neglect produce dysphoria. Figure 4.2 illustrates the next steps in the spiral (LaRose, Lin, & Eastin, 2003). Depression leads to further seeking of self-reactive outcomes to relieve dysphoric moods, leading to further deficiencies in self-reaction and mounting use, and so on. Moreover, depression also has a direct impact on deficient self-reaction since depressed people tend to slight the success of their own efforts to restore effective self-regulation (Bandura, 1999). That can accelerate the downward spiral with each turn of the cycle.

Thus, to assess whether someone is in imminent danger of forming a problematic Internet habit, clinicians might explore whether the online behavior in question has become the primary means of relieving dysphoric moods and probe for signs of depression associated with mounting use. In conventional UGs terms, that happens when "pass time" gratifications are especially salient. Rather than administering an UGs inventory like that shown in Table 4.1, that might be determined by asking about what was done to relieve recent episodes of boredom, stress, or depression. If online activities are frequently mentioned, that would be an indication of a potential problem. Indications that the behavior has become automatic in nature also provide early warning signals. The Self-Report Habit Index (SRHI) (Verplanken & Orbell, 2003) has been shown to be a reliable and valid measure of psychological habit strength, assessed through the level of agreement with statements such as the behavior is performed without thinking or would cause distressful feelings if it was not performed. If the symptoms of Internet addiction or indicators of Compulsive Internet Use (Caplan, 2005) are evaluated on multipoint, agree-disagree scales, then low to moderate levels of endorsement (i.e. at or near the mid point of the scales) could be an indication of progression from a normal pattern of media use to a potentially harmful and pathological one.

Why Isn't Everyone an Internet Addict?

At this point it is appropriate to wonder why Internet addictions are not more common and indeed why everyone is not engaged in pathological online habits. After all, the Internet is a veritable cornucopia of appealing leisure activities tailored to every imaginable taste and available almost everywhere on a 24/7 basis. Short of bottoming out and resorting to professional help, how can the cycle be broken?

One possibility is that some online activities may be inherently more prone to abuse than others, and only those who become involved with the most inherently addictive ones develop problems. For example, the social skill account of problematic Internet use (Caplan, 2005, 2006) recognizes that many accounts of abuse are associated with social uses of the Internet. It argues that problematic uses are a function of deficiencies in social skills, leading to a preference for online social interaction, then to compulsive use (what has been called deficient self-reaction here), and finally to negative consequences such as the loss of a grade in school or trouble at work. Following that argument, social networking and instant messaging applications should be the most prone to problems. However, a comparative analysis of favorite Internet activities that incorporated both the social skills account and the previously cited model of habitual Internet use found that the downloading of music and video files was potentially the most problematic activity. But also, the differences among favorite activities were generally small, although social networking and instant messaging were more associated with deficient self-observation (but not with self-reactive outcome expectations or deficient self-reaction) than downloading, gaming, or online shopping (LaRose, Kim, & Peng, 2010). Following the logic of the model presented earlier, any pleasurable online activity could develop into a problematic habit if it is consistently used to relieve dysphoria.

Perhaps a better answer to the question of why pathological Internet use is not more common is that most individuals are able to maintain effective self-control or restore it when it is disrupted. Many respond to the warning signs emitted by their spouses, bosses, or bank statements by summoning the resolve to moderate the offending behavior. But also, Internet habits are to some degree self-limiting. The pleasurable activities that initially dispel dysphoric moods wear out quickly (LaRose, 2008), triggering a search for new activities and the moderation or discontinuance of old habits. In addition, the negative consequences that attend deepening involvement with habitual activities also may restore effective self-observation (LaRose, Kim, & Peng, 2010) and inspire renewed efforts to bring online behaviors that are operating "on automatic" once again under the control of conscious thought processes.

IMPLICATIONS FOR THE PREVENTION OF INTERNET ABUSE

The present analysis is predicated on studies of Internet use among normal populations, so it is beyond our scope to further consider the etiology of pathological forms of Internet use or to speculate about effective treatments for them. However, it is known that habits, even nonpathological ones, are difficult to break once formed (Verplanken & Wood, 2006), so it behooves us to consider how they might be prevented from forming in the first place and disrupted after their formation but before harmful cycles of self-medication by means of Internet occur.

It was argued previously that deficient self-regulation is the key to understanding the development of uncontrolled Internet habits. Effective self-regulation may also be the key to moderating uncontrolled online behavior. Interventions aimed at bolstering self-regulation of television viewing, another medium said to have addictive qualities, have reduced television consumption and the negative effects of excessive viewing, including obesity and violent tendencies, among children (Jason & Fries, 2004; Robinson & Borzekowski, 2006).

Since habits are formed by repetition under stable circumstances, one obvious strategy for disrupting habits is to alter the contexts in which the triggering cues are likely to occur. For example, varying the time, location, preceding activities, and the company one keeps when accessing favorite online activities should weaken habits. However, extreme disruptions in the context of a behavior, comparable to turning off TV for a week in Robinson and Borzekowski (2006), may be necessary, and extreme acts of willpower may be required to execute such changes. It might be possible to take advantage of naturally occurring changes in the context of Internet behavior such as the beginning of a new school year or work schedule or the purchase of a new computer to bring about the necessary contextual change. The context of Internet use might also be altered automatically by the use of web site filters that block access to problem-causing content. Societal-level policies that facilitate Internet habits might also be changed, such as imposing usage-sensitive charges on Internet use or so-called sin taxes on the consumption of certain kinds of content.

A variety of persuasion techniques similar to those developed in health interventions might also have an impact on habit formation. Since lack of attention to a behavior is one of the earmarks of habits, keeping a diary of one's online activities or inspecting activity logs on web sites that provide them to users would draw attention to behavior and undermine habits. Reflection on the mood states that preceded indulgence in a favorite online activity, mounting use, or sessions that last longer than intended (or remembered) would provide an early warning of habits that are in danger of spinning out of control. Another possibility is to use self-help or public education approaches to build upon the natural defenses uncovered by LaRose et al. (2010), in which awareness of negative consequences linked to Internet use appeared to reawaken attentiveness to Internet behavior. Alternatively, self-efficacy beliefs related to diminishing Internet use could be bolstered through persuasion, access to testimonials from successful quitters, or gradual reductions in use. Or societal or group norms (e.g., within a family or specific school) for Internet use might be emphasized. These strategies would likely only work when habits are still forming, however. When habits are strong, individuals filter out information that might persuade them to change their behavior (Verplanken & Wood, 2006). However, persuasion tactics such as these might amplify the effectiveness of context changes.

Finally, self-regulation has been likened to muscle-building. Overexertion temporarily depletes self-regulatory resources, whereas sustained, incremental exercise of the resource seems to strengthen it. And, just as strengthening the muscles in our arms by lifting weights in the gym gives us more strength to lift objects in our homes, the strengthening of self-regulation in one behavioral domain generalizes to others (Baumeister, Schmeichel, & Vohs, 2007). That suggests that restoring self-regulation to one form of media consumption (e.g., television) or even in completely different behavior domains (e.g., eating or exercise habits) might enhance the ability to regulate Internet behavior as well.

SUMMARY AND CONCLUSION

Internet users initially actively select online activities that gratify needs such as entertainment, information, social interaction, and diversion. With repetition, favorite online activities gradually become automatic, habitual behaviors that may be activated with limited awareness, attention, intentionality, or controllability in response to contextual cues. Habitual behaviors may be explained in terms of deficiencies in self-observation and self-reactive influence that supplant the conscious pursuit of expected gratifications of online activities as determinants of Internet use. Habits that become a primary means of relieving dysphoric moods have the greatest potential for spinning out of control by undermining the ability of individuals to regulate their own behavior through self-reactive influence. Self-help programs and public education campaigns may be effective in controlling habits in the early stages of their formation. However, entrenched habits are resistant to change and may require substantial alterations in the context of Internet use before change can occur. The relationship of uses and gratifications (UGs) of Internet use to self-regulation of online behavior is thus crucial in the development of Internet habits that disrupt lives and also in the prevention of problematic forms of use.

Therapists can use these models to assess why each client becomes addicted to the Internet. Understanding the personal motivations among clients will help build effective recovery strategies that are individualized to each client. Finally, recovering addicts often struggle with how to overcome difficult situations or emotional problems while abstaining from alcohol, drugs, sex, or food. They miss the escape hatch their addictions provided, and while learning to live without them, may turn to the Internet as a new and socially acceptable way to cope. What they do not often realize is that by doing so they have perpetuated the addictive cycle. Addicts often look to the Internet as a way to escape reality without really dealing with the underlying problems that cause the addictive behavior. They turn to the Internet instead of dealing with relationship problems, money problems, work problems, or school problems. The same issues that drove them to drink or overeat or gamble are still not being resolved.

Using the Internet becomes a quick fix and an instant cure that washes away troubling feelings, feelings that they have not learned to deal with. Based on these models, we see that Internet addicts can lose themselves in anything that piques their interest, allowing the difficulties they face to fade into the background as their attention becomes focused on the Internet. However, while they can obtain significant gratification from Internet use, they are simply substituting one addiction for another and engaging in avoidant behavior. It keeps addicts from dealing with issues contributing to the addiction, leading to a vicious cycle. By applying these models, both the client and therapist can raise awareness of the reasons why the Internet is so alluring and determine a proper course of recovery.

REFERENCES

Bandura, A. (1986). *Social foundations of thought and action: A social cognitive theory.* Englewood Cliffs, NJ: Prentice Hall.

Bandura, A. (1991). Social cognitive theory of self-regulation. *Organizational Behavior and Human Decision Processes, 50,* 248–287.

Bandura, A. (1999). A sociocognitive analysis of substance abuse: An agentic perspective. *Psychological Science, 10,* 214–217.

Baumeister, R. F., Schmeichel, B. J., & Vohs, K. D. (2007). Self-regulation and the executive function: The self as controlling agent. In A. W. Kruglanski & E. T. Higgins (Eds.), *Social psychology: Handbook of basic principles* (2nd ed.) (pp. 516–540). New York: Guilford Press.

Caplan, S. E. (2005). A social skill account of problematic Internet use. *Journal of Communication, 55,* 721–736.

Caplan, S. E. (2006). Relations among loneliness, social anxiety, and problematic Internet use. *CyberPsychology & Behavior, 10,* 234–242.

Charney, T. R., & Greenberg, B. S. (2001). Uses and gratifications of the Internet. In C. Lin & D. Atkin (Eds.), *Communication, technology and society: New media adoption and uses* (pp. 379–407). Cresskill, NJ: Hampton Press.

Eastin, M. A., & LaRose, R. L. (2000). Internet self-efficacy and the psychology of the digital divide. *Journal of Computer Mediated Communication, 6*. Available from http://www.ascusc.org/jcmc/vol6/issue1/eastin.html

Flanagin, A. J., & Metzger, M. J. (2001). Internet use in the contemporary media environment. *Human Communication Research, 27*, 153–181.

Jason, L. A., & Fries, M. (2004). Helping parents reduce children's television viewing. *Research on Social Work Practice, 14*, 121–131.

Katz, E., Gurevitch, M., & Haas, H. (1973). On the use of the mass media for important things. *American Sociological Review, 38*, 164–181.

Korgaonkar, P., & Wolin, L. (1999). A multivariate analysis of Web usage. *Journal of Advertising Research, 39*, 53–68.

LaRose, R. (2008). Habituation. In W. Donsbach (Ed.), *The international encyclopedia of communication* (Vol. 5, pp. 2045–2047). Malden, MA: Wiley-Blackwell.

LaRose, R. (2010, forthcoming). Media habits. *Communication Theory.*

LaRose, R., & Eastin, M. S. (2004). A social cognitive theory of Internet uses and gratifications: Toward a new model of media attendance. *Journal of Broadcasting and Electronic Media, 48*, 358–377.

LaRose, R., Kim, J. H., & Peng, W. (2010, forthcoming). Social networking: Addictive, compulsive, problematic, or just another media habit? In Z. Pappacharissi (Ed.), *The networked self.* New York: Routledge.

LaRose, R., Lin, C. A., & Eastin, M. S. (2003). Unregulated Internet usage: Addiction, habit, or deficient self-regulation? *Media Psychology, 5*, 225–253.

LaRose, R., Mastro, D., & Eastin, M. S. (2001). Understanding Internet usage—A social-cognitive approach to uses and gratifications. *Social Science Computer Review, 19*, 395–413.

Leung, L. (2004). Net-generation attributes and seductive properties of the Internet as predictors of online activities and Internet addiction. *CyberPsychology & Behavior, 7*, 333–344.

Limayem, M., Hirt, S. G., & Cheung, C. M. K. (2007). How habit limits the predictive power of intention: The case of information systems continuance. *MIS Quarterly, 31*, 705–738.

Lin, C. A. (1999). Online-service adoption likelihood. *Journal of Advertising Research, 39*, 79–89.

Marlatt, G. A., Baer, J. S., Donovan, D. M., & Kivlahan, D. R. (1988). Addictive behaviors: Etiology and treatment. *Annual Review of Psychology, 39*, 223–252.

McIlwraith, R., Jacobvitz, R., Kubey, R., & Alexander, A. (1991). Television addiction—Theories and data behind the ubiquitous metaphor. *American Behavioral Scientist, 35*, 104–121.

Meerkerk, G. J., van den Eijnden, R. J. J. M., Vermulst, A. A., & Garretsen, H. F. L. (2009). The Compulsive Internet Use Scale (CIUS): Some psychometric properties. *Cyberpsychology and Behavior, 12*, 2009.

Newell, J. (2003). The role of habit in the selection of electronic media (Doctoral dissertation, Michigan State University).

Palmgreen, P., Wenner, L., & Rosengren, K. (1985). Uses and gratifications research: The past ten years. In K. Rosengren, L. Wenner, & P. Palmgreen (Eds.), *Media gratifications research* (pp. 11–37). Beverly Hills, CA: Sage.

Papacharissi, Z., & Rubin, A. M. (2000). Predictors of Internet usage. *Journal of Broadcasting and Electronic Media, 44,* 175–196.

Robinson, T. N., & Borzekowski, D. L. G. (2006). Effects of the SMART classroom curriculum to reduce child and family screen time. *Journal of Communication, 56,* 1–26.

Rubin, A. M. (1983). Television uses and gratifications: The interactions of viewing patterns and motivations. *Journal of Broadcasting, 27,* 37–51.

Rubin, A. M. (1984). Ritualized and instrumental television viewing. *Journal of Communication, 34,* 67–77.

Ruggerio, T. E. (2000). Uses and gratifications theory in the 21st century. *Mass Communication and Society, 3,* 3–37.

Saling, L. L., & Phillips, J. G. (2007). Automatic behaviour: Efficient not mindless. *Brain Research Bulletin, 73,* 1–20.

Song, I., LaRose, R., Lin, C., & Eastin, M. S. (2004). Internet gratifications and Internet addiction: On the uses and abuses of new media. *CyberPsychology & Behavior, 7,* 384–394.

Stafford, T. F., & Stafford, M. R. (2001). Identifying motivations for the use of commercial web sites. *Information Resources Management Journal, 14,* 22–30.

Stone, G., & Stone, D. (1990). Lurking in the literature: Another look at media use habits. *Mass Communications Review, 17,* 25–33.

Verplanken, B., & Orbell, S. (2003). Reflections on past behavior: A self-report index of habit strength. *Journal of Applied Social Psychology, 33,* 1313–1330.

Verplanken, B., & Wood, W. (2006). Interventions to break and create consumer habits. *Journal of Public Policy & Marketing, 25,* 90–103.

CHAPTER 5

Addiction to Online
Role-Playing Games

LUKAS BLINKA and DAVID SMAHEL

MASSIVE MULTIPLAYER online role-playing games (MMORPGs) are one example of Internet applications that have become increasingly popular. These games are played in online worlds, where an individual acts through a created virtual personality, a so-called avatar. The popularity of these games can be seen from data on the most popular MMORPG, World of Warcraft, which has over 11.5 million official subscribers. Based on data from the Entertainment Software Association (2007), the number of online gamers doubled between 2006 and 2007. MMORPGs are a type of so-called massively multiplayer online (MMO) game; MMOs include, for example, the well-known game Second Life. MMOs are not always games in the strict sense of the word; for example, users of Second Life often claim that "Second Life is not a game but a second life." According to some statistics, MMO games were played by 48 million players in April 2008 (Voig, Inc., 2008).

The forerunners of MMORPG games were so-called multiuser dungeons (MUDs), which have inspired many books about virtual worlds as well as researchers (Kendall, 2002; Suler, 2008; Turkle, 1997, 2005). The main difference is that MUDs ran in text form while current MMORPG games are worlds running in high graphic resolution. It is not clear what the differences between text MUDs and the current graphic MMORPG games are concerning the impact on players, but what we know for sure is that MMORPGs are played by a much larger number of players today than MUDs ever were.

In this chapter we primarily deal with MMORPG games that have proven to be a very significant free-time activity of some of today's adolescents,

---

The authors acknowledge the support of the Faculty of Social Studies, Masaryk University.

younger adults, and adults (e.g., Ng & Wiemer-Hastings, 2005; Smahel, Blinka, & Ledabyl, 2008). At the same time, MMORPGs are often presented as being potentially dangerous due to possible addiction (Rau, Peng, & Yang, 2006; Wan & Chiou, 2006a, 2006b), and as such they attract a lot of attention of the scientific community, the general public, and media.

In other parts of the chapter, we will also list examples from 16 interviews with MMORPG players that we carried out in May 2009. The semistructured interviews with 12 men (aged 15 to 28) and four women (aged 15 to 19) was carried out face-to-face in seven cases and online through Skype or ICQ in nine cases. The interviews were analyzed with use of grounded theory. Samples from these interviews have been included in the discussion to complement the obtained results.

In this chapter we first deal with a description of the virtual worlds in MMORPGs, so that the reader can get a better idea of what these worlds look like. We then follow with showing who the players of these games are and their motivations for playing. Afterward we present the concept of addiction in the context of MMORPGs and factors facilitating addiction both on the side of individual players and on the side of the game. We also present a short questionnaire that can be used for basic diagnostics of online games addiction symptoms and its following evaluation based on interviews with players. In the last section we discuss the phenomenon of self-perceived addiction (i.e., a MMORPG player's perception of potential addiction).

WHAT ARE MMORPGs?

MMORPGs are usually fantasy role-playing games played on the Internet, where several thousand various players from all around the world are present at the same time. A player controls his or her character, which can fulfill various tasks, advance its capabilities, and interact with other players' characters. A player can perform a wide range of activities, from building his or her avatar's character to interacting with other players in both positive ways (conversation) and negative ways (aggression). The motivation for playing MMORPGs also varies (as described further), as well as manners of playing these games (e.g., Yee 2006b). A player can explore a vast world, which is persistent in its character—it remains in existence even when the player logs off. This world is consistently in development, disregarding the presence of the player, which in a certain sense pressures the player to stay in touch with the virtual world. If players are absent for a longer period of time, they become out of touch with the virtual world and lose their influence and power to affect the world. The player also loses power compared to fellow players who are playing more often and advancing faster. In the words of an 18-year-old male player: *"The more I want to improve, the more time I should invest in the game. That's how the game works, unfortunately, and I always keep thinking that I could, that I should spend even more time online and do things now that I would otherwise do tomorrow."* Success in the game is often closely tied with long-term and everyday presence in the game.

It is the unbounded scope of the world, the practical impossibility of finishing the game, and the emphasis on communication and cooperation with other players that make MMORPGs different from traditional computer games, and it is also the reason for considering it a whole new environment and subject. The biggest difference between MMORPGs and other computer games is notable in the intensity of play: MMORPGs are played 25 hours per week on average, whereas other computer games and video games are played over 20 hours per week by only 6% of players, and 84% of players spend less than six hours per week playing (Ng & Wiemer-Hastings, 2005). The high intensity of play is apparently the main factor for considering gaming problematic and potentially addictive. It remains an open question, however: What actually keeps players in the game for such long periods of time? Are they necessarily addicted due to their long stay in the game, or could there be some other explanation? Now we will have a closer look at who plays MMORPGs and how much time they spend in the virtual world.

WHO PLAYS AND HOW MUCH?

There exists a generally established image of a typical gamer as a young or adolescent man. Some findings (e.g., Griffiths, Davies, & Chappell, 2003; Smahel, Blinka & Ledabyl, 2008; Yee, 2006b), however, disprove this archetype: The average age of MMORPG players is generally around 25 years, and there are more adult than adolescent players. Most often the gamers are men—their representation exceeds 90%, especially for younger players. The representation of women increases with age, and it reaches approximately 20% among adult gamers (Griffiths, Davis, & Chappell, 2003). One notable fact is that the average age of female gamers (approximately 32 years) is significantly higher than the average age of male gamers. It seems that female players usually become involved in the game through their partners (Yee, 2006a). Female gamers of adolescent age are very rare. The increase in their numbers during emerging adulthood and young adulthood suggests that they were introduced to the game by their social surroundings (usually male partners).

At a first glance, the numbers on intensity of play are quite interesting. As has been noted, the average intensity of play per week is approximately 25 hours (Griffiths, Davies, & Chappell, 2004; Smahel, Blinka, & Ledabyl, 2008); 11% of players, however, spend over 40 hours per week in the game world, which corresponds to a full-time job or high school attendance (Ng & Wiemer-Hastings, 2005); 80% of gamers play over eight hours in one session at least from time to time (Ng & Wiemer-Hastings, 2005); and 60% play over 10 hours in one session (Yee, 2006a). One of the gamers in our interviews noted that he has played 30 hours in one session. It can thus be said that MMORPGs present, at least from a time perspective, a very significant part of the lives of their players—since the intensity of play limits available time for other activities. Furthermore, this is apparently not just a short episode in the lives of the players. Griffiths, Davies, & Chappell (2004) found out that the average time of play is approximately two years for adolescent players (aged up to 20) and 27 months for older players. As for intensity of play, adolescents tend to play more than their adult counterparts (26 hours per week for those under 20 compared to 22 hours for those over 26). However, the group of players aged 20 to 22 spends the most time playing online games, with an average of almost 30 hours per week. Based on Cole & Griffiths (2007), women play significantly less, namely up to 10 hours per week less than men.

A very low representation of women among MMORPG players is unusual compared to other online games. Based on data from the Entertainment Software Association (2008), women form 44% of all online players (i.e., almost half). Women, however, prefer puzzle and card games online, which represent half of all online games. The data suggest that online role-playing games such as World of Warcraft are played by approximately 11% of online players. This group of players, however, plays very intensively, which is why this small group is so significant. Games with low intensity of play are usually considered only a type of relaxation, whereas MMORPGs generally have more complex motivations for play. Let's have a closer look at them now.

MOTIVATION FOR PLAYING MMORPGs

MMORPGs are relatively complex virtual worlds, which offer wide and varying possibilities for entertainment. Yee (2006b) summarized the significant components of play into three main categories: achievement, social, and immersion, with a range of possible dimensions. The first component, achievement, includes management of game mechanisms. MMORPGs are relatively complicated, and it usually takes a period of time for players to become familiar with the game mechanisms. Optimization of these game mechanisms is then often the topic of discussion forums on the Internet, where players also tend to spend a lot of time. Achievement includes the notion of advancement—the progression of a player's avatar, both in experience levels (leading to new abilities) and by obtaining better equipment. Overall this gives more power to the player and a higher status in the game world. The last part of the achievement component is competition—the process of competing with other players.

The second MMORPG component comprises the social dimension of virtual worlds. Online gaming is social in principle; solo play is allowed but not encouraged: *"MMORPGs are mainly about people—when I started playing, it was absolutely fantastic."* Players gather into larger groups, usually called "guilds," although the terminology is different in certain online games. Playing together with others then leads to a certain social commitment. Seay et al. (2003) showed that players in guilds play four hours per week more than unguilded players, on average. The game itself also serves as a chat; players communicate not only about the game but about all sorts of other topics as well, via both text messages and voice chat. The Internet also supports self-disclosure of players. Yee (2006b) notes that 23% of male and 32% of female players at some time disclosed personal and intimate information in the game. This openness, however, varies with age. Whereas older individuals are mostly careful, over one-half of adolescents speak about their personal real-life experiences in the game. Meeting with a fellow player in real life is then more common for women (almost 16%) than for men (5%). A higher tendency to meet in real life is found in older players. Another thing to note is that, especially for adolescents, intensive playing can have a negative effect on offline social life—younger players have a higher tendency to immure themselves in the game.

The third motivation component is immersion. A shared element of all MMORPGs is a complex and vast world; a wide range of players thus focuses on exploring this world (mostly based on the fantasy genre). Immersion also occurs when identifying with one's avatar—adjusting his or her appearance, expanding his or her equipment, role-playing, and so on.

All of these components are in some way present in every MMORPG, and various players prefer each component in varying degrees. Griffiths et al. (2004), for example, claimed that violence in games is preferred by adolescent players. The preference of violence, aggression, and competition in games decreases with age, and women also have a lower preference for these notions. The social component of the game is preferred more by adult players. Some players with a high potential for addictive behavior can then consider the game their "second life," citing an 18-year-old player who spends 70 hours per week in the game: *"The game in itself comprises all sorts of interests, as if it almost was a second life. You can do anything you could imagine there, perhaps everything except for sex. I can even fish there."* For these types of players, all the aforementioned motivations combine together. A less frequent but perhaps even more interesting motivation is the targeted damaging of other players' avatars, as described by a 19-year-old man playing 65 hours per week: *"I usually play to cause harm = I like to murder, steal, and do anything immoral in the game (it helps me relax at the end of the day)."* This player does not communicate with others, but the game rather functions as a manner of relaxation for him, and as he himself states: *"I can't imagine being mean in real life. I'd say that in this respect, the game allows me to try unexplored possibilities."* In this context we can then consider internal psychological motivations for playing MMORPGs, including psychological identification with one's avatar and the virtual representation of a player. The deep psychological motivations for a player who uses MMORPGs for stress relief are more likely a question for clinical interviews.

The avatar itself is an important game element; players, however, have various approaches to their avatars. Adolescents have the Largent tendency not to distinguish between themselves and their avatars (Blinka, 2008). Thus they pay less attention to differences between themselves and their game avatars, and consider success in the game (e.g., in confrontation with other avatars) their personal success. This apparently could be related to the origination of self-efficacy and self-esteem, both of which are most significant during adolescence. The compensative function of avatars is also most prominent in the lower age category—meaning that players consider their avatars as an idealized, superior form of themselves, according to Blinka. This is influenced by the fact that individuals with lower self-esteem find MMORPGs very attractive—they provide a quick form of relief from the uncomfortable feelings of low self-esteem. Various studies have already confirmed that a connection exists between potential addiction and the identification of a player with his or her avatar (Smahel et al., 2008), and there are also connections among low self-esteem, self-efficacy, and extensive play (Bessière, Seay, & Kiesler, 2007; Wan & Chiou, 2006b).

ADDICTION TO THE INTERNET AND MMORPGs

Due to the length and intensity of MMORPG play, it might be very tempting to consider these players addicted. There are factors that facilitate the creation of addiction. Ko, Yen, Yen, Lin, & Yang (2007) identified the factors that increase the risks of creation of a potential addiction to the Internet: dysfunctional families, low self-esteem, spending over 20 hours per week online, and playing online games. Those authors thus claim that MMORPGs facilitate the creation of addiction and overuse (the authors have considered a limit of 20 hours per week), and if a player is also affected by the other risk factors (i.e., being in a dysfunctional family or having low self-esteem), the creation of an addiction is significantly more probable. Based on Mitchell, Becker-Blease, and Finkelhor (2005), out of all the people seeking specialized psychological help due to compulsive use of the Internet, about one-fifth (21%, to be precise) are online gamers. Problems related to online play then form approximately 15% of all cases of specialized psychological help due to problems related to the Internet (other problems include, e.g., Internet overuse, use of pornography, and virtual infidelity). Adolescents (55%) are slightly prevalent over adults, and men (74%) are more common than women.

We now present the components of Internet addiction created by Mark Griffiths based on the general addiction *DSM IV* criteria (Griffiths, 2000a, 2000c; Widyanto & Griffiths, 2007). Internet users can be considered addicted if they fulfill or score high in all the following criteria/dimensions. These dimensions are often used generally for the development of questionnaires for identifying Internet addiction, but are at the same time fully valid for the case of addiction to MMORPGs (e.g., Smahel et al., 2008). The listed dimensions are at the same time symptoms of online addiction and they can be used to conclude concrete effects on MMORPG players.

The following is a list of components of addiction to a game or the Internet:

- *Salience*—when the activity becomes the most important thing in an individual's life. It can be divided into cognitive (when an individual often thinks about the activity) and behavioral (e.g., when an individual neglects basic necessities such as sleep, food, or hygiene to perform the activity).

- *Mood change*—subjective experiences affected by the carried-out activity.
- *Tolerance*—the process of requiring continuously higher doses of activity to achieve the original sensations. The player thus needs to play more and more.
- *Withdrawal symptoms*—negative feelings and sensations accompanying termination of the activity or impossibility of performing the required activity.
- *Conflict*—interpersonal (usually with one's closest social surroundings, family, partner) or intrapersonal conflict caused by the carried-out activity. It is often accompanied by a deterioration of school or work results, abandoning previous hobbies, and so on.
- *Relapse and reinstatement*—the tendency to return to addictive behavior even after periods of relative control.

Although there is agreement on the use of these indications, it is not yet clear how many of them (whether all or only some of them and in what ratios) should be enough for identifying an individual as addicted. For example, Grüsser, Thalemann, and Griffiths (2007) noted a 12% addiction rate of MMORPG players when demonstrating three and more signs of addiction. Charlton and Danforth (2004, 2007) discovered two factors in these components via factor analysis. The first is actual addiction (or the main factors of addiction); this factor included especially the recurring nature of play, withdrawal symptoms, conflict with one's surroundings, and behavioral salience. The second factor, which could perhaps be called "excessive captivation by the game" (or peripheral factors of addiction) is not related to pathological play. It is connected with the components of tolerance, mood change, and cognitive salience. Addiction is mainly understood as a compulsion in the area of reduced mental tension, whereas "excessive captivation by the game" represents entertainment. The key component seems to be conflict; for example, Beard and Wolf (2001) defined Internet addiction as "uncontrollable, damaging use of this technology," and they consider conflict to be the basic and required dimension for identifying a player as addicted. In the case of adolescents, however, this could be tricky. Several studies (e.g., Mesch, 2006a, 2006b) have shown that the presence of a computer and Internet access leads to intergenerational tension in families. Parents lose part of their control over their children, who often have better understanding of new technologies. At the same time parents are worried about the fact that their children spend their time on the Internet doing other things than what the parents had hoped or expected. This often leads to conflicts, which are to a certain extent caused by the parents and not actual overuse of the Internet by the adolescent. Deciding when conflict indicates problematic or compulsive play thus becomes crucial. For adolescents, this type of conflict needs to be distinguished from common intergenerational conflicts.

FACTORS OF ADDICTION IN THE GAME

It remains an open question whether any Internet application can be considered a source of problematic behavior, in this case addiction to the Internet. Nevertheless, the number of players and the intensity of play of MMORPGs do invite such suspicions. Several studies have pinpointed the main factor of this as the *flow phenomenon*, which explains the intensity of play and following addiction (Chou & Ting, 2003; Rau, Peng, & Yang, 2006; Wan & Chiou, 2006a). Flow is usually described as a difficult activity requiring a certain level of skill and effort, usually related to some form of competition with others. Although it is a subjective phenomenon, its creation is related to characteristic traits of MMORPGs—online social communication and a permanent system of tasks, rewards, and feedback (the role-playing factor). The carried-out activity also blends with one's consciousness—the player fully focuses only on the game and does not pay attention to anything else, and the game then feels "smooth." During flow, other sensations are usually suppressed or completely ignored; these include pain, tiredness, hunger, thirst, and excretion (players often play over eight hours continuously). A typical indicator is an altered perception of time; the activity feels like a several-minutes-long episode, whereas in reality it could have been several hours long. Interruption while playing in such a state is considered very unfavorable and often is the source of conflicts between players and their social surroundings. Concentration on playing the game, together with the altered perception of time and curiosity, leads to excessive play (Chou & Ting, 2003). Time is not one of the factors of addiction; however, there exists a moderate association between time spent in the game and addictive behavior (Smahel et al., 2008). The amount of time spent in the game is thus related to potential addiction; excessive time spent playing, however, does not mean that a player is addicted.

Rau, Peng, and Yang (2006), for example, claim that experienced as well as inexperienced players have difficulties leaving the game due to the flow effect and the related alteration of time perception—they are not aware of the length of their play, because they are consumed by the game. The results also indicate that inexperienced players can enter flow faster (already in the first hour of play), whereas more experienced players need more time. A similarity arises with one of the factors of addiction—increasing tolerance, meaning the player needs an ever increasing amount of time in the game to achieve the sought sensations. As noted by Wan and Chiou (2006a), the relationship of the flow phenomenon to addiction to online games might not be direct and definite. It even seems that sometimes it could be reversed: The authors state that the players with symptoms of addiction experience flow less often. The flow state is strongest and most frequent when a player begins playing. The more intensively and longer one plays, the lower is the frequency of flow. It can even be assumed that truly addicted players sometimes do not have positive sensations from the game, as stated by a 25-year-old man in our research: *"You're so bored that you're not interested in doing anything, but you still keep playing. When you play World of Warcraft a lot, it becomes your second life. So whether you decide to be bored outside or in WoW, it basically changes nothing."* In this sense, the game is the place where a player may be, after all, less bored than in real life. The game is empty, but real life is even emptier. We can conjecture that these sensations could be related to depressions. Flow is probably a significant factor for the initial engagement of players rather than for addiction. The development of pathological play requires suitable conditions on the player's side.

It can also be said that the extent of MMORPG play is partially caused by the social dimension of these games, which break the stereotype of an addicted player as a lonely, unsociable individual or a nerd (e.g., Kendall, 2002). On the contrary, studies have shown that potential addiction positively correlates with the social aspect of online games. Based on Cole and Griffiths (2007), approximately 80% of players play with their real-life friends. About 75% have found good friends in the online game, and 43% have met them face-to-face. As confirmed by an 18-year-old male player: *"The community of players is important; it allows us to create our reputations as players over time and reminds us what we have achieved over the past years."*

We have demonstrated a moderate correlation ($r = 0.44$) in our research between addiction and the preference of the MMORPG social group—the more players claimed they felt "more important and more respected in the virtual group," the more factors of addiction they displayed (Smahel, 2008). In total, 31% of all players agree that they feel more important in the MMORPG social group than in real-life social groups. This number is higher for adolescents aged 12 to 19, where a whole 50% agree compared to 35% of young adults (aged 20 to 26) and 16% of adults (above 27). Adolescents thus have a higher tendency to prefer the virtual group, which is also related to their higher tendency for addictive behavior.

MMORPGs seem to be a considerably social activity. On one hand it is positive that the game does not lead players into social isolation (it does the opposite, actually), but on the other hand the social network keeps players playing for a much longer time. A certain role is also played by the dissociation of social ties (Smahel et al., 2008)—the tendency toward addiction grows with the tendency of dividing friendships originating in the virtual world from those originating in real life. It can be said that the more players divide their virtual life from their real one, the greater is their tendency toward addiction. The most endangered group is the age group of adolescents, which also displays the greatest tendency toward dividing real life from the virtual world. It remains an open question whether we are not witnessing various approaches to reality for which we now have only a pathological interpretation. Is it correct to consider someone's preference for a virtual life pathological if the person at the same time lives a normally functioning life in the real world? That is, unless these two facts are mutually exclusive.

A certain role is also played by the infinity of MMORPG games—it is basically impossible to finish these games, since they are continuously under development. Since the game incorporates players' characters so strongly into its mechanics, it keeps changing and developing constantly. An example is the virtual free-market economics in the game worlds—the prices of various items and services follow complex rules and are affected by many real-life factors (whether it is a holiday, time of the day, etc.), as well as game factors. The software company developing the game also continuously performs various upgrades, usually new features, items, locations, challenges, and so on. The player is thus de facto forced to keep gathering new items (which are better than the old ones) and search new locations to keep his or her social standing in the game. This causes the equipment of players to gradually become obsolete unless an upgrade is found; for example, year-old equipment is almost useless due to the ease of obtaining better items in new locations. This endless and continuing development forces players in the game to continuously remain active; they usually have invested large amounts of time and energy (and sometimes money), and to stop playing would mean throwing all that away, including social contacts (other players are often at least virtually the best friends of addicted players), prestige, and status, which players often lack in the real world. In the words of one player who spends 80 hours weekly playing: *"My classmates and peers actually run into pubs and I run into that game instead, and there I can do as I please—it could be the same kind of thing."*

FACTORS OF ADDICTION ON THE PLAYER'S SIDE

Another direction in studying MMORPG addiction is an emphasis not on the properties of games and virtual reality itself, but rather on players. Studies point mainly to two psychological factors—lower self-esteem and self-efficacy. At the same time we can say that obtaining positive self-esteem and self-efficacy is one of the developmental goals of adolescence, which is probably related to the fact that young players consider the game community more important than older ones do (Smahel, 2008).

The factor of lower self-esteem seems to be crucial in the creation of addiction; this has been shown in many studies, however mostly indirectly. For example, Bessière, Seay, and Kiesler (2007) compared differences in players' perceptions of their current self, ideal self, and game character. The results have then shown that their current self was perceived worse than the game character, and the game character was perceived worse than their ideal self. The differences increased based on the level of depressiveness and the level of self-esteem in particular. Respondents with high self-esteem had notably lower discrepancies between their views of themselves and their game characters, while there were higher discrepancies for respondents with lower self-esteem. The ideal self then was about the same distance away for both groups. This could mean that more depressive players and players with lower self-esteem idealize their game characters and perhaps have a tendency to solve their own perceived weaknesses through the game and thus a tendency to become stuck in the game. Wan and Chiou (2006b) also consider self-efficacy a very significant factor, especially for adolescent players.

The virtual environment of online games allows a lower emphasis on self-control, permitting the subconsciousness of players to express itself more—supported not only by the anonymity but also by the aforementioned flow states. Players of role-playing games often daydream about the game, their characters, and various situations. These fantasies are then considered by players to be one of the most beneficial and strongest moments the game has brought them and the reason they look forward to playing. Players themselves claim they are motivated by fun, experimenting, and so on, but as for subconscious motivations, players with addictive symptoms are motivated by self-expression of a full and efficient self, something they lack in real life (Wan & Chiou, 2006b). These authors explain addiction in the game via a mechanism that is principally close to the feeling of bliss obtained through psychoanalysis. A similar mechanism is described by Allison et al. (2006), where in the case of an 18-year-old hospitalized player the researchers show that his excessive play sessions lasting up to 18 hours per day were mostly a solution to his problems with self-esteem and social drawbacks. His character, a "shaman capable of reviving the dead and calling lightning," then represented a compensation for his deficits, allowing the player to create a full-fledged self in the game. Although he had social phobias, he successfully socialized in the game. Unfortunately, this player was not able to transfer such a full self and the obtained self-efficacy into real life.

The authors, in accordance with Sherry Turkle (1997), thus liken the relationship of the player to his character to a *transfer* as defined by deep psychology. A transfer is a sort of space between an individual (his inner world) and the outer reality, meaning the transfer does not fully belong to either of these places. The game character is on one hand controlled by the player, but on the other hand it is not part of the player, and this could explain why some players are not capable of fully controlling their play. The relationships between players and their game characters can, however, have various forms, and the developmental aspect also plays a certain role here (Blinka, 2008). Especially younger players use their game characters as tools for gaining prestige in the game world and are thus more susceptible to becoming stuck in the game. The relationships between players and their characters can even have therapeutic potential from a certain point of view. Players in the game unknowingly compensate for certain aspects that they lack in themselves; if therapy could identify these aspects, reflect them, and then transfer them into real life, the game could be used to treat their problems, which could paradoxically lead to less time spent in the game. Turkle showed a similar use of the therapeutic potential of games on MUDs, the aforementioned predecessors of MMORPGs (Turkle, 1997).

Wolvendale (2006) spoke directly of the attachment of players to their game characters. This is a very similar relationship to the one we have to absent individuals—they are not in reality present, but by keeping them in our minds, they are real in consequences. The game character is similarly absent or perhaps unreal, but the feelings one keeps toward it are real. The character might be a self-created object and as such it can be considered unreal; however, MMORPGs are based on the interactions of game characters representing the players' identities. Their graphical representation also creates a stronger feeling of their actual existence; for example, players tend to maintain personal space between avatars even if there is no actual benefit to such behavior in the game.

QUESTIONNAIRE OF ADDICTION ON ONLINE GAMING

For a simple discernment of the level of addiction of a player, we have made the following questionnaire based on the aforementioned components of addiction by *DSM-IV* (Griffiths, 2000a, 2000b) and experience from our studies (Smahel, 2008; Smahel, Blinka, & Ledabyl, 2008; Smahel, Sevcikova, Blinka, & Vesela, 2009). All of the six criteria are included, with two small changes: withdrawal symptom is a part of mood modifications (third question) and relapse is a part of time restrictions (ninth question). We verified sufficient reliability of the used items (alpha > 0.90) (Smahel et al., 2009). Table 5.1 shows 10 questions covering five dimensions of addiction to online gaming. Possible answers are (1) never, (2) rarely, (3) often, and (4) very often. The dimension is present if the player answers at least one question of the

Table 5.1
Questionnaire of Gaming Addictive Behavior

Factors	Questions
Salience	Do you ever neglect your needs (like eating or sleeping) because of online gaming?
	Do you ever imagine you are in the game when you are not?
Mood modification	Do you feel unsettled or irritated when you cannot be in the game?
	Do you feel happier and more cheerful when you finally get to the game?
Tolerance	Do you feel like you are spending ever more time in the online game?
	Do you ever catch yourself playing the game without being really interested?
Conflicts	Do you ever argue with your close ones (family, friends, partners) because of the time you spent in the game?
	Do your family, friends, job, and/or hobbies suffer because of the time you spend in online gaming?
Time restrictions	Have you ever been unsuccessful in trying to limit time spent in the game?
	Does it happen to you that you stay in the game for a longer time than originally planned?

dimension "often" or "very often." The player is considered as having all symptoms of addictive behavior if all five dimensions are present. The player is considered "endangered by addictive behavior" if three dimensions plus conflict are present. This questionnaire can be easily used as a simple test for symptoms of addictive behavior in online gaming but it can never replace clinical interview. There are also players who score low in the questionnaire because they unconsciously (and sometimes also consciously because of social pressure) underestimate their results.

SELF-PERCEPTION OF ADDICTION

Addiction to MMORPGs is not just a theoretical, abstract notion. The notion of addiction in relation to MMORPGs has entered general awareness. For example, Google found 4.5 million results when searching for "addiction WoW" at the end of May 2009. There are hundreds of videos on YouTube about this phrase. Yee (2006b) has stated that approximately half of players consider themselves addicted. The older gamers had a lower tendency for doing so: 67% of adolescent girl gamers, 47% of adolescent boy gamers, and 40% of adult gamers have labeled themselves addicted to the game. From qualitative interviews with excessive players (Blinka, 2007), the tendency to do so also seemed apparent; however, this has not yet been quantitatively confirmed. Basically, younger players more often label themselves addicted, but they do not consider this significant and reject possible negative impacts of such addiction. Older players are more often aware of possible negative aspects of addiction, but more often deny being actually addicted to the game. The term *addiction* usually comprises three factors for players: The first is excessive play compared to the referential group of players, which is tricky due to the fact that the referential group of players can sometimes play more than 10 hours a day. As stated by one of the players in our interviews: *"I went to bed at night and the other players went to bed the other day in the morning."* Another factor constitutes conflicts with one's surroundings, and the third is cognitive salience, meaning that a player constantly thinks, dreams, or daydreams about the game. In the words of one of the players, *"When I was addicted, I didn't think about anything else and I played whenever I could."*

One can also ask to what extent somebody labeling himself or herself addicted could actually be related to addictive behavior. In our quantitative study (Smahel, Blinka, & Ledabyl, 2007), we found agreement between self-definition as an addicted individual and addictive behavior in about 21% of players; such is thus the ratio of players who both have symptoms of addiction and consider themselves addicted. Almost a quarter of players then claim to be addicted but do not show symptoms of addiction—probably due to the popular overuse of the word *addiction*. Many players base their judgment of whether they are addicted solely on the amount of time spent playing. From a therapeutic standpoint, 6% of players do not consider themselves addicted but display symptoms of addiction. This group does not acknowledge their addictive behavior, and that fact should be elaborated on therapeutically. The remaining 49% of players do not consider themselves addicted and do not display symptoms of addiction. A total of 27% of MMORPG players in our study indicated all five factors of addiction—a relatively high share considering the fact that, for example, World of Warcraft is played by over 11 million players.

CONCLUSION: WHAT CAN THERAPISTS DO?

In this chapter we have dealt with playing MMORPGs in the context of addiction to the game. Now let's look at possible implications for therapists as well as clinical or social workers who could come into contact with excessive players of MMORPGs. Empirical data on therapeutic work with MMORPG players is still rare, so we will now draw mostly from our experience with and knowledge of MMORPGs and their context.

We have shown that MMORPGs are played primarily by men in young adulthood and that time spent in the game often reaches 30 and more hours per week. Motivations for playing MMORPGs are various, ranging from competition in the context of creation of powerful characters and exploring the online world to recognition in the virtual social group of players, often within so-called guilds. The player's virtual character, or avatar, becomes a part of the player and the player communicates in the game through it. The virtual character in a sense incorporates into the real personality of the player, based on the current state of the player's development and identity. Players then feel a wide range of emotions toward their avatars. Since players spend a lot of time in the game, they often label themselves addicted. About half of players think that they are addicted to the game (Yee, 2006a). Usually this is only a trendy and excessive use of the word *addiction*, since a large share of these players do not display symptoms of addiction to the game. Symptoms of addiction to the game are, however, displayed by approximately a quarter of MMORPG players (Smahel, 2008; Smahel et al., 2008).

We have also presented a simple questionnaire for determining these symptoms, which can be used for basic orientation. However, for determining whether someone is truly suffering from addiction, the best option is to participate in a clinical interview. Many players undervalue or overvalue answers in questionnaires, and playing in the context of the whole of the player's life must be taken into account. Therapists should ask questions regarding the function of playing in the player's life and the hidden motives for playing. It seems that for many players with developed addictions to MMORPGs that this addiction only hides other problems of the player in real life. This hypothesis has, however, not yet been empirically verified, although it does come from informative interviews with therapists. One of the therapists, for example, stated that he had an adult client asking about his depressions. Only after half a year of treatment did it become apparent that this client played

MMORPGs every day, morning to evening. He was at the same time very ashamed of this and did not want to talk about it. Playing MMORPGs could be not only the client's main problem, but also a symptom hidden behind another problem (e.g., depressions, anxiety). Playing online games is actually a relatively safe symptom, since although physical needs sometimes do get neglected to a certain degree, no physical harm is caused directly—as is the case in overuse of drugs or alcohol.

Therapists also have a new option of working with the player's relationship to the avatar and also the context of social links in the game. Understanding the function of the virtual social space of the player is apparently crucial: Is it a compensation for relationships in the real world? Or is it a way of supporting the player's self-esteem and self-efficacy? The therapists should ask themselves what the online world brings the player and how can the player use this in real life. Potential addiction usually has a certain function for players, in some manner that fits in their real lives—similarly to other addictions or psychological problems. Addiction to MMORPGs is specific due to the virtual presence of the player in a community and also due to the relationship to the online character, but apparently is not special as far as therapeutic principles and procedures are concerned. Our recommendation to therapists of potential MMORPG addicts thus leads to using their proven procedures for other types of addictions or problems and possibly combining them with the options provided by the virtual world. Meeting the client in the virtual world could lead to a better understanding of the player's problems and have certain therapeutic potential, as shown by Turkle in the example of text online worlds (Turkle, 1997).

The future remains a big question as far as the development of addiction to online games goes. If we look back, 10 years ago MMORPGs were practically nonexistent and playing within complex online worlds was relatively rare, mostly in the context of the aforementioned MUDs. We can thus ask: What will happen in the next 5 to 20 or more years? The development of technologies and online worlds is so fast that it is hard to guess what the future may bring. It is practically certain, though, that online addiction has been on the rise in recent years. We expect that the virtual reality as a form of escape from the real world will become more and more common, and MMORPGs will be no exception. If the borders between reality and virtual reality keep blurring, be it by improving the graphics of games or quality of monitors or by the development of new technological tools altogether such as monitors in glasses, sensor gloves, or other examples, we can expect further significant development and deepening of these phenomena. Players will find it even more difficult to distinguish between the real world and the virtual one, and their immersion in the game will be even greater. The importance of exploring MMORPGs in the context of addiction will thus rise greatly. This chapter can thus be seen as a prompt to people who come into contact with the phenomenon of MMORPGs, whether in clinical practice or in their research, not to underestimate virtual worlds and not to demonize them. Virtual worlds are, first and foremost, simply another place for people to find fulfillment, be it for better or worse.

The authors acknowledge the support of the Czech Ministry of Education, Youth and Sports (MSM0021622406).

REFERENCES

Allison, S. E., Walde, L. V., Shockley, T., & O'Gabard, G. (2006). The development of self in the era of the Internet and role-playing games. *American Journal of Psychiatry, 163*, 381–385.

Beard, K. W., & Wolf, E. M. (2001). Modification in the proposed diagnostic criteria for Internet addiction. *CyberPsychology & Behavior, 4*(3), 377–383.

Bessière, K., Seay, F. A., & Kiesler, S. (2007). The ideal elf: Identity exploration in World of Warcraft. *CyberPsychology & Behavior, 10*(4), 530–535.

Blinka, L. (2007). I'm not an addicted nerd! Or am I? A narrative study on self-perceiving addiction of MMORPGs players. Paper presented at the Cyberspace 2007. Retrieved from http://ivdmr.fss.muni.cz/info/storage/blinka-mmorpg.ppt

Blinka, L. (2008). The relationship of players to their avatars in MMORPGs: Differences between adolescents, emerging adults and adults [Electronic Version]. *CyberPsychology: Journal of Psychosocial Research on Cyberspace, 2*. Retrieved from http://cyberpsychology.eu/view.php?cisloclanku=2008060901&article=5

Charlton, J. P., & Danforth, I. D. W. (2004). Differentiating computer-related addictions and high engagement. In J. Morgan, C. A. Brebbia, J. Sanchez, & A. Voiskounsky (Eds.), *Human perspectives in the Internet society: Culture, psychology, gender* (pp. 59–68). Southampton, UK: WIT Press.

Charlton, J. P., & Danforth, I. D. W. (2007). Distinguishing addiction and high engagement in the context of online game playing. *Computers in Human Behavior, 23*(3), 1531–1548.

Chou, T., & Ting, C. (2003). The role of flow experience in cyber-game addiction. *CyberPsychology & Behavior, 6*(6), 663–675.

Cole, H., & Griffiths, M. D. (2007). Social interactions in massively multiplayer online role-playing gamers. *CyberPsychology & Behavior, 10*(4), 575–583.

Entertainment Software Association. (2007). Essential facts about the computer and video game industry [Electronic version]. Retrieved from http://www.theesa.com/facts/pdfs/ESA_EF_2007.pdf

Entertainment Software Association. (2008). Essential facts about the computer and video game industry [Electronic version]. Retrieved from http://www.theesa.com/facts/pdfs/ESA_EF_2008.pdf

Griffiths, M. (2000a). Does Internet and computer "addiction" exist? Some case study evidence. *CyberPsychology & Behavior, 3*(2), 211–218.

Griffiths, M. (2000b). Excessive Internet use: Implications for sexual behavior. *CyberPsychology & Behavior, 3*(4), 537–552.

Griffiths, M. (2000c). Internet addiction—Time to be taken seriously? *Addiction Research, 8*(5), 413–418.

Griffiths, M., Davies, M. N. O., & Chappell, D. (2003). Breaking the stereotype: The case of online gaming. *CyberPsychology and Behavior, 6*(1), 81–91.

Griffiths, M., Davies, M. N. O., & Chappell, D. (2004). Online computer gaming: A comparison of adolescent and adult gamers. *Journal of Adolescence, 27*(1), 87–96.

Grüsser, S. M., Thalemann, R., & Griffiths, M. D. (2007). Excessive computer game playing: Evidence for addiction and aggression? *CyberPsychology & Behavior, 10*(2), 290–292.

Kendall, L. (2002). *Hanging out in the virtual pub: Masculinities and relationships online.* Berkeley: University of California Press.

Ko, C.-H., Yen, J.-Y., Yen, C.-F., Lin, H.-C., & Yang, M.-J. (2007). Factors predictive for incidence and remission of Internet addiction in young adolescents: A prospective study. *CyberPsychology & Behavior, 10*(4), 545–551.

Mesch, G. S. (2006a). Family characteristics and intergenerational conflicts over the Internet. *Information, Communication & Society, 9*(4), 473–495.

Mesch, G. S. (2006b). Family relations and the Internet: Exploring a family boundaries approach. *Journal of Family Communication, 6*(2), 119–138.

Mitchell, K. J., Becker-Blease, K. A., & Finkelhor, D. (2005). Inventory of problematic Internet experiences encountered in clinical practice. *Professional Psychology: Research and Practice, 35*(5), 498–509.

Ng, B. D., & Wiemer-Hastings, P. (2005). Addiction to the Internet and online gaming. *CyberPsychology & Behavior, 8*(2), 110–113.

Rau, P.-L. P., Peng, S.-Y., & Yang, C.-C. (2006). Time distortion for expert and novice online game players. *CyberPsychology & Behavior, 9*(4), 396–403.

Seay, F. A., Jerome, W. J., Lee, K. S., & Kraut, R. (2003). Project Massive 1.0: Organizational commitment, sociability and extraversion in massively multiplayer online games [Electronic version]. Retrieved from http://www.cs.cmu.edu/~afseay/files/44.pdf.

Smahel, D. (2008). Adolescents and young players of MMORPG games: Virtual communities as a form of social group. Paper presented at the XIth EARA conference. Retrieved May 5, 2009, from http://www.terapie.cz/smahelen

Smahel, D., Blinka, L., & Ledabyl, O. (2007). MMORPG playing of youths and adolescents: Addiction and its factors. Paper presented at the Association of Internet Researchers, Vancouver 2007: Internet research 8.0: let's play. Retrieved from http://ivdmr.fss.muni.cz/info/storage/smahel2007-vancouver.pdf

Smahel, D., Blinka, L., & Ledabyl, O. (2008). Playing MMORPGs: Connections between addiction and identifying with a character. *CyberPsychology & Behavior, 2008*(11), 480–490.

Smahel, D., Sevcikova, A., Blinka, L., & Vesela, M. (2009). Abhängigkeit und Internet-Applikationen: Spiele, Kommunikation und Sex-Webseiten [Addiction and Internet applications: Games, communication and sex web sites]. In B. U. Stetina & I. Kryspin-Exner (Eds.), *Gesundheitspsychologie und neue Medien.* Berlin: Springer.

Suler, J. (2008). *The psychology of cyberspace.* Retrieved August 20, 2008, from http://www-usr.rider.edu/suler/psycyber/psycyber.html

Turkle, S. (1997). *Life on the screen: Identity in the age of the Internet.* New York: Touchstone.

Turkle, S. (2005). *The second self: Computers and the human spirit* (20th anniversary ed.). Cambridge, MA: MIT Press.

Voig, Inc. (2008). MMOGData: Charts [Electronic version]. Retrieved October 16, 2008, from http://mmogdata.voig.com/

Wan, C.-S., & Chiou, W.-B. (2006a). Psychological motives and online games addiction: A test of flow theory and humanistic needs theory for Taiwanese adolescents. *CyberPsychology & Behavior, 9*(3), 317–324.

Wan, C.-S., & Chiou, W.-B. (2006b). Why are adolescents addicted to online gaming? An interview study in Taiwan. *CyberPsychology & Behavior, 9*(6), 762–766.

Widyanto, L., & Griffiths, M. (2007). Internet addiction: Does it really exist? (Revisited). In J. Gackenbach (Ed.), *Psychology and the Internet: Intrapersonal, interpersonal, and transpersonal implications* (2nd ed.). (pp. 141–163). San Diego, CA: Academic Press.

Wolvendale, J. (2006). My avatar, my self: Virtual harm and attachment. Paper presented at the Cyberspace 2005, Brno, Moravia.

Yee, N. (2006a). The demographics, motivations and derived experiences of users of massively-multiuser online graphical environments. *Presence: Teleoperators and Virtual Environments, 15*, 309–329.

Yee, N. (2006b). The psychology of massively multi-user online role-playing games: Motivations, emotional investment, relationships and problematic usage. In R. Schroeder & A. Axelsson (Eds.), *Avatars at work and play: Collaboration and interaction in shared virtual environments*. Dordrecht, Netherlands: Springer.

CHAPTER 6

Gambling Addiction on the Internet

MARK GRIFFITHS

G AMBLING IS a popular activity across many cultures. Surveys into gambling on a national level have tended to conclude that there are more gamblers than nongamblers, but that most participants gamble infrequently (e.g., Wardle, Sproston, Orford, Erens, Griffiths, Constantine, & Pigott, 2007). Estimates based on survey data from countries all over the world indicate that the majority of people have gambled at some time in their lives (Meyer, Hayer, & Griffiths, 2009; Orford, Sproston, Erens, & Mitchell, 2003). The introduction of remote gambling (e.g., Internet gambling, mobile phone gambling, interactive television gambling) has greatly increased the potential accessibility of gambling all over the world. Government commission studies in a number of countries, including the United States, United Kingdom, Australia, and New Zealand, have all concluded that in general increased gambling availability has led to an increase in problem (pathological) gambling, although the relationship is complex and nonlinear (Abbott, 2007).

Estimates of the number of problem gamblers vary: for example, 0.6% in the United Kingdom, 1.1% to 1.9% in the United States, and 2.3% in Australia (Wardle et al., 2007). These surveys have also indicated that problem gambling is twice as common among males as it is among females, that nonwhites have higher rates than whites, and that those with a poor education are more likely to be pathological gamblers (Abbott et al., 2004; Griffiths, 2007). In 1980, pathological gambling was recognized as a mental disorder in the third edition of the *Diagnostic and Statistical Manual* (*DSM-III*) under the section "Disorders of Impulse Control" along with other illnesses such as kleptomania and pyromania (American Psychiatric Association, 1980). Since then, the criteria for pathological gambling have undergone two revisions (*DSM-III-R* [American Psychiatric Association, 1987] and *DSM-IV* [American Psychiatric Association, 1994]) and are now modeled on more general addiction criteria.

INTERNET GAMBLING

It has been claimed that remote types of gambling have provided the biggest cultural shift in gambling in the past decade (Griffiths, Parke, Wood, & Parke, 2006) and that the introduction of Internet gambling has the potential to lead to increased levels of problematic gambling behavior (Griffiths, 2003; Griffiths & Parke, 2002). To date, knowledge and understanding of how the medium of the Internet affects gambling behavior are sparse. Globally speaking, proliferation of Internet access is still an emerging trend and it will take some time before the effects on gambling behavior surface. However, there is a strong foundation to speculate on the potential hazards of Internet gambling. The impact of gambling technology has been widespread, and there are many observed trends around the world that appear to have resulted from technological innovation (e.g., gambling coming out of gambling environments, gambling becoming a more asocial activity, widespread deregulation, and increased opportunities to gamble) (Griffiths, 2006). At the time of writing, there are around 3,000 sites worldwide, with a large number of these located in just a few particular countries such as Antigua and Costa Rica, where there are around 1,000 sites (Griffiths, Wardle, Orford, Sproston, & Erens, 2009).

In many countries there appears to be a slow shift of gambling being taken out of gambling environments and into the home and the workplace. Historically, what we have witnessed is a shift from destination resorts (such as Las Vegas and Atlantic City) to individual gaming establishments in most major cities (e.g., betting shops, casinos, amusement arcades, bingo halls). More recently there has been a large increase in single-site gambling opportunities (e.g., slot machines in nongaming venues, lottery tickets sold in mainstream retail outlets) and gambling from home or work (e.g., Internet gambling). It is also clear that the newer forms of gambling like Internet gambling are activities that are done almost exclusively from nongambling environments.

EMPIRICAL STUDIES ON INTERNET GAMBLING

To date, there have been a relatively small number of studies on Internet gambling and even fewer that have examined problem gambling and online gambling addictions. However, a variety of different studies have examined different aspects of Internet gambling. These have included national studies on adult Internet gambling (e.g., Gambling Commission, 2008; Griffiths, 2001; Griffiths, Wardle, et al., 2009); national studies on adolescent Internet gambling (e.g., Griffiths & Wood, 2007); regional studies of Internet gamblers (e.g., Ialomiteanu & Adlaf, 2001; Wood & Williams, 2007); studies on self-selected samples of Internet gamblers (e.g., Griffiths & Barnes, 2008; International Gaming Research Unit, 2007; Matthews, Farnsworth, & Griffiths, 2009; Wood, Griffiths, & Parke, 2007a); studies examining behavioral tracking data of Internet gamblers from online gaming sites (e.g., Broda et al., 2008; LaBrie, Kaplan,

LaPlante, Nelson, & Shaffer, 2008; LaBrie, LaPlante, Nelson, Schumann, & Shaffer, 2007); Internet gambling case studies (Griffiths & Parke, 2007); studies examining very specific forms of gambling such as online poker (Griffiths, Parke, Wood & Rigbye, 2009; Wood et al., 2007a; Wood & Griffiths, 2008); and studies examining Internet gambling and social responsibility features (Griffiths, Wood, & Parke, 2009; Smeaton & Griffiths, 2004).

The first national prevalence survey was published in 2001 when Internet gambling was almost nonexistent. In this study, Griffiths (2001) reported that only 1% of British Internet users were Internet gamblers and all of these were gambling only occasionally (i.e., less than once a week). More recently, a survey by the Gambling Commission (2008) reported that 8.8% of the 8,000 British adults surveyed said they had participated in at least one form of remote gambling (through a computer, mobile phone, or interactive/digital TV) in the previous month with no change in the participation rate from the previous year's survey. Those participating in remote gambling were more likely to be male than female, and were more likely to be aged 18 to 34 years.

The largest survey of Internet gamblers was carried out by the International Gaming Research Unit (2007). A total of 10,865 Internet gamblers completed an online survey (58% male and 42% female), with the majority of respondents being between the ages of 18 and 65 years. Respondents from 96 countries participated, and a broad range of occupations were represented. It was reported that the typical Internet casino player was likely to be female (54.8%), be aged 46 to 55 years (29.5%), play two or three times per week (37%), have played for two to three years (22.4%), play for between one and two hours per session (26.5%), and wager between $30 and $60 per session (18.1%). It was also reported that the typical Internet poker player was likely to be male (73.8%), be aged 26 to 35 years (26.9%), play two or three times per week (26.8%), have played for two to three years (23.6%), and play for between one and two hours per session (33.3%). However, online gambling addiction was not assessed. Despite the size of the survey, it should be noted that the sample was not representative as it comprised a self-selected sample.

In relation to problem gambling, a U.S. survey by Ladd and Petry (2002) was carried out examining gambling among 389 self-selected individuals from university health and dental clinics. The study found that 90% of the sample had gambled within the prior year and that 70% had gambled within the previous two months of the survey. It was also reported that 31 individuals (8%) had gambled on the Internet at some point in their lives and that 14 of them (3.6%) engaged in Internet gambling weekly. Mean scores on the South Oaks Gambling Screen showed that the Internet gamblers had significantly higher scores than the non-Internet gamblers (7.8 compared to 1.8). The authors concluded that Internet gamblers were significantly more likely to be problem gamblers than non-Internet gamblers. However, there were many limitations to the study, the most major being the use of a self-selected sample in dental waiting rooms. Research carried out by Wood and Williams (2007) on a self-selected sample of Internet gamblers ($n = 1,920$) in North America highlighted a strong relationship between Internet gambling and problem gambling, with 43% of the sample meeting the criteria for either moderate or severe problem gambling.

Griffiths and Barnes (2008) examined some of the differences between Internet gamblers and non-Internet gamblers. A self-selected sample of 473 respondents (213 males and 260 females) aged between 18 and 52 years (mean age = 22 years; SD = 5.7 years) participated in an online survey. Problem gamblers ($n = 26$) were significantly more likely to have gambled on the Internet (77%) than not (23%). Griffiths and Barnes suggested that the structural and situational characteristics of Internet gambling may be having a negative psychosocial impact on Internet gambling. This is most notably because of the increased number of gambling opportunities, convenience, 24-hour access and flexibility, increased event frequencies, smaller intervals between gambles, instant reinforcements, and the ability to forget gambling losses by gambling again immediately.

Wood, Griffiths, and Parke (2007a) examined a self-selected sample of student online poker players using an online survey ($n = 422$). Results showed that online poker playing was undertaken at least twice per week by a third of the participants. Almost one in five of the sample (18%) was defined as a problem gambler using the *DSM-IV* criteria. Findings demonstrated that problem gambling in this population was best predicted by negative mood states after playing, gender swapping while playing (i.e., men pretending to be female when gambling online or women pretending to be male when gambling online), and playing to escape from problems. They also speculated that their data suggested a new type of problem gambler—gamblers who win more than they lose. Here, the negative detriments to the gamblers' lives are caused by the loss of time (e.g., gamblers playing online poker for 14 hours a day and having little time for anything else in their lives).

Matthews, Farnsworth, and Griffiths (2009) carried out a pilot study on 127 student Internet gamblers. In addition to questions asking for basic demographic data, their questionnaire included the Positive and Negative Affect Schedule (PANAS) and the South Oaks Gambling Screen (SOGS). Results showed that approximately one in five online gamblers (19%) was defined as a probable pathological gambler using the SOGS. Among this sample, results also showed that problem gambling was best predicted by negative mood states after gambling online, and negative mood states more generally.

Griffiths, Wardle, et al. (2009) provided the first-ever analysis of a representative national sample of Internet gamblers. Using participant data from the 2007 British Gambling Prevalence Survey ($n = 9,003$ adults aged 16 years and over), all participants who had gambled online, who had bet online, and/or who had used a betting exchange in the prior 12 months ($n = 476$) were compared with all other gamblers who had not gambled via the Internet.

Overall, results showed a number of significant sociodemographic differences between Internet gamblers and non-Internet gamblers. When compared to non-Internet gamblers, Internet gamblers were more likely to be male, relatively young adults, single, well educated, and in professional/managerial employment. Further analysis of *DSM-IV* scores showed that the problem gambling prevalence rate was significantly higher among Internet gamblers (5%) than non-Internet gamblers (0.5%). It was also found that some items on the *DSM-IV* were more heavily endorsed by Internet gamblers, including gambling preoccupation and gambling to escape. Griffiths, Wardle, et al.'s results suggest that the medium of the Internet may be more likely to contribute to problem gambling than gambling in offline environments.

Another UK national prevalence survey examined Internet gambling among adolescents. In a survey of 8,017 children aged between 12 and 15 years old, Griffiths and Wood (2007) reported that 8% of their sample ($n = 621$) had played a National Lottery game on the Internet. Boys were more likely than girls to say they had played National Lottery games on the Internet (10% and 6%, respectively), as were young people who were Asian or black. Not surprisingly, young people classified as problem gamblers (as defined by the *DSM-IV-J*) were more likely than social gamblers to have played a National Lottery game on the Internet (37% compared with 9%). When asked which of a series of statements best describes how they played National Lottery games on the Internet, nearly three in 10 adolescents who played online reported playing free games (29%), one in six reported that the system let them register (18%), slightly fewer played along with their parents (16%), and one in 10 used their parents' online National Lottery account either with their permission (10%) or without it (7%). However, it should be noted that a third of online players said they "couldn't remember" (35%). Overall these findings indicate that, of all young people (and not just players), 2% have played National Lottery games online with their parents or with their permission and 2% have played independently or without their parents. Those who have played independently are most likely to have played free games, with just 0.3% of young people having played National Lottery games on their own for money.

FACTORS INFLUENCING ONLINE GAMBLING ADDICTIONS

The previous section showed that problem gambling online exists. According to Griffiths (2003), there are a number of factors that make online activities like Internet gambling potentially seductive and addictive. Such factors include anonymity, convenience, escape, dissociation/immersion, accessibility, event frequency, interactivity, disinhibition, simulation, and asociability. Outlined next are some of the main variables that may account for acquisition and maintenance of some online behaviors (adapted from Griffiths, 2003; Griffiths, Parke, Wood, & Parke, 2006). It would also appear that virtual environments have the potential to provide short-term comfort, excitement, or distraction.

Accessibility   Access to the Internet is now commonplace and widespread, and can be done easily from the home or the workplace. Increased accessibility may also lead to increased problems. Increased accessibility of gambling activities enables the individual to rationalize involvement in gambling by removing previously restrictive barriers such as time constraints emanating from occupational and social commitments. With reductions in time required to make selections, place wagers, and collect winnings, gambling as a habitual activity appears more viable, as social and occupational commitments are not necessarily compromised (Griffiths et al., 2006).

Affordability   Given the wide accessibility of the Internet, it is now becoming cheaper and cheaper to use the online services on offer. Griffiths et al. (2006) noted that the overall cost of gambling has been reduced significantly through technological developments. For example, the saturation of the online gambling industry has led to increased competition, and the consumer is benefiting from the ensuing promotional offers and discounts available on gambling outlay. Regarding interactive wagering, the emergence of peer-to-peer gambling through the introduction of betting exchanges has provided the customer with commission-free sporting gambling odds, which in effect means the customer needs to risk less money to obtain potential revenue. Finally, ancillary costs of face-to-face gambling, such as parking, tipping, and purchasing refreshments, are removed when gambling within the home, and therefore the overall cost of gambling is reduced, making it more affordable.

Anonymity   The anonymity of the Internet allows users to privately engage in gambling without the fear of stigma. This anonymity may also provide the user with a greater sense of perceived control over the content, tone, and nature of the online experience. Anonymity may also increase feelings of comfort since there is a decreased ability to look for, and thus detect signs of insincerity, disapproval, or judgment in facial expression, as would be typical in face-to-face interactions. For activities such as gambling, this may be a positive benefit, particularly when losing, as no one will actually see the face of the loser. Griffiths et al. (2006) believed that anonymity, like increased accessibility, may reduce social barriers to engaging in gambling, particularly skill-based gambling activities such as poker that are relatively complex and often possess tacit social etiquette. The potential discomfort of committing a structural or social faux pas in the gambling environment because of inexperience is minimized because the individual's identity remains concealed.

Convenience   Interactive online applications provide convenient mediums to engage in online behaviors. Online behaviors will usually occur in the familiar and comfortable environment of home or workplace, thus reducing the feeling of risk and allowing even more adventurous behaviors that may or may not be potentially addictive. For the gambler, not having to move from the home or the workplace may be of great positive benefit.

Escape   For some, the primary reinforcement to engage in Internet gambling will be the gratification they experience online. However, the experience of Internet gambling itself may be reinforced through a subjectively or objectively experienced high. The pursuit of mood-modifying experiences is characteristic of addictions. The mood-modifying experience has the potential to provide an emotional or mental escape and further serves to reinforce the behavior. Excessive involvement in this escapist activity may lead to addiction. In a qualitative interview-based study of 50 problem gamblers, Wood and Griffiths (2007b) identified that gambling to escape was the primary motivator for problem gamblers' continued excessive gambling. Online behavior can provide a potent escape from the stresses and strains of real life.

Immersion and Dissociation   The medium of the Internet can provide feelings of dissociation and immersion and may facilitate feelings of escape. Dissociation and immersion can involve lots of different types of feelings, including losing track of time, feelings of being someone else, blacking out, and being in a trancelike state. In extreme forms it may include multiple-personality disorders. All of these feelings when gambling on the Internet may lead to longer play either because "time flies when you are having fun" or because the psychological feelings of being in an immersive or dissociative state are reinforcing. A study that compared problem gambling with video game playing in adolescents found that those who had the most severe gambling problems were most likely to experience dissociative states both when playing video games and when gambling (Wood, Gupta, Derevensky, & Griffiths, 2004). Another study examining adult video game players (Wood, Griffiths, & Parke, 2007b) found that experiences of time loss while playing video games were entirely dependent upon the structural characteristics of the game independent of gender, age, or frequency of play. Therefore, as online gambling utilizes the same technology and many of the same structural characteristics as video games, the potential for online gambling to facilitate dissociative experiences may be far greater than has been the case for traditional forms of gambling.

Disinhibition   Disinhibition is clearly one of the Internet's key appeals, as there is little doubt that the Internet makes people less inhibited (Joinson, 1998). Online users appear to open up more quickly online and reveal themselves emotionally much faster than in the offline world. Walther (1996) referred to this phenomenon as *hyperpersonal communication*. Walther argued that this occurs because of four features of online communication:

1. The communicators usually share social categories so they will perceive each other as similar (e.g., all online poker players).
2. The message senders can present themselves in a positive light, and so may be more confident.

3. The format of online interaction (e.g., there are no other distractions, users can spend time composing messages, they can mix social and task messages, and they don't waste cognitive resources by answering immediately).
4. The communication medium provides a feedback loop whereby initial impressions are built upon and strengthened.

For the gamblers, being in a disinhibited state may lead to more money being gambled, particularly if they are motivated to maintain their initial personas (e.g., as a skillful online poker player).

Event Frequency   The event frequency of any gambling activity (i.e., the number of opportunities to gamble in a given time period) is a structural characteristic designed and implemented by the gaming operator. The length of time between each gambling event may indeed be critical as to whether some people might develop problems with a particular type of gambling. Obviously gambling activities that offer outcomes every few seconds (e.g., slot machines) will probably cause greater problems than activities with outcomes less often (e.g., biweekly lotteries). The frequency of playing when linked with the two other factors—the result of the gamble (win or loss) and the actual time until winnings are received—exploit certain psychological principles of learning (Skinner, 1953). This process (operant conditioning) conditions habits by rewarding behavior; that is, through presentation of a reward (e.g., money), reinforcement occurs. Rapid event frequency also means that the loss period is brief, with little time given over to financial considerations; and, more importantly, winnings can be regambled almost immediately. Internet gambling has the potential to offer visually exciting effects similar to slot machines and video lottery terminals (two of the most problematic forms of gambling).

Furthermore, the event frequency can be very rapid, particularly if the gambler is subscribed or visits several sites. Griffiths et al. (2006) concluded that the high event frequency in skill-based games like online poker provides increased motivation to participate in such gambling activities. Online poker, in relative terms, provides significant opportunity for an individual to manipulate the outcome of the gambling event. However, the individual's profitability is still determined to an extent by random probability. The online poker gambler may rationalize that with the increased frequency of participation, deviations from expected probability will be minimized (i.e., bad luck), increasing the effect of skill in determining gambling outcomes over the long term. Because of technological developments, poker gamblers can participate in several games simultaneously, and with reduced time limits for decision making in comparison to traditional poker games, games are also completed at a substantially faster rate.

Interactivity   The interactivity component of the Internet may also be psychologically rewarding and different from other more passive forms of entertainment (e.g., television). It has been shown that increased personal involvement in a gambling activity can increase the illusion of control (Langer, 1975), which in turn may facilitate increased gambling. The interactive nature of the Internet may therefore provide a convenient way of increasing such personal involvement.

Simulation Simulations provide an ideal way in which to learn about something and tend not to have any of the possible negative consequences. However, Internet gambling simulations may have effects that were not originally thought of. For instance, many online gambling sites have a practice mode format, where a potential customer can place a pretend bet in order to see and practice the procedure of gambling on that site. Although this activity cannot be regarded as actual gambling as there is no real money involved, it can be accessed by minors and possibly attract an underage player into gambling. Also, gambling in practice modes available within the gambling web site may build self-efficacy and potentially increase perceptions of control in determining gambling outcomes, motivating participation in the real cash counterparts within the site (Griffiths et al., 2006).

Asociability One of the consequences of technology and the Internet has been to reduce the fundamentally social nature of gambling to an activity that is essentially asocial. Those who experience problems are more likely to be those playing on their own (e.g., those playing to escape). Retrospectively, most problem gamblers report that at the height of their problem gambling it was a solitary activity. Gambling in a social setting could potentially provide some kind of safety net for overspenders—a form of gambling where the primary orientation of gambling is for social reasons with the possibility of some fun and a chance to win some money (e.g., bingo). However, it could be speculated that those individuals whose prime motivation was to constantly play just to win money would possibly experience more problems. One of the major influences of technology appears to be the shift from social to asocial forms of gambling. From this it could be speculated that as gambling becomes more technological, gambling problems will increase due to its asocial nature. However, it could also be argued that for some people, the Internet (including online gambling) provides a social outlet that they would not otherwise have. This is particularly true for women who may feel uncomfortable going out on their own, unemployed people, and retired people.

Because of the apparent vacuous social component within remote gambling, Griffiths et al. (2006) emphasize that alternative methods of peer interaction are available within interactive gambling activities that retain the socially reinforcing aspects of the behavior. Individuals can communicate via computer-mediated communication within the game itself and even outside of gambling through involvement in online gambling Web communities. An increasing trend is for online gambling web sites to provide a customer forum to facilitate peer interaction and therefore increase the social element of the game. Some firms even have introduced an Internet radio facility that entertains their customers as they gamble, while simultaneously drawing attention to significant winners within the site. Effectively, the structural design of remote gambling removes the social safety net that is integral to maintaining responsible gambling practice without reducing the socially rewarding aspects inherent in traditional gambling environments (Griffiths et al., 2006).

Furthermore, there are many other specific developments that look likely to facilitate uptake of remote gambling services, including sophisticated gaming software, integrated e-cash systems (including multicurrency), multilingual sites, increased realism (e.g., real gambling via webcams, player and dealer avatars), live remote wagering (for both gambling alone and gambling with others), and improving customer care systems.

INTERNET ADDICTION AND INTERNET GAMBLING ADDICTION

For almost 15 years it has been alleged that social pathologies are beginning to surface in cyberspace—that is, technological addictions (Griffiths, 1995, 1998). Technological addictions can be viewed as a subset of behavioral addictions and feature all the core components of addiction (e.g., salience, mood modification, tolerance, withdrawal symptoms, conflict, and relapse [Griffiths, 2005]). Young (1999) claimed that Internet addiction is a broad term that covers a wide variety of behaviors and impulse control problems and is categorized by five specific subtypes (cybersexual addiction, cyber-relationship addiction, net compulsions, information overload, and computer addiction). Griffiths (2000b) has argued that many of these excessive users are not Internet addicts but just use the Internet excessively as a medium to fuel other addictions. Put very simply, gambling addicts who engage in their chosen behavior online are not addicted to the Internet. The Internet is just the place where they engage in the behavior.

However, in contrast to this, there are case study reports of individuals who appear to be addicted to the Internet itself (Griffiths, 2000a). These are usually people who use Internet chat rooms or play fantasy role-playing games—activities that they would not engage in except on the Internet itself. These individuals to some extent are engaged in text-based virtual realities and take on other social personas and social identities as a way of making them feel good about themselves. In these cases, the Internet may provide an alternative reality to the users and allow them feelings of immersion and anonymity that may lead to an altered state of consciousness. This in itself may be highly psychologically and/or physiologically rewarding.

To a gambling addict, the Internet could potentially be a very dangerous medium. For instance, it has been speculated that structural characteristics of the software itself might promote addictive tendencies. Structural characteristics promote interactivity and to some extent define alternative realities to the users and allow them feelings of anonymity—features that may be very psychologically rewarding to such individuals. This area has particular relevance to the area of gambling in the shape of Internet gambling. Despite evidence that both gambling and the Internet can be potentially addictive, there is no evidence (to date) that Internet gambling is doubly addictive, particularly as the Internet appears to be just a medium to engage in the behavior of choice. What the Internet may do is facilitate social gamblers who use the Internet (rather than Internet users per se) to gamble more excessively than they would have done offline.

INTERNET GAMBLING: PSYCHOSOCIAL ISSUES

Internet gambling is global and accessible, and has 24-hour availability. In essence, technological advance in the form of Internet gambling is providing *convenience gambling*. Theoretically, people can gamble all day every day of the year. This will have implications for the social impact of Internet gambling and consequences for problem gamblers. Griffiths and Parke (2002) previously outlined some of the main social impact issues concerning Internet gambling. These are briefly described next.

PROTECTION OF THE VULNERABLE

There are many groups of vulnerable individuals (e.g., adolescents, problem gamblers, gambling addicts, drug or alcohol abusers, the learning impaired, etc.) who in offline gambling would be prevented from gambling by responsible members of the gaming industry. Furthermore, Wood and Griffiths (2007b) also identified a number of problem gamblers who had developed specific online gambling problems while staying at home because they were either unemployed, retired, or looking after children. However, many Internet gambling sites provide little in the way of protective gatekeeping (Smeaton & Griffiths, 2004). In cyberspace how can a gaming operator be sure that adolescents do not have access to Internet gambling by using an older sibling's credit card? How can an operator be sure that a person does not have access to Internet gambling while under the influence of alcohol or other intoxicating substances? How can an operator prevent a problem gambler who may have been barred from one Internet gambling site from simply clicking to the next Internet gambling link?

INTERNET GAMBLING IN THE WORKPLACE

Internet gambling is one of the newer opportunities for gambling in the workplace. An increasing number of organizations have unlimited Internet access for all employees, and many employees have their own computer terminals in their own offices, which allows such activity to take place without arousing suspicion. Internet gambling is a somewhat solitary activity that can happen without the knowledge of both management and the employee's coworkers.

This has potentially large implications for work efficiency and productivity. It is an issue that employers will have to take seriously, and they will need to develop effective gambling policies for the workplace environment; see Griffiths (2002) for an overview of issues concerning Internet gambling in the workplace.

ELECTRONIC CASH

For most gamblers, it is very likely that the psychological value of electronic cash (e-cash) will be less than real cash (and similar to the use of chips or tokens in other gambling situations). Gambling with e-cash may lead to what psychologists call a *suspension of judgment*. The suspension of judgment refers to a structural characteristic that temporarily disrupts the gambler's financial value system and potentially stimulates further gambling (Parke & Griffiths, 2007). This is well known by those in commerce (people typically spend more on credit and debit cards because it is easier to spend money using plastic) and by the gaming industry. This is the reason that chips are used in casinos and why tokens are used on some slot machines. In essence, chips and tokens disguise the money's true value (i.e., decrease the psychological value of the money to be gambled). Tokens and chips are often regambled without hesitation, as the psychological value is much less than the real value. Evidence would seem to suggest that people will gamble more using e-cash than they would with real cash.

INCREASED ODDS OF WINNING IN PRACTICE MODES

One of the most common ways that gamblers can be facilitated to gamble online is when they try out games in the demo, practice, or free play mode. Research carried out by Sevigny, Cloutier, Pelletier, and Ladouceur (2005) showed it was significantly more commonplace to win while gambling on the first few goes on a demo or free play game. They also reported that it was commonplace for gamblers to have extended winning streaks during prolonged periods while playing in the demo modes. Obviously, once gamblers start to play for real with real money, the odds of winning are considerably reduced.

UNSCRUPULOUS OPERATORS

Many concerns about the rise of Internet gambling and implications for problem gamblers have to do with unscrupulous practices operated by some Internet gambling sites. A major issue concerns the trustworthiness of the site itself. For instance, on a very basic trust level, how can Internet gamblers be sure they will receive any winnings from an unlicensed Internet casino operating out of Antigua or the Dominican Republic? There are, however, other issues of concern, including the potentially unscrupulous practices of embedding, circle jerks and pop-ups, online customer tracking, and use of trusted nongambling brands. These are briefly overviewed next.

Embedding   One seemingly common practice is the hidden embedding of certain words on an Internet gambling site's web page through the use of meta-tags. A meta-tag is a command hidden in the web page to help search engines categorize sites (i.e., telling the search engine how the site operator wants the site indexed). One common way to get extra traffic flowing through a web page is to embed common words that people might be searching for on the Internet (e.g., *Disney*). Some Internet gambling sites appear to have embedded the term *compulsive gambling* in their web pages. In essence, what such unscrupulous sites are saying is "Index my casino site in with compulsive gambling sites" so people will hit this site when they are looking for information related to problem gambling. Those looking for help with a gambling problem will get these sites showing up in front of them. This is a particularly unscrupulous practice that at the moment is perfectly legal and most impacts problem gamblers.

Circle Jerks and Pop-Ups   Another potentially unscrupulous tactic used by both Internet sex and gambling sites is telescoping windows often referred to as "circle jerks." If someone online accesses a particular type of site and tries to get out of it, another box offering a similar type of service will usually pop up. Many people find that they cannot get out of the never-ending loop of sites except by shutting down the computer. Obviously, those sites that use circle jerks hope that a person will be tempted to access a service they are offering while their site is on the screen. This is also related to the continual pop-ups that appear while surfing the Internet, offering users free bets in online casinos and tempting those who may not have thought about online gambling before. Pop-ups such as these can also be a big temptation for a recovering problem gambler.

Online Customer Tracking   Perhaps the most worrying concern over Internet gambling is the way sites can collect other sorts of data about the gambler. Internet gamblers can provide tracking data that can be used to compile customer profiles. Such data can tell commercial enterprises (such as those in the gambling industry) exactly how customers are spending their time in any given financial transaction (i.e., which games they are gambling on, for how long, and how much money they are spending). This information can help in the retention of customers, and can also link up with existing customer databases and operating loyalty schemes. Companies who have one central repository for all their customer data have an advantage. It can also be accessed by different parts of the business. Many consumers are unknowingly passing on information about themselves, which raises serious questions about the gradual erosion of privacy. Customers are being profiled according to how they transact with service providers. Linked loyalty schemes can then track the account from the opening established date.

The technology to sift and assess vast amounts of customer information already exists. Using very sophisticated software, gaming companies can tailor their services to the customer's known interests. When it comes to gambling, there is a very fine line between providing what the customer wants and exploitation. The gaming industry sells products in much the same way that any other business sells things. These companies are now in the business of brand marketing, direct marketing (via mail with personalized and customized offers), and introducing loyalty schemes (which create the illusion of awareness, recognition, and loyalty) (Griffiths, 2007; Griffiths & Wood, 2008).

On joining loyalty schemes, players supply lots of information, including name, address, telephone number, date of birth, and gender (Griffiths & Wood, 2008). Those who operate Internet gambling sites are no different. They will know gamblers' favorite games and the amounts they have wagered. Basically operators can track the playing patterns of any gambler. They will know more about the gamblers' playing behavior than the gamblers themselves. They will be able to send the gamblers offers and redemption vouchers, complimentary accounts, and the like. The industry claims that all of these things are introduced to enhance the customer experience. Benefits and rewards to the customer include cash, food and beverages, entertainment, and general retail. However, more unscrupulous operators will be able to entice known problem gamblers back onto their premises with tailored freebies (such as the inducement of free bets in the case of Internet gambling).

Although there are negatives, behavioral tracking does offer a potential upside for helping problem gamblers by spotting them via their online game play. There are two routes that gaming companies can go in identifying and helping online problem gamblers. First, they could use a social responsibility tool that has already been developed, the most obvious example being PlayScan (Svenska Spel; see Griffiths, Wood, & Parke, 2009; Griffiths, Wood, Parke, & Parke, 2007). The second is to develop a bespoke identification scheme such as the Observer system designed by 888.com. In contrast to offline gambling, behavioral tracking presents an opportunity for gaming operators and researchers to examine the actual and real-time behavior engaged in by gamblers. Furthermore, such tracking technologies may provide implications for future diagnostic criteria for problem gambling if it can be shown that problem gambling can be reliably identified online without the use of established problem gambling screening instruments.

Use of Trusted Nongambling Brands   Some trusted nongambling sites now provide links and endorsements to either their own gambling sites or those of affiliates. For instance, Wood and Griffiths (2007b) identified a case of an online problem gambler who had been led to an online gambling site by watching a popular (and trusted) daytime television program that promoted its own online gaming site.

ONLINE HELP AND TREATMENT
FOR INTERNET GAMBLERS

Although an overview of treatment for problem gamblers is beyond the scope of this chapter, it is worth noting that online treatment interventions may be an effective medium in helping online gambling addicts. Griffiths and Cooper (2003) reviewed the main issues in the area and examined the advantages and disadvantages of online therapy, and the implications for the treatment of problem gamblers. There appear to be three main types of web sites where psychological help for problem gamblers is provided—information and advice sites, web sites of traditional helping agencies (e.g., Gamblers Anonymous), and individual therapists. Despite a number of possible downsides to online therapy (e.g., establishing client rapport, possible client referral problems, confidentiality issues), there are many positive advantages, including convenience, cost-effectiveness for clients, overcoming barriers that may prevent people seeking help in the first place, and overcoming social stigma.

Wood and Griffiths (2007a) reported one of the earliest studies that evaluated the effectiveness of an online help and guidance service for problem gamblers, GamAid. GamAid is an online advisory, guidance, and signposting service whereby the client can either browse the available links and information provided or talk to an online advisor. If the problem gambler connects to an online advisor, then a real-time image of the advisor appears on the client's screen in a small webcam box. Next to the image box is a dialogue box where the client can type messages to the advisor and in which the advisor's replies appear. Although the client can see the advisor, the advisor cannot see the client. The advisor also has the option to provide links to other relevant online services, and these appear on the left-hand side of the client's screen and remain there after the client logs off from the advisor. The links that are given are in response to statements or requests made by the client for specific, and where possible, local services (e.g., a local debt advice service or a local Gamblers Anonymous meeting).

In Wood and Griffiths' study, a total of 80 clients completed an in-depth online evaluation questionnaire, and secondary data were gathered from 413 distinct clients who contacted a GamAid advisor. They reported that the majority of clients who completed the feedback survey were satisfied with the guidance and counseling service. Most participants agreed that GamAid provided information for local services where they could get help, agreed that they had or would follow the links given, felt the advisor was supportive and understood their needs, would consider using the service again, and would recommend the service to others. Being able to see the advisor enabled the client to feel reassured, while at the same time this one-way feature maintained anonymity as the advisor could not see the client.

An interesting aside is the extent to which GamAid was meeting a need not met by other gambling help services. This was examined by looking at the profiles of those clients using GamAid in comparison with the most similar service currently on offer, that being the UK GamCare telephone help line. The data recorded by GamAid advisors during the evaluation period found that 413 distinct clients contacted an advisor. The types of gambling engaged in and the preferred location for gambling showed little similarity to the data collected in the two British national prevalence surveys to date (Sproston, Erens, & Orford, 2000; Wardle et al., 2007). Unsurprisingly (given the medium of the study), online gambling was the single most popular location for clients to gamble, with 31% of males and 19% of females reporting that they gambled this way. By comparison, the GamCare help line found that only 12% of their male and 7% of their female callers gambled online. Therefore, it could be argued that the GamAid service is the preferred modality for seeking support for online gamblers. This is perhaps not surprising given that online gamblers are likely to have a greater degree of overall competence in using, familiarity with, and access to Internet facilities. Problem gamblers may therefore be more likely to seek help using the medium that they are most comfortable in.

GamAid advisors identified gender for 304 clients, of whom 71% were male and 29% were female. By comparison, the GamCare help line identified that 89% of callers were male and 11% were female. Therefore, it would appear that the GamAid service might be appealing more to women than other comparable services. There are several speculative reasons why this may be the case. For instance, online gambling is gender neutral and may therefore be more appealing to women than more traditional forms of gambling, which (on the whole) are traditionally male-oriented (with the exception of bingo) (Wardle et al., 2007).

It is likely that online gamblers are more likely to seek online support than are offline gamblers. Women may feel more stigmatized as problem gamblers than males and/or be less likely to approach other help services where males dominate (e.g., Gamblers Anonymous). If this is the case, then the high degree of anonymity offered by GamAid may be one of the reasons it is preferred. Most of those who had used another service reported that they preferred GamAid because they specifically wanted online help. Those who had used another service reported that the particular benefits of GamAid were that they were more comfortable talking online than on the phone or face-to-face. They also reported that (in their view) GamAid was easier to access, and the advisors were more caring.

Online therapy is clearly not for all problem gamblers, and those participating should at the very least be comfortable expressing themselves through the written word. In an ideal world, it would not be necessary for those in serious crisis—some of whom could be problem gamblers (where nonverbal cues are vital)—to need to use computer-mediated communication-based forms of help. However, because of the Internet's immediacy, if this kind of therapeutic help is the only avenue available to individuals or the only thing they are comfortable using, then it is almost bound to be used by those with serious crises.

INTERNET GAMBLING IN A MULTIMEDIA WORLD

The rise and challenges of Internet gambling and online gambling addictions cannot be seen in isolation, particularly as there is ever-increasing multimedia integration among the Internet, mobile phones, and interactive television (i-TV). It may be that people are more likely to spend money in particular media. For instance, the Internet can be described as a "lean forward" medium. This means that the users (who are usually alone) take an active role in determining what they do. Computers are better at displaying text than television and have a wider range of fine-tuning controls through the mouse and keyboard. This makes them more suitable for complex tasks such as obtaining insurance quotations or travel itineraries. In contrast, the television is a "lean back" medium where the viewer (often as part of a group) is more passive and seeks less control over what is going on. The television is better at displaying moving images than computers are. This may have implications for the types of gambling done in particular media.

Furthermore, i-TV may also help in one other important area—trust. People appear to trust their television even though it is accessing the Internet in the same way as a computer. However, as argued before, i-TV is a "lean back" service. If a person is relaxed sitting back on the sofa, it will make television the key to creating a true mass market for online commercial activity (including gambling). In addition, some i-TV services can be linked to actual television programs (such as betting on horse races). Browsing and buying by i-TV are still in their infancy but look set to expand significantly in the future.

CONCLUSIONS

Technology has always played a role in the development of gambling practices and will continue to do so. Analysis of the technological components in gambling activities indicates that situational characteristics impact most on acquisition and that structural characteristics impact most on development and maintenance. Furthermore, the most important of these factors appear to be accessibility of the activity and event frequency. It is when these two characteristics combine that the greatest problems could occur in remote gambling. It can be argued that games that offer a fast, arousing span of play, frequent wins, and the opportunity for rapid replay are associated with problem gambling.

There is no doubt that frequency of opportunities to gamble (i.e., event frequency) is a major contributory factor in the development of gambling problems (Griffiths, 1999). Addictions are essentially about rewards and the speed of rewards. Therefore, the more potential rewards there are, the more addictive an activity is likely to be. However, there is no precise frequency level of a gambling game at which people become addicted, since addiction will be an integrated mix of factors in which frequency is just one factor in the overall equation. Furthermore, Parke and Griffiths (2004) point out that the most effective way to control the effects of the idiosyncratic features of

Internet gambling on development of problematic gambling behavior is to provide individuals with a scrutinized, regulated Internet gambling industry. All over the world, recognition of the inability to successfully prohibit Internet gambling has led various jurisdictions to turn attention to developing harm-minimization regulations.

REFERENCES

Abbott, M. W. (2007). Situational factors that affect gambling behavior. In G. Smith, D. Hodgins, & R. Williams (Eds.), *Research and measurement issues in gambling studies* (pp. 251–278). New York: Elsevier.

Abbott, M. W., Volberg, R. A., Bellringer, M., & Reith, G. (2004). *A review of research aspects of problem gambling*. London: Responsibility in Gambling Trust.

American Psychiatric Association. (1980). *Diagnostic and statistical manual of mental disorders* (3rd ed.). Washington, DC: Author.

American Psychiatric Association. (1987). *Diagnostic and statistical manual of mental disorders* (3rd ed., rev.). Washington, DC: Author.

American Psychiatric Association. (1994). *Diagnostic and statistical manual of mental disorders* (4th ed.). Washington, DC: Author.

Broda, A., LaPlante, D. A., Nelson, S. E., LaBrie, R. A., Bosworth, L. B., & Shaffer, H. J. (2008). Virtual harm reduction efforts for Internet gambling: Effects of deposit limits on actual Internet sports gambling behaviour. *Harm Reduction Journal, 5,* 27.

Gambling Commission. (2008). *Survey data on remote gambling participation*. Birmingham, UK: Gambling Commission.

Griffiths, M. D. (1995). Technological addictions. *Clinical Psychology Forum, 76,* 14–19.

Griffiths, M. D. (1998). Internet addiction: Does it really exist? In J. Gackenbach (Ed.), *Psychology and the Internet: Intrapersonal, interpersonal and transpersonal applications* (pp. 61–75). New York: Academic Press.

Griffiths, M. D. (1999). Gambling technologies: Prospects for problem gambling. *Journal of Gambling Studies, 15,* 265–283.

Griffiths, M. D. (2000a). Does Internet and computer "addiction" exist? Some case study evidence. *CyberPsychology & Behavior, 3,* 211–218.

Griffiths, M. D. (2000b). Internet addiction—Time to be taken seriously? *Addiction Research, 8,* 413–418.

Griffiths, M. D. (2001). Internet gambling: Preliminary results of the first UK prevalence study. *Journal of Gambling Issues, 5.* Retrieved June 17, 2009 from http://www.camh.net/egambling/issue5/research/griffiths_article.html

Griffiths, M. D. (2002). Internet gambling in the workplace. In M. Anandarajan & C. Simmers (Eds.), *Managing Web usage in the workplace: A social, ethical and legal perspective* (pp. 148–167). Hershey, PA: Idea Publishing.

Griffiths, M. D. (2003). Internet gambling: Issues, concerns and recommendations. *CyberPsychology & Behavior, 6,* 557–568.

Griffiths, M. D. (2005). A "components" model of addiction within a biopsychosocial framework. *Journal of Substance Use, 10,* 191–197.

Griffiths, M. D. (2006). Internet trends, projections and effects: What can looking at the past tell us about the future? *Casino and Gaming International, 2*(4), 37–43.

Griffiths, M. D. (2007). Brand psychology: Social acceptability and familiarity that breeds trust and loyalty. *Casino and Gaming International, 3*(3), 69–72.

Griffiths, M. D., & Barnes, A. (2008). Internet gambling: An online empirical study among gamblers. *International Journal of Mental Health Addiction, 6,* 194–204.

Griffiths, M. D., & Cooper, G. (2003). Online therapy: Implications for problem gamblers and clinicians. *British Journal of Guidance and Counselling, 13,* 113–135.

Griffiths, M. D., & Parke, J. (2002). The social impact of Internet gambling. *Social Science Computer Review, 20,* 312–320.

Griffiths, M. D., & Parke, J. (2007). Betting on the couch: A thematic analysis of Internet gambling using case studies. *Social Psychological Review, 9*(2), 29–36.

Griffiths, M. D., Parke, A., Wood, R. T. A., & Parke, J. (2006). Internet gambling: An overview of psychosocial impacts. *Gaming Research and Review Journal, 27*(1), 27–39.

Griffiths, M. D., Parke, J., Wood, R. T. A., & Rigbye, J. (2009). Online poker gambling in university students: Further findings from an online survey. *International Journal of Mental Health and Addiction,* in press.

Griffiths, M. D., Wardle, J., Orford, J., Sproston, K., & Erens, B. (2009). Sociodemographic correlates of Internet gambling: Findings from the 2007 British Gambling Prevalence Survey. *CyberPsychology & Behavior, 12,* 199–202.

Griffiths, M. D., & Wood, R. T. A. (2007). Adolescent Internet gambling: Preliminary results of a national survey. *Education and Health, 25,* 23–27.

Griffiths, M. D., & Wood, R. T. A. (2008). Gambling loyalty schemes: Treading a fine line? *Casino and Gaming International, 4*(2), 105–108.

Griffiths, M. D., Wood, R. T. A., & Parke, J. (2009). Social responsibility tools in online gambling: A survey of attitudes and behaviour among Internet gamblers. *CyberPsychology & Behavior, 12,* 413–421.

Griffiths, M. D., Wood, R. T. A., Parke, J., & Parke, A. (2007). Gaming research and best practice: Gaming industry, social responsibility and academia. *Casino and Gaming International, 3*(3), 97–103.

Ialomiteanu, A., & Adlaf, E. (2001). Internet gambling among Ontario adults. *Electronic Journal of Gambling Issues, 5.* Retrieved June 17, 2009 from http://www.camh.net/egambling/issue5/research/ialomiteanu_adlaf_articale.html

International Gaming Research Unit (2007). The global online gambling report: An exploratory investigation into the attitudes and behaviours of Internet casino and poker players. Report for e-Commerce and Online Gaming Regulation and Assurance (eCOGRA).

Joinson, A. (1998). Causes and implications of disinhibited behavior on the Internet. In J. Gackenback (Ed.), *Psychology and the Internet: Intrapersonal, interpersonal, and transpersonal implications* (pp. 43–60). New York: Academic Press.

LaBrie, R. A., Kaplan, S., LaPlante, D. A., Nelson, S. E., & Shaffer, H. J. (2008). Inside the virtual casino: A prospective longitudinal study of Internet casino gambling. *European Journal of Public Health.* doi:10.1093/eurpub/ckn021

LaBrie, R. A., LaPlante, D. A., Nelson, S. E., Schumann, A., & Shaffer, H. J. (2007). Assessing the playing field: A prospective longitudinal study of Internet sports gambling behavior. *Journal of Gambling Studies, 23*, 347–363.

Ladd, G. T., & Petry, N. M. (2002). Disordered gambling among university-based medical and dental patients: A focus on Internet gambling. *Psychology of Addictive Behaviours, 16*, 76–79.

Langer, E. J. (1975). The illusion of control. *Journal of Personality and Social Psychology, 32*, 311–328.

Matthews, N., Farnsworth, W. F., & Griffiths, M. D. (2009). A pilot study of problem gambling among student online gamblers: Mood states as predictors of problematic behaviour. *CyberPsychology & Behavior*, in press.

Meyer, G., Hayer, T., & Griffiths, M. D. (2009). *Problem gaming in Europe: Challenges, prevention, and interventions*. New York: Springer.

Orford, J., Sproston, K., Erens, B., & Mitchell, L. (2003). *Gambling and problem gambling in Britain*. Hove, East Sussex, UK: Brunner-Routledge.

Parke, A., & Griffiths, M. D. (2004). Why Internet gambling prohibition will ultimately fail. *Gaming Law Review, 8*, 297–301.

Parke, J., & Griffiths, M. D. (2007). The role of structural characteristics in gambling. In G. Smith, D. Hodgins, & R. Williams (Eds.), *Research and measurement issues in gambling studies* (pp. 211–243). New York: Elsevier.

Sevigny, S., Cloutier, M., Pelletier, M., & Ladouceur, R. (2005). Internet gambling: Misleading payout rates during the "demo" period. *Computers in Human Behavior, 21*, 153–158.

Skinner, B. F. (1953). *Science and human behavior*. New York: Free Press.

Smeaton, M., & Griffiths, M. D. (2004). Internet gambling and social responsibility: An exploratory study. *CyberPsychology & Behavior, 7*, 49–57.

Sproston, K., Erens, B., & Orford, J. (2000). *Gambling behaviour in Britain: Results from the British Gambling Prevalence Survey*. London: National Centre for Social Research.

Walther, J. B. (1996). Computer-mediated communication: Impersonal, inter-personal, and hyperpersonal interaction. *Communication Research, 23*, 3–43.

Wardle, H., Sproston, K., Orford, J., Erens, B., Griffiths, M., Constantine, R., & Pigott, S. (2007). *British Gambling Prevalence Survey 2007*. London: National Centre for Social Research.

Wood, R. T. A., & Griffiths, M. D. (2007a). Online guidance, advice, and support for problem gamblers and concerned relatives and friends: An evaluation of the GamAid pilot service. *British Journal of Guidance and Counselling, 35*, 373–389.

Wood, R. T. A., & Griffiths, M. D. (2007b). A qualitative investigation of problem gambling as an escape-based coping strategy. *Psychology and Psychotherapy: Theory, Research and Practise, 80*, 107–125.

Wood, R. T. A., & Griffiths, M. D. (2008). Why Swedish people play online poker and factors that can increase or decrease trust in poker websites: A qualitative investigation. *Journal of Gambling Issues, 21*, 80–97.

Wood, R. T. A., Griffiths, M. D., & Parke, J. (2007a). The acquisition, development, and maintenance of online poker playing in a student sample. *CyberPsychology & Behavior, 10*, 354–361.

Wood, R. T. A., Griffiths, M. D., & Parke, A. (2007b). Experiences of time loss among videogame players: An empirical study. *CyberPsychology & Behavior, 10,* 45–56.

Wood, R. T. A., Gupta, R., Derevensky, J., & Griffiths, M. D. (2004). Video game playing and gambling in adolescents: Common risk factors. *Journal of Child & Adolescent Substance Abuse, 14,* 77–100.

Wood, R. T. A., & Williams, R. J. (2007). Problem gambling on the Internet: Implications for Internet gambling policy in North America. *New Media & Society, 9,* 520–542.

Young, K. (1999). Internet addiction: Evaluation and treatment. *Student British Medical Journal, 7,* 351–352.

CHAPTER 7

Cybersex Addiction and Compulsivity

DAVID L. DELMONICO and ELIZABETH J. GRIFFIN

THE WORLDWIDE Internet population grew 380% from 2008 to 2009. It is estimated that nearly 75% of the entire North American continent has access to the Internet. The Internet is a microcosmic representation of the real world, both sexually and nonsexually. Nearly everything found sexually in the real world translates in some way onto the Internet. With such a large audience, commercial producers of cybersex activities see the potential to profit from this segment with practically no overhead costs. In fact, in 2006 Internet pornography accounted for nearly $3 billion (23%) of the total market share of pornography in the United States (Family Safe Media, 2010). As a result of the increased number of people online, as well as the availability of sexual material online, researchers and clinicians have reported a significant increase in the number of individuals seeking help for their cybersex addiction and cybersex compulsivity.

Cybersex problems cross all demographic boundaries. Recent studies estimate that one of every three visitors to adult pornography web sites is likely to be female, and nearly 60% of those who use the search term *adult sex* on Internet search engines are female (Family Safe Media, 2010). Other groups, such as those under the age of 18, are also seeking sexual material online. The top search terms used by teens online include *teen sex* and *cyber sex* (Family Safe Media, 2010). The average annual income for consumers of Internet pornography is a reported $75,000 plus. These statistics challenge our cultural assumptions about online sexual activity and who engages in it.

It is important to remember that not all online sexual activity should be viewed as having a negative impact on its consumers. Cooper, Delmonico, & Burg (2000) estimated that nearly 80% of those who engage in online sexual activity could be considered "recreational users," and do not self-report any significant problems related to their online behavior. Both youth and adults report using the Internet to research sexual information on issues such as preventing the spread of sexually transmitted infections, purchasing and reviewing options for contraception, exploring healthy sexuality, and so forth. However, for the 20% of individuals who struggle with problematic online sexual behavior, the consequences can be devastating and long lasting. Some individuals become compulsive with collecting and viewing pornography, others cross legal boundaries, while still others find themselves spending 10+ hours each day online in search of intimacy or romance. It is these 20% on which this chapter focuses. The purpose of this chapter is to provide a foundational overview of the current thinking related to the psychology of the Internet, as well as fundamental assessment and management concepts essential to working with an individual struggling with problematic online sexual behavior.

TECHNOLOGY AND SEX ONLINE

This section emphasizes the importance of understanding basic and current technologies in order to conduct accurate and thorough assessments with clients. Clinical interviews will be incomplete and inaccurate if the mental health professional does not gather information regarding the client's use of technology. Further, management and treatment planning may overlook some of the most basic interventions for problematic online sexual behavior if evaluations do not include technology-related components.

One of the first concepts to understand is the fact that every online technology can be used for a sexual purpose. It has been true of Twitter, Second Life, Facebook, and even eBay, just to name a few. While this section cannot address every online technology, it does introduce common methods and venues where sex online becomes problematic.

WORLD WIDE WEB

The most common method for accessing sex on the Internet is through the World Wide Web. Internet browsers (e.g., Firefox, Internet Explorer, Chrome, etc.) interpret and display text, graphics, and multimedia on a user's monitor. Sexually oriented web pages are commonly used to display pornographic images, but may also be used for sexualized chatting, video streaming (live), or accessing other sexual areas of the Internet discussed later.

NEWSGROUPS

Newsgroups can be used for sexual purposes by allowing individuals to share sexualized text, photos, videos, or sounds on the Internet with others who have similar sexual interests. There are thousands of newsgroups divided into specific topic areas, many of which are used to exchange sexualized content.

CHAT AREAS

There are a variety of methods for accessing online sexual chat areas. Regardless of the method, the common characteristic of all chat areas is their ability to allow multiple individuals to gather in a common "room" and engage in live conversation, or to relay files back and forth via the chat connection. Many chat areas include video or audio conferencing options as part of the chat process. It is not uncommon for individuals in chat rooms to have sexualized conversations, to view sexualized video, or to send pornographic files back and forth to one another. Examples of common chat areas include Yahoo! Chat, Internet Relay Chat (IRC), and Excite Chat.

A subset of chat areas are the common messenger programs, such as America Online Instant Messenger (AIM) or Yahoo! Messenger. These allow individuals to have a list of so-called buddies with whom they can have individual live conversations.

PEER-TO-PEER FILE SHARING

Software packages such as Limewire have made file sharing a popular hobby. Although music is the most common file type shared in these networks, pornographic images, videos, and software are also commonly shared.

SOCIAL NETWORKING SITES

Social networking sites allow for individuals to create groups of online "friends" with whom they can exchange messages, chat, send photos/videos, share music, and so on. There are a variety of genres in social networking sites, including finding old classmates, finding romantic partners (dating sites), or meeting new people with similar interests. Common social networking sites include MySpace.com, Facebook.com, Bebo, e-Harmony, Classmates.com, YouTube, and Photobucket, but there are many others. Social networking sites can also be used to engage in sexualized activities, or to arrange for offline sexual purposes. These sites were made popular by teens and young adults, but the demographics of such sites show that all age groups online now regularly use some form of social networking on the Internet.

Another common subset of social networking is known as micro-bloggers; the most common one is Twitter. Micro-blogging allows individuals to sign up to follow another individual's online version of a diary, but each entry is made with no more than 140 typed characters. Companies, movie stars, rock bands, and others "tweet" to their fans, as do sexual dominatrices, pornography companies, and others who wish to meet for sexual purposes.

ONLINE GAMING

Online games, whether played at a computer or via a portable gaming device (Xbox 360, PlayStation Portable, iPod, etc.) often include the ability to text or audio-chat while playing the game. Such technology can include sexualized discussions, comments, or arranging for offline sexual activities. The wide range of ages in these venues makes them particularly popular for adults talking sexually to minors.

MOBILE INTERNET ACCESS

Computers are only one way to access the Internet. Cell phones, smart phones, personal data assistants (PDAs) such as Palm Pilot, iPods, and other devices allow users to connect to the Internet from anywhere at any time. Many of the aforementioned methods and venues can be accessed via these portable devices, and therefore sex online is literally in the palm of your hand. The built-in features, such as digital cameras, also make these devices one way to capture sexual experiences in the real world and share them instantly with millions of users around the world.

PSYCHOLOGY OF THE INTERNET

The first book describing the psychology of the Internet was written by Wallace (1999). The book outlined how the Internet changes the way people think, feel, and behave in the online world. Perhaps the foremost scholar in the area of cyberpsychology is John Suler. Suler (2004) has written extensively on how the online world differs from the offline world. The writings are objective and place little value on whether the concepts presented are good or bad; rather, they simply are descriptive of how the Internet changes the environment and the individual.

Suler (2004) coined the term *online disinhibition effect* to describe the phenomenon that people communicate and behave differently online than in the real world. He operationalized the online disinhibition by delineating six characteristics often present when online disinhibition occurs. These disinhibiting elements are often a cornerstone for why individuals engage in online sexual behavior, and the risks they are willing to take in such behaviors. These concepts are listed next.

You Don't Know Me/You Can't See Me   These two concepts are related to the social psychology idea of anonymity and its role in people's behavior. Anonymity in the online world allows people to explore and experiment with their sexuality beyond what they often feel comfortable doing in the real world. When people separate their actions from their identity, they feel less inhibited or accountable for their actions.

See You Later This concept is related to the sense that online consequences can be avoided by simply closing the application or turning off the computer. When individuals feel it is easy to escape consequences, it allows them to take more risks than they may normally take in real life. For those exploring their sexuality online, this translates into more risky online sexual activities.

It's All in My Head/It's Just a Game These two concepts combine to fuel the fantasy world often associated with the Internet. The line between reality and fantasy is frequently difficult to define for Internet users, and when sexual behavior is involved, this line becomes even more blurred. The belief that all online sexual behavior is fantasy oriented allows users to have more cognitive dissonance when they view their own online sexual behaviors.

We're Equals In the real world, hierarchies exist to define clear boundaries and to help understand the rules and roles in relationships. However, the Internet often negates these hierarchies, leaving individuals unclear about the rules for online interactions. Everyone—regardless of status, wealth, race, gender, or age—starts off on a level playing field.

* * *

In addition to online disinhibition, another concept used to describe the psychological changes that occur when an individual is online is deindividuation. This term has been in social psychology literature since the early 1970s (Zimbardo, 1970). Deindividuation is feeling anonymous in one's environment, resulting in behaviors contrary to one's typical pattern of behavior. Johnson and Downing (1979) concluded that anonymity causes individuals to pay more attention to their external cues and environment, and less to their own self-awareness and internal guides. The field of Internet psychology has applied this concept to the electronic world. McKenna and Green (2002) reported that people "tend to behave more bluntly when communicating by email or participating in other electronic venues such as news groups, than they would in a face-to-face situation" (p. 61). Deindividuation combined with the online disinhibition effect creates a powerful force in the online world where individuals write, speak, and behave in ways that are often ego-dystonic to their real-world interactions.

Others have proposed similar models for understanding problematic online sexual behavior. Young et al. (2000) presented the ACE model for understanding this phenomenon. ACE is an acronym for accessibility, convenience, and escape. Cooper (1998) suggested that the Triple A Engine can help explain the strong attraction that compels individuals to engage in problematic online behaviors. The Triple A Engine is represented by accessibility, anonymity, and affordability. The common characteristics of these models center around four main themes: ability to be anonymous, ease of accessing information, ability to engage in fantasy, and ease of escaping potential consequences.

ASSESSMENT OF CYBERSEX ISSUES

The following sections address the issues that should be considered for all clients who may be experiencing Internet-related problems. Although the first section is not specifically about Internet-related issues, the information gained from the Non-Internet Assessment can be useful in understanding the underlying issues associated with problematic Internet behavior. The section on Global Internet Assessment will allow the clinician to identify and isolate specific Internet-related issues that need to be addressed as part of the management and treatment process for problematic sexual behavior online.

NON-INTERNET ASSESSMENT

It is estimated that 70% to 100% of individuals who report struggling with paraphilic or sexually impulsive behavior also report a comorbid Axis I condition, the most common being anxiety disorders (96%) and generalized mood disorders (71%) (Raymond, Coleman, & Miner, 2003). Carnes (1991) reported that of 1,000 self-identified sexual addicts, 65% to 80% of subjects reported an additional Axis I disorder. Therefore, assessment of commonly associated disorders is a significant part of the assessment process. The literature indicates that common co-occurring disorders include depression, anxiety, bipolar disorders, obsessive-compulsive disorders, addictive disorders, and attentional issues (ADD/ADHD) (Kafka & Hennen, 2003; Raymond, Coleman, & Miner, 2003). Also, the screening for underlying personality disorders is critical in determining the path of treatment. Detection of such disorders relies on a comprehensive clinical interview and a standard battery of psychological testing. It is assumed that helping professionals reading this chapter are competent in either conducting such general assessment or referring clients for formal assessment.

GLOBAL INTERNET ASSESSMENT

The assessment of an individual's sexual use of the Internet is often overlooked when conducting a clinical evaluation. All clients, regardless of the presenting problem, should be screened for potential Internet-related issues. Given the large number of individuals accessing the Internet, more and more individuals are struggling with some aspect of their online behavior—sexual or otherwise. The focus of the Global Internet Assessment is to determine the types of individuals' online sexual behaviors, the frequency of the behaviors, and the impact of the behaviors on their lives.

As stated previously, it is important to remember that not all cybersex behavior is unhealthy or problematic (see Cooper, Delmonico, & Burg, 2000). The fundamental question is whether an individual has moved from healthy use of cybersex behavior into more problematic categories. Schneider (1994) posited three basic criteria that can be used to help distinguish these

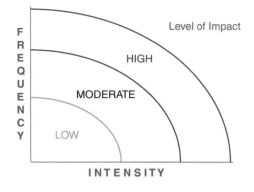

Figure 7.1 Level of Impact of Cybersex Activity

categories. They include: (1) an individual's loss of freedom to choose whether to stop or continue a sexual behavior, (2) continuation of a sexual behavior despite its negative consequences, and (3) obsessive thinking associated with the sexual behavior. In addition to these criteria, another consideration is the interaction between the reported intensity of an individual's online behavior and how frequently he or she engages in such behavior. Figure 7.1 offers a visual illustration of how these two variables can be used to assess the level of impact that cybersex activity has on an individual's life.

This graph assists the helping professional in understanding that low-frequency/high-intensity cybersex behaviors may have the same impact on an individual as high-frequency/low-intensity cybersex behaviors. Repeated, frequent exposure to online sexual behavior, even if reported to have a low intensity, can have as much significant impact and consequence as infrequent behaviors reported to have a high level of intensity (obsessively thinking or planning the behavior, using the activity for fantasy, etc.). One instrument useful in considering not just frequency, but also the level of impact cybersex behavior is having on an individual is the Internet Sex Screening Test (ISST).

INTERNET SEX SCREENING TEST

The Internet Sex Screening Test was developed as a self-administered tool to help individuals assess their own cybersex behavior (Delmonico & Miller, 2003). It is a short screening test to give the helping professional basic data on whether the client should be further assessed for problematic cybersex use.

The Internet Sex Screening Test consists of 25 core items and nine general offline sexual compulsivity items. Delmonico and Miller (2003) reported that factor analysis yielded eight distinct subscales with low to moderate internal consistency reliability (.51 to .86). These subscales include the following:

1. *Online sexual compulsivity.* This factor was developed to assess Schneider's three previously mentioned criteria: (1) loss of freedom to choose,

(2) continuation despite significant consequences, and (3) obsessive thinking.

2. *Online sexual behavior: social.* This factor measures online sexual behavior that occurs in the context of a social relationship or involves an interpersonal interaction with others while online (e.g., chat rooms, e-mail, etc.).

3. *Online sexual behavior: isolated.* This factor measures online sexual behavior occurring with limited interpersonal interaction with others (e.g., surfing web sites, downloading pornography, etc.).

4. *Online sexual spending.* This factor examines the extent to which subjects spend money to support their online sexual activities, and the consequences associated with such spending.

5. *Interest in online sexual behavior.* This factor examines general interest in sexual behavior online.

6. *Non-home use of the computer.* This factor measures the extent to which individuals use computers outside of their homes for sexual purposes (e.g., use at work, friend's home, cybercafé, etc.).

7. *Illegal sexual use of the computer.* This factor examines cybersex behaviors considered illegal or borderline illegal, including downloading child pornography or exploiting a child online.

8. *General sexual compulsivity.* The final factor performs a brief screening for *offline* sexual compulsivity.

Delmonico and Miller (2003) reported a significant relationship between offline and online sexual activity. Questions on this factor were adapted from the Sexual Addiction Screening Test (SAST) (Carnes, 1989). The ISST is included in Figure 7.2 and is available as public domain for use and reproduction. For more information on the subscales and individual reliability values, see Delmonico and Miller (2003). The Internet Sex Screening Test may also be found in electronic form at http://www.internetbehavior.com.

Subject self-report is a major limitation of most screening instruments. This must be taken into consideration, and the helping professionals should rely on their clinical judgment about variables such as honesty, denial, and awareness when interpreting the results of the ISST.

INTERNET ASSESSMENT QUICKSCREEN

While the ISST provides relatively objective data about an individual's cybersex behavior and offline sexual compulsivity, such test data is only one data point among many that should be considered by the clinician. Another less objective, but highly meaningful, assessment technique is a semistructured interview of the client. In order to assist clinicians with the semistructured interview specific to cybersex-related issues is the Internet Assessment (Delmonico & Griffin, 2005). This instrument is helpful since many clinicians avoid structured interviews around topics on which they have limited

Internet Sex Screening Test

Directions: Read each statement carefully. If the statement is mostly TRUE, place a check mark on the blank next to the item number. If the statement is mostly false, skip the item and place nothing next to the item number.

_____ 1. I have some sexual sites bookmarked.

_____ 2. I spend more than five hours per week using my computer for sexual pursuits.

_____ 3. I have joined sexual sites to gain access to online sexual material.

_____ 4. I have purchased sexual products online.

_____ 5. I have searched for sexual material through an Internet search tool.

_____ 6. I have spent more money for online sexual material than I planned.

_____ 7. Internet sex has sometimes interfered with certain aspects of my life.

_____ 8. I have participated in sexually related chats.

_____ 9. I have a sexualized username or nickname that I use on the Internet.

_____10. I have masturbated while on the Internet.

_____11. I have accessed sexual sites from other computers besides my home.

_____12. No one knows I use my computer for sexual purposes.

_____13. I have tried to hide what is on my computer or monitor so others cannot see it.

_____14. I have stayed up after midnight to access sexual material online.

_____15. I use the Internet to experiment with different aspects of sexuality (e.g., bondage, homosexuality, anal sex, etc.).

_____16. I have my own website which contains some sexual material.

_____17. I have made promises to myself to stop using the Internet for sexual purposes.

_____18. I sometimes use cybersex as a reward for accomplishing something (e.g., finishing a project, stressful day, etc.).

_____19. When I am unable to access sexual information online, I feel anxious, angry, or disappointed.

_____20. I have increased the risks I take online (give out name and phone number, meet people offline, etc.).

_____21. I have punished myself when I use the Internet for sexual purposes (e.g., time-out from computer, cancel Internet subscription, etc.).

_____22. I have met face-to-face with someone I met online for romantic purposes.

_____23. I use sexual humor and innuendo with others while online.

_____24. I have run across illegal sexual material while on the Internet.

_____25. I believe I am an Internet sex addict.

_____26. I repeatedly attempt to stop certain sexual behaviors and fail.

_____27. I continue my sexual behavior despite it having caused me problems.

_____28. Before my sexual behavior, I want it, but afterwards I regret it.

_____29. I have lied often to conceal my sexual behavior.

_____30. I believe I am a sex addict.

_____31. I worry about people finding out about my sexual behavior.

_____32. I have made an effort to quit a certain type of sexual activity and have failed.

_____33. I hide some of my sexual behavior from others.

_____34. When I have sex, I feel depressed afterwards.

Figure 7.2   Internet Sex Screening Test (Original)

Internet Sex Screening Test Scoring Directions

1. Sum the number of check marks placed in items 1 through 25. Use the following scale to interpret the final number.

1 to 8 = You may or may not have a problem with your sexual behavior on the Internet. You are in a low-risk group, but if the Internet is causing problems in your life, seek a professional who can conduct further assessment.

9 to 18 = You are at risk for your sexual behavior to interfere with significant areas of your life. If you are concerned about your sexual behavior online, and you have noticed consequences as a result of your online behavior, it is suggested that you seek a professional who can further assess and help you with your concerns.

19+ = You are at highest risk for your behavior to interfere with and jeopardize important areas of your life (social, occupational, educational, etc.). It is suggested that you discuss your online sexual behaviors with a professional who can further assess and assist you.

2. Items 26 through 34 are an abbreviated version of the Sexual Addiction Screening Test (SAST). These items should be reviewed for general sexual addiction behavior, not specifically for cybersex. Although there is no cutoff score calculated for these items, a high score on items 1 through 25 paired with a high number of items in 26 through 34 should be seen as an even greater risk for sexual acting-out behavior on the Internet. Please note: Items 26 through 34 should not be calculated in the total score for part 1.

3. No item alone should be an indicator of problematic behavior. You are looking for a constellation of behaviors, including other data, that may indicate the client is struggling with their Internet sexuality. For example, it would not be unusual to have sexual sites bookmarked or to have searched for something sexual online, but paired with other behaviors, it may be problematic.

Figure 7.2   (*Continued*)

understanding. Cybersex- and technology-related issues tend to rank high on this list.

The Internet Assessment Quickscreen (IA-Q) (see Figure 7.3) can provide a basic overview of common issues that emerge for cybersex users. The interview is divided into two sections. The first measures the extent of an individual's knowledge of the Internet and online sexual behaviors. The second addresses social, sexual, and psychological aspects of cybersex behavior. Questions are based around six thematic dimensions:

1. *Arousal.* This subscale addresses the arousal templates that individuals pursue when engaged in their online sexual behaviors.
2. *Tech-savvy.* Assessing how tech-savvy an individual is can be helpful in understanding a client's online capabilities, and help the clinician maintain vigilance for the possibility clients are being dishonest in their self-reports.
3. *Risk.* There are many reasons why people engage in cybersex, including the rush associated with taking more risks than usual in the online environment. This theme addresses this issue.

Internet Assessment Quickscreen (Form Q)

A Structured Interview for Assessing Problematic Online Sexual Behavior

Section I: Internet Knowledge and Behavior

1. Over the past six months, on average how many hours per week is your computer logged on to the Internet? On average, how many of those online hours do you sit in front of your computer and use the Internet (not necessarily for sexual purposes)?

2. Over the past six months, on average how many hours per week have you actively engaged in Internet sex, including downloading images, sexual chats, etc.?

3. Have you ever posted/traded any sexual material on or through the Internet? This would include self photos, photos of others, sexual stories, videos, audio clips, sexual blogs, sexual profiles, etc.

4. Have you ever viewed child pornography or images of individuals who appeared to be less than 18 years old?

5. Have you ever tried to conceal yourself or the places you have been online (e.g., clearing your history or cache, using programs to hide/clean your online tracks, deleted/renamed downloaded files, use anonymous services, stealth surfers, etc.)?

6. Have you ever had offline contacts with individuals (children, teens, or adults) you met online (e.g., phone calls, sending/receiving through the mail, or face-to-face meetings, etc.)?

7. Have you ever had any of the following types of programs installed on any computer you have used: peer-to-peer (e.g., Kazaa), Internet relay chat (e.g., Mirc), news reader (e.g., FreeAgent), webcam (e.g., PalTalk)?

Section II: Social, Sexual, and Psychological

8. Has your offline sexuality ever been impacted by your online sexual behaviors?

9. Has there ever been a relationship between your masturbation and cybersex behaviors?

10. Have you ever noticed a progression in your sexual risk-taking behavior (either online or offline) as a result of your cybersex behavior?

11. Have you ever experienced consequences, or jeopardized important life areas (e.g., work, family, friends) as a result of your online sexual behaviors?

12. Has your partner ever complained about your Internet sexual behavior?

13. Have you ever become more isolated (physically or emotionally) from family and friends as a result of your online sexual behaviors?

14. Have you ever noticed your Internet sexual behaviors affecting your mood, either positively or negatively?

15. Have you ever wished you could stop using sex on the Internet, but are unable to set limits or stop the behavior?

Figure 7.3   Internet Assessment Quickscreen (IA-Q)

4. *Illegality.* Questions around this theme help identify individuals who may have crossed the line into illegal behaviors—an important consideration for treatment planning.
5. *Secrecy.* Secrecy is often associated with compulsive behaviors, and as the behaviors increase in frequency and intensity, so does secrecy. This theme attempts to assess how secretive an individual's online behavior has become.
6. *Compulsivity.* Questions in this theme help identify individuals whose behaviors appear compulsive, need driven, and ritualistic. High levels of compulsivity can often mean more difficult treatment cases.

Structured interviews are only as good as the interviewer; therefore, while the Internet Assessment is a self-report instrument, knowledgeable and skilled clinicians will be able to use the Internet Assessment to help reveal the breadth and depth of the issues involved for a particular client.

Both the Internet Sex Screening Test (ISST) and the Internet Assessment Quickscreen (IA-Q) have more extensive versions available as part of a comprehensive "Cybersex Clinician Resource Kit." The extended versions of these instruments can provide more detailed and useful information to a treating clinician. For more information about the resource kit, visit http://www.internetbehavior.com.

SEXUAL OFFENSE BEHAVIOR ONLINE

A minority of individuals who engage in cybersex activities also engage in illegal sexual behaviors online. Illegal behaviors online are typically limited to viewing, creating, or distributing child pornography, or attempting to meet with a minor for offline sexual activity. If a client presents with either of these issues, without exception a comprehensive sex offender evaluation should be completed by a qualified clinician. Since not all individuals who engage in these types of behaviors are attracted to children, the evaluator can determine whether the client has sexual interest or arousal with regard to children, has offline sexual-offense-related concerns, or poses a risk for hands-on offense behavior. A referral is likely necessary if such an evaluation falls outside the helping professional's area of expertise. For more information about sex offenders online, see Delmonico and Griffin (2008c).

MANAGING PROBLEMATIC CYBERSEX BEHAVIOR

Treating the underlying causes of problematic cybersex goes beyond the scope of this chapter (e.g., intimacy, grief and loss, spirituality, depression, anxiety). This section emphasizes issues related to managing problematic cybersex. Management is the first step in addressing problematic cybersex and should be implemented before more long-term treatment for the underlying issues can be fully effective.

COMPUTER AND ENVIRONMENT MANAGEMENT

Basic strategies can be implemented to manage and prevent problematic cybersex. Not all of these strategies are necessary for each client, but the following list provides examples of behaviors to be reviewed with clients to determine which would be most effective in managing their online sexual behavior. The clients should also be engaged in the process of developing items helpful to their specific situations. In general, these computer/environment management strategies are most effective with clients who are highly motivated, able to see the negative impact of their cybersex behavior, and without a history of compulsive sexual behavior. Example strategies include:

- Ensuring the computer is used only in high-traffic areas.
- Limiting the days and times of use (e.g., no use after 11:00 P.M. or on weekends).
- Using the computer only when others are nearby (e.g., not when home alone).
- Specifying locations where the Internet can or cannot be used (e.g., not at hotels).
- Making sure the monitor is visible to others (e.g., coworkers).
- Installing screen savers or backgrounds of important people (e.g., family, partner).

It is unrealistic to think that clients will completely stop using the Internet; therefore, small changes like those listed can be helpful in initially managing their cybersex behaviors.

ELECTRONIC MANAGEMENT

Several electronic management solutions are available to help clients manage their cybersex behavior. These include programs that block or filter Internet content and programs designed to monitor an individual's Internet behavior and report it to a third party.

Filtering and Blocking   There are a variety of software programs available to filter the content of Internet activity. Most are designed to protect children from inappropriate content; however, the programs can also be useful to clients who are attempting to limit their Internet activity. Although most programs can be easily thwarted, they can serve as a front line of protection to get clients to think before they act. For a comprehensive listing of Internet filtering software, visit http://internet-filter-review.toptenreviews.com/.

In addition to software programs for filtering, some Internet service providers (ISPs) screen out content before it reaches the personal computer. While this is more difficult to disable, it offers far less flexibility to the client to customize the content and activities that are filtered. To find such service providers, search Google for "filtered ISP."

Computer Monitoring   Monitoring software tracks an individual's computer use and generates a report that can be viewed by a third party. Blocking software may be combined with monitoring software to allow for filtering of Internet content, while also monitoring Internet activity. The accountability partner may be a friend, group member, sponsor, or other responsible individual, but should not be the spouse or partner; when the partner is involved as the accountability partner, negative dynamics often occur in the relationship. A list of top monitoring software and a review of each can be found at http://www.monitoringadvisor.com/.

As previously discussed, there are many ways to access the Internet, and when considering filtering and monitoring options, it is important to remember portable devices that allow access to the Internet (cell phone, BlackBerry, smart phone, Xbox 360, etc.). While it is difficult to manage these portable devices, filtering software is now available for cell phones (see http://www.mobicip.com) and some of the other portable devices. Simply knowing that these devices exist and discussing their appropriate use with clients is an important aspect of management.

ACCEPTABLE USE POLICIES

Most people think about acceptable use policies (AUPs) as they apply to managing employees' Internet use in the work environment. However, the AUP is an effective tool in clinical practice for the management of individuals struggling with their cybersex behaviors. It is no longer feasible to tell people not to use the Internet, so clinicians should help clients establish clear boundaries. An AUP establishes clear boundaries for appropriate Internet behaviors. The AUP should be created with the cooperation of the client, and should include a variety of areas, such as time of day, number of hours online, off-limit technologies, and use of filtering/monitoring software. Delmonico and Griffin (2008b) wrote a comprehensive article on how helping professionals can work with families to develop AUPs for children, adolescents, and adults. These concepts can be easily adapted for individuals who struggle with their online sexual behaviors. Helping professionals who wish to develop an AUP with a client should refer to the Delmonico and Griffin article.

INTEGRATING ASSESSMENT AND MANAGEMENT

This chapter has presented ways to assess and manage the individual who presents with cybersex-related problems. As most experienced clinicians understand, these two areas are not mutually exclusive of one another, and assessment should guide and direct the treatment planning, and in this case the management process.

At the completion of a comprehensive evaluation, the clinician should have:

- Information regarding the relationship between frequency and intensity of the individual's online sexual behavior.
- An overall score from the Internet Sex Screening Test and the cutoff values to determine if cybersex is a significant problem for the client.
- A subscale score from the Internet Sex Screening Test to help determine if the individual exhibits signs of offline sexually compulsive behaviors.
- Responses from the semistructured clinical interview to help assess problematic cybersex behaviors associated with the following themes: types of arousal, level of tech-savvy skills, online risk behaviors, illegal behaviors, level of secrecy, and level of online compulsivity.

In addition to these results from the technology-specific assessment protocol, clinicians must also take into account information gathered from the psychosocial-sexual interview conducted as part of the comprehensive assessment plan. Based on the information gathered from assessment, helping professionals should be able to make a clinical judgment regarding the level of management needed for a particular client. For example, a client who demonstrates significant levels of compulsivity in all areas (frequency and intensity, ISST, Internet Assessment, etc.) would likely need significant levels of computer/environmental management; long-term, more intense treatment; and a thorough evaluation for the use of medications in treatment, as opposed to an individual who scores only moderately high on the ISST and reports just some difficulty in managing the frequency and intensity of his or her online sexual behavior. This latter individual would likely benefit from some of the computer/environment management techniques outlined earlier, combined with individual or group therapy for an abbreviated period of time. These are two simplified examples. Often these cases are far more complex, and frequently involve comorbid conditions that complicate the treatment planning.

Comorbid issues such as anxiety, depression, attention-deficit concerns, and other Axis I and Axis II diagnoses often make the issue of treatment for cybersex compulsives more complicated. Consultation with a psychiatrist knowledgeable of addictive and sexual issues is critical to treatment process, since cybersex compulsives are not likely to respond well to management or treatment if comorbid issues go untreated.

Medications can be a critical component in managing and treating the comorbid conditions uncovered in the assessment process. The best management and treatment techniques will be ineffective if chemical imbalances associated with the cybersex behavior are present.

Current research on the use of medications to treat sexual compulsivity concludes that the use of medications can be helpful in treating the comorbid conditions that often accompany problematic sexual behavior (e.g., depression, anxiety, obsessive-compulsive issues) (Kafka, 2000). Although little research has been done to confirm that these medications will be useful in cybersex compulsives, anecdotally, clinicians report similar results in assisting the cybersex compulsives with medications such as selective serotonin reuptake inhibitors (SSRIs) (Kafka, 2000); serotonin norepinephrine reuptake inhibitors (SNRIs) (Karim, 2009); and opiate blockers (naltrexone) (Raymond, Grant, Kim, & Coleman, 2002). Although medications may be useful in all cybersex cases, they are particularly useful in cases where an individual has developed a severe cybersex compulsivity. Consultation with a psychiatrist knowledgeable in these issues is critical to the cybersex management process.

YOUTH ONLINE

This chapter has focused primarily on the assessment and management of adults who struggle with their online sexual behaviors. While space is limited in this chapter, it would be remiss not to mention the issues facing youth with regard to problematic online sexual behavior.

Cybersex predators are commonly presented in the media as the key risks to young people who go online. However, the biggest risk facing youth is the lack of adult knowledge and supervision of online behavior, combined with the developmental issues (e.g., risk-taking behavior, sexual curiosity, decision making, problem solving, etc.) common to most young people. Wolak, Finkelhor, Mitchell, & Ybarra (2008) found that certain online behaviors of youths placed them at higher risk for sexual exploitation.

- Interacting with unknown people.
- Having unknown people on buddies or friends lists.
- Using the Internet to make rude or nasty comments.
- Sending personal information to unknown people met online.
- Downloading images from file-sharing programs.
- Visiting X-rated sites on purpose.
- Using the Internet to embarrass or harass people.
- Talking online to unknown people about sex.

Although the research emphasized these behaviors as being associated with sexual exploitation, it may also be true that such behaviors place young people at risk for developing their own online sexually compulsive behaviors. Although Internet prevention and safety programs are more widespread, their focus is often on the cyber-predator and not on the ways young people may get themselves into trouble sexually (online pornography, sexting, cyber-harassment, etc.). Delmonico and Griffin (in press) discussed such limitations with Internet safety prevention programs, and present more effective ways to prevent online sexual problems in today's youth.

Teens spend an average of seven hours per day exposed to various technologies (cell phone, Internet, gaming, etc.) (Rideout, Foehr, & Roberts, 2010). Given the frequency of exposure to the online world, it is critical for clinicians to assess the possible impact that medium is having on a youth's life. The issue of the Internet (and other forms of media) should be addressed with all young people regardless of the presenting problem. It is not unusual that the presenting problem is exacerbated by a youth's media use. Instruments such as the Internet Sex Screening Test—Adolescents (ISST-A) (Delmonico & Griffin, 2008a) can be helpful in having clinical conversations with young people about their online behaviors.

The management strategies presented in this chapter can be useful for both adults and youths. Young people tend to be more technologically savvy, and may require additional supervision of their online behaviors. Adults need to be more conscious and less intimidated about the issues of supervising adolescents online. The earlier the management techniques begin, the more effective the results. Having conversations with young children (preschool and older) is the most effective strategy in developing open communication and supervision of an older youth's online behavior.

CONCLUSIONS

This chapter set out as a primer for helping professionals who know little about assessing and managing individuals who present with cybersex-related behavior problems. It provided a brief overview and introduction to a complex issue that continues to evolve. The latest technologies include sexual devices that connect to a computer and allow for sexual interactions with partners over the Internet. Vibrators, simulated vaginas, and other sex toys can be controlled by real-life partners in chat rooms, or videos programmed to manipulate the sex toy to match the scene portrayed on the screen via the Internet. It is unclear how such technologies may impact sexual development and relationships in the future; however, it is clear that individuals will continue to present with issues related to problematic cybersex. It is also unclear what impact early exposure to online sexual material and activity will have on children and youth of today. Clinicians should make a commitment to learn more about these issues and the impact they have on individuals and relationships. As a primer, this chapter has provided an overview of critical concepts related to understanding, assessing, and managing individuals who present with problematic online behavior concerns.

REFERENCES

Carnes, P. J. (1989). *Contrary to love*. Center City, MN: Hazelden Educational Publishing.

Carnes, P. J. (1991). *Don't call it love*. Center City, MN: Hazelden Educational Publishing.

Cooper, A. (1998). Sexuality and the Internet: Surfing into the new millennium. *CyberPsychology & Behavior, 1*(2), 181–187.

Cooper, A., Delmonico, D. L., & Burg, R. (2000). Cybersex users, abusers, and compulsives: New findings and implications. *Sexual Addiction & Compulsivity: The Journal of Treatment and Prevention, 7*(1–2), 5–30.

Delmonico, D. L., & Griffin, E. J. (2005). *Internet assessment: A structured interview for assessing online problematic sexual behavior.* Unpublished instrument, Internet Behavior Consulting.

Delmonico, D. L., & Griffin, E. J. (2008a). Cybersex and the e-teen: What marriage and family therapists should know. *Journal of Marital and Family Therapy, 34*(4), 431–444.

Delmonico, D. L., & Griffin, E. J. (2008b, Fall). Setting limits in the virtual world: Helping families develop acceptable use policies. *Paradigm Magazine for Addiction Professionals, 12–13,* 22.

Delmonico, D. L., & Griffin, E. J. (2008c). Sex offenders online. In D. R. Laws & W. O'Donohue (Eds.). *Sexual deviance* (2nd ed.). New York: Guilford Press.

Delmonico, D. L., & Griffin, E. J. (in press). Myths and assumptions of Internet safety programs for children and adolescents. In K. Kaufman (Ed.). *Preventing Sexual Violence: A Sourcebook.*

Delmonico, D. L., & Miller, J. A. (2003). The Internet sex screening test: A comparison of sexual compulsives versus non-sexual compulsives. *Sexual and Relationship Therapy, 18*(3), 261–276.

Family Safe Media. (2010). Pornography statistics. Retrieved January 25, 2010, from http://www.familysafemedia.com/pornography_statistics.html

Johnson, R. D., & Downing, L. L. (1979). Deindividuation and valence of cues: Effects on prosocial and antisocial behavior. *Journal of Personality and Social Psychology, 37,* 1532–1538.

Kafka, M. P. (2000). Psychopharmacological treatments for non-paraphilic compulsive sexual behavior: A review. *CNS Spectrums, 5,* 49–50, 53–59.

Kafka, M. P., & Hennen, J. (2003). Hypersexual desire in males: Are males with paraphilias different from males with paraphilia related disorders? *Sexual Abuse: A Journal of Research and Treatment, 15,* 307–321.

Karim, R. (2009). Cutting edge pharmacology for sex addiction: How do the meds work? A presentation for the Society for the Advancement of Sexual Health, San Diego, California.

McKenna, K. Y. A., & Green, A. S. (2002). Virtual group dynamics. *Group Dynamics: Theory, Research, and Practice, 16*(1), 116–127.

Raymond, N. C., Coleman, E., & Miner, M. H. (2003). Psychiatric comorbidity and compulsive/impulsive traits in compulsive sexual behavior. *Comprehensive Psychiatry, 44,* 370–380.

Raymond, N. C., Grant, J. E., Kim, S. W., & Coleman, E. (2002). Treating compulsive sexual behavior with naltrexone and serotonin reuptake inhibitors: Two case studies. *International Clinical Psychopharmacology, 17,* 201–205.

Rideout, V. J., Foehr, U. G., & Roberts, D. F. (2010). Generation M^2: Media in the lives of 8- to 18-year-olds. Retrieved January 26, 2010, from http://www.kff.org/entmedia/mh012010pkg.cfm

Schneider, J. P. (1994). Sex addiction: Controversy within mainstream addiction medicine, diagnosis based on the *DSM-III-R* and physician case histories. *Sexual Addiction and Compulsivity: Journal of Treatment and Prevention, 1*(1), 19–44.

Suler, J. (2004). The online disinhibition effect. *CyberPsychology & Behavior, 7,* 321–326.

Wallace, P. (1999). *The psychology of the Internet*. New York: Cambridge University Press.

Wolak, J., Finkelhor, D., Mitchell, K. J., & Ybarra, M. L. (2008). Online "predators" and their victims: Myths, realities, and implications for prevention and treatment. *American Psychologist, 63*(2), 111–128.

Young, K. S., Griffin-Shelley, E., Cooper, A., O'Mara, J., & Buchanan, J. (2000). Online fidelity: A new dimension in couple relationships with implications for evaluation and treatment. *Sexual Addiction & Compulsivity: The Journal of Treatment and Prevention, 7*(1–2), 59–74.

Zimbardo, P. (1970). The human choice: Individuation, reason, and order versus deindividuation, impulse, and chaos. In W. J. Arnold & D. Levine (Eds.), *Nebraska symposium on motivation* (Vol. 17, pp. 237–307). Lincoln: University of Nebraska Press.

PART II

Psychotherapy, Treatment, and Prevention

CHAPTER 8

The Addictive Properties
of Internet Usage

DAVID GREENFIELD

MANY STUDIES have confirmed the existence of compulsive or addictive use of the Internet (e.g., Aboujaoude, Koran, Gamel, Large, & Serpe, 2006; Chou, Condron, & Belland, 2005; Greenfield, 1999a; Shaw & Black, 2008; Young, 2007). Young (1998a) was the first to find that excessive use of the Internet for nonacademic and nonprofessional reasons was associated with detrimental effects to academic and professional performance. Greenfield (1999b) found that approximately 6% of those who use the Internet seem to do so compulsively, often to a point of serious negative consequences. There are, however, still many questions as to appropriate nosology for the labeling of the effects of Internet abuse. Although the most popular media term currently in use seems to be *Internet addiction*, other terms that have been used include Internet addiction disorder, pathological Internet use, Internet abuse, Internet-enabled behavior, compulsive Internet use, digital media compulsion, and virtual addiction (Greenfield, 1999c). This list is by no means exhaustive, but should serve to illustrate the complexity of the current state in labeling this clinical phenomenon.

Perhaps the most accurate labels to date would be *Internet-enabled compulsive behavior* or *digital media compulsion*, as many behaviors previously associated only with the Internet have now been incorporated into many of the newer digital devices such as personal digital assistants (PDAs), iPhones, BlackBerries, MP3 players, and Internet-enabled console/portable game devices and smart phones, as well as desktop, laptop, and netbook computers. The basic psychological factors that account for the addictive nature of the Internet apply mainly to these interrelated technologies. Because the area of Internet and digital media technology is changing rapidly, it should be noted that when referring to the Internet, all Internet-enabled digital technologies are included. The lines that define Internet use and abuse have begun to blur in that many media and entertainment technologies utilize Internet or Web-based access and therefore share many of the addictive elements that are discussed throughout this chapter.

For simplicity's sake, throughout this chapter the term *Internet addiction* will be used, and it may be inferred that all digital media devices are thereby subsumed under this label. With regard to Internet addiction, we continue to struggle with appropriate terminology. Further clarification is required to reflect the psychophysiological phenomenon of Internet addiction symptom patterns and to more accurately reflect what occurs behaviorally and physiologically when abusing Internet and digital media technology.

ADDICTIVE FEATURES OF INTERNET USE

The Internet is not completely new. It is not new in that it is not the first easily accessible, affordable, time-distorting, interactive, anonymous, and pleasurable activity we have come up with. What are new, however, are the intensity, accessibility, and availability with which all of these characteristics are utilized with Internet-enabled technologies. Toward that end, most activities (behaviors) and substances that produce pleasurable effects tend to be repeated. The consequence from a behavior being positively reinforced is what makes it likely that the behavior will be repeated. Positive reinforcement occurs when the presence of some reinforcer increases the likelihood of the preceding response (Schwartz, 1984). This pattern follows basic tenets of operant conditioning (Ferster & Skinner, 1957). It is only natural for people to increase their use (and hence abuse) of the Internet due to its pleasurable nature and reinforcement structure; this reinforcement structure will be further elaborated later in this chapter.

The neurotransmitter that seems most associated with the experience of pleasure is dopamine; we know from years of research that drugs, alcohol, gambling, sex, eating, and even exercise involve changes in this neurotransmitter (Hartwell, Tolliver, & Brady, 2009). In essence, what we become addicted to is the intermittent and unpredictable flooding of dopamine that becomes classically associated with the substance or behavior being utilized. This is where the Internet fits in.

With substance or alcohol abuse or dependence there are other factors, including physiological intoxication, tolerance, and withdrawal. We also know there are physically damaging results from drug or alcohol abuse. The Internet shares some but not all of these features and contains several new and unique characteristics as well. With Internet addiction we may see aspects of tolerance and withdrawal with concomitant physical discomfort (mostly in the form of anxiety-like symptoms or elevated irritability) when patients remove or alter their Internet use patterns. Many patients report such withdrawal symptoms when discontinuing or decreasing their use of the Internet and other digital media technologies; often such symptoms and reactions are corroborated by close family members and friends.

Before discussing Internet addiction in more depth, a review of some general constructs of addiction is in order. The term *addiction* does not typically appear in the psychiatric, psychological, or addictions nomenclature. Rather, the more commonly accepted terms are *abuse* and *dependence*, with the latter marked with features of tolerance and withdrawal along with other markers of physiological habituation. To meet the criteria for what might closely resemble a substance-based addiction, there must be: (1) engaging in an intoxicating/pleasurable behavior (with an intention to alter mood and consciousness), (2) a pattern of excessive use, (3) negative or deleterious impact in a major sphere of living, and (4) the presence of tolerance and withdrawal features. There are other markers as well, but these are the most significant, comparable to compulsive gambling or other impulsive control disorders (Young, 1998b).

Regardless of how we label the problem, there appears to be several central hallmarks that represent this clinical syndrome. The highlight of the Internet *addictive* or *compulsive* pattern would involve not only the presence of tolerance (requiring more time online, greater or varying degrees of stimulating content, or more frequent use) but also the presence of some form of withdrawal pattern. This withdrawal pattern for Internet addiction involves a heightened state of psychological and physiological arousal and discomfort when separated from the Internet. These behaviors have been observed both in objective observation as well as by subjective self-report by many patients.

Another important criterion involves using the Internet for psychoactive or intoxicative purposes in order to alter mood or consciousness. With regard to the Internet, there are two intoxicative components. First, we have the actual *hit* or dopamine elevation, and second, we have intoxication in the form of the imbalance or avoidance in the rest of one's life. This would manifest as an impact on one or more major spheres of living (e.g., relationships, work, academic performance, health, finances, or legal status). If the Internet use does not impact a major living sphere, then it is probably not an issue that would warrant the designation as an addiction; however, many individuals don't abuse these technologies to the point where a serious impact occurs but do experience a *life-imbalance*. It is important to note that because Internet addiction is not directly a *tissue-damaging addiction*, most of the deleterious effects are due to the imbalances created by excessive time spent with the technology.

Desire to Stop, Inability to Stop, Attempts to Stop, and Relapse (DIAR)

A simple algorithm of addiction criteria that is useful is *DIAR* (Greenfield, 2009), which stands for *desire* to stop, *inability* to stop, *attempts* to stop, and *relapse* to previous use pattern. This is the pattern we often see with many, if not most, addictions. DIAR is a notable marker for Internet addiction, in addition to tolerance and withdrawal markers.

TOLERANCE AND WITHDRAWAL

Block (2007, 2008) suggests including Internet addiction in the compulsive-impulsive spectrum disorder category and argues for inclusion in the next revision of the APA *Diagnostic and Statistical Manual (DSM)*. He argues this in part because one of the most notable factors in most addictions (dependencies), of any type, is the presence of tolerance and withdrawal. It is well documented that many, if not most, substance-based addictions involve a degree of physiological and psychological tolerance to pre-established levels of consumption; along with tolerance, some form of psychological or physiological withdrawal is typically found (Young, 1998b). The end result is that Internet addiction will be included in the DSM-V appendix for further study.

In substance-based addictions, tolerance eventually leads to the experience of physiological and psychological withdrawal symptoms when the substance is decreased or removed from use. The patient often feels a combination of uncomfortable (and at times life-threatening) physical symptoms, along with significant psychological discomfort, including anxiety, irritability, emotional lability, and alterations in mood and behavior. Internet addiction poses some unique variations on the experience of tolerance and withdrawal. With tolerance, there are several factors in the consumption (use) of Internet and other digital media technologies that seems to mimic what occurs with substance-based addictions. The addictive potential of a substance is enhanced by the rapidity of its absorption into the bloodstream; it also appears that the rapid access and short latency between clicking and receiving digital images, audio, and other content seem to increase the addictive potential of the Internet. The high speed by which the desired image or content appears seems to enhance the addictive nature of the Internet—thereby increasing the degree of withdrawal symptoms.

Withdrawal symptoms seem to vary depending on the individual, but Internet withdrawal almost always includes a degree of verbal protest at the removal of the technology, especially if said removal is done by a parent or loved one. Typically, such protestations include bouts of strong emotion, frustration, a sense of loss, separation, feeling ill at ease, and a sense of missing something. Sometimes physical expressions of anger and manipulation, coercion, or blackmail can occur. The overwhelming symptom pattern seems to be anxiety based (Young, 1998b). At times, abject disobedience may occur; this can frequently be seen in children and adolescents whose parents remove the technology. Indeed, there are many reports where children or adolescents have become physically or verbally violent when they are prohibited from Internet use.

Other withdrawal symptoms include elevations of anxiety, anger, depression, irritability, and social isolation. The difficulty with the experience of withdrawal from Internet and other digital media technologies is that it is nearly impossible to achieve a level of complete abstinence. Modern living precludes the avoidance of the Internet on a consistent basis. The desired outcome of abstinence, which is often the goal in alcohol and substance abuse treatment, is not a practical probability with Internet addiction. Rather, what is hopefully achieved is the creation of a moderated pattern of use. This moderated pattern has been called *conscious computing* (Greenfield, 2008). The experience of conscious computing is the development and integration of healthy Internet and media technology use. This concept was first observed in the numerous German nonprofit organizations providing public education and prevention materials espousing healthy computing behaviors. A moderated pattern affords a greater degree of conscious self-control and balanced use, and it is this conscious use that afford greater self-control and balanced use.

The goal of treatment then becomes education and prevention to help reestablish (within reasonable limits) a more moderate use pattern. Conscious use and self-awareness is the critical process by which this change occurs. Such behavioral changes are not easily achieved, and further discussion of this process will be left to chapters dealing directly with treatment strategies.

NEUROCHEMICAL FACTORS

There is a great deal of research currently (Hollander, 2006) that discusses the impact of the elevation of dopamine and other neurotransmitters in the addictive cycle; there is more specific brain research emerging that demonstrates with functional magnetic resonance imaging (fMRI) scanning clear neurophysiologic changes from online addiction. New studies have found that the neural substrate of cue-induced game urge and craving in online addiction is similar to that of cue-induced craving in substance abuse (Chih-Hung et al., 2009). It now appears that the addiction may actually be to the elevated levels of dopamine itself in the brain, not simply to the substance or behavior. It is this elevation of dopamine that the heavy Internet user becomes habituated to (Arias-Carrión & Pöppel, 2007). In essence, the intoxicating charge people get from using the Internet or other digital media technologies helps ignite what we classify as addiction. Many pleasurable behaviors become addictive, and because the Internet and other digital media technologies produce significant experiences of pleasure under this theory, the use of these can produce or possess an addictive potential.

The issue of diagnosing an Internet addiction is much simpler when we note that alteration of mood and consciousness occurs when we use or abuse the Internet and other digital media technologies. This pleasurable mood change increases the likelihood of further use and abuse. The nexus of an addictive behavior cycle is that pleasurable actions are followed by intoxication (elevated dopamine). This dopamine elevation is then followed by an addictive pattern, which leads to negative life consequences (including shame and guilt); this consequence pattern then serves to increase the desire to alter mood and consciousness in order to achieve psychic numbing and self-medication, thus facilitating further use or abuse.

DIGITAL MEDIA ATTRACTIVENESS

The following is a compilation of factors that appear to be characteristic of the addictive potential of the Internet and other digital media technologies (Greenfield, 1999b). The five main factors that make digital media attractive are:

1. Content factors
2. Process and access/availability factors
3. Reinforcement/reward factors
4. Social factors
5. Gen-D factors

CONTENT FACTORS

There is a plethora of highly stimulating (addictive) content available on the Internet. Most of this content is not unique to the Internet. The most addictive aspects of the Internet today, in terms of the percentage of people requiring clinical treatment, are sexual content and video or computer gaming. The abuse of these two content areas is by no means new or limited to the Internet; however, when accessing such content using the Internet, a synergistic process occurs wherein the addictive potential of these content areas becomes significantly amplified. When content is consumed online and through other digital media technologies, it in essence becomes the psychoactive raw material for Internet addiction. We know that the Internet medium itself has addiction-enhancing properties and the content that is consumed on the Internet is typically fun and desirable. The most common contents consumed include music, information, sports, shopping, financial and other news, gambling, games, sexual content and so on. Many, if not most, of these content areas are inherently pleasurable; gaming, gambling, shopping, and sex are perhaps at the top, and have a history of being overused, abused, or addicted (Young, 1998a).

With the advent of Internet technology, the ability to easily and frequently access such content has enhanced its addictive potential considerably. If content is the raw material, then the *Internet medium* is the psychological syringe that delivers the content into our nervous system for consumption. There has never been a more efficient and direct input into our minds and nervous systems than the Internet. Now, with the advent and proliferation of high-speed connections and mobile Internet portals such as smart phones, PDAs, iPhones, BlackBerries, and many other portable devices, accessibility is even further enhanced.

Even iPods and other MP3 players are now Internet ready. The seamless ease of access to the Internet from anywhere places the user as part of the Internet network itself. People have literally become nodes on a vast impersonal network system, and this system is now mobile and portable. The mobility of current Internet access is based on our desire to have convenience and to have a sense of freedom and choice; it is this desire that fosters the illusion that more access and opportunity equals a better/happier lifestyle—that more is better. But that is a paradox. The more choices we seem to have, the less healthy we seem to become. The more choices we have, the more stress we have (Weissberg, 1983). We have seen this same phenomenon with the availability of a variety of food product choices. More is simply not better.

The availability and variety of previously inaccessible, illegal, or hard-to-find content enhances the Internet's attractiveness considerably. Finding what you want, especially if it is hard to find, is very intoxicating. In addition, the absence of delay of gratification in the ability to access such hard-to-find and potent content makes the Internet that much more compelling. "God in a box" (Greenfield, 2007) is a term used in some discussions of Internet use. It seems an almost magical experience to have a thought, curiosity, or desire, and to simply click with near-instantaneous manifestation of thought to reality. It also captures the near-deified level of worship that the Internet and other digital technologies receive. The threshold one crosses is very narrow and easily traversed on the Internet, and on the other side of this threshold is the world's most stimulating content, and therein lies much of the Internet's power and potency.

Process and Access/Availability Factors

The ability to experience one's personal power (extended and amplified via the Internet) in experiencing a fantasy, or to act out a persona, is highly intoxicating. The experience of enacting a sexual fantasy with the relative *ease, disinhibition,* and *anonymity* that the Internet affords is quite powerful (Cooper, Delmonico, & Burg, 2000, Greenfield & Orzack, 2002). Multi-user games, which utilize the Internet to allow social and game interactivity, appear to be even more addictive as they utilize the Internet platform. The vast majority of Internet-based games add additional attractive elements of social interaction, real-time competition, challenge, accomplishment, social hierarchy, and stimulating content—along with a very sophisticated variable reward schedule. Gaming content itself can be quite stimulating and addictive, but when combined with the Internet modality the synergistic effect seems to produce a still stronger addictive experience.

The Internet operates with a high degree of unpredictability and novelty, and it is this unpredictability that facilitates the compelling nature of the Internet.

Much of our Internet use pattern operates on a subconscious level—well below awareness; it is this automated use that supports a significant degree of time distortion and dissociation (loss of the perception of ourselves) when on the Internet (Greenfield, 1999b; Suler, 2004; Toronto, 2009). Indeed, estimates as high as 80 percent of individuals who use the Internet lose track of time and space while online (Suler, 2004). Early studies found that 80 percent of Internet addicts (43 percent of nonaddicts) reported feeling less inhibited when online (Greenfield, 1999b), and more current studies have found that 8.2 percent used the Internet as a way to escape problems or relieve negative moods (Aboujaoude et al., 2006). This disinhibition effect further supports the Internet as a psychoactive medium; this consciousness- and mood-altering effect seems to operate irrespective of content. The attractiveness of the Internet modality seems, in part, to be separate from the content that is being consumed. Individuals who might consume sexual content, participate in gaming, or do shopping might do so with a greater degree of disinhibition and impulsivity when utilizing the Internet modality, compared to other use modalities (Suler, 2004).

Greenfield (1999b) found three main factors that seem to account for a good deal of the Internet addiction variance. The first factor could be subsumed under the broad category of *access/availability* or *process* factors. Cooper (1998) discusses this factor under his rubric of the Triple A Engine, where *affordability* and *anonymity* are included as well.

Within the general construct of access and availability is the fact that the Internet is always open, and this is a highly compelling feature. We know that the brain seems to enjoy the ability to have what appears to be unfettered access without constraints of time or space. Additionally, the factors involved in the interactive nature of the Internet modality itself seem to increase its attractiveness. Our research also demonstrated the second factor of perceived anonymity (Greenfield, 2009). It is the perception of anonymity in the online communication process that seems to facilitate disinhibition (Cooper, Boies, Maheu, & Greenfield, 2000). This is particularly notable in the areas of sexual behavior, gambling, shopping, and gaming. Disinhibition is also a factor in e-mail, chat, instant messaging, and text communications as well. There appears to be less restriction of inhibition during lexagraphic communication compared with the verbal modality.

We know from cognitive science and neuropsychology that disinhibition can occur when the brain is neuropsychologically compromised—basically in an altered state of consciousness. It stands to reason that this, to a milder extent, is what occurs when communicating online. In essence, compulsive online use is functioning in an altered state of consciousness. Additionally, the ability to access hidden or subconscious aspects of one's personality or persona that are not normally accessible appears to have strong addiction-facilitating effects. Fantasy and role-play via the Internet are highly appealing and are especially noteworthy in gaming, sexual chatting (cybering), and in social networking situations. An additional area that falls under the access/availability category is the relative low cost of accessing Internet content areas (Cooper, 1998). Access is thus enhanced by the relative low cost of Internet access, thereby lowering the threshold to using and abusing the Internet. It is easier to abuse things that are cheaper.

No discussion of access and availability factors can be complete without the inclusion of the *convenience* factor. The Internet is available with nearly seamless and unfettered access 24 hours, seven days a week. Ease of access and availability is growing with the widespread adoption of portable and mobile broadband access. Cell phones, PDAs, and portable game and MP3 devices, in addition to laptops and their newest cousin, the netbook, are all geared toward portable Internet applications.

The ability to instantly obtain anything and to gratify any intellectual, communicative, or consumer urge in a seemingly anonymous fashion makes the Internet almost irresistible for many people. This is especially true for sexual content and experiences. The threshold to cross over from impulse (desire) to action (what is viewed, downloaded, played, or purchased online) is greatly reduced when online. There in essence is no barrier to cross, since the time needed to pick and click online is so short. There is also much less accountability due to the perception (however inaccurate) of anonymity and privacy. The degree of resistance that one might ordinarily have to fulfill a fantasy or desire is absent or greatly reduced when online, and this can have the effect of distorting reality. For the Internet addict, reality distortion is often perceived as a desirable outcome, as it supports the fantasy experience through the Internet's virtual interface. Once addicted, individuals may tend to view their virtual reality as more valid than real-time living. This is especially true for Internet and computer gamers. This distortion supports an overall level of denial, which can hamper the addicts' ability to recognize any negative impact in their lives. This is intoxication in its purest form!

Psychological inertia is often experienced as pleasurable (thus further feeding the addictive cycle) in that it blocks us from addressing what might be viewed as self-defeating. The Internet changes all of this because there is almost no lag or threshold to cross and we experience the Internet as a form of instant gratification. The need for delay or to modulate our desires is often absent with the use of the Internet. In a sense, thought becomes reality, instantly, which is quite compelling.

The final access/availability construct is boundaries. There are no boundaries with online content. All other forms of media have a discrete beginning and end. There are almost always markers for the passage of time or limits to content in newspapers, magazines, television shows, books, or other forms of media. By contrast, you are never done with anything on the Internet. There are no time markers while online, which is often compared to being in a casino with high stimulation, variable rewards, and no time structure. There is always another link, web site, or reference to find; always another e-mail to open, image to view, or song to download. There is always more. This unending availability of content represents unfinished business to the brain and is highly compelling. There is a tendency to move toward completion of all tasks for the brain—to complete the gestalt called the Zeigarnik effect (Zeigarnik, 1967). This unconscious attention to unfinished or incomplete information (which the Internet is replete with) is yet another compelling feature of the Internet.

REINFORCEMENT/REWARD FACTORS

As previously noted, Internet technology operates on a variable ratio reinforcement schedule (VRRS). All aspects of information sought after and found on the Internet occur within this variable ratio reinforcement environment. The Internet operates with a high degree of unpredictability and novelty, and it is this unpredictability that facilitates the compelling nature of the Internet's attractiveness.

The reinforcement/reward factor seems to be the most significant element in contributing to the addictive nature of the Internet and other digital media technologies. The Internet functions on a variable ratio reinforcement schedule. Whether it's gaming, sexual content, e-mail, shopping, or general information surfing, they all support unpredictable and variable reward structures. The saliency and desirability of the targeted online content, as well as the time and frequency when that content might be obtained, all affect the addictive experience to the content. There appear to be numerous synergistic factors that occur when the VRRS is combined with mood-enhancing or stimulating content, further cementing the addictive cycle.

The Internet is in part addictive because of its psychoactive properties. Inherent to any reinforcement system are the secondary gains that occur from a habitual pleasure pattern such as Internet addiction and compulsive media use. The secondary gains are those aspects of indirect benefit that serve to further reinforce the addictive pattern (elevation of dopamine). These secondary benefits may present in the form of avoidance of anxiety-provoking social interaction or effortful school or work performance, or as psychosocial exits from family or primary relationships. They can also be expressed as increased social stature within a social network or online game community.

Many elements of the Internet that are most attractive to people operate on a variable ratio reinforcement schedule. Young (1998b) was one of the first to note similarities between gambling behavior and heavy Internet use. It stands to reason that pleasurable Internet experiences operate within an environment where intermittent degrees of reinforcement are the rule. Here a pleasurable charge is received with both an unpredictable frequency as well as an unpredictable saliency. We experience this pleasure in the form of clicking on and thus finding and receiving desired content, mastering a challenging game, searching for and finding desirable pornography, or unpredictably receiving a desired text, instant message, chat, or e-mail. The same is true for searching on Facebook, MySpace, Twitter, and so on. All these hits are unpredictable, intermittent, and of varying attractiveness (saliency). It is this combination of unpredictable content salience and the variable reward structure that makes the Internet so addictive (Greenfield, 2008).

Even basic Internet modalities such as e-mail operate on this very powerful reinforcement schedule (e.g., you never know if that e-mail is going to be from a desired source with good news, junk mail, or a bill to pay). We know from behavioral science research (Ferster & Skinner, 1957) that the VRRS is highly resistant to extinction, and because the Internet frequently provides variable rewards, this extinction resistance further reinforces the addiction cycle. Each time we log on to the Internet to surf, play a game, check e-mail, send an instant message, chat, text on a cell phone, or search for anything, we are invoking this powerful reinforcement principle (Young, 2007).

Combining this reinforcement system with highly stimulating content found in gaming or pornography will likely yield an even greater positive charge and an even greater resistance to extinction, thus reinforcing an addictive cycle (Greenfield & Orzack, 2002; Young, 2007). It appears that synergistic interaction occurs (Cooper, Boies, Maheu, & Greenfield, 2000), wherein the power of both the content and the Internet process are thereby amplified. Greenfield (1999b) begins to describe two types of Internet addicts with regard to sex: primary and secondary. Primary type typically consists of a sexually compulsive pattern of behavior that predates the use of the Internet for achieving sexual satisfaction. Here the Internet serves to function as a means by which a more efficient and expeditious sexual arousal and satisfaction cycle can be achieved. This Internet-enabled pattern often creates an accelerated development of compulsive sexual behavior. Here we see the synergistic process whereby the stimulating content of sexual material is enhanced by the psychoactive nature of the Internet medium itself.

In the secondary type, there is often no prior history of compulsive sexual behavior, but the development of the compulsive pattern seems to initiate almost concurrently with the introduction of the Internet. It is as if a spontaneous arousal/compulsion cycle ignites, often born out of the seeds of curiosity, sexual desire, and ease of access/availability or anonymity. With secondary-type compulsives, there is usually no history of prior sexual addiction or compulsion; here the Internet appears to activate a disinhibited process and support the addictive cycle. In such cases, the Internet process seems to lower the threshold for certain individuals to develop a problem that they likely would not have developed without the Internet medium. This is the Internet's strength and weakness, in that the immediacy of gratification can affect one's ability to inhibit previously managed drives and desires.

Most computer and Internet game manufacturers, as well as the sex industry, understand these behavioral principles, and they understand their use within the development of a game or other stimulating media, such as pornography. Most of the issues that we find with Internet addiction involve the unconscious and compulsive use of this technology with little or no awareness of the passage of time (dissociation/time distortion) or the negative consequences of this distortion (Suler, 2004). It is known from clinical analysis that much of the deleterious effect of heavy Internet use seems to be from the dissociated use of the technology, and the imbalance this creates in our lives.

SOCIAL FACTORS

The Internet is both socially connecting and simultaneously socially isolating (Greenfield, 1999a-c; Kimkiewicz, 2007; Kraut & Kiesler, 2003; van den Eijnden, Meerkerk, Vermulst, Spijkerman, & Engels, 2008; Young, 2004). This statement speaks to one of the major attractions of the Internet. The Internet affords titrated social connection within a highly circumscribed social networking medium. In a sense, users can tailor their degree of social interaction in a way that maximizes comfort and mediates connection, while minimizing social anxiety and limiting necessary social contextual cues.

With heavy Internet users (especially in the high school and young adult population) the Internet affords an easy way to participate in a well-controlled social environment with less need for real-time social interaction (Ferris, 2001; Leung, 2007). The Internet narrows and simplifies the social-emotional intelligence cues needed to a more manageable interaction level. For most users it lessens and attenuates the level of attention, interaction, emotional risk, and intimate connection needed in the social relationship. It reduces interpersonal relating to a tolerated level. For individuals with learning disabilities, attention deficit disorders, pervasive developmental disorders, social anxiety, and phobias, the Internet becomes a safe, predictable, circumscribed environment. It holds our attention, provides endless novel stimulation, minimizes real-time social interaction, and provides unbounded reinforcements and social rewards. It is no wonder why patients have such difficulty in modifying something that is so much fun and so adaptive.

It is important to note here that there is room for healthy, balanced Internet and digital media use, including social networking, texting, instant messaging, e-mail, and the like. Peltoniemi (2009) in Finland uses the Internet, texting, and social networking to assist children and young adults in learning to moderate their use and abuse; his organization, ICT-Services for Media Addiction, Prevention and Treatment in Finland, utilizes the very technology it is trying to limit to reach its audience; Peltoniemi is doing this because this is the main communications medium for this digital generation, or *Gen-D* (Greenfield, 2009). These digital communications modalities have become the norm for most of our youth (Walsh, White, & Young, 2008), and if managed reasonably, they can become less harmful and remain a part of modern social interaction.

No technology has ever existed before that connects us socially while simultaneously disconnecting us. This is the first time in recorded history that the capacity to express and broadcast oneself is literally in the hands of anyone with access to the Internet. The ability to broadcast oneself (as evidenced by viral levels of blogging and YouTube-ing) is intoxicating and provides, for the first time, broadcast capacity to everyone on the planet. Everyone's 15 minutes of fame is expanded exponentially, and the largest adopters of this technology are the Gen-Ds. The ability to efficiently social network is supported by the popularity of social networking sites such as Facebook, MySpace, Twitter, Friendster, and other social networking/consumer integrations. All of these sites support the social efficacy of the Internet and represent some of the Internet's greatest strengths in its ability to efficiently distill and enhance social interaction in an instant.

However, there are clear drawbacks to such efficiency. For one, doing all this social networking is both addictive and very time-consuming, and therefore unbalancing.

In addition, the type of social interaction accomplished virtually seems to be quite different from other types of real-time social interaction; and it may not provide the same positive and health-enhancing benefits that real-time social interaction does.

Additional social factors include the wide level of acceptability and availability of Internet technologies in our culture, and the prevalence of personal computers, laptops, notebooks, portable digital devices, and especially Internet-ready cell phones. These technologies are woven into the social fabric of anyone under 30 years of age, who treat such devices as we elders would a toaster—with a comfort and familiarity that is natural. Internet-ready devices such as cell phones and PDAs speak to the normalization of the popular culture of Internet technology. If one wishes to be part of the mainstream, one needs to be connected to the Internet. This sociotechnical peer pressure is not to be ignored. Many of our peers, coworkers, teachers, and superiors have expectations for people to maintain constant availability, and among our youth culture having a cell phone and Internet access is becoming standard issue.

A few short years ago it was becoming widely accepted that individuals would have access to their e-mail while at home and in the workplace. This expectation has recently expanded to include the portable and constant availability of e-mail and other data. It is now expected that individuals can and should access their e-mail remotely at any time and any place. All these expectations lead to, at minimum, an increase of psychophysiological stress and at worst contribute to the potential for Internet addiction.

As wireless technology continues to untether us from land-based/wired computers and Internet access, there will be further employer expectations and social pressures exerted upon us to stay connected all the time. Early research studies conducted found that social factors were a contributing factor in the development of Internet addiction disorder (Kraut et al., 1999). A key factor is the inherent human desire to socially connect. As social creatures, we are invariably drawn toward social interaction; the need to connect and communicate is hardwired into our biology. All forms of Internet and digital media communication are in part an electronic extension of this natural proclivity.

When it comes to sex and pornography, the Internet has become a virtual Petri dish for sexual expression and sexual excess (Cooper, Scherer, Boies, & Gordon, 1999; Greenfield, 2009). However, little is known of the long-term impact from digital versions of social connection compared to more direct real-time connection. It would be overly simplistic to say that all forms of digital and Internet social interaction are insufficient and inferior. And most people do not become addicted to these technologies, though many abuse them. However, the increased availability, ease of access, and normalization of these technologies increases the potential for problems to occur.

The ability to e-mail or text a friend or family member or to instant message someone may not necessarily be problematic. These new communication technologies have, in a sense, replaced talking on the phone or hanging out at the mall or malt shop for previous generations. The discerning question seems to be how much is too much and how we define too much. Many individuals, including parents, teachers, and spouses, ask: How much *is* too much? The answer always has to do with the ultimate impact on the overall balance and quality of living. Individuals do not present themselves for treatment unless there is some deleterious consequence in one of the major spheres of their lives. Often, an initial negative consequence is a considerable breach or negative impact on one or more of their primary relationships, a decrease in work or school performance, or a negative legal consequence.

In Germany, there is an active public education and prevention movement offered through government and nonprofit social service agencies to advocate healthy computing. The German government has taken to include Internet and media addiction as part of its overall drug, alcohol, and addiction education/treatment program. In Spain, the authorities are introducing programs to treat and prevent Internet addiction and are organizing professional training conferences. The United States does not yet have this same level of public awareness and organized prevention programs. This is in part due to how Americans use and abuse the Internet; most of their use is in the privacy of their own homes and not in the public arena as it is in many other counties. There also is a different health care and prevention philosophy and value system in the United States. In many Asian countries, such as China, Korea, and Singapore, there are near-epidemic levels of Internet addiction behavior, and they are addressing the issue as a public health threat.

GEN-D FACTORS

There are a numerous factors that appear to contribute to the Internet's addictive experience, and many of these are contributed to by our social or family context. From a clinical perspective, most treatment cases that occur involve negative consequences in primary or family relationships. Within the family constellation there is often a reversal of the generational hierarchy. When it comes to Internet and digital technology, today's children and adolescents have been raised with this technology. They are *Generation-Digital*, or *Gen-D*. (Greenfield, 2009). They are highly familiar with the computer, the Internet, and most other digital devices, and they often have more comfort and confidence with this technology than their adult parents have. It is more typical for the parent to impart knowledge and experience downward toward the younger generation. Here we have just the opposite.

The Internet functions to our Gen-D children in a seamless and natural manner, and they often have a greater Internet and digital knowledge base than their parents. For the first time in modern history, the generational knowledge and power hierarchy has been reversed. This increased familiarity and comfort, along with high levels of use, creates a power imbalance in the family system, which has a significant impact on how the technology is handled in the home. Often, the parent will have little or no knowledge of what is going on or how it all works and not be aware of the level of activity or abuse. Parents often don't know what is normal or what is reasonable, and they don't want their children to be left behind the digital growth curve. This lack of knowledge and lack of technological power further contributes to possible abuse and addiction to these technologies.

In the cases of children, adolescents, and young adults, the clinician's role is to educate and empower parents, caregivers, school personnel, and employers on how these technologies work, and to educate them on Internet/video gaming, gambling, online sexuality, social networking; as well as on general issues of overusing or abusing the Internet and other digital media devices. Without such information it is difficult to regain the power balance within the family system and take appropriate control of the family's technology.

CONCLUSION

We live in changing times. Our world is becoming smaller and we should feel more connected to those around us, but at times the very digital media technologies that purport to connect us to others often have an alienating, isolating, and addicting effect.

These digital communication and entertainment technologies (Internet, e-mail, cell phones, PDAs, iPods, gaming devices) are fun and can be helpful in our lives, but they all have addictive and abusable properties that can alter our mood and consciousness, distract us, and provide an exit from living in the present. These devices have the capacity to numb us and time-shift, thereby moving our attention from the present to somewhere else.

There is ever-present availability and unending access to overloaded information and communication; there are no boundaries, and there is no place to hide and recharge our internal psychological batteries. Being able to track and be tracked through every movement one makes via text or tweet takes a lot of time, energy, and attention and still leaves us with what might be classified as a two-dimensional social interaction. The implication when users are online, texting, tweeting, or using any other digital-based communication format, is that they are not where they are, but rather somewhere else; that they are not in the present and that their attention and energy are divided. This has the uncanny effect of making one feel that the user is physically there but not really present.

The rationale of multitasking is not valid in that we find that multiple tasks indeed divide our attention as well. There is no increase in efficiency, as it simply takes longer to accomplish all the activities when we are multitasking. This partial attention everywhere is a bit unnerving and leaves interactions with the electronically tethered somewhat less than satisfying.

The idea of disconnecting in order to connect to others seems ludicrous, as real-time social interaction and connection cannot be digitized or time-shifted without some negative impact. With moderation, there is a place for cell phones, PDAs, and portable Internet access portals. We know the Internet and digital media devices alter mood and consciousness and are therefore powerful devices, and therefore should be respected and limited. Technology is useful, but is not without its impact on our health and well-being.

We are not designed to be in a constant state of nervous system arousal and with all our portable devices all operating on a variable ratio reinforcement pattern. We feel as if we cannot turn them off and we begin to feel we cannot live without them. The question really becomes: Can we live well with them? Living our lives in virtual environments through gaming or in virtual worlds like Second Life leaves many questions. How can we live a second life when we really aren't living our first life? It seems we are running away from something, perhaps from ourselves. We are trying to numb ourselves or deal with boredom, or we feel disconnected from ourselves and our lives. So we stay connected, but also disconnected, distracting ourselves in a seemingly endless fashion. We go to bed using our technology and begin our day with it as well. We wonder why we feel depressed and drained and need Prozac. We live our lives unconsciously, wired and wireless, and then we medicate ourselves with the same technology when we feel bad.

We know that many marriages and relationships have been significantly impacted by the use and abuse of the Internet and other digital media devices. In France it was recently reported that 50 percent of all divorces have some type of Internet or digital media issue associated with them, and it was ruled that text messages can be used as evidence in divorce proceedings. Often these technologies become digital distractions from the real-time work of connection, intimacy, and communication. Having the portability and accessibility can be practical, entertaining, and fun, but highly distracting.

The future will likely see Internet and digital media addiction increasing. As the technology continues to become faster, cheaper, and more portable, it is likely that abuse and addiction will continue to grow. We are only on the edge of the true portability and mobility that is to come; it will not be long before our cell phone or PDA will be small and wearable or implantable along with a link for all our financial transactions. No more card swiping, no more cell phone to carry, just a small chip wired into our sense organs. Sound like science fiction? What was science fiction 40 years ago is used every day today. The only limits are our desire and our imagination, but technology for technology's sake is foolish at best and dangerous at worst. History is replete with examples of how our greatest technological breakthroughs became new problems.

Some foresight into the use of these technologies may help prevent these problems. The longer we fail to see the power that Internet technologies have in our lives, the more likely we will be unconscious as to the negative impact they can produce from their use and abuse. The ability for us to recognize the potential positive and negative impact is what will allow us to manage our use in a more positive and conscious manner. In the long run, we must learn to live our lives with conscious computing and to integrate all of our digital media technologies into a healthier balance. We can manage our Internet and digital media technology so it doesn't manage us.

REFERENCES

Aboujaoude, E., Koran, L. M., Gamel, N., Large, M. D., & Serpe, R. T. (2006). Potential markers for problematic Internet use: A telephone survey of 2,513 adults. *CNS Spectrums: The International Journal of Neuropsychiatric Medicine, 11,* 750–755.

Arias-Carrión, O., & Pöppel, E. (2007). Dopamine, learning and reward-seeking behavior. *Acta Neurobiologiae Experimentalis, 67*(4), 481–488.

Block, J. (2007). Prevalence underestimated in problematic Internet use study. *CNS Spectrums: The International Journal of Neuropsychiatric Medicine, 12,* 14–15.

Block, J. (2008). Issues for DSM-V: Internet addiction. *American Journal of Psychiatry, 165,* 306–307.

Chih-Hung, K., Gin-Chung, L., Hsiao, S., Ju-Ju, Y., Ming-Jen, Y., Wei-Chen, L., et al. (2009). Brain activities associated with gaming urge of online gaming addiction. *Journal of Psychiatric Research, 43,* 739–747.

Chou, C., Condron, L., & Belland, J. C. (2005). A review of the research on Internet addiction. *Educational Psychology Review, 17*(4), 363–388.

Cooper, A. (1998). Sexuality and the Internet: Into the next millennium. *CyberPsychology & Behavior, 1,* 181–187.

Cooper, A., Boies, S., Maheu, M., & Greenfield, D. (2000). Sexuality and the Internet: The next sexual revolution. In F. Muscarella & L. Szuchman (Eds.), *Psychological perspectives on human sexuality: A research based approach* (pp. 519–545). New York: John Wiley & Sons.

Cooper, A., Delmonico, D. L., & Burg, R. (2000). Cybersex users, abusers, and compulsives: New findings and implications. *Sexual Addiction & Compulsivity, 7,* 5–29.

Cooper, A., Scherer, C., Boies, S., & Gordon, B. (1999). Sexuality on the Internet: From sexual exploration to pathological expression. *Professional Psychology: Research and Practice, 30*(2), 154–164.

Ferris, J. (2001). Social ramifications of excessive Internet use among college-age males. *Journal of Technology and Culture, 20*(1), 44–53.

Ferster, C. B., & Skinner, B. F. (1957). *Schedules of reinforcement.* New York: Appleton-Century-Crofts.

Greenfield, D. N. (1999a). The nature of Internet addiction: Psychological factors in compulsive Internet use. Paper presentation at the 1999 American Psychological Association Convention, Boston, Massachusetts.

Greenfield, D. N. (1999b). Psychological characteristics of compulsive Internet use: A preliminary analysis. *CyberPsychology & Behavior, 8*(5), 403–412.

Greenfield, D. N. (1999c). *Virtual addiction: Help for Netheads, cyberfreaks, and those who love them.* Oakland, CA: New Harbinger Publications.

Greenfield, D. N. (2008). *Virtual addiction: Clinical implications of digital & Internet-enabled behavior.* Presentation at the International conference course about new technologies: Addiction to new technologies in adolescents and young people, Auditorium Clinic Hospital, Madrid, Spain.

Greenfield, D. N. (2009). *Living in a virtual world: Global implications of digital addiction.* Berliner Mediensuch-Konferenz—Beratung und Behandlung für mediengefährdete und geschädigte Menschen, Berlin, Germany, March 6–7, 2009.

Greenfield (2007, January 26). In Kimkiewicz, J. Internet junkies: hooked online, *Harford Courant,* pp. D1.

Greenfield, D. N., & Orzack, M. H. (2002). The electronic bedroom: Clinical assessment for online sexual problems and Internet-enabled sexual behavior. In A. Cooper (Ed.), *Sex and the Internet: A guidebook for clinicians* (pp. 129–145). New York: John Wiley & Sons.

Hartwell, K. J., Tolliver, B. K., & Brady, K. T. (2009). Biologic commonalities between mental illness and addiction. *Primary Psychiatry, 16*(8), 33–39.

Hollander, E. (2006). Behavior and substance addictions: A new proposed DSM-V category characterized by impulsive choice, reward sensitivity and fronto-striatal circuit impairment. *CNS Spectrums: The International Journal of Neuropsychiatric Medicine, 11,* 814.

Kimkiewicz, J. (2007, January 26). Internet junkies: Hooked online. *Hartford Courant,* D1.

Kraut, R., & Kiesler, S. (2003). The social impact of Internet use. *Psychological Science Agenda, 16*(3), 8–10.

Kraut, R., Patterson, M., Lundmark, V., Kiesler, S., Mukopadhyay, T., & Schewrlis, W. (1999). Internet paradox: A social technology that reduces social involvement and psychological well-being? *American Psychology, 53,* 1017–1031.

Leung, L. (2007). Stressful life events, motives for Internet use, and social support among digital kids. *CyberPsychology & Behavior, 10*(2), 204–214.

Peltoniemi, T. (2009). Berliner Mediensuch-Konferenz—Beratung und behandlung für mediengefährdete und geschädigte Menschen, Berlin, Germany, March 6–7, 2009.

Schwartz, B. (1984). *Psychology of learning and behavior* (2nd ed.). New York: W.W. Norton.

Shaw, M. Y., & Black, D. W. (2008). Internet addiction: Definition, assessment, epidemiology and clinical management. *CNS Drugs, 22,* 353–365.

Suler, J. (2004). The online disinhibition effect. *CyberPsychology & Behavior, 7*(3), 321–325.

Toronto, E. (2009). Time out of mind: Dissociation in the virtual world. *Psychoanalytic Psychology, 26*(2), 117–133.

van den Eijnden, R. J. J. M., Meerkerk, G.-J., Vermulst, A. A., Spijkerman, R., & Engels, R. C. M. (2008). Online communication, compulsive Internet use, and psychosocial well-being among adolescents: A longitudinal study. *Developmental Psychology, 44*(3), 655–665.

Walsh, S. P., White, K. M., & Young, R. M. (2008). Over-connected? A qualitative exploration of the relationship between Australian youth and their mobile phones. *Journal of Adolescence, 31*, 77–92.

Weissberg, M. (1983). *Dangerous secrets: Maladaptive responses to stress.* New York: W.W. Norton.

Young, K. S. (1998a). *Caught in the Net: How to recognize the signs of Internet addiction and a winning strategy for recovery.* New York: John Wiley & Sons.

Young, K. S. (1998b). Internet addiction: The emergence of a new clinical disorder. *CyberPsychology & Behavior, 1*, 237–244.

Young, K. S. (2004). Internet addiction: The consequences of a new clinical phenomenon. In K. Doyle (Ed.). *American behavioral scientist: Psychology and the new media* (Vol. 1., pp. 1–14). Thousand Oaks, CA: Sage.

Young, K. S. (2007). Cognitive-behavioral therapy with Internet addicts: Treatment outcomes and implications. *CyberPsychology & Behavior, 10*(5), 671–679.

Zeigarnik, B. V. (1967). On finished and unfinished tasks. In W. D. Ellis (Ed.), *A sourcebook of Gestalt psychology* (pp. 300–315). New York: Humanities Press.

CHAPTER 9

Psychotherapy for Internet Addiction

CRISTIANO NABUCO DE ABREU and DORA SAMPAIO GÓES

F EW ARE the psychotherapeutic approaches currently available for Internet addiction treatment, and those existing are still little known in the literature. Because this form of addiction has not yet been included in official medicine and psychology manuals, its research and knowledge are not extensive. However, although its emergence is recent, its manifestation in our practices, at schools, and in mental health outpatient units is increasingly observed. Thus, for the present chapter, psychotherapeutic intervention descriptions were searched in the Pubmed (U.S. National Library of Medicina, National Institutes of Health), Lilacs (Latin American and Caribbean databases in Health Sciences), Scielo (Scientific Electronic Library Online), and Google Academic databases, and in the general literature. Interventions performed in detoxification centers, for example, which are not described in the literature, were not addressed here. Our goal is to present to readers the existing studies, as well as the description of the therapeutic dimension of such applications. Then, we describe the standard psychotherapeutic intervention procedure that has been used in the population for approximately three years in our Impulse Disorders Outpatient Unit at the University of São Paulo, Institute of Psychiatry.

THE NATURE OF THERAPY WITH INTERNET ADDICTION

When it comes to psychotherapeutic interventions, results still provide very incipient data, and no one form of psychological intervention can be suggested as being the most recommended (gold standard) for the treatment of Internet addiction. It is suggested that the support therapies (those giving emotional support to patients, focusing on the here and now) would be of great value, as well as the counseling therapies,[1] which could be used and coupled with family interventions as a manner of repairing the damage caused in the emotional relations. Although very few research studies have been described, the most frequently investigated approaches are cognitive behavioral therapy (CBT)[2] and motivational interview[3] (Beard, 2005; Wieland, 2005; Young, 1999).

Regarding the use of CBT, Davis (2001) described a proposal for understanding interventions by offering a more detailed description of the cognitive schemes involved in the change process (specific and generalized environmental factors, personal vulnerability, dependence styles, as well as intervention possibilities).

Within his proposal, the pathological Internet use shows two basic possibilities: (1) specific pathological use, describing the excessive use and abuse of specific Internet features by patients, such as unrestrictive access to chat rooms, MSN, social networks (facebook, orkut e.g.), erotic web sites, games (e.g., MMORPGs), eBay and shopping (e.g., eBay), and (2) generalized pathological use, relative to the time spent by users surfing the Internet (i.e., without a defined focus of interest and action). Davis (2001) stated that this dependence is settled at the moment when patients feel they have no social and family support, thereby developing the so-called maladaptive cognitions (which are

---

[1]Therapeutic counseling is delivered in a private, highly confidential setting. In the counseling session, patients have the opportunity to express their difficulties, dissatisfactions, conflicts, and questions to the counselor. In turn, counselors carefully listen to them, respecting their points of view. Through this process, counselors can then elicit an external vision of their questioning, help them explore creative alternatives for their options, and accompany them in the choice and decision-making process without posing biased judgments.

[2]Currently, cognitive behavioral therapy (CBT) is described as a structured, directive therapeutic approach that has clear, well-defined goals, is focused on the present time, and is used in the treatment of the most various psychological disorders. CBT's main objective is to produce changes in the patients' thoughts and meaning systems (beliefs), with the purpose of bringing about a longer-lasting emotional and behavioral transformation, rather than a short-lived decrease of symptoms. Thus, the cognitive conceptions have developed the most diverse proposals and created *cognitive adjustment* tools, such as the "dysfunctional thought records," "cognitive restructuring" techniques, "irrational belief identification" process, and a range of techniques supporting the practice of correcting or replacing dysfunctional thought patterns for more functional analysis and logics ones. Therefore, it is fundamental for the cognitive references that meaning *distortions* do not evolve in such a way to become maladaptive (Abreu, 2004).

[3]"Motivational interview" is a method of directive assistance that is centered in the patient being willing to promote an internal motivation to change a behavior by exploring and troubleshooting the ambivalence that the patient presents with. This method involves the patient showing a spirit of collaboration, participation, and autonomy with a sense of walking through it side by side with the therapist and being able to participate in his or her change process rather than just following directions. Motivational interview is a special means to help people recognize and take action on their current or potential problems. It is particularly useful in people who are reluctant to change and ambivalent about change. The goal is to help people in a manner that they can troubleshoot the ambivalence present and move on in their natural path to behavioral change. This is a direct, patient-centered counseling form that pursues behavioral change by assisting patients to explore and troubleshoot their difficulties (Payá & Figlie, 2004).

the mental evaluations or screeners of interpretation) about themselves and the world.

It should be highlighted that the clinical intervention option for cognitive-behavioral models has a justified cause. Because cognitive behavioral therapy shows good results in the treatment of other impulse-control disorders, such as pathological gambling, compulsive shopping (Caplan, 2002; Dell'Osso, Allen, Altamura, Buoli, & Hollander, 2008; Dell'Osso, Altamura, Allen, Marazziti, & Hollander, 2006; Hollander & Stein, 2005; Mueller & de Zwaan, 2008; Shaw & Black, 2008; Young, 2007), bulimia nervosa, and binge eating—disorders that are similar in their impulsiveness and compulsion characteristics—this approach naturally appears as a first-choice option, although *trials* of the treatment of Internet addiction involving control groups are still nonexistent (Hay, Bacaltchuk, Stefano, & Kashyap, 2009; Munsch et al., 2007).

Young (1999), the precursor and one of the pioneers in the study of Internet addiction, with numerous experiences at the Center for Online Addiction, offers some intervention strategies based on the cognitive behavioral therapy assumptions, and one of the focuses is moderation and controlled use of the Internet. According to the author, the therapy should use time management techniques that help patients to recognize, organize, and manage their time spent online, as well as techniques that help to set rational goals of utilization. In addition, it aims at collaboratively developing gratifying offline activities with patients, as well as some other coping techniques mostly targeted at enabling patients to deal with their difficulties and developing a support system and a system for more appropriate use.

A technique suggested by Young is the development of a personal inventory. As Internet addicts tend to neglect their hobbies and other interests due to the time spent searching for virtual interests, the individual is encouraged to complete an inventory containing the activities that used to be carried out and were disregarded after the problem emerged. This aims to help patients reflect from an experience contrast point of view (past versus future) that can assist them to better observe their decision-making process. This activity may help individuals become aware of their choices and thus motivated to try to resume the previous activities that have been lost.

The author also believes that time reorganization is an important tool in treating this dependence, and the therapist's role should be to help patients with specific identification and use, as well as to set a new agenda. Young reports from such interventions that it would be possible to therapeutically work by *practicing the opposite*, that is, making patients break their current Internet use routine and develop a new, more adaptive behavioral pattern. For example, if the patient goes online as soon as he or she arrives home from work and remains online until it is time to go to bed, the clinician may suggest that he or she take a break for dinner, watch the news, and only then go back to the computer. Therefore, this is a helpful form to reduce or discontinue the use.

Another technique is to identify some stimulant to log off ("External Stoppers Technique"); with the new agenda already developed for the Internet use, the clinician suggests, for example, the use of an alarm clock to function as a warning for the patient that it is time to turn off the computer and carry out some other offline activity, such as going to work or school or, when it is late at night, simply going to bed to have some rest and try to sleep.

It is worth reminding that people with this type of addiction may experience many difficulties trying to discontinue their routine of use during treatment due to the change in time perception, or even because they experience a state of flow, just to mention some examples. Thus, in order to facilitate these discontinuation processes, goals that could help them keep their focus on the objectives as agreed upon with therapists are identified, but with the use of markers that divert the patients' attention. This technique, called setting goals, allows patients to have their attention diverted for brief time periods. Therefore, structured usage sessions could be scheduled through the definition of achievable goals. For example, if the patient remains online all day long on Saturdays and Sundays, a schedule with brief sessions of use followed by brief, although frequent, discontinuations could be designed. In Young's proposal, the use of a schedule of use is encouraged, provided that it is accomplishable.

When these plans fail, however, abstinence is another possible form of intervention. Some applications might serve as triggers for the reinforcement of continuous use. This means that patients should stop navigating particular web sites or even certain applications (e.g., MSN, Facebook, online games) that are most attractive for them, discontinuing the use from time to time, shifting to alternative forms such as sending and receiving e-mails, news search, bibliographical sources for their school works, and so forth.

The use of reminder cards is also an important tool to assist patients to keep their focus on the abstinence or reduction of uncontrolled use goals. For example, a card containing the five major problems caused by Internet addiction, as well as the five major benefits from reducing the use (or ultimately refraining from using a given application) should be listed. Then, the clinician instructs the patient to keep this card sufficiently near so that, if in a risky situation, he or she can review the card and be reminded about the positive consequences from refraining from the navigation, as well as the negative consequences from maintaining uninterrupted online activity.

Also from CBT interventions, Young (2007) reports a 12-session follow-up of 114 patients, who were evaluated in sessions 3, 8, and 10 (and in the six-month follow-up) with the use of the Internet Addiction Test (IAT) and the Client Outcome Questionnaire in order to evaluate: (1) motivation to reduce abusive use, (2) ability to control online use, (3) involvement with offline activities, (4) improvement of interpersonal relationships, and, finally, (5) improvement of offline sexual life (when applicable). Results show that online time management was the most difficult (96%) as reported by patients, followed by relationship problems (85%) due to the amount of time spent at the computer, and sexual problems (75%) due to less interest in real-life partners because of the online sex preference. The author's conclusion indicates that CBT is effective in treating patients when it concerns Internet addiction-related symptom reduction, and that after six months patients were still able to overcome the obstacles to continuous recovery, despite the absence of a control group (Young, 2007).

Another intervention was described in the literature by Chiou (2008) with the purpose of analyzing the effects of the freedom of choice and the quantity of reward based on the cognitive dissonance theory precepts.[4] One hundred and fifty-eight teenage students experienced in online games were investigated with the use of the Online Games Addiction Scale for Adolescents developed by Wan and Chiou (2006) . Participants were randomized to groups regarding (1) freedom of choice (with vs. without) and (2) quantity of reward (high vs. medium vs. low). The experiment was conducted in brief sessions in which six randomly selected participants discussed online games addiction. Following this intervention, the participants were invited to analyze their arguments, as well as to write down the pros and cons for online games. As a manner of manipulating the reward, the participants were told that they would receive a prize for the completion of this task. Results show that lower rewards in the condition involving freedom of choice caused higher changes in the adolescents' behavior; that is, the author concluded that this could be a way to induce adolescents to reduce the use of online games (Chiou, 2008; Stravogiannis & Abreu, 2009).

Rodrigues, Carmona, and Marín (2004) described a case study also based on CBT techniques and associated with the motivational interview. At first, the reported patient sought help for her addiction problem; however, through a functional analysis,[5] precipitating factors such as problems with her husband and children and the maladaptive response to them were identified. The intervention was targeted to (1) figure out the problem and prepare the patient for change; (2) help her with the decision-making process and help her cope with the problem at hand; (3) deliver psychological treatment through stimulus control techniques, such as breaking connection habits, setting new

---

[4]Cognitive dissonance is a theory about human motivation that states it is psychologically uncomfortable to keep contradictory cognitions. The theory proclaims that dissonance, because it is uncomfortable, motivates the person to replace his or her cognition, attitude, or behavior. Leon Festinger proposed that dissonance and consonance are relationships between cognitions (i.e., between opinions, beliefs, awareness of the environment, and awareness of the person's own actions and feelings). Two opinions, beliefs, or items of awareness are dissonant when they do not match with each other; that is, they are incompatible. Festinger says there are three ways to deal with the cognitive dissonance, which are not considered mutually exclusive. They are: (1) One can try to replace one or more beliefs, opinions, or behaviors involved in the dissonance. (2) One can try to acquire new information or beliefs that will increase the existing consonance, thereby reducing the total dissonance. (3) One can try to forget or reduce the importance of those cognitions that maintain a dissonant relationship.

[5]The analysis of functional relationships represents a natural phenomena interpretation and investigation model that is present in the Skinnerian project of psychology constitution as behavioral science. Thus, the functional analysis refers to the investigation of the relationships between an individual's responses to objectively identified environmental stimuli. It is essential in studies that objectives include predicting and/or controlling behavior repertoires in specific situations.

goals to achieve it, withdrawing a specific application or web site; and, finally, (4) developing an improved interpersonal problem coping ability. The result of the intervention was a generalized increase of the resources to cope with family difficulties, as well as higher autonomy and consequent amplification of activities.

Zhu, Jin, and Zhong (2009) conducted a controlled study using CBT. With 47 patients diagnosed with Internet addiction, the following two intervention modalities were proposed: (1) 10 CBT sessions and (2) 10 CBT sessions combined with electroacupuncture (EA). Anxiety, depression, Internet addiction, and overall health condition scales were applied. Using psychologic intervention alone or combined with EA significantly reduced anxiety and improved self-conscious health status in patients with Internet addiction, but the effect obtained by the combined therapy was better.

Using interpersonal psychotherapy,[6] Liu and Kuo (2007) evaluated five educational institutions in Taiwan with a sample consisting of 555 individuals, in an attempt to identify predicting Internet addiction factors. The main objective was to achieve symptom relief and improvement in interpersonal relationships. Therefore, parent-child adjustment scales adapted for Taiwan by Huang, interpersonal relationship scales developed by Huang, and Young's social anxiety and Internet addiction scales (1998) were used. The results showed that (1) interpersonal relationships are significantly related with or even considered as a direct reflex of the interaction pattern observed in the parent-child interaction, (2) this interpersonal relationship shows a significant influence on social anxiety, and (3) the triad comprising parent-child relationship, interpersonal relationships, and social anxiety substantially impacts the emergence of Internet addiction and its severity. The authors concluded by stating that these findings are consistent with the point of view shared by various Internet addiction investigators that this pathology would be a poorer type of coping response, and therefore, it is used as a way to precariously wind around the difficulties encountered in the real world. It was observed in this investigation that those Internet users showed higher rates of social anxiety and emotional numbing, which indicated frustrated previous relationships.

Based on Young's (1999) ACE Cybersexual Addiction Model, which was developed to explain how cyberspace induces a favorable atmosphere for online sexually adulterous and promiscuous behaviors, Young et al. (2000) described cybersexual addiction and its implications for couples therapy. According to

---

[6]Mainly based on the ideas from Sullivan's interpersonal psychoanalysis school, on Freud's studies of grief, and on Bowlby's attachment theory. Initially developed for the treatment of depression major, interpersonal psychotherapy was shown to be highly effective as a therapy for a number of other disorders. Interpersonal psychotherapy tries to be centered on a problematic area as the treatment focus. Four of the problematic areas often found in depressed patients are (1) grief (loss due to death); (2) interpersonal disputes (with partner, children, other family members, friends, workmates); (3) shift of roles (new job, leaving home, completion of studies, relocating, divorce, economic changes, or other family-related changes); (4) interpersonal deficits (loneliness, social isolation).

the ACE model, three variables may lead to virtual adultery: anonymity, convenience, and escape.

Anonymity favors the user's involvement in erotic chats without fearing to be discovered by the spouse. The person therefore experiences a sense of control over the online conversation's content and form, the type that typically occurs in the privacy of the individual's home, office, or bedroom. Cyberspace's privacy, according to the author, allows the person to secretly share thoughts, desires, and feelings, which may open a door for a flirt and may often lead to virtual adultery.

The *convenience* of online applications such as chat rooms, instant messages, and so on provides a favorable means to meet other people. Conversations may begin with an exchange of e-mails or encounters in chat rooms, and may become intense and passion-ridden, possibly leading to the occurrence of phone calls and potential real-world dates.

Seemingly, sexual satisfaction serves as a reinforcer of online sexual behaviors, but the major reinforcement in such cases, according to Young, is the ability to fuel a world of online fantasies that might offer an emotional or mental *escape* from the everyday stresses and strains. For example, a woman with a broken marriage might make use of chat rooms in order to escape from the feeling of emptiness and to feel important or even desired by her virtual partners.

Virtual affairs and cybersexual encounters often appear as a symptom of difficulties preceding the Internet presence in a couple's life. An impoverished communication with the spouse, some other kind of sexual dissatisfaction, parenting difficulties, and financial issues are common problems in marriages; however, such difficulties provide powerful triggers for the search of virtual affairs.

Virtual encounters also favor the expression of privations experienced by couples, such as sexual fantasies, romance, and passion that may have become absent in the current relationship. Thus, dealing with virtual problems becomes an easier solution for spouses than facing the existing difficulties in the marriage. The virtual partner, then, offers the necessary understanding and comfort for feelings driven by anger, sorrow, or otherwise that were not spoken out in the real relationship. Young et al. (2000) concluded by stating that in psychotherapy with couples, clinicians should contribute for communication improvement and for the couple to be able to set an open, honest dialogue that is exempted from hard feelings like guilt or anger. Some suggestions include:

- *Setting specific goals.* Goals should be set in order to evaluate each one's expectations toward the use of the computer and commitment to the current relationship's reconstruction.
- *Using "I" statements in order to not blame the other.* The therapist should emphasize the use of nonjudgmental, nonaccusatory language. This way, the clinician should help patients to rephrase their opinion and feeling

expressions. For example, instead of saying, "You never pay attention to me because you are always at this computer!" one could replace it for "I feel abandoned when you spend too much of our time together at the computer." As practicing the use of "I," the therapist also recommends that patients focus their statements on the present moment and avoid negative words, as these would function as new triggers for renewed disharmony.

- *Empathy.* Help couples truly listen to the significant other. When a partner tries to explain the reasons for his or her actions, it is important to help the other partner hold back feelings of anger or loss of trust so that he or she can as openly as possible listen in order to expand the communication and, as a result, the mutual understanding.

Considering Alternatives   In case face-to-face dialogue is difficult, the clinician may suggest other forms of communication, such as writing letters or even emails. Writing allows for higher flow thought and feeling expressions without the other's interruption. It also facilitates a less defensive and more open reading. With the purpose of assisting patients to develop effective coping strategies in the treatment of Internet addiction, the individual format of psychotherapy may be used, as well as groups in the form of support groups or therapy groups, self-help programs, or family guidance groups (Davis, 2001; Dell'Osso et al., 2006; Young, 1988; Young, 1999).

According to the perspectives presented above, we may consider the contributions as still minor in terms of number; however, they are expressive in their proposals and interventions. Therefore, further follow-up studies to determine which psychotherapeutic approach could be considered as more effective in a short term and as having good consistency to sustain long-term effectiveness are needed. Because the distinct psychotherapy models feature different mechanisms involved in the change process, a more direct therapeutic efficacy comparison is likely to take some time to be tested. It is, however, worth highlighting that, although distinct models have been described, moderation and controlled use of the Internet constitutes the focus of services in most of them.

STRUCTURED COGNITIVE THERAPY

Internet addiction is treated in our outpatient service through the Structured Cognitive Psychotherapy Program (Abreu & Góes, in press), which has been applied for over three years to the population. From the theoretical and practical axes of the cognitive therapy, this intervention is delivered in groups including adolescents and adults for 18 weeks. As the psychotherapy progresses, patients are also followed up by psychiatrists whenever needed for the treatment of associated comorbidities. In addition, in the case of treatment for adolescents, a family intervention group is also planned to occur simultaneously (Barossi, Meira, Góes, & Abreu, 2009). Because Internet addiction, according to several authors, already is indicated for future inclusion in *DSM-V* (impulse control disorders category) (Block, 2008), our goal in psychotherapy is primarily to restore the control over an appropriate use of the Internet (i.e., to implement an adaptive routine of controlled healthy use) (Abreu, Karam, Góes, & Spritzer, 2008). Furthermore, as the Internet becomes more and more present in people's everyday lives, whether in the form of social networks due to academic needs or in simpler forms of daily communication, the virtual life turns into a virtually new instance of life experiences in the 21st century; therefore, intending to thoroughly ban it—as with the treatment of alcohol or drug abuse—is nothing but a lack of knowledge about the Internet's real dimensions and extensions.

INITIAL PHASE

By considering the characteristics described earlier, it is clear that the so-called virtual weaning cannot rely on any form of acceptance or collaboration from patients unless the severity of the case is not yet very pronounced. Therefore, in the initial phases of group treatment, the negative impacts resulting from excessive use are little addressed; instead, the *facilities* and *benefits* from this contact are emphasized (see Table 9.1, week 2). Then, various aspects are discussed, such as the importance of the Internet for each one's life or the advantages from using it. Obviously, this attitude of the professionals surprises all of the patients; they are expecting to hear any discouraging message about

Table 9.1
Structured Cognitive Psychotherapy Model for the Treatment of
Internet Addiction

Week	Topics
—	Application of inventories
1	Program presentation
2	Analysis of the Internet's positive aspects
3	Everything has a consequence or price.
4–5	Do I like to or need to navigate the Web?
6–7	What the experience of needing is like (*problem*)
8	Analysis of the most often visited web sites and the subjective sensations experienced
9	Understanding the triggering mechanism
10	Life line technique (*pattern*)
11	Deepening into deficient aspects
12	Working on emerging topics
13	Working on emerging topics
14	Working on emerging topics
15–16	Alternative actions (coping) (*process*)
17	Preparation for termination
18	Termination and application of inventories

Source: Abreu and Góes (in press).

the Internet, not the advantages of using it. And best of all is that the effect is immediate. Following this first contact, everybody progressively starts to express the relevance of the Internet to their lives and openly discusses the quantity of (positive) change experienced after this period. When analyzing each person's discourse, the role played by the Internet in the individual's life becomes clear. It is an understatement to mention the aspects linked to loneliness lessening or an alternative manner of social inclusion, renewed ability to cope with problems, or even mood regulation (*"The Internet is my virtual Prozac"*), factors that have already been widely described in the literature (Chak & Leung, 2004; Ko et al., 2006; Shaffer, Hall, & Bilt, 2000). Thus, by promoting this type of discussion, it is evidenced that the virtual life is a major option, and as a result, addressing its bad side would be naive, to say the least.

Psychotherapy researchers (Safran, 1998) have long warned about the construct called *therapeutic alliance*. According to Safran, this working alliance (or interpersonal trust building between patient and therapist) takes place within the first four meetings; that is, in order for the psychotherapy to be successful, the work in this phase should be careful, since the psychotherapy outcome depends on it. Therefore, good results or a great amount of personal change will be related with the construction of a good alliance. Early withdrawal or low levels of personal change are related with a poor alliance. For this reason, in this phase we do not use any intervention that might contain confront, doubt, or even disbelief elements toward the patients' accounts. This is what we do in the first four sessions.

In this initial phase in which the alliance is still being built, the social and psychological *consequences* from Internet use are addressed; that is, the complaints that are most frequently heard from family members, friends, and workmates are voiced (week 3). The (usually failed) relationship histories are therefore elicited, and this makes the Internet a potential, healthier space for relationships. Interestingly, the group's exposure to these elements interferes positively with the group dynamics. Saying that the most refractory members inevitably end by recognizing in the others the very same difficulties, thereby creating true social glue among the participants of the therapeutic group, is an understatement. Therefore, at this point, any difficulty of cooperation or collaboration that had initially been shown starts to significantly fade away.

In the following sessions, we move toward exploring the *personal implications* from excessive use, as it is observed, for example, in the following dialogues: *"I get online because I feel I am accepted there," "There, I find a more dignifying life," "In the Internet I have a partner who really wants me," "In the Internet I feel as fulfilled as I could never be in real life."* Thus, patients begin to notice that the choice for the virtual life is nothing but an alternative, although maladaptive, way to cope with pressure, fear, or exposure situations. This is the way that the vicious circle comprehending this addiction starts to be identified. In this phase it is common that the Internet's roles are questioned—that is, if the Internet is actually an *option* or a crying *need* (weeks 4 and 5).

Interestingly, at this point patients themselves already begin to establish a cause-effect relationship between their avoidant behaviors and the use of the Web; that is, they can now identify that the behavior linked to excessive use (and what they had initially classified as a benefit) is, in fact, a set of failed coping behaviors or unsatisfied needs, eliciting a clear lack of personal management toward the environment and turning the Internet into a new possible (but not adequate) way of coping.

INTERMEDIARY PHASE

Having established a therapeutic alliance and ensured the relationship among group members and the professionals, we start with the psychotherapeutic interventions themselves. However, prior to going into them, the role of a *guardian angel* is established. This person is randomly chosen by the professionals (the guardian angel is chosen by the patients or the therapists when necessary), and his or her role is to take care of any of the group participants who are not feeling assured and not reporting being well on the meeting day during the week. The group members are instructed that this contact will be made through phone calls or even personal meetings. The guardian angel is encouraged to be present in difficult and stressful situations, providing the required support and backup. In this manner, a type of positive reinforcing relationship among people that is obviously hardly present in the life of each of them is developed. By working like this, we gradually introduce new experiences that can compete with those achieved only through the Internet. This caregiver's role may be rotated among people whenever needed, thereby increasing the possibilities of bond among the group's participants.

Although the relationships previous to and resulting from the abusive Internet use are now clearer for the group members, none of them has yet been the target of any therapeutic intervention; therefore, the interventions will now be more specific, with the purpose of changing the dysfunctional responses. In this phase, patients are asked to complete a weekly diary containing the experiences lived during the week, particularly recording those concerning the unsatisfied *emotional needs* that are eventually found in the virtual world (weeks 6, 7, and 8). They record the following: situations triggering the desire for the Internet, hours spent, associated thoughts, feelings experienced, and all types of information that help them map the chain of behaviors resulting from these unsatisfied needs.

This record will serve as the material to discuss the adverse conditions with the group and to receive the appropriate guidance from the professionals on how to deal with such situations the next time they occur. Thus, each week, one or two patients in the group describe the situations, which are then worked on by the group in general and will serve as targets for specific techniques of therapeutic intervention (cognitive restructuring, assertiveness training, role-play, etc.).

The procedure used in this psychotherapy is in line with the precepts described by Mahoney (1992), once it aims to perform the work on the three Ps: *problem*, *pattern*, and *process*. In the beginning of the clinical process, the objective is to focus on the problem with all of its particularities and variations (four first sessions). Next in this intermediary phase, the analysis of the overall patterns is deepened—those patterns that are long-standing in the patients' lives and are directly responsible for the emergence of the same problems presented in different shapes; that is, they are composed of the same recurrent coping strategies put in action by the same situational triggers (week 9). In this sense, we feel satisfied when patients are able to hold a clear vision of the maladaptive personal mechanics and, as a result, can act in a manner distinct from that used in the past, which made the Internet their only option for coping.

A technique that is often used currently is the *life line technique* (Gonçalves, 1998), in which patients are asked to complete a full record of their lives (from birth to the present date) (week 10). A horizontal line is drawn on a piece of paper and the most significant periods of time are written above it (with the respective ages) and, under the line, the significant facts and impressions (positively or negatively speaking). This horizontal graph increases the possibilities of identifying the emotional wounds and leads patients to better visualize the repetition of the problems faced across their lives. This makes it easier for them to notice that the personality of each person is gradually developed during his or her life. The graph resembles a railroad system, with a main line across which a number of stations (or situations) are placed toward a given direction but that soon divides into several alternative routes, some of which deviate from the main route while others run on a convergent course. The abusive Internet use would be then considered as a new form of manifestation of an old behavior pattern (second P).

With this, we try to show each patient that a full trail of attitudes (and mainly relationships) has been built and has defined the possible perspectives of interaction with the world in a repetitive manner. So, understanding why the Internet turns into a great escape and a better place for emotional management and control becomes an easier task.

A critical assumption in our focus is that human beings are predisposed for interpersonal relationships, and much of the maladaptive learning comes from individuals' attempts to avoid the disintegration of certain important interpersonal relationships (Safran, 1998).

When looking into this process as a whole, a deeper analysis of the processes (third P) is developed, through which such patterns and problems had been built and manifested throughout the individual's life. This is when the *change perspectives* are emotionally and visually outlined for each person (weeks 11–14). The aim here is the following:

- At first, the therapist needs to provide a safe haven in which patients can explore themselves, as well as the relationships that were established in the past or might be developed in the future.

- Join patients in the exploration and encourage them to examine the situations lived and roles played by them, as well as their reactions to those situations.
- Elicit from patients the ways they construe, inadvertently, the reactions of the world around them, on the grounds of the dysfunctional models resulting from their past life (their emotional and cognitive modus operandi).
- Define the Internet's role in this dysfunctional coping process.
- Once this world map is made, the behavioral pattern is changed and, as a result, we interfere with the abusive behavior in the Internet use.

Once therapists have established a safe environment for each of the patients in the group, the basic conditions for the progression of a good psychotherapy will be assured. The safety offered by the professionals and group members is considered to be an important intervention tool, at a practical level, to convey and understand the meanings as they facilitate the new information processing. In fact, as with any other psychotherapy process, at this point little is discussed about the aspects initially responsible for the lives of each one in the group (abusive Internet use), but now the *personal coping perspectives* in emotional terms and in challenging situations take place (week 15). Given the progression of discussions, the level of emotional exchange, and the challenges and change promises expressed to the group, the role played by the Internet becomes second ranked.

FINAL PHASE

The final phase is characterized by the follow-up of the changes achieved by each member or by the reinforcement of those still requiring further attention. Obviously, not all patients will show the same type or same quantity of change; however, the social role played by the group becomes a preponderant factor (week 16). Broader coping styles and relationship styles are more carefully examined at this point. Additional attention is given to families (in the case of adolescents) and romantic partners (in the case of adults), by analyzing the changes from occurrences prior to the beginning of the treatment and recorded, and now possibly present in a distinct manner. This contrast effect indicating the changes achieved through psychotherapy (week 17) grants to everybody the possibility of constructing an answer to the question: *What life do I want to live?*

Of course, most of the abusive Internet users show exacerbated forms of personal vulnerability (low tolerance to frustration, high damage avoidance, social anxiety, low self-esteem), and among other deficiencies, the World Wide Web becomes one of the best ways to reduce real life's stress and fear. Addicts at any age use the Web as a social and a communication tool, as they have a higher pleasure and satisfaction experience when they are online (virtual experience) than when they are offline (Young, 2007). Such patients stop eating regularly, lose their sleep-wake cycle, stop going out of the house, let their work and personal relationships become impaired, relate only with people they know in the virtual world, and so on. Therefore, it is not so surprising that these people easily stay online for over 12 hours a day, reaching relatively often 35 consecutive hours online; gather in the course of one year more than four million erotic photos; or receive over three thousand e-mails on just one day. Indeed, the geography of life is changed. It should be highlighted that the interventions described earlier are applicable to an adult population within an outpatient rather than in an inpatient setting.

When treating adolescents simultaneously to the structured program (Table 9.2), parents and/or caregivers are summoned for follow-up, because it is our understanding that, in these cases, family interventions are the supporting actor for a good prognosis. The sequence of topics used in the Guidance Program for Parents and Internet-Addicted Adolescents (Barossi, Meira, Góes and Abreu, 2009) is described in Table 9.2.

The program aims to favor parents' adhesion to adolescents' treatment and develop alternative actions to deal with the conflicts in order to achieve a more functional parent-child communication. The program consists of 12 meetings at two-week intervals (90 minutes long) with the adolescents' parents, who also attend a weekly group with other professionals of the team. At each meeting, the goals are introduced to the parent group, following the schedule as adjusted to the process evolution.

For the group work development, audiovisual resources, bibliographic material, and group dynamics are used to facilitate reflection and communication among the members. At the end of the process there is a follow-up phase consisting of three additional monthly meetings.

The process designed in the therapeutic program contributes to the development of a more empathic parent-child relationship, broadening the possibilities for a joint troubleshooting of the problems associated with excessive Internet use by adolescents. The group's attendance should be highlighted, so that it remains regular up to the end of the process.

CONCLUSION

There are several psychotherapeutic treatment proposals for patients with Internet addiction. The intervention plans holding the highest representativeness make use of cognitive behavioral therapy as their theoretical basis. This preference occurs because of CBT's high effectiveness reported in the treatment of other psychiatric disorders. However, despite this preference, there are no trials to date that have included control groups to test the effectiveness of this theoretical model.

Due to the increasingly more frequent use of the Internet by all age groups of the population, further studies to determine which treatments and approaches are more effective for each age group, as well as for the various types of Internet addiction are warranted. Long-term follow-up studies are critical to elicit and indicate the most effective intervention strategies.

Table 9.2

Structured Cognitive Psychotherapy Model for the Treatment of Internet Addiction in Adolescents and Parents

	Meeting Goal (adolescents)	Meeting Goal (parents)
1	Express feelings and thoughts.	Write down on a record sheet the experiences shared with the child.
2	Reduce the frequency of criticisms and increase the empathy among the group.	Describe the child's adequate and inadequate behaviors; indicate the adequate ones and try not to reinforce the inadequate ones.
3	Learn about the potential reasons and interests associated with the use of the Internet.	Observe the child's use of the Internet on different days. Write down the experiences on the record sheet.
4	Evaluate negative beliefs and expectations that are hindering the management of new behaviors.	Write down in a diary the personal sensations when negative behaviors come up.
5	Distinguish the adolescent's inadequate behaviors due to parental care deficit or excess.	Identify and describe potential influences of the abusive Internet use.
6	Differentiate rights from privileges given in parenting.	Survey the rights and privileges granted to the child.
7	Functionally analyze the adolescents' and the parents' or caregivers' behaviors.	Compare their parenting methods with those adopted by their parents (trans-generational pattern)
8	Identify problem-solving procedures	Apply a problem-solving exercise.
9	Learn new social skills and educational practices.	Experience alternative forms of parenting.
10	Develop a family support repertoire for the maintenance of the changes achieved.	Keep consistent with the parenting methods adopted with the child.
11	Acquire family support for vulnerability factors.	Recognize the relapse risk factors and use the strategies learned at the therapeutic program.
12	Evaluate interventions of behavioral and emotional changes and consequences.	Report on the experience with the meetings.
	Follow up.	Identify the effects on the reduction of the use and/or relapses.

REFERENCES

Abreu, C. N. (2004). Introdução às terapias cognitivas. In C. N. Abreu & H. Guilhardi, *Terapia comportamental e cognitivo-comportamental: Práticas clínicas* (pp. 277–285). São Paulo: Editora Roca.

Abreu, C. N., & Góes, D. S. (in press). Structured cognitive psychotherapy model for the treatment of Internet addiction: Research and outcome.

Abreu, C. N., Karam, R. G., Góes, D. S., & Spritzer, D. T. (2008). Internet and videogame addiction: A review. *Revista Brasileira de Psiquiátria, 30*(2), 156–167.

Barossi, O., Meira, S., Góes, D. S., & Abreu, C. N. (2009). Internet addicted adolescents' parents guidance program—PROPADI. *Revista Brasileira de Psiquiatría*.

Beard, K. (2005). Internet addiction: A review of current assessment techniques and potential assessment questions. *CyberPsychology & Behavior, 8*(1), 7–14.

Block, J. (2008). Issues for DSM-V: Internet addiction. *American Journal of Psychiatry, 165,* 306–307.

Caplan, S. E. (2002). Problematic Internet use and psychosocial well-being: Development of a theory-based cognitive-behavioral measurement instrument. *Computers in Human Behavior, 18*(5), 553–575.

Chak, K., & Leung, L. (2004). Shyness and locus of control as predictors of Internet addiction and Internet use. *CyberPsychology & Behavior, 7*(5), 559–570.

Chiou, W. B. (2008). Induced attitude change on online gaming among adolescents: An application of the less-leads-to-more effect. *CyberPsychology & Behavior, 11*(2), 212–216.

Davis, R. A. (2001). A cognitive-behavioral model of pathological Internet use. *Computers in Human Behavior, 17*(2), 187–195.

Dell'Osso, B., Allen, A., Altamura, A. C., Buoli, M., & Hollander, E. (2008). Impulsive-compulsive buying disorder: Clinical overview. *Australian and New Zealand Journal of Psychiatry, 42*(4), 259–266.

Dell'Osso, B., Altamura, A. C., Allen, A., Marazziti, D., & Hollander, E. (2006). Epidemiologic and clinical updates on impulse control disorders: A critical review. *European Archives of Psychiatry and Clinical Neuroscience, 256*(8), 464–475.

Gonçalves, O. F. (1998). *Psicoterapia cognitiva narrativa: Manual de terapia breve.* Campinas, Brazil: Editorial Psy.

Hay, P. P., Bacaltchuk, J., Stefano, S., & Kashyap, P. (2009). Psychological treatments for bulimia nervosa and binging. *Cochrane Database Systematic Reviews 7*(4), CD000562.

Hollander, E., & Stein, D. J. (2005). *Clinical manual of impulse-control disorders.* Arlington, VA: American Psychiatric Publishing.

Huang, Z., Wang, M., Qian, M., Zhong, J., & Tao, R. (2007). Chinese Internet addiction inventory: Developing a measure of problematic Internet use for Chinese college students. *CyberPsychology & Behavior, 10,* 805–811.

Ko, C. H., Yen, J. Y., Chen, C. C., Chen, S. H., Wu, K., & Yen, C. F. (2006). Tridimensional personality of adolescents with Internet addiction and substance use experience. *Canadian Journal of Psychiatry, 51*(14), 887–894.

Liu, C. Y., & Kuo, F. Y. (2007). A study of Internet addiction through the lens of the interpersonal theory. *CyberPsychology & Behavior, 10*(6), 779–804.

Mahoney, M. J. (1992). *Human change processes: Scientific foundations of psychotherapy.* New York: Basic Books.

Mueller, A., & de Zwaan, M. (2008, August). Treatment of compulsive buying. *Fortschritte der Neurologie Psychiatrie, 76*(8), 478–483.

Munsch, S., Biedert, E., Meyer, A., Michael, T., Schlup, B., Tuch, A., & Margraf, J. (2007). A randomized comparison of cognitive behavioral therapy and behavioral weight loss treatment for overweight individuals with binge eating disorder. *International Journal of Eating Disorders, 40*(2), 102–113.

Payá, R., & Figlie, N. B. (2004). Entrevista motivacional. In C. N. Abreu & H. Guilhardi, *Terapia comportamental e cognitivo-comportamental: Práticas clínicas* (pp. 414–434). São Paulo: Editora Roca.

Rodriguez, L. J. S., Carmona, F. J., & Marín, D. (2004). Tratamiento psicológico de la adicción a Internet: A propósito de un caso clínico. *Revista Psiquiatría de Faculdad de Medicina de Barna, 31*(2), 76–85.

Safran, J. (1998). *Widening the scope of the cognitive therapy: The therapeutic relationship, emotion and the process of change.* New York: Jason Aronson.

Shaffer, H. J., Hall, M. N., & Bilt, J. V. (2000). Computer addiction: A critical consideration. *American Journal of Orthopsychiatry, 70*(2), 162–168.

Shaw, M., & Black, D. W. (2008). Internet addiction: Definition, assessment, epidemiology and clinical management. *CNS Drugs, 22*(5), 353–365.

Stravogiannis, A., & Abreu, C. N. (2009). Internet addiction: A case report. *Revista Brasileira de Psiquiatria, 31*(1), 76–81.

Wan, C.S., Chiou, W.B. (2006). Psychological motives and online games addiction: a test of flow theory and humanistic needs theory for Taiwanese adolescents. *CyberPsychology & Behavior; 9*: 317–24.

Wieland, D. M. (2005, October–December). Computer addiction: Implications for nursing psychotherapy practice. *Perspectives in Psychiatric Care, 41*(4), 153–161.

Young, K. S. (1998). Internet addiction: The emergence of a new clinical disorder. *CyberPsychology & Behavior, 1*(3), 237–244.

Young, K. S. (1999). *Internet addiction: Symptoms, evaluation, and treatment.* Retrieved July 20, 2006, from http://www.netaddiction.com/articles/symptoms.pdf

Young, K. S. (2007). Cognitive behavior therapy with Internet addicts: Treatment outcomes and implications. *CyberPsychology & Behavior 10*(5), 671–679.

Young, K. S., Cooper, A., Griffiths-Shelley, E., O'Mara, J., & Buchanan, J. (2000). Cybersex and infidelity online: Implications for evaluation and treatment. Retrieved July 23, 2009, from http://www.netaddiction.com/articles/symptoms.pdf

Zhu, T. M., Jin, R. J., & Zhong, X. M. (2009). Clinical effect of electroacupuncture combined with psychologic interference on patient with Internet addiction disorder. Zhongguo Zhong Xi Yi Jie He Za Zhi. Mar;29(3): 212-4.

CHAPTER 10

Working with Adolescents Addicted to the Internet

KEITH W. BEARD

A DOLESCENTS MAY be particularly attracted to the Internet. This chapter reviews current research on adolescents and their Internet use. It includes a discussion of the typical online behaviors of adolescents, the benefits of using the Internet, and problems that can result from adolescents' online activities. Warning signs and symptoms that may indicate a significant problem in adolescents' Internet use are reviewed. The chapter also considers developmental issues, social dynamics (i.e., family factors and peer interactions), and cultural components that have been associated with adolescent Internet addiction. Finally, there is a review of how to treat adolescents who are addicted to the Internet, including ways to assess for a problem with the Internet and specific intervention strategies that might be used. There is a particular focus on potential family therapy interventions that could be used.

INTRODUCTION

The use of the Internet has exploded and continues to grow exponentially. One group has been particularly attracted to this unique form of technology—adolescents. Adolescents may be attracted to the Internet for several reasons. Lam, Zi-wen, Jin-cheng, and Jin (2009) suggested that stress-related variables are a reason for adolescents to get overly involved with the Internet. Adolescents may have limited coping skills, and the Internet is a convenient and available way for them to try to deal with the tension. Another reason is the ability to express one's true self, which can be particularly attractive to an adolescent dealing with identity development and self-concept issues (Tosun & Lajunen, 2009). The perceived anonymity of the

Internet is also an attractive aspect for adolescents, allowing them to engage in behaviors they might not do or have access to in the real world (Beard, 2008). For example, adolescents may be much more willing to engage in the bullying or harassing of others, gain access to pornography, be exposed to sexual behaviors, and find opportunities to be rebellious toward authority figures (Dowell, Burgess, & Cavanaugh, 2009; Kelly, Pomerantz, & Currie, 2006).

This chapter reviews current research on adolescents and the Internet, including the online behaviors of adolescent, the benefits and problems that can result from their online activities, and warning signs and symptoms that may signify problematic use in adolescents. It also reviews the factors and social dynamics that have been associated with adolescent Internet addiction. Finally, there is a review of treatment options for adolescents, with a focus on family therapy interventions.

ONLINE BEHAVIORS

There are 31 million adolescents in the United States (Tsao & Steffes-Hansen, 2008), with 90% of them having Internet access (Harvard Mental Health Letter, 2009), and more than half of adolescents interacting through social networks online (Williams & Merten, 2008). With this large number of adolescents involved with the Internet, it is important to examine and understand their online behaviors.

Lenhart, Madden, and Rainie (2006) report that nearly half of adolescents who are using the Internet do so in their homes and with a broadband connection. Accessing the Internet at school or a friend's house are other popular places to get online.

The types of online activities that adolescents engage in have broadened (Lenhart et al., 2006). For the most part, adolescent boys and girls engage in the same types of Internet activities (Gross, 2004). The exception to this is file-sharing and downloading content from the Internet, which is dominated by adolescent boys (Lenhart et al.).

Eastin (2005) found that adolescents use the Internet for information, entertainment, and communication. Their information use was measured in his study with items that asked the participants about how they had used the Internet to gather information. Entertainment usage was assessed through items that revolved around playing video games, listening to music, and watching movies. Communication behaviors were assessed by examining items that asked about participants' e-mailing and use of chat areas for social purposes. To a lesser degree, adolescents used the Internet to help develop their identities (e.g., successfully being able to find information online can help develop a sense of self-efficacy), improve their moods (e.g., entertainment media on the Internet could offset or lessen dysphoric moods), and improve their careers or social settings (e.g., gathering information about job opportunities and using the Internet to chat, meet, or e-mail with others). Adolescents also used the Internet to view aesthetically pleasing sights, waste time, and make life easier.

In early studies, Gross (2004) reported that adolescents' interactions online are with friends who are also part of their daily lives and affiliated with their lives outside of the Internet. They also reported that their online social inter-action takes place in private, through the two most popular communication applications (e-mail and instant messages), and the topics discussed are fairly common yet personal topics, such as friends and gossip (Gross, 2004; Lenhart et al., 2006). Interestingly, nearly 82% of adolescents (roughly 16 million) have blocked someone from communicating with them, as opposed to only 47% of adults (Lenhart et al., 2006).

Subrahmanyam, Smahel, and Greenfield (2006) monitored 583 adolescents in teen-only chat rooms that were portrayed as rooms for adolescents to hang out in and had no dedicated topics, as opposed to rooms that had dedicated topics such as romance, sports, and music. Over a two-month period, the researchers would enter the chat rooms as passive observers until 15 pages of transcript were collected per session. The transcripts were blindly coded for analysis. From 38 chat sessions collected, they recorded one sexual remark per minute and one obscenity every two minutes. However, even with this level of sexual and obscene behaviors, when looking at overall online ado-lescent behavior, bullying and harassment continued to be the most frequent problems online (Harvard Mental Health Letter, 2009).

Around 57% of adolescents who are online have created content for the Internet (Lenhart et al., 2006). Gross (2004) reported that 55% of online adoles-cents have used and created social networking profiles. When these personal profile pages of adolescents were reviewed, it was found that 58% included a picture on their pages, 43% revealed their full names, 27.8% listed the schools they attend, 11% revealed their places of employment, 10% listed their phone numbers, and 20% disclosed other online contact information such as their e-mail addresses (Hinduja & Patchin, 2008; Williams & Merten, 2008). Ado-lescents know that they shouldn't engage in some online behaviors or that they shouldn't disclose this personal information. Lenhart et al. (2006) found that 64% of adolescents admit that they do things online that they know their parents would not approve of them doing. Not surprisingly, 81% of parents said that their adolescents aren't careful with their online behavior and give out too much information.

Williams and Merten (2008) also found that 84% of online profiles de-scribed some type of risk-taking behaviors involving substances like alcohol, illegal drugs, stealing, vandalism, or some other type of crime. Some 27% of the profiles reviewed included statements about harm to self or others, including suicidal thoughts, discussions on fights or gangs, or images of weapons.

Williams and Merten (2008) further discovered that online profiles of ado-lescents had an average 194 friends in their social network and interacted with others an average of every 2.79 days. They proposed that online social net-works are a primary way for adolescents to engage in interpersonal commu-nication and maintain relationships on a regular basis. Williams and Merten described how blogging has become a standard form of communication among adolescents, comparable to cell phone use, e-mailing, and instant messaging. Teens are more likely to blog and read blogs than adults, with older girls blogging the most in the adolescent cohort (Lenhart et al., 2006). When Williams and Merten examined these blogs by adolescents, they found that themes often revolve around topics of romantic relationships, sexuality, friends, parents, conflicts with others, academics, popular culture, self-expression, eating disorders, depression, and self-harm. The researchers expanded on this finding by reviewing other research that found the top two reasons adolescents create blogs. The first is the need for creative self-expression, and the second is to document and share personal experiences.

While the momentum of adolescents using the Internet has continued to increase, Lenhart et al. (2006) found that 13% of American teens do not use the Internet and almost half of those not using the technology have used it before but have since stopped. About one in 10 adolescents report having a bad experience online, that their parents restrict their use, or that they feel unsafe online. These nonusing teens were also likely to report not using the Internet because of a lack of interest, not enough time, or the inability to access the Internet.

BENEFITS

Although it is easy to focus on the negatives, the Internet is not all bad. It has helped adolescents in many ways, and these benefits should be remembered. Some researchers (Beard, 2008; Williams & Merten, 2008) have explained how the Internet can help adolescents by allowing for increased positive communication and social interactions with others. This has allowed old relationships with peers and relatives to be reconnected and maintained, as well as permitted the opportunities for new friendships to develop. The Internet has also allowed people to find emotional support that may have been lacking. For example, Internet use was observed in one study as a way to help new students feel welcome to their new schools and initiate new friendships (Williams & Merten). Beard felt that the Internet has been a way for those who are isolated geographically to meet others and feel a part of a larger community. The Internet has also been a place for entertainment, with an abundance of games, images, news, and web sites to view. There are also educational benefits to this technology for adolescents. The Internet has allowed adolescents to access information that may have previously been difficult or nearly impossible to review. Likewise, this technology has allowed for adolescents to learn and be exposed to new and diverse cultures and ideas.

With regard to physical and mental health, Beard (2008) went on to say that the Internet can be a way for some people to get relief from anxiety and depression symptoms. Spending time online could help the person get some relief through distraction by engaging in online activities instead of dwelling on their symptoms. The Internet could also help the person gain needed support and education about their physical or mental health issue. It has even been suggested that the Internet may increase a person's sense of self-worth and self-esteem because it allows for others to demonstrate their knowledge and offer assistance and support to those who need help with their physical or mental difficulties.

Beard (2008) stated that this increased sense of self-worth and self-esteem could also occur when assistance is given to others based on their technology needs. For example, those who are knowledgeable can offer advice or demonstrate how to use various applications or programs to those less knowledgeable. The Internet has also allowed people to increase their knowledge about technology. For example, people can access reviews of new technology to ascertain the pros and cons of using or purchasing the technology, they can read user manuals or helpful sites on how their technology is used, or they can be more willing to upgrade to newer technology because of comfort or success over mastering previous technology. It has even been proposed that the Internet is a medium that has allowed for improvement of writing abilities and intellectual growth for a number of people. For example, people who might not normally write or journal can blog and obtain comments on their writing or even submit written works to sites for others to review and give feedback on. People may grow intellectually by having access to an abundance of material on unlimited topics or through discovering new information through Web searches on topics of interest.

PROBLEMS

Unfortunately, there are some negative consequences associated with the Internet. Beard (2002, 2008) said that although a benefit of the Internet is the plethora of information and the ability to access it, there are also issues with some of the content that can be obtained on the Internet. Exposure to excessive information can lead to misinformation, gossip, and dangerous information being quickly obtained and easily perpetuated. For example, it is relatively easy to inaccurately self-diagnose a physical problem or learn how to engage in self-harming behaviors without getting caught. There can also be difficulties trying to obtain desired information because of the overabundance of web sites that have to be reviewed and sorted through in order to find the wanted content. Besides dealing with a surplus of material, uncensored and unfiltered information can lead to other issues. For example, there could be increased access to pornographic material, which might also result in problems arising in multiple areas of the person's personal, academic, and professional life.

Beard (2002, 2008) commented on the potential degradation of the family and other interpersonal relationships because time that could be spent together is spent online. This could result in impatience, arguments, and strains in the relationships. Researchers (Beard, 2002; Beard & Wolf, 2001; Park, Kim, Cho, 2008; Young, 2009) have talked about the change in family relationships in more depth. With increased Internet use, the quantity and quality of family communication declines. There is less opportunity to talk with each other since the adolescent is spending more and more time online. The adolescent may ignore or miss aspects of the communication with family members because of preoccupation with online activities. Additionally, adolescents may begin to lie to their family and friends about their Internet use. Park et al. (2008) went on to talk about the decrease in family cohesion with adolescents addicted to the Internet. The bond that family members have with each other may begin to loosen, causing those dealing with the addicted adolescent to feel separated or disconnected. Besides communication and interpersonal relationship problems, the level of Internet use has also led to problems in schoolwork, extracurricular activities, and employment.

One main attraction to the Internet is the sense of anonymity that comes with using this technology. Adolescents can misrepresent themselves by constructing a personal profile online and depict themselves as how they see themselves or how they want others to view them (Williams & Merten, 2008). Since people can test out new identities and misrepresent themselves online, adolescents may be disappointed if an online friend is never met or disappointed after he or she is met (Turkle, 1996). Another danger that can result from misrepresentation is interactions with sexual predators, who can easily engage adolescents in this relatively anonymous environment (Beard, 2008; Dombrowski, LeMasney, & Ahia, 2004).

Beard and Wolf (2001) stated that a negative consequence of the Internet is the maladaptive use of this technology, commonly referred to as Internet addiction. Xiang-Yang, Hong-Zhuan, and Jin-Qing (2006) recognized that the inappropriate use of the Internet harms the user physically and mentally, and this harm is especially damaging for the youth. The notion of Internet addiction in youth has been viewed as something of importance by our society and research community and something that should be further examined. Li (2007) conducted a study in Zhengzhou City of Henan Province in China and found that problematic Internet use is occurring. The incidence of Internet addiction among the urban middle school students was 5% with no significant differences found in gender, grade, and the nature of the school environment. Further research is needed to determine what cultural risk factors exist with problematic Internet use and how factors such as gender and age can impact addiction among adolescents.

Since these potential negative consequences of using the Internet may occur and excessive Internet use could develop, some have attempted to limit the amount of time or types of activities that adolescents can do on the Internet. Tynes (2007) said that although it is important to recognize and understand these negative consequences, it is also important to remember that for the majority of adolescents, we may be doing them a disservice by limiting their use of the Internet. The educational and psychosocial benefits often outweigh the potential dangers that this medium provides. Therefore, the potential benefits should be kept in mind when considering the negative aspects of this technology.

WARNING SIGNS AND SYMPTOMS OF PROBLEMATIC INTERNET USE

Many of the warning signs and symptoms that apply to people in general would be relevant to issues with Internet addiction found in adolescents. However, this population may also have some unique warning signs and symptoms that should be highlighted. As previously mentioned, as problems with the Internet develop, several areas of the adolescent's life may suffer, such as school performance, extracurricular activities, hobbies, and after-school employment (Beard, 2008). One reason this decrease in performance occurs is the lack of adequate rest because of online activities (Young, 1998a, 2009). Other warning signs that a problem is developing have been proposed (Beard, 2008; Beard & Wolf, 2001; Young, 1998a, 2009). These signs include behaviors such as poor self-care and weight loss or gain. The adolescent may have increased anger, irritability, edginess, apathy, and mood change. The adolescent may also start to be overly sensitive to questions about online use and act out, especially when time on the Internet is limited by adults.

Beard (2008) felt that changes or conflicts with parental and other real-world interpersonal relationships may occur as problems with the Internet develop. There may be changes in friendships and less time spent with others. Free time is replaced with online activities, resulting in strained relationships. As the adolescent withdraws from others, emotional attachment with those online may increase. The adolescent may even begin to justify the online behavior and resulting real-world relationship problems by believing that the excessive Internet use is really enhancing the person's peer relationships. As a result, the adolescent becomes more dependent on the social contact obtained while online. Additionally, the more adolescents engage in online activities, the more importance they tend to associate with the Internet (Williams & Merten, 2008).

The perceptions that adolescents have on how useful and beneficial the Internet is in their lives has been found to be a predicting factor in whether an adolescent could become addicted to the Internet (Xuanhui & Gonggu, 2001). With this specific population in mind, Ko, Yen, Chen, Chen, and Yen (2005) developed a diagnostic criterion intended for the diagnosis of Internet addiction in adolescents. They hoped that this criterion could provide mental health professionals with a way to communicate and make comparisons between patients. Their criterion consists of nine diagnostic conditions based on three main areas: (1) characteristic symptoms of Internet addiction, (2) functional impairment secondary to Internet use, and (3) exclusive criteria. Their diagnostic criterion shows some promise with high diagnostic accuracy, specificity, negative predictive value, acceptable sensitivity, and acceptable positive predictive value. Although this is a good start, further studies are needed if criteria for this specific population are to be established. These studies need to add additional validity, utility, and acceptance of the proposed criteria.

Some researchers (Beard, 2008; Young, 1998a) have pointed out that the Internet may not be the cause of the problem. Instead, the problem could be how the Internet is used, the sites accessed, the feelings created from being online or on a site, or the reinforcement obtained from online behavior. Likewise, problematic Internet use may be an indication of other problems in the adolescent's life. For example, Young (1997, 1998a) suggested that the Internet may attract adolescents with attention-deficit/hyperactivity disorder (ADHD) because of the abundance of stimulating and rapidly changing material that can be found online. Several researchers (Beard, 2008; Jang, Hwang, & Choi, 2008; Morahan-Martin, 1999; Young, 1997, 1998a) have stated that adolescents may use the Internet to help alleviate depression, anxiety, obsessive-compulsive disorder, social phobia, guilt, loneliness, family discord, and other real-life problems. Unfortunately, as a result of this avoidance behavior, the problems may grow and now feel even more difficult to endure. This could result in the adolescent feeling a deeper need to go online to ease these states.

RISK FACTORS AND SOCIAL DYNAMICS

There are a variety of risk factors and social issues that adolescents face, and as a result, these aspects of their lives could contribute to their Internet addiction. The time period of adolescence provides unique issues and obstacles that the adolescent must deal with during this phase of life. How well and effectively the adolescent conquers and maneuvers through these factors and issues can have a lasting impact on their online behavior.

Developmental Aspects   Adolescents are developing social skills during this period that can be used throughout the life span. There has also been some concern that the Internet may help an adolescent escape from face-to-face social interactions and hinder the development of certain social skills that will be needed later in life (Beard & Wolf, 2001).

Adolescents are also dealing with many developmental challenges during this period of life. One of these developmental tasks is the formation of a unified identity. As briefly mentioned earlier, on the Internet, people can create new identities to demonstrate how they view themselves or how they want to be viewed, as well as misrepresent themselves (McCormick & McCormick, 1992; Williams & Merten, 2008). Researchers (Beard, 2002, 2008; Young, 1997, 1998a, 1998b) have stated that this aspect of the Internet is attractive to adolescents and they could be particularly susceptible to this behavior since they are often discontented with their looks and internal factors. The Internet gives the adolescent a chance to try on different personas to determine what fits for them and potentially meet unfulfilled needs. Adolescents can develop online personas through various applications such as online role-playing games and chat rooms.

The anonymity of these sites allows the adolescent to take on screen names or alternative handles that do not represent who they are in real life. Although not as anonymous, Kramer and Winter (2008) discussed how users of social networking sites have the opportunity to consider which aspects of their personalities they want to present in their profiles or which photos convey the best images of them. As a result, they have more control over their self-presentations and can be more strategic than they can in face-to-face encounters. Surprisingly, the researchers found that these self-presentations have been fairly accurate, indicating that there is not as much interest in playing with one's identity on these types of social networking sites.

Additionally, there has been some fear that engaging in this behavior of trying on different personas could potentially delay the appropriate resolution of an identity crisis. Young (1997, 1998a, 1998b) also warned that as the online identity develops, the adolescent may begin to blur the distinction between one's real-world personality and the online persona. Others have argued that even though these new identities and behaviors can be of concern to adults, the behaviors may not be as detrimental as once feared and could be a safe and positive way for self-expression and experimentation (Williams & Merten, 2008). How much this medium has really been used to explore identity issues has also been questioned. Gross (2004) found that when adolescents pretended to be someone else online, it was more likely to be motivated by a desire to play a joke on friends than to explore a desired or future identity.

Family Dynamics   The Internet could potentially provide a backdrop for several critical family problems (Oravec, 2000). Young (2009) commented on how family stability can be disrupted through events such as separation or divorce. The adolescent may stop participating and interacting in real-life relationships, instead focusing on online relationships that the adolescent feels good about and lessening the interaction with unfulfilling real-life relationships.

Family dynamics, disruptions, and stress can promote the onset of addictive behavior as well as influence how the family enables, encourages, and overlooks the addictive behavior (Stanton & Heath, 1997; Yen, Yen, Chen, Chen, & Ko, 2007; Young, 2009). For example, young people in families that have conflict and poor communication styles are more likely to turn to the Internet as a way to avoid conflict and gain support (Beard, 2008; Yen et al., 2007; Young, 2009), and adolescents who have parents and siblings who habitually abuse substances are more likely to seek out the Internet (Yen et al., 2007; Young, 2009). Turning to the Internet may be an attempt to cope and gain some psychological relief from the dynamics, disruptions, and stress within the family (Beard, 2008; Eastin, 2005).

Families may also rationalize the adolescent's problematic Internet use as a phase and convince themselves that the problem will resolve itself over time (Young, 1998a). Additionally, family factors have been found with Internet addiction in adolescents and substance use. Adolescents whose parents abuse substances are more likely to have an increased risk of using the Internet as a means to cope with problems (Yen, Ko, et al., 2008; Yen, Yen, Chen, Chen, & Ko, 2007).

The family's view of the Internet could also play a role. Young (1998a) stated that many parents are unaware of the online behaviors of their children.

Other parents have banned Internet use for fear of the content that their children may be exposed to online. Neither being unaware nor prohibiting online activity will help parents deal with the issues that may arise from their child's Internet use. Likewise, the adolescent's primary caregiver may view the Internet only in positive terms, or the caregiver may also be engaging in problematic Internet use. As a result, the caregiver is serving as a model for excessive online behavior (Beard, 2008).

Interpersonal and Cultural Factors   Most people have a need to feel connected to others, and the Internet has provided a new way for this to occur. Beard (2008) felt that adolescents may be particularly attracted to the Internet because they often feel isolated. As a result, the bonds that are formed over the Internet gain even more significance in the adolescent's life. Unfortunately, the Internet may provide only the illusion of a close relationship since these connections may be artificial and easily severed with the click of a mouse.

Adolescents may also deal with peers modeling, expecting, and pressuring them to engage in various online activities or behaviors (Beard, 2008). As previously mentioned, adolescents will often use e-mail and instant messages with friends (Gross, 2004). They also engage in online gaming where they can play against their peers (Young, 2009). Applications that involve two-way communication (e-mail, messaging, and gaming) are thought to be the applications that are most addictive (Beard & Wolf, 2001). As a result of these interpersonal factors, the adolescent may insist on regularly engaging in certain online activities, for various amounts of time, in order to maintain a sense of acceptance and social status.

Additionally, Beard (2008) felt that there are cultural pressures for adolescents to use the Internet more and more. Adolescents receive messages from our culture that they need to become a part of a technologically advanced society if they want to succeed. There is also pressure to use technology in school and work in order to get ahead, be competitive, and be better than others.

Research is actively being done in Taiwan, Korea, and China regarding adolescents and addictive online behavior (Jang et al., 2008; Ko, Yen, Chen, et al., 2005; Lam, Zi-wen, Jin-cheng, & Jin, 2009; Li, 2007; Xiang, et al., 2006; Xuanhui & Gonggu, 2001; Yen, Ko, et al., 2008; Yen, Yen, et al., 2007). These studies have helped us begin to see how various factors in some cultures are influencing the development and maintenance of Internet addiction. Whether these factors are universal or culture specific has yet to be explored. However, this research is a good starting point for us to begin looking at the cultural components that impact Internet addiction.

TREATMENT

Before treatment can begin, assessment of the adolescent should occur and be ongoing. Beard (2005) described the use of a clinical interview and a standardized assessment instrument as a way to understand the signs, symptoms, and development of the problematic Internet behavior. His assessment protocol is based on the biopsychosocial model of behavior. As a result, there are suggested questions related to biological, psychological, and social factors that could be contributing to the adolescent's Internet use. The biological questions focus on biological symptoms or problems that may occur in a person engaging in an addictive behavior (e.g., Does your Internet use interfere with your sleep?). The psychological questions focus on how classical and operant conditioning as well as thoughts, feelings, and behaviors may play a role in initiating and maintaining behavior of those addicted to the Internet (e.g., Have you ever used the Internet to help improve your mood or change your thoughts?). The social questions focus on familial, social, and cultural dynamics that prompt excessive Internet use (e.g., How has your Internet use caused problems or concerns with your family?). Besides these areas, Beard also included questions related to the presenting problem (e.g., When did you begin to notice problems with your Internet use?) and questions related to relapse potential (e.g., What seems to trigger Internet use?).

Some researchers (Caplan, 2002; Davis, 2002; Ko, Yen, Yen, Chen, Yen, & Chen, 2005; Widyanto, Griffiths, Brunsden, & McMurran, 2008; Young, 1995, 1998a) have developed Internet addiction self-report inventories that can be completed by the adolescent or someone knowledgeable about the adolescent's online behavior. Although these instruments are a good start and some research has been completed on the psychometric properties of some of these instruments, additional research on the validity and reliability of these instruments could be done. Once an assessment is completed and an appropriate diagnosis can be given, then treatment planning and implementation with the adolescent can begin.

Marlatt (1985) believed that effective treatment for addictive behavior should revolve around the assumption that people can learn effective ways to change their behavior regardless of how the problem developed. Since addictive behaviors are often the result of multiple factors, interventions need to include strategies from a wide array of options, including behavioral, cognitive, and lifestyle changes. For example, the adolescent may need some help in making specific modifications to the environment so that the problematic Internet use will not continue.

As Beard (2005) pointed out, the use of technology and the Internet is becoming more and more ingrained in our society. It may be impossible for the adolescent to completely stop all use of the Internet and to not have some contact with online content. Therefore, the idea of just pulling the plug and going cold turkey for the Internet addict is not very realistic. Instead, the focus on treatment should be exploring ways to engage in controlled Internet use. This could be done by helping the adolescent define clear limits on his or her Internet use. Likewise, the adolescent should be aware of and learn to identify triggers that could cause a relapse so that maladaptive behavior patterns can be avoided and stopped from recurring. The adolescent may need to be reminded of treatment strategies and interventions to help control Internet use, as well as where to seek help if more support is needed.

FAMILY THERAPY

Beard (2008) stated that when working with adolescents, the therapist is often working and intervening with the caregivers and other family members. As a result, family therapy is often a primary treatment modality. Liddle, Dakof, Turner, Henderson, and Greenbaum (2008) described the Multidimensional Family Therapy (MDFT) model to treatment of an addicted adolescent. With this model the therapy services are provided in various settings and formats such as in the office, in the home, brief formats, intensive outpatient therapy, day treatment, and residential treatment. A therapy session may involve the adolescent alone, the parent(s) alone, or with the adolescent and parent(s) together. Who is involved with a particular therapy session is based on the specific issue to be addressed in that session. MDFT can be delivered from one to three times per week, and the course of treatment is typically four to six months based on the treatment setting, the severity of the adolescent's problems, and the family functioning.

In their study, Liddle, Dakof, Turner, Henderson, and Greenbaum (2008) treated the family across four domains (adolescent, parent, interactional, and extrafamilial). The adolescent domain focused on getting the client engaged in treatment, improving communication skills with parents and adults, developing skills related to coping with everyday problems, emotion regulation and problem solving, improving the client's social skills as well as his or her school and work performance, and establishing alternatives to addictive behavior. The parent domain focused on getting the parents engaged in treatment, improving their behavioral and emotional involvement with the adolescent, developing more effective parenting skills such as monitoring the adolescent's behavior and clarifying their expectations of the adolescent, setting limits and consequences, and addressing the psychological needs of the parents. Additionally, caregivers may want to examine their own Internet behaviors and explore ways that they may model appropriate Internet use (Beard, 2008). Liddle et al. (2008) went on to describe how the interactional domain is focused on decreasing family conflicts, increasing emotional attachments, and enhancing communication and problem-solving skills. Finally, the extrafamilial domain focused on developing family competency in the social systems in which the adolescent is involved (e.g. educational setting, juvenile justice, settings where the adolescent spends spare time).

Beard (2008) added that it is also necessary to examine previous and current family problems since these may be factors in why the adolescent sought out the Internet and began to use the technology in a problematic way. Also, aiding the family in how to handle crises and problems as well as stabilizing the family unit are often goals of treatment.

Just as Liddle et al. (2008) and others (Beard, 2008; Young, 2009) have described, communication skills need to be worked on within the family unit. Beard said that lecturing the adolescent is typically a futile and unproductive intervention. Family members need to learn how to effectively listen to the adolescent, acknowledge the feelings and thoughts the adolescent is experiencing, and convey messages in a way that the adolescent understands and is receptive to hearing. By increasing appropriate communication, the family will be better able to understand the issues at hand and how best to deal with them. Likewise, caregivers may want to take a proactive stance and begin talking to their adolescents early on about the Internet, just as they might do when talking to them about drugs and alcohol.

Young (1995) suggested that the family be educated on how the Internet can be addictive for some people. The family is also encouraged to help the adolescent find new interests and hobbies, take time for himself or herself, and find other activities to fill in the time gained by decreasing the amount of Internet use. Stanton and Heath (1997) suggested that the families need to be supportive and learn how to validate the adolescent for any effort being made. At the same time, they do not want to enable problematic Internet use or aid the adolescent with excuses for why he or she missed school or failed an assignment.

Researchers (Beard, 2009; Young, 1998a, 2009) have advised that mental health workers help the caregivers establish appropriate rules, clear limits, and goals for Internet use. Caregivers also need to be consistent with the new rules and limits that are established. Software can even be used to help monitor Internet use and ensure that the rules and limits are being followed appropriately. If this is not occurring, then the issue can be addressed in treatment and how to alter the variables that caused the limits to not be followed can be explored. Likewise, the caregivers need to learn how to work together. If there is a division between them, then the adolescent may use this to create an even bigger divergence.

Working with siblings may also be vital since they are a part of the family system. It is possible that since siblings are in the same environment as the addicted adolescent, they could be enabling the addictive behavior of the client or be engaging in addictive behavior themselves. This should be examined during the assessment and treatment process. Even if the siblings are not engaging in addictive behavior, implementing some of these strategies within the whole family unit may be useful in helping establish a more structured home environment and better communication among family members. Young (2009) also talked about using a sibling as someone who could assist with implementing some of the treatment interventions. For example, a sibling may be a good person for the addicted adolescent to practice or role-play new communication skills with in a comfortable setting.

Young (1995, 1998a) further recommended that families look for support groups for Internet addiction. If these cannot be located in the immediate area, then other support groups such as Al-Anon could provide information about dealing with any addiction in the family. Seeing that others are dealing with addictive behaviors can help normalize the family experience, increase a sense of validation, and decrease the sense of isolation often associated with addiction. Likewise, caregivers may want to seek support from parent associations affiliated with schools in order to connect with other caregivers who are experiencing similar difficulties. Although it may sound contradictory, families may find support online through various sites that have been developed to provide education, information, and support for families dealing with addiction as well as sites that focus on the treatment of Internet addiction.

CONCLUSION

Problematic Internet use is an issue for some adolescents. The causes of Internet addiction are complex and multifaceted (Wang, 2001). The need to continue the examination and awareness of problematic Internet use in adolescents, as well as in other populations, is something that those in the mental health field should do. Mental health professionals should also keep an open mind, take these issues seriously, and actively assess potential problems with every new patient. As the research in this area continues, we will further enhance our ability to assess, diagnose, and treat those dealing with Internet-related issues. Difficulties for adolescents that could arise with the use of new technologies should be examined in a proactive manner instead of waiting after the fact and trying to deal with the issues that have already developed. Technology is going to continue to be an integral part of our everyday lives. Being aware of the potential positive and negative impacts of the Internet can only bring positive results to adolescents and those involved with them.

REFERENCES

Beard, K. W. (2002). Internet addiction: Current status and implications for employees. *Journal of Employment Counseling, 39,* 2–11.

Beard, K. W. (2005). Internet addiction: A review of current assessment techniques and potential assessment questions. *CyberPsychology & Behavior, 8,* 7–14.

Beard, K. W. (2008). Internet addiction in children and adolescents. In C. B. Yarnall (Ed.), *Computer science research trends* (pp. 59–70). Hauppauge, NY: Nova Science Publishers.

Beard, K. W. (2009). Internet addiction: An overview. In J. B. Allen, E. M. Wolf, & L VandeCreek (eds.) *Innovations in clinical practice: A 21st century sourcebook,* vol. 1. (pp. 117–134). Sarasota, FL: Professional Resource Press.

Beard, K. W., & Wolf, E. M. (2001). Modification in the proposed diagnostic criteria for Internet addiction. *CyberPsychology & Behavior, 4,* 377–383.

Caplan, S. E. (2002). Problematic Internet use and psychosocial well-being: Development of a theory based cognitive-behavioral measurement instrument. *Computers in Human Behavior, 18,* 5553–5575.

Davis, R. A. (2002). Validation of a new scale for measuring problematic Internet use: Implications for preemployment screening. *CyberPsychology & Behavior, 5,* 331–345.

Dombrowski, S. C., LeMasney, J. W., & Ahia, C. E. (2004). Protecting children from online sexual predators: Technological, psychoeducational, and legal considerations. *Professional Psychology: Research and Practice, 35,* 65–73.

Dowell, E. B., Burgess, A. W., & Cavanaugh, D. J. (2009). Clustering of Internet risk behaviors in a middle school student population. *Journal of School Health, 79,* 547–553.

Eastin, M. S. (2005). Teen Internet use: Relating social perceptions and cognitive models to behavior. *CyberPsychology & Behavior, 8,* 62–75.

Gross, E. F. (2004). Adolescent Internet use: What we expect, what teens report [Special issue: Developing children, developing media: Research from television to the Internet from the Children's Digital Media Center; A special issue dedicated to the memory of Rodney R. Cocking]. *Journal of Applied Developmental Psychology, 25*(6), 633–649.

Harvard Mental Health Letter. (2009). Reducing teens' risk on the Internet. *Harvard Mental Health Letter, 25*(10), 7.

Hinduja, S., & Patchin, J. W. (2008). Personal information of adolescents on the Internet: A quantitative content analysis of MySpace. *Journal of Adolescence, 31*(1), 125–146.

Jang, K. S., Hwang, S. Y., & Choi, J. Y. (2008). Internet addiction and psychiatric symptoms among Korean adolescents. *Journal of School Health, 78,* 165–171.

Kelly, D. M., Pomerantz, S., & Currie, D. H. (2006). "No boundaries"? Girls' interactive, online learning about femininities. *Youth & Society, 38,* 3–28.

Ko, C. H., Yen, J. Y., Chen, C. C., Chen, S. H., & Yen, C. N. (2005). Proposed diagnostic criteria of Internet addiction for adolescents. *Journal of Nervous and Mental Disease, 193*(11), 728–733.

Ko, C. H., Yen, J. Y., Yen, C. F., Chen, C. C., Yen, C. N., & Chen, S. H. (2005). Screening for Internet addiction: An empirical research on cut-off points for the Chen Internet Addiction Scale. *Kaohsiung Journal of Medical Science, 21,* 545–551.

Kramer, N. C., & Winter, S. (2008). Impression management 2.0: The relationship of self-esteem, extraversion, self-efficacy, and self-presentation within social networking sites. *Journal of Media Psychology, 20*(3), 106–116.

Lam, L. T., Zi-wen, P., Jin-cheng, M., & Jin, J. (2009). Factors associated with Internet addiction among adolescents. *CyberPsychology & Behavior, 12,* 551–555.

Lenhart, A., Madden, M., & Rainie, L. (2006). Teens and the Internet. *Pew Internet & American Life Project.*

Li, Y. (2007). Internet addiction and family achievement, control, organization. *Chinese Mental Health Journal, 21*(4), 244–246.

Liddle, H. A., Dakof, G. A., Turner, R. M., Henderson, C. E., & Greenbaum, P. E. (2008). Treating adolescent drug abuse: A randomized trial comparing multidimensional family therapy and cognitive behavior therapy. *Addiction, 103*(10), 1660–1670.

Marlatt, G. A. (1985). Relapse prevention: Theoretical rationale and overview of the model. In G. A. Marlatt & J. Gordon (Eds.), *Relapse prevention* (pp. 3–70). New York: Guilford Press.

McCormick, N. B., & McCormick, J. W. (1992). Computer friends and foes: Content of undergraduates' electronic mail. *Computers in Human Behavior, 8*, 379–405.

Morahan-Martin, J. M. (1999). The relationship between loneliness and Internet use and abuse. *CyberPsychology & Behavior, 2*, 431–439.

Oravec, J. A. (2000). Internet and computer technology hazards: Perspectives for family counseling. *British Journal of Guidance & Counseling, 28*, 309–224.

Park, S. K., Kim, J. Y., & Cho, C. B. (2008). Prevalence of Internet addiction and correlations with family factors among South Korean adolescents. *Adolescence, 43*(172), 895-909.

Stanton, M. D., & Heath, A. W. (1997). Family and marital therapy. In J. Lowinson, P. Ruiz, R. Millman, and J. Langrod (Eds.), *Substance abuse: A comprehensive textbook* (3rd ed.). (pp. 448–454). Baltimore, MD: Williams & Wilkins.

Subrahmanyam, K., Smahel, D., & Greenfield, P. (2006). Connecting developmental construction to the Internet: Identity presentation and sexual exploration in online teen chatrooms. *Developmental Psychology, 42*(3), 395–406.

Tosun, L. P., & Lajunen, T. (2009). Why do young adults develop a passion for Internet activities? The associations among personality, revealing "true self" on the Internet, and passion for the Internet. *CyberPsychology & Behavior, 12*, 401–406.

Tsao, J. C., & Steffes-Hansen, S. (2008). Predictors for Internet usage of teenagers in the United States: A multivariate analysis. *Journal of Marketing Communications, 14*(3), 171–192.

Turkle, S. (1996). Parallel lives: Working on identity in virtual space. In D. Grodin & T. R. Lindolf (Eds.), *Constructing the self in a mediated world: Inquiries in social construction*. Thousand Oaks, CA: Sage.

Tynes, B. M. (2007). Internet safety gone wild? Sacrificing the educational and psychosocial benefits of online social environments. *Journal of Adolescent Research, 22*(6), 575–584.

Wang, W. (2001). Internet dependency and psychosocial maturity among college students. *International Journal of Human-Computer Studies, 55*, 919–938.

Widyanto, L., Griffiths, M., Brunsden, V., & McMurran, M. (2008). The psychometric properties of the Internet Related Problem Scale: A pilot study. *International Journal of Mental Health and Addiction, 6*(2), 205–213.

Williams, A. L., & Merten, M. J. (2008). A review of online social networking profiles by adolescents: Implications for future research and intervention. *Adolescence, 43*(170), 253–274.

Xiang-Yang, Z., Hong-Zhuan, T., & Jin-Qing, Z. (2006). Internet addiction and coping styles in adolescents. *Chinese Journal of Clinical Psychology, 14*(3), 256–257.

Xuanhui, L., & Gonggu, Y. (2001). Internet addiction disorder, online behavior, and personality. *Chinese Mental Health Journal, 15*, 281–283.

Yen, J., Ko, C., Yen, C., Chen, S., Chung, W., & Chen, C. (2008). Psychiatric symptoms in adolescents with Internet addiction: Comparison with substance use. *Psychiatry and Clinical Neurosciences, 62*, 9–16.

Yen, J., Yen, C., Chen, C., Chen, S., & Ko, C. (2007). Family factors of Internet addiction and substance use experience in Taiwanese adolescents. *CyberPsychology & Behavior, 10*, 323–329.

Young, K. S. (1995). Internet addiction: Symptoms, evaluation, and treatment. Retrieved January 9, 2002, from http://www.netaddiction.com/articles/symptoms.html

Young, K. S. (1997). What makes the Internet addictive: Potential explanations for pathological Internet use. Retrieved October 25, 2001, from http://www.netaddiction.com/articles/hatbitforming.html

Young, K. S. (1998a). The center for online addiction—Frequently asked questions. Retrieved January 9, 2002, from http://www.netaddiction.com/resources/faq.html

Young, K. S. (1998b). *Caught in the Net*. New York: John Wiley & Sons.

Young, K. S. (2009). Understanding online gaming addiction and treatment issues for adolescents. *American Journal of Family Therapy, 37*, 355–372.

CHAPTER 11

Internet Infidelity: A Real Problem

MONICA T. WHITTY

I T IS now well established that Internet infidelity is a real problem. This chapter examines the unique features of Internet infidelity and how these features have altered as the Internet has evolved. It first considers how intimacy is established online and the unique aspects of an online affair. It then considers the sexual and emotional components of infidelity and attempts a generic definition for Internet infidelity. Different forms of online infidelity are highlighted, including the use of infidelity dating sites and social networking sites. It also questions whether all online activities that mimic offline infidelities ought to be considered unfaithful. It may well be that some activities are simply play rather than belonging to the realm of reality. This chapter also highlights that digital technologies can be utilized to establish an offline affair and looks at how these technologies can aid in maintaining offline affairs. Finally, a treatment rationale is posited, looking at what we know so far about Internet infidelity as well as what we might learn from research on more traditional offline infidelities. It is argued here that our entire understanding of the nature of infidelity (both new and more traditional forms) needs to be completely reexamined given the importance of digital technologies in many people's lives.

ONLINE INTIMACY

Over the past 10 years, research has confirmed that real relationships initiate and develop in an assortment of places online (see Whitty & Carr, 2006 for an overview). Some of these spaces are anonymous, such as chat rooms and discussion groups (McKenna, Green, & Gleason, 2002; Parks & Floyd, 1996; Whitty & Gavin, 2001), while some spaces are set up to match up individuals (Whitty, 2008a). It is far less common, of course, these days to be completely anonymous in cyberspace. Research has found that not only are real relation-ships formed online in most spaces, but that sometimes these relationships can develop more quickly and intimately than offline relationships. These rather intense relationships are referred to as *hyperpersonal relationships* (Tidwell & Walther, 2002; Walther, 1996, 2007).

Walther and his colleagues have discussed in detail how under certain conditions individuals develop hyperpersonal relationships. Their view is unique in the way they focus on technological affordances rather than on the problems associated with communicating via digital technologies. They argue that users can take advantage of the fact that computer-mediated com-munication (CMC) is editable, which allows the user to alter what has been written prior to sending the message. Furthermore, individuals typically have more time to construct a message, which is not a luxury one has in face-to-face (FtF) communication. This is of course less true of some spaces online, such as Instant Messenger (IM), where the expectations to respond are different compared to others spaces such as e-mail. Importantly, they point out that users can and often do exchange messages in physical isolation, which can mask involuntary cues, such as nonverbal leakage. Another key point made by these scholars is that individuals can devote more attention to CMC than FtF communication affords. The face, body, voice, and so forth do not need to be scanned during CMC, which gives individuals more time to focus on the message itself. Walther and colleagues argue that each of these technological affordances provides individuals with the opportunity to manage impres-sions; that is, CMC allows individuals to present a more likable self than what is perhaps known in FtF situations. Hence, it is no surprise that hyperpersonal relationships are frequently reported online.

IDEALIZING ONLINE RELATIONSHIPS

Developing close and intimate relationships online has certain advantages. As already stated, relationships that develop online often move successfully to the offline realm. Moreover, cyberspace can also allow individuals to learn about their sexuality (McKenna & Bargh, 1998); to learn how to flirt (Whitty, 2003a); and to gain social support (Hampton & Wellman, 2003). However, as has been previously pointed out, we also need to be aware of the dark side of online relating (Whitty & Carr, 2005, 2006). Given the hyperintimacy that can be achieved during CMC, there is the danger that these relationships, while they remain online, might appear more appealing and enticing; this can lead to idealization. This is problematic for a variety of reasons; however, the concern in this chapter is the issue of infidelity.

Drawing from Walther and colleagues' hyperpersonal theory as well as object-relations theory, it has been argued that some relationships become so personal that they become idealized (Whitty & Carr, 2005, 2006). This idealization can lead to inappropriate relationships. As already highlighted, because of certain features of CMC, individuals can be strategic in their self-presentations, creating potentially a more likable person than perhaps they are more commonly known as in other spaces. Having people respond more positively to this more, well-crafted, likable self, could be more appealing than the more mundane self of everyday life. Moreover, if the individual that person is communicating with is employing the same strategy, they too might seem a more likable person than people known in one's everyday life; hence, the seductive appeal of CMC, which could lead to an online affair. Internet infidelity can be understood in many different ways (as will be defined later on in this chapter), but for now let us consider an online affair to be having a relationship that remains online with another whom that person has fallen in love with and/or sexually desires.

Melanie Klein's work on splitting is also useful in explaining the appeal of online relationships (Whitty & Carr, 2005, 2006). She believed that splitting was one of the most primitive or basic defense mechanisms against anxiety. According to Klein (1986), the ego prevents the bad part of the object from contaminating the good part of the object by splitting it off and disowning a part of itself. An infant in its relationship with the mother's breast conceives it as both a good and a bad object. The breast gratifies and frustrates, and the infant will simultaneously project both love and hate onto it. On the one hand, the infant idealizes this good object, but on the other hand, the bad object is seen as terrifying, frustrating, and a persecutor threatening to destroy both the infant and the good object. The infant projects love and idealizes the good object but goes beyond mere projection in trying to induce in the mother feelings toward the bad object for which she must take responsibility (that is, a process of projective identification). This stage of development Klein termed the *paranoid-schizoid position*. The infant may, as another defense mechanism for this less developed ego, seek to deny the reality of the persecutory object. While in our normal development we pass through this phase, this primitive defense against anxiety is a regressive reaction that, in a sense of always being available to us, is never transcended. The good objects in the developed superego come to represent the fantasized ego ideal and thus "the possibility of a return to narcissism" (Schwartz, 1990, p. 18).

In line with Klein's object-relations theory, it might be useful to understand the individual with whom one is having an online affair to be the good object. Given that the interactions that take place in cyberspace can often be seen as separate from the outside world (Whitty & Carr, 2006), it is potentially easier to split an online affair off from the rest of the individual's world. The online relationship can potentially cater to an unfettered, impotent fantasy that is difficult to measure up to in reality. Hence, the online affair can potentially lead to a narcissistic withdrawal.

It has been argued that offline infidelity occurs because there are problems in the relationship, or because of certain personality characteristics (see Fitness, 2001). Buss and Shackelford (1997) have identified some key reasons why people betray their partners, including complaints that one's partner sexualizes others, exhibits high levels of jealousy and possessiveness, is condescending, withholds sex, or abuses alcohol. These are perhaps the same reasons individuals are motivated to initiate online affairs. However, drawing from Klein's theory, it has been argued that online affairs are perhaps easier to maintain than offline affairs; that the online relationship can become idealized through the process of splitting, while simultaneously denying the bad aspects of the person one is having the affair with and at the same time the bad aspects in oneself. It is possibly easier to idealize an individual online (the good object) when one can more easily filter out the potential negative aspects of the relationship (the bad object). The relationship can be turned on or off at one's leisure and the communication content, to some extent, can be more easily controlled. Moreover, the Internet does provide an environment where it is easier to construct a more positive view of the self and avoid presenting the negative aspects of the self. In contrast, it is not so easy to indulge in one's fantasies of perfection in an offline affair, as one still has to deal with the real person. Given the nature of these affairs as psychologically different from offline affairs, it is argued later in this chapter that therapy needs to take into account these differences; however, before considering treatment approaches, it is important to examine exactly what is meant by Internet infidelity.

DEFINING INTERNET INFIDELITY

For a number of years, scholars considered whether Internet infidelity was a real phenomenon (e.g., Cooper, 2002; Maheu & Subotnik, 2001; Whitty, 2003b; Young, 1998). These days there is general agreement that people can and do cheat on their partners on the Internet. However, there are conflicting views on which behaviors might be considered to be unfaithful. Before considering this question, allow me first to highlight some useful definitions.

Shaw (1997) defined Internet infidelity as "of course, behaviorally different from other kinds of infidelity; however, the contributing factors and results are similar when we consider how it affects the way partners relate" (p. 29). A more specific definition has been offered by Young, Griffin-Shelley, Cooper, O'Mara, and Buchanan (2000), who stated that a cyber-affair is "a romantic and/or sexual relationship that is initiated via online contact and maintained predominantly through electronic conversations that occur through email and in virtual communities such as chat rooms, interactive games, or newsgroups" (p. 60). In contrast, Maheu and Subotnik (2001) provide a generic definition for infidelity:

> Infidelity happens when two people have a commitment and that commitment is broken—regardless of where, how or with whom it happens. Infidelity is the breaking of a promise with a real person, whether the sexual stimulation is derived from the virtual or the real world. (p. 101)

The Internet will continue to evolve, so a statement about the specific places online that individuals might cheat (e.g., e-mail, social networking sites, and so forth) is difficult to include in any definition of Internet infidelity. Nevertheless, as will be later argued in this chapter, it is also important to consider the nature of the space. Therefore, it is considered here that:

Internet infidelity occurs when the rules of the relationship are broken by acting inappropriately in an emotional and/or a sexual manner with at least one person other than one's partner. The rules might differ for different couples, but there are some fundamental rules that are often unspoken and are typical expectations of most committed relationships. When it comes to Internet infidelity, the Internet might be the exclusive, main, or partial space where the inappropriate emotional or sexual interactions take place.

UNFAITHFUL ACTS THAT TAKE PLACE ONLINE

As with offline infidelity, the types of behaviors that are considered unfaithful online are classified as either emotional or sexual. However, we need to be mindful that there is a range of sexual and emotional activities that one can engage in and that not all of these are necessarily considered to be unfaithful by all individuals.

Cybersex is one of the sexual acts that can be conducted online. Cybersex is generally understood to be involving "two online users engaging in private discourse about sexual fantasies. The dialogue is typically accompanied by sexual self-stimulation" (Young et al., 2000, p. 60). Another similar definition is that cybersex is "obtaining sexual gratification whilst interacting with another person online" (Whitty, 2003b, p. 573). Of course this does not need to be limited to two individuals. Previous research has consistently found this to be understood as an act of infidelity (Mileham, 2007; Parker & Wampler, 2003; Whitty, 2003b, 2005). This is not limited to studies that ask participants if they would be upset if they learned their partner was engaging in such activities. Mileham (2007), for example, interviewed 76 men and 10 women whom she had recruited from Yahoo!'s Married and Flirting and MSN's Married but Flirting chat rooms. Married people inhabit these sites and engage in cyber-flirting and cybersex and sometimes organize to meet offline. She found that some of these participants acknowledged that online activities could be perceived as unfaithful.

Another type of sexual act online that is considered infidelity is hot chatting (Whitty, 2003b). Durkin and Bryant (1995) have defined hot chatting as a kind of erotic talk that moves beyond lighthearted flirting. Parker and Wampler (2003) have found a range of other online sexual interactions that participants believed to be unfaithful, including interacting in adult chat rooms and becoming a member of an adult web site.

Interestingly, research is fairly consistent on whether pornography is considered unfaithful. While partners are typically unhappy to learn that their partner is being aroused by viewing pornography, in the main, viewing pornography online or offline is considered by few to be an act of infidelity (Whitty, 2003b). Parker and Wampler (2003) found that visiting adult chat rooms but not interacting, and visiting various adult web sites were also not considered to be relationship transgressions. Perhaps this has something to do with the passiveness of the act, where one is simply watching another rather than interacting with another. Moreover, there is no real possibility of this leading to any interactions with the person being watched.

Although the research is fairly consistent about the view that sexual acts such as cybersex and hot chatting are unfaithful, it is still important to question why this is the case. In previous research I have considered this question and drawn from research on offline infidelity to speculate a potential explanation (Whitty, 2003b, 2005). This research has found that "mental exclusivity" is as important as "sexual exclusivity" (Yarab & Allgeier, 1998). Roscoe, Cavanaugh, and Kennedy (1988) found that undergraduates believed that engaging in sexual interactions such as kissing, flirting, and petting with someone else other than their partner ought to be considered unfaithful. Moreover, Yarab, Sensibaugh, and Allgeier (1998) revealed an array of unfaithful sexual behaviors in addition to sexual intercourse, including passionately kissing, sexual fantasies, sexual attraction, and flirting. Interestingly, Yarab and Allgeier (1998) found that when considering sexual fantasies, the greater the threat of the sexual fantasy to the current relationship, the more likely the fantasy was to be rated as unfaithful. For instance, fantasizing about a partner's best friend was considered by most to be a greater threat, and therefore more unfaithful, than fantasizing about a movie star. Returning to the question posed earlier, the empirical research outlined here suggests that it is the sexual desire for another that is the act of betrayal. Hence, displays of that sexual desire as well as fantasizing about the object of one's desire can be upsetting for one's spouse. But this desire needs to be seen as potentially mutual. Therefore, if I have sexual fantasies about Brad Pitt or a male gigolo, then my partner is far less likely to be concerned than if I fantasize about having sex with his best friend or a stranger I have cybersex with online. Of course, not all sexual activities are deemed as equally upsetting. In my previous research, for example, it was found that sexual intercourse was rated slightly higher as an act of infidelity than cybersex (Whitty, 2003b). Hence, penetrative sex might be seen as a fait accompli and therefore more upsetting than other sexual activities.

Emotional infidelity can be just as upsetting a form of betrayal as sexual infidelity. Emotional infidelity is understood in the main to be falling in love with another person. It can also be understood as inappropriate emotional closeness with another, such as the sharing of intimate secrets. Emotional infidelity has been seen to be equally upsetting whether it takes place online or offline (Whitty, 2003b). In my previous work, where participants performed a story completion task, I found that emotional infidelity was expressed in the stories as much as sexual infidelity (Whitty, 2005). This is clearly illustrated in the following extract from this study:

"It is cheating," she said rather calmly.

"No, I'm not cheating. It's not like I'm bonking her anyway. You're the one I'm with and, like I said, I have *NO* intentions of meeting her." He hopped into bed.

"It's 'emotional' cheating," she said, getting annoyed.

"How so?" he asked, amusement showing in his eyes.

"Cheating isn't necessarily physical. That's one side of it. . . ." He pulled the sheets over himself and rolled over. "Well . . . I know you have not met her *yet*, that's why, but I'm still a little annoyed, Mark." She sat on the edge of the bed.

"Don't be mad. You're the one I love. So *how* is it emotional cheating?" He sat up.

"You're keeping stuff from me. Relationships are about trust! How can I trust you if you keep stuff from me about the 'Internet girl'?" (pp. 62–63)

INFIDELITY DATING SITES

As already highlighted, there are many different ways people can cheat on their partners in cyberspace. However, we also need to be mindful that the Internet can be used as a tool to locate someone with whom to conduct an offline affair. Online infidelity matchmaking sites are good examples of spaces where individuals can meet to find someone with whom to have an affair offline (either an ongoing affair or a one-night stand). These sites look and operate similarly to the sites set up for singles to meet partners. Of course, traditional online dating sites have also been used to locate others with whom to have one-night stands or ongoing affairs, but when they are, the persons seeking out the affairs are typically deceptive about their marital status. The infidelity online dating sites do not try to disguise the agenda of the site. For example, Marital Affair (n.d.) states that the site delivers "an online dating service for married and single people looking to increase activity in their private lifestyles with uncomplicated adult fun." The Ashley Madison Agency (n.d.), which claims to be the world's premier discreet dating service, has the slogan "Life is short, have an affair." The site Meet2cheat (n.d.) states that "since 1998, we have dedicated ourselves to the professional, serious and discrete facilitation of erotic adventures of all kinds on a national and international basis. Our experience and widely known service enable you to live out your fantasies in a fully uncomplicated way."

In a thematic analysis, I have compared the profiles of an infidelity dating site with a more generic online dating site (Whitty, 2008b). Some interesting similarities between the sites were that it was typical for individuals to include a list of their hobbies and interests, a shopping list of qualities they were looking for in another, and a statement that they were honest and genuine people. This is an example of a statement of honesty from one of the profiles on the infidelity dating site:

> I don't play games with people's emotions or lives. You're looking at the most realistic person who's searching for friendship and a possible future lover and soulmate.

An interesting difference was the obvious lack of photographs and the plea for secrecy. For example, one of the profiles on the infidelity site stated:

> Not looking for any strings other than those that being a good pal bring along. I am not interested in any boat rocking and discretion is a priority.

Those on the infidelity site were also much more likely to state that they were willing to travel for their date. As one wrote:

> Travel for work and away from home a lot, so anyone in the London, Surrey, or southeast, or anywhere else for that matter, who would like to get in touch, please do.

The emphasis on a good sexual relationship was more evident on the infidelity profiles. For example:

> PLEASE TAKE TIME TO READ MY PROFILE. first thing i am not a hunk ... but i am a funny guy AND I WILL MAKE YOU LAUGH PROMISED!! I AM ALSO GOOD IN BED ... i am missing one of the best parts SEX, my marriage is a shamble (my wife is not interested in any part of it and has not been for a long time we are only together for financial reasons). i have got a very high sex drive i'd like to find a woman 35/60 (looks unimportant) who likes sex and laughter.

Finally, an unexpected finding was the emphasis on a number of the infidelity profiles that they were moral individuals. As one person writes:

> Morals? How did that end up on here? Ok, we can still do what we're doing but take the moral high ground on others?!?! It's just a positioning exercise.

SOCIAL NETWORKING SITES

Social networking sites are another place that individuals could potentially locate others to have an affair with. These potential others could already be known to that person. For instance, a social networking site might be used to initiate flirtation with or learn more about a person than what they would typically self-disclose face-to-face (FtF). This might instill enough confidence in an individual to initiate an affair with another. In a brief report, Muise,

Christofides, and Desmarais (2009) found a significant relationship between the amount of time spent on Facebook and jealousy-related feelings experienced on Facebook. They found that it was the ambiguity in communication between a partner and one of the ex-partners that was more likely to trigger jealousy. One of their participants expressed this ambiguity as: "I have enough confidence in her [his partner] to know my partner is faithful, yet I can't help but second-guess myself when someone posts on her wall. ... It can contribute to feelings of you not really 'knowing' your partner" (p. 443). While the authors did not consider this, it may well be that this jealousy has some rational basis. The Internet has made it much easier for ex-partners and past lovers to reconnect, whereas previously the past relationship typically remained as part of one's history. Social networking sites allow one to reconnect. These places are often perceived to be private even though they are in a public space (Whitty & Joinson, 2009); consequently, more information could be revealed to others than would typically have been made known formerly.

USING THE INTERNET TO INITIATE AND FACILITATE AN OFFLINE AFFAIR

Much of the early research on Internet infidelity either assumed or found that many of these unfaithful activities were initiated between strangers. This obviously still takes place, and the online infidelity sites are a good example of this. However, as already considered with social networking sites, affairs these days can initiate online, even when the individuals know one another offline. Moreover, it could be argued that digital technologies have made it easier for affairs to take place offline. Instant Messenger might be used for erotic talk, and subtle text messages can be sent to organize a quick meeting. All this communication can easily take place in the home where one's spouse is present. So it is important to note that digital technologies have changed the nature of even more traditional offline affairs.

IT'S ALL FUN AND GAMES UNTIL SOMEONE LOSES A MARRIAGE

Morris (2008) reported the story of an English couple who divorced because of the husband's alter ego hot chatting with another woman in Second Life. Second Life is a massively multiplayer online role-playing game (MMORPG) where individuals create their own avatars (persona) and interact in a fantasy world. Morris wrote that the couple initially met online, after which their avatars become partners in Second Life—that is, until Taylor (aka Laura Skye in Second Life) caught her husband, Pollard (aka Dave Barmy in Second Life) having cybersex with a prostitute in Second Life. As Morris reports:

> Horrified, Taylor ended the online relationship between Skye and Barmy but stayed with Pollard in real life.

It was then that fact and fiction really began to collide. Taylor decided to test Dave Barmy—and thus Pollard's loyalty—by turning to a virtual female private eye called Markie Macdonald. A "honey trap" was set up in which an alluring avatar chatted Barmy up. He passed the test with flying colors, talking about Laura Skye all night. Barmy and Skye got back together in cyberspace, marrying in a ceremony held in a pretty tropical grove. In real life at their flat in Cornwall, Taylor wept as she watched the service, and in 2005—real life again—the couple married in the less glamorous surroundings of the St. Austell registry office. But Taylor sensed something was wrong and eventually found Dave Barmy chatting affectionately to a woman who was not Laura Skye. She found it even more disturbing than his earlier tryst, as there seemed genuine affection in it and—in real life—she filed for divorce.

Although Taylor obviously believed that her husband had cheated on her, we still need to consider whether the majority of people would see things in the same light. In her case the two lived intense lives together in a fantasy world (considered to be a game). Perhaps Taylor found it difficult to separate play from reality. Research has yet to determine whether there are some activities online that are considered to be confined to the realm of play and hence do not impact on real life. However, it would seem to be an important question to investigate.

THERAPEUTIC IMPLICATIONS

Numerous treatment approaches have been developed to assist individuals and couples affected by Internet infidelity. In a thorough review of therapists' assessment and treatment of Internet infidelity, Hertlein and Piercy (2008) pointed out a variety of approaches by both male and female therapists. Therapists' treatment varied depending on their age, gender, and religiosity. Importantly, Hertlein and Piercy stated:

> The spectrum of Internet infidelity can include a wide variety of behaviors. On one end of the spectrum may be spending time on the computer rather than one's primary relationship, while at the other end may the physical meeting and subsequent intercourse of two people who met online. Some behaviors that are considered infidelity by one couple may not be considered infidelity or problematic by another couple. (p. 491)

As this chapter highlights, digital technologies can be used in numerous ways to initiate, conduct, and facilitate infidelities. What is unique about online infidelities is the greater potential for online affairs to become more idealized. Moreover, the rules of what is a relationship transgression are less clear with regard to some online behavior. While individuals might be equally upset by sexual activities conducted online versus offline, Whitty and Quigley (2008) argue that cybersex is nonetheless qualitatively different from sexual intercourse and these different understandings need further investigation.

Where the infidelity takes place is also unique. Its being conducted in one's own home, for instance, could arguably have quite a different impact on a relationship, especially with regard to reestablishing trust.

Gender differences have been found for why people cheat as well as which type of infidelity is more upsetting. Parker and Wampler's 2003 study, which considered sexual online activities, found that women viewed these activities more seriously than did men. My own study found that women overall were more likely to believe that sexual acts were an act of betrayal than were men (Whitty, 2003b). Although more research is needed to investigate gender differences, the available research suggests that any treatment rationale should be mindful of these differences.

This chapter has highlighted the range of ways individuals can utilize digital technologies to conduct affairs; however, we also need to be aware of the range of ways individuals can be caught out via digital technologies. Partners could check their spouses' text messages or IM history if they are suspicious of any infidelities. There are numerous software packages available that monitor and record other people's PC activity, including viewing and recording people's e-mails, chat messages, and web sites visited, as well as the monitoring and recording of keystrokes, and even individuals' passwords. Spytech online (n.d.) advertises its spy software as a way to catch out one's cheating spouse:

> Our monitoring software can quickly detect and give you the evidence you need to prove that your spouse is remaining faithful to you—or cheating on you. Our spy software tools, such as SpyAgent and Realtime-Spy, can operate in total stealth—defeating the built-in Windows task manager and popular spyware detection tools. These abilities mean you will not have to worry about your spouse discovering you are monitoring them—and even if you inform them they will still not be able to tell how. Logs can even be stored in an encrypted format, so they can only be viewed with our software.

The question for suspicious partners is whether they should utilize digital technologies to check on their spouse if they are suspicious. Previous research has found that how an infidelity is revealed has important implications for the future of the relationship. Afifi, Falato, and Weiner (2001) found that unsolicited partner disclosure was beneficial because it allowed the transgressor full opportunity to apologize, provide accounts, and employ repair strategies. Unsolicited third-party discovery and red-handed discovery gave far less opportunity for relationship repair. Although more research is needed on the discovery of infidelities, Afifi et al.'s research suggests that employing digital technologies to spy on one's partner is not the best solution if the couple hopes to repair the relationship.

Discovery is not the only issue that is important to consider with regard to relationship repair after an infidelity is revealed. As with any relationship transgression, the reasons why it happened in the first place need to be considered. How blame is portioned as well as how trust is reestablished also need to be addressed. With regard to Internet infidelity, it has been argued that the computer itself is at times blamed, and computers are sometimes taken out of the home (Whitty & Carr, 2005, 2006). While this approach might have been effective in earlier days, these days, with the ubiquity and easy access of the Internet, such a strategy is almost impossible to employ. New treatment approaches, therefore, need to consider the evolving nature of the Internet and how best to cope with it in the lives of spouses who have been affected by Internet infidelity.

CONCLUSION

There is much we still need to learn about Internet infidelity. Moreover, we need to be constantly aware of the changing nature of the Internet. Web 2.0 has brought about a much more interactive Internet (using applications to increase interactivity), and it will continue to develop in more sophisticated ways. Social networking sites and the applications on mobile phones are good examples of how the Web has changed to be more interactive. This form of Web is more social and hence could result in more infidelities. However, on the other side of the coin, this new technology allows one to check up on and monitor one's partner more than ever before. The question for therapists to consider is whether such monitoring is a psychologically healthy activity (especially given that it is symbolic of a lack of trust). Although this chapter has focused on the issue of Internet infidelities, because of the ubiquity of cyberspace the nature of any form of infidelity needs to be completely reexamined. Affairs are potentially easy to initiate and maintain because of digital technologies, and these technologies must surely play a significant role in most forms of infidelity.

REFERENCES

Afifi, W. A., Falato, W. L., & Weiner, J. L. (2001). Identity concerns following a severe relational transgression: The role of discovery method for the relational outcomes of infidelity. *Journal of Social and Personal Relationships, 18*(2), 291–308.

Ashley Madison Agency. (n.d.). Retrieved December 22, 2009, from www.AshleyMadison.com/

Buss, D. M., & Shackelford, T. K. (1997). Susceptibility to infidelity in the first year of marriage. *Journal of Research in Personality, 31*, 193–221.

Cooper, A. (2002). *Sex & the Internet: A guidebook for clinicians*. New York: Brunner-Routledge.

Durkin, K. F., & Bryant, C. D. (1995). "Log on to sex": Some notes on the carnal computer and erotic cyberspace as an emerging research frontier. *Deviant Behavior: An Interdisciplinary Journal, 16*, 179–200.

Fitness, J. (2001). Betrayal, rejection, revenge and forgiveness: An interpersonal script approach. In M. Leary (Ed.), *Interpersonal rejection* (pp. 73–103). New York: Oxford University Press.

Hampton, K., & Wellman, B. (2003). Neighboring in Netville: How the Internet supports community and social capital in a wired suburb. *City and Community, 2*(4), 277–311.

Hertlein, K. M., & Piercy, F. P. (2008). Therapists' assessment and treatment of Internet infidelity cases. *Journal of Marital and Family Therapy, 34*(4), 481–497.

Klein, M. (1986). *The selected works of Melanie Klein* (J. Mitchell, Ed.). London: Penguin Books.

Maheu, M., & Subotnik, R. (2001). *Infidelity on the Internet: Virtual relationships and real betrayal*. Naperville, IL: Sourcebooks.

Marital Affair. (n.d.). Retrieved December 22, 2009, from http://www. maritalaffair. co.uk/married.html

McKenna, K. Y. A., & Bargh, J. A. (1998). Coming out in the age of Internet: Identity "de-marginalization" through virtual group participation. *Journal of Personality and Social Psychology, 75*, 681–694.

McKenna, K. Y. A., Green, A. S., & Gleason, M. E. J. (2002). Relationship formation on the Internet: What's the big attraction? *Journal of Social Issues, 58*, 9–31.

Meet2cheat. (n.d.). Retrieved December 22, 2009, from http://www.meet2cheat. co.uk/advantage/index.htm

Mileham, B. L. A. (2007). Online infidelity in Internet chat rooms: An ethnographic exploration. *Computers in Human Behavior, 23*(1), 11–21.

Morris, S. (2008, November 13). Second Life affair leads to real life divorce. Guardian.co.uk. Retrieved December 22, 2009, from http://www.guardian. co.uk/technology/2008/nov/13/second-life-divorce

Muise, A., Christofides, E., & Desmarais, S. (2009). More information than you ever wanted: Does Facebook bring out the green-eyed monster of jealousy? *CyberPsychology & Behavior, 12*(4), 441–444.

Parker, T. S., & Wampler, K. S. (2003). How bad is it? Perceptions of the relationship impact of different types of Internet sexual activities. *Contemporary Family Therapy, 25*(4), 415–429.

Parks, M. R., & Floyd, K. (1996). Making friends in cyberspace. *Journal of Communication, 46*, 80–97.

Roscoe, B., Cavanaugh, L., & Kennedy, D. (1988). Dating infidelity: Behaviors, reasons, and consequences. *Adolescence, 23*, 35–43.

Schwartz, H. (1990). *Narcissistic process and corporate decay: The theory of the organization ideal*. New York: New York University.

Shaw, J. (1997). Treatment rationale for Internet infidelity. *Journal of Sex Education and Therapy, 22*(1), 29–34.

Spytech online. (n.d.). Retrieved March 29, 2006, from http://www.spytech-web. com/spouse-monitoring.shtml

Tidwell, L. C., & Walther, J. B. (2002). Computer-mediated communication effects on disclosure, impressions, and interpersonal evaluations: Getting to know one another a bit at a time. *Human Communication Research, 28*, 317–348.

Walther, J. B. (1996). Computer-mediated communication: Impersonal, interpersonal and hyperpersonal interaction. *Communication Research, 23*, 3–43.

Walther, J. B. (2007). Selective self-presentation in computer-mediated communication: Hyperpersonal dimensions of technology. *Computers in Human Behavior, 23*, 2538–2557.

Whitty, M. T. (2003a). Cyber-flirting: Playing at love on the Internet. *Theory and Psychology, 13*(3), 339–357.

Whitty, M. T. (2003b). Pushing the wrong buttons: Men's and women's attitudes towards online and offline infidelity. *CyberPsychology & Behavior, 6*(6), 569–579.

Whitty, M. T. (2005). The "realness" of cyber-cheating: Men and women's representations of unfaithful Internet relationships. *Social Science Computer Review, 23*(1), 57–67.

Whitty, M. T. (2008a). Revealing the "real" me, searching for the "actual" you: Presentations of self on an Internet dating site. *Computers in Human Behavior, 24*, 1707–1723.

Whitty, M. T. (2008b). Self presentation across a range of online dating sites: From generic sites to prison sites. Keynote address, London Lectures 2008, December 9, 2008.

Whitty, M. T., & Carr, A. N. (2005). Taking the good with the bad: Applying Klein's work to further our understandings of cyber-cheating. *Journal of Couple and Relationship Therapy, 4*(2/3), 103–115.

Whitty, M. T., & Carr, A. N. (2006). *Cyberspace romance: The psychology of online relationships*. Basingstoke, UK: Palgrave Macmillan.

Whitty, M. T., & Gavin, J. (2001). Age/sex/location: Uncovering the social cues in the development of online relationships. *CyberPsychology & Behavior, 4*(5), 623–630.

Whitty, M. T., & Joinson, A. N. (2009). *Truth, lies, and trust on Internet*. London: Routledge/Psychology Press.

Whitty, M. T., & Quigley, L. (2008). Emotional and sexual infidelity offline and in cyberspace. *Journal of Marital and Family Therapy, 34*(4), 461–468.

Yarab, P. E., & Allgeier, E. (1998). Don't even think about it: The role of sexual fantasies as perceived unfaithfulness in heterosexual dating relationships. *Journal of Sex Education and Therapy, 23*(3), 246–254.

Yarab, P. E., Sensibaugh, C. C., & Allgeier, E. (1998). More than just sex: Gender differences in the incidence of self-defined unfaithful behavior in heterosexual dating relationships. *Journal of Psychology & Human Sexuality, 10*(2), 45–57.

Young, K. S. (1998). *Caught in the Net: How to recognize the signs of Internet addiction and a winning strategy for recovery*. New York: John Wiley & Sons.

Young, K. S., Griffin-Shelley, E., Cooper, A., O'Mara, J., & Buchanan, J. (2000). Online infidelity: A new dimension in couple relationships with implications for evaluation and treatment. *Sexual Addiction & Compulsivity, 7*, 59–74.

CHAPTER 12

Twelve-Step Recovery in Inpatient Treatment for Internet Addiction

SHANNON CHRISMORE, ED BETZELBERGER,
LIBBY BIER, and TONYA CAMACHO

T HE DISEASE of chemical dependency (i.e., signs and symptoms, consequences, treatment, etc.) is well documented. Less has been documented regarding problematic Internet usage, specifically the use of inpatient treatment when working with those individuals diagnosed with Internet addiction. The purpose of this chapter is to examine the use of an inpatient treatment model used in a treatment center treating chemical dependency and process addictions (including gambling, Internet, video game, shopping/spending, sex, and food addictions, as well as chronic pain with addiction). This chapter also explores the use of a group format, not only in professional settings but also in the 12-step community. In order to better understand the uses of treatment and group therapy of persons suffering from Internet addiction, an initial overview will be given regarding Internet addiction, Emotions Anonymous (EA), as well as special populations. At present, Internet addiction has not been recognized by the *Diagnostic and Statistical Manual of Mental Disorders* (*DSM-IV-TR*) (American Psychiatric Association, 2000), and there is some debate about its inclusion in *DSM-V* (Block, 2008). Many terms have been used to refer to this behavior, such as *compulsive Internet use*, *Internet overuse*, and *Internet misuse*. For the purposes of this chapter, *Internet/computer addiction* will be used interchangeably with these terms.

In 1996, the Illinois Institute for Addiction Recovery (IIAR) began treating those suffering from Internet addiction after seeing the power of screening

We wish to acknowledge the following for their assistance on this chapter: Pam Hillyard, Director; Phil Scherer, Site Manager; Coleen Moore, Marketing and Admissions Manager; and Bryan Denure, Site Manager.

for other process addictions, especially pathological gambling. At the time, pay-per-minute Internet access through sites such as America Online (AOL) contributed to significant financial debt among individuals who were struggling to control their Internet usage. Please note that for the remaining sections of this chapter we are focusing on the IIAR's experience in treating those suffering from Internet/computer addiction. Therefore, only the IIAR's recommendations and strategies for treatment will be discussed. Other treatment approaches are outside the realm of this chapter.

IMPACT OF INTERNET ADDICTION

While most employers provide Internet access to their employees in hopes of increasing productivity, research supports a growing concern about compulsive Internet usage while at work. Harris Interactive, Inc. (2005) conducted a survey of employees and human resources (HR) managers regarding employee Internet use. They found that nearly one-third of time spent on the Internet is not related to work; 80% of companies reported that their employees had abused their Internet privileges in various ways, such as downloading pornography; and employees rated online shopping, news, pornography, gambling, and auctions as the most addictive online activities in addition to e-mailing and instant messaging. Internet misuse is costing more than $85 billion a year in reduced productivity. However, this does not take into account family costs such as divorce, domestic violence, abuse, time away from family activities, or suicide, to name a few. What also needs to be considered in this cost are the consequences of drug and alcohol dependence. A dual diagnosis of drug and alcohol dependence was present in 41% of a sample of patients treated for Internet addiction at the Illinois Institute for Addiction Recovery (Scherer, 2009). These findings should be taken with caution, however, because most of the individuals treated for Internet addiction at the IIAR initially came to treatment for a drug or alcohol problem, and the presence of an Internet addiction was detected through screening tools. Depressive symptoms are also common among individuals with Internet addiction. Of those treated at IIAR, 88% had a dual disorder in the depression spectrum (e.g., bipolar disorder, dysthymic disorder, or major depressive disorder) (Scherer, 2009). Depressive symptoms are strongly associated with pathological Internet usage, and those with increased levels of depression are more susceptible to becoming addicted to the Internet (Ha et al., 2007; Young & Rodgers, 1998).

Not only entertainment, but also concerns come with society's increased reliance on technology and the Internet over time. Overall, most people are able to browse the Internet, converse via instant messages or in chat rooms, or play online interactive video games for social or entertainment purposes, experiencing no negative consequences. However, there are those people who suffer consequences related to their Internet behaviors when they lose control and end up engaging in problematic or even pathological use of the Internet.

This is where professionals and 12-step groups are available to offer assistance and support.

EMOTIONS ANONYMOUS

In putting together the IIAR treatment program for Internet/computer addiction, there was a dilemma. As a 12-step-based program, the IIAR had to find some way of applying the 12-step principles to this rather new concept of addiction to the Internet/computer.

Process Addiction = Chemical Addictions
- Loss of control.
- Unsuccessful attempts to cut down or stop the behavior.
- A great deal of time spent thinking about or engaging in the behavior.
- Continuing the behavior despite related consequences.
- Withdrawal symptoms such as irritability, headaches, or restlessness.
- A need for increased amounts of the substance or behavior.
- Changes in social, occupational, or recreational activities as a result of the behavior.

Internet addiction, like chemical addictions, is a primary, progressive disease.

Making the Diagnosis
- Attempts at control: Y or N
- Dishonesty related to computer use: Y or N
- Impairment of significant life areas: Y or N
- Questionable behavior: Y or N
- Increase in tolerance: Y or N
- Euphoria and guilt: Y or N
- Withdrawal syndrome: Y or N
- Preoccupation: Y or N
- Escape and relief from computer use: Y or N

At the time, there was relatively minimal literature on the subject of addiction to the computer and/or Internet and certainly no recovery program designed around the 12 steps. The IIAR theorized that many people becoming obsessed with this rather new technology were also suffering from mental health disorders such as depression or anxiety or social isolation.

The book *Emotions Anonymous* was discovered. "Emotions Anonymous is a fellowship of people who share their experiences, feelings, strengths, weaknesses, and hopes with one another in order to solve their emotional problems and to discover a way to live at peace with unsolved problems" (Emotions Anonymous Fellowship, 2007).

Emotions Anonymous (EA) started in 1971 in Minneapolis, Minnesota, but its roots go back to 1965 when Marion F. read a newspaper article about an organization that had adopted the 12 steps of Alcoholics Anonymous (AA) for overcoming emotional problems (Emotions Anonymous Fellowship, 1995). Marion had suffered for years with emotional and physical problems. Thinking this might be an answer for her, she was disappointed to learn there were no meetings of this group in the Minneapolis area. Marion F.'s journey through recovery led her to start the first Neurotics Anonymous group in Minneapolis in 1966, which ultimately led to the founding of Emotions Anonymous. As the EA book went to print for its latest printing in 2007, there were over 1,300 EA groups in over 35 countries around the world (Emotions Anonymous Fellowship, 2007).

EA states openly in its literature that "all are welcome in EA . . . we may have come to EA simply because life was uncomfortable and we are looking for a better way. Or, we may have been in the depths of despair . . . the symptoms that led us to seek help are diverse" (Emotions Anonymous Fellowship, 1995). Philosophically, EA appears to be welcoming to a wide variety of people, but with the structure (steps) and guidance (traditions) of the AA program. While it has been a struggle finding face-to-face meetings for IIAR for patients to attend in their home areas, these patients have found the book to be invaluable. Patients report having similar experiences from reading the EA book that are often heard from alcoholics about the AA Big Book.

Because fewer EA meetings are available, the clinician should require those suffering from Internet addiction to seek assistance and support from other 12-step meetings such as AA and utilize their desire to not use today to attend the meeting. Those suffering from Internet addiction often struggle to identify with alcoholics and other addicts and would rather not attend anything but EA if they have not experienced problems with chemicals in the past; however, because of fewer EA meetings and the high risk of relapse, it is imperative for individuals suffering from Internet addiction to receive continued support of the 12-step program whether or not it is solely from EA. Some people suffering from Internet addiction choose to abstain from all mood-altering chemicals and behaviors in order to avoid the potential for cross-addiction (replacing one addiction with another). Sometimes it may also be helpful for these individuals to obtain two sponsors—one through EA (the sponsor can be of the opposite sex if a sponsor of the same sex is not available) and one for step work (this one needs to be a same-sex sponsor from another 12-step program).

EA does not have a specific group for family members, such as Al-Anon or Gam-Anon. However, family members and significant others are encouraged to attend a 12-step support group in order to cope with their loved one's addiction, as well as learn how to set healthy boundaries. Family members of persons suffering from Internet addiction are encouraged to reach out to groups such as Families Anonymous, Codependents Anonymous, or Al-Anon. These groups provide a place for family members to share their experiences and receive support from others who are dealing with their loved ones' addictive behaviors as well.

SPECIAL POPULATIONS

There are discrepancies about the typical profile of an Internet addict. Stereotypically, the Internet addict is thought to closely resemble a so-called computer geek—a young, introverted male who is knowledgeable about computers. However, fewer than half (47%) of the patients treated at the IIAR for Internet addiction fit into the category of males under 30 years old (Scherer, 2009). However, when all patients under 30 years old are considered, the percentage rises to 65%, and when broken down into gender, 71% were males (Scherer, 2009). While these results represent a very small sample size and cannot necessarily be generalized to the entire population of Internet addictions, it is possible that an Internet addict is more likely to be male or to be a young person but not necessarily a young male. Other studies support the notion that males are more likely to be problematic Internet users (Mottram & Fleming, 2009).

A clear set of personality characteristics predicting who will become problematic Internet users does not exist. It is also unclear whether individuals with certain characteristics are drawn to spending prolonged periods of time on the Internet or they develop these characteristics as a result of becoming addicted. However, research does support certain characteristics that are more common in individuals with problematic Internet usage. Internet addicts typically spend more time online, are members of more online clubs and organizations, and make more new, online friends than nonaddicted Internet users (Shek, Tang, & Lo, 2009). Not only are these individuals spending more time engaged in Internet-related activities, but they are also substituting Internet-related activities for other recreational activities such as doing things with friends, watching television, and so on. Other studies suggest that individuals with abstract thinking skills may be drawn to the stimulating nature of the Internet (Young & Rodgers, 1998). There is some debate about whether extroversion is related to developing Internet addiction. While individuals are engaging in online activities alone, the interactive nature of the Internet may provide enough stimulation and contact with other people to satisfy the extrovert. Introverted individuals, by contrast, may be overwhelmed by the connectedness with other people online. Shy, introverted individuals may find comfort in the anonymity afforded to them through the use of an online medium, but it still appears that they struggle to initiate conversations and self-disclosure (Brunet & Schmidt, 2008).

FEMALES

In the general population, the percentage of women using the Internet still falls slightly below the percentage of men (Fallows, 2005). Studies conducted on Internet addiction indicate that rates are higher among men than women (Zhang, Amos, & McDowell, 2008). These findings can also be supported by those seeking treatment for Internet addiction (29% females versus 71% males) at the Illinois Institute for Addiction Recovery (Scherer, 2009). Women have been more likely to be involved in online activities that are seen as social by the user. Social activities online would include chat rooms and instant messaging, as well as social networking web sites such as Facebook, MySpace, LinkedIn, and Twitter. Women may also find themselves escaping the stressors of life through general Web surfing. Typically, women with Internet/computer addiction appear to suffer from family and relationship problems to a greater degree than their male counterparts. Many women are the primary caretakers for children in the household. As they are engaged in more problematic use of the Internet, they are pulled away from family activities and other caretaking roles. This absence is likely to have a more negative impact on the family system when the female Internet addict is the primary caretaker. This could also be a contributing factor to why fewer women enter into treatment for Internet addiction.

TEENAGERS

Teenagers typically present to treatment as a result of problems with online gaming activities, and are most often male (67% male versus 33% female). Of all patients treated for Internet addiction at the IIAR over the past three years, only 35% fell into the category of aged 19 years and younger. When the age range is adjusted to include all persons under 30 years old, the percentage changes drastically, with 65% of the total patients treated falling into this category (Scherer, 2009). Most male teenagers treated at the IIAR for Internet addiction over the past three years have been treated for online gaming. Teens are more likely than older Internet users to engage in games known as massively multiplayer online role-playing games (MMORPGs), in which multiple players connect to a common server or Internet source to all play the same game at the same time (Smahel, Blinka, & Ledabyl, 2008). These games are intense and highly interactive and can involve countless hours of online play, all of which places individuals at greater risk of becoming addicted. Players are able to communicate through text on the screen and/or through audio. Common MMORPGs include World of Warcraft, EverQuest, Ultima Online, Dungeons and Dragons, and Final Fantasy. If the individual suffering from Internet/computer addiction does not play MMORPGs, he is most likely to play individual computer or console games such as Nintendo, Game Boy, Xbox, and PlayStation.

Over the past three years, there have been few female teens ($n = 2$) who have entered into treatment for Internet addiction at IIAR. These teenage females have played a combination of MMORPGs and Sims games. Sims games are simulation games that allow players to create their own new identities or personas and watch the new characters play out their lives. Teenage females are more likely to engage in the social networking web sites such as MySpace than play Internet games.

SCREENING AND ASSESSMENT TOOLS

This current section identifies screening and assessment tools as well as other issues of a person suffering from Internet/computer addiction. The first step in treatment is spent gathering information through psychological screenings, a biopsychosocial interview, medical history, and a concerned person questionnaire (CPQ), among other information-gathering techniques.

Although the *DSM-IV-TR* does not specifically recognize Internet addiction as a distinct diagnosis, it does allow for the inclusion of such addictive behaviors to be coded under the Impulse-Control Disorder, Not Otherwise Specified (NOS) diagnosis. As such, it is important for clinicians to be acutely aware of the diagnostic features present under the array of impulse-control disorders. When assessing an individual who is engaging in excessive Internet use, it is important to have a clear definition of what constitutes an NOS diagnosis. Unlike the other formal diagnoses under the category of impulse-control disorders, the NOS diagnosis does not specifically identify a set of criteria that need to be met for a formal diagnosis. Instead, the *DSM-IV-TR* merely offers a guideline to clinicians rather than a clear set of criteria. During the assessment process, it is the clinician's responsibility to review the information with the treatment team to ensure proper diagnosis by ruling out other potential presenting disorders before an NOS diagnosis can be made. Presenting features of any impulse-control disorder include inability to resist urges to engage in destructive behaviors and/or euphoric feelings either during or after the behavior. As with other addictive behaviors, individuals experience severe consequences in various aspects of their lifestyles. They frequently experience relationship discord as a result of excessive Internet use, as well as problems with employment and loss of interest in other activities they once found important.

In treating individuals suffering from Internet addiction, it is imperative to screen for other addictions, such as alcohol, drugs, sex, pathological gambling, food, and compulsive shopping/spending, as well as other mental health disorders. Often, individuals will report they need to be assessed for Internet/computer addiction when they are engaging in online addictive behaviors related to gambling, shopping, or sex. It is important to determine whether use of the Internet or computer is problematic, or if the individual is utilizing the Internet as his or her vehicle to engage in pathological gambling, compulsive shopping/spending, or downloading pornography. In these cases, treatment for Internet addiction would miss the underlying behaviors that are problematic.

It is estimated that 86% of those suffering from Internet addiction have some other *DSM-IV-TR* diagnosis present (Block, 2008). Of those individuals treated for Internet addiction at the IIAR over the past three years, 94% were also diagnosed with another *DSM-IV-TR* diagnosis; 81% of these individuals had some type of mood disorder (major depressive disorder, dysthymic disorder, or bipolar disorder); 44% had a chemical dependency diagnosis; and 56% had another process addiction diagnosis (compulsive shopping/spending, pathological gambling, sexual addiction, or eating disorder).

A psychiatric evaluation is appropriate and essential to determine any co-morbidity issues, as well as need for medication. As discussed earlier, there are extremely high rates of comorbidity among this population, and a thorough psychiatric evaluation can provide both the patient and the clinician with valuable information for treatment planning and relapse prevention. This evaluation may also determine if a patient is at risk of harm to self or others especially during this time. For patients identifying thoughts of harming themselves or another person, it would also be advisable to complete a suicide risk assessment to determine precautions necessary and have the patient contract for safety.

Along with the psychiatric evaluation and the psychological screenings, it is helpful to complete a mental status examination to determine the patient's orientation to person, place, and time, as well as screen for any organic disorders. These screening tools will assist in the development of the patient's treatment plans. It is important to treat the whole person; if not, it is an injustice to the patient and his or her risk of relapse will increase. If a clinician is not aware of other addictions or mental health diagnoses and is treating only the disease of alcoholism, but the patient also suffers from Internet addiction, the patient may remain sober from alcohol while Internet usage increases. Therefore, the patient is not truly in recovery. The clinician may experience confusion, wondering why the patient remains unhealthy and does not appear to be making progress.

Within the first 24 hours of treatment, the nurse completes a nursing assessment and the attending physician completes a history and physical. Some considerations about medical well-being in working with a person suffering from Internet addiction might be:

- A diabetic engaging in compulsive or problematic Internet usage who does not leave the computer to eat or check blood sugars and, as a result of this, needs medical attention to regulate his or her blood sugars.
- A person suffering from Internet addiction who is neglecting to take his or her blood pressure medications and, therefore, experiences high blood pressure; when the patient comes into treatment, he or she needs to be evaluated for the appropriateness of medication and continued monitoring.

The biopsychosocial assessment allows for the therapist to gather more information from the patient to determine a course of treatment. This assessment covers history on the following issues: family, legal, educational, occupational, sexual, abuse (as well as any domestic violence issues), chemical or other addictive behavior, emotional, spiritual, and environmental (e.g., Where do you live? Who has financial control in your household? Are there any financial concerns while in treatment?). Recreation/leisure activities prior to coming into treatment are also assessed, as well as goals for after treatment and the patient's strengths and weaknesses.

The Virtual Addiction Test (VAT) developed by David Greenfield (1999) is just one particular screening tool that can be used to examine the potential for Internet addiction in a wider segment of patients. Using a tool such as the VAT offers several advantages to patients who may be struggling to identify their Internet use as problematic. It provides patients with a noninvasive means of looking at their behavior. Given the resistance many patients experience, such an opportunity for personal reflection can provide for more open dialogue during the formal assessment process. The screen is short and easy to understand, allowing the patient to clearly and concisely answer questions "yes" or "no" without getting into heady rationalizations for their behavior. When the screen is used as an adjunct to the formal assessment, it can help guide the clinician to identify areas of concern. Conversely, it provides the clinician with valuable information into the potential insight or lack thereof into the problematic behavior. Screening tools such as the VAT are also valuable when screening other patients who present with other impulse-control disorders or substance-related disorders. As with any comprehensive assessment process, screening for other potential disorders is important and can be done easily through the use of such screens.

Another screening tool, the Internet Addiction Test (IAT), can be used to determine the level of severity of a person's addictive use of the Internet (Young, 2006). This is a self-administered, 20-item test, in which patients can indicate the frequency of their Internet-related behaviors and the degree to which these behaviors have impacted their lives. For example, the IAT asks a patient to explore loss of control, dishonesty, and secrecy about Internet usage; inability to cut down; and negative emotions, to name a few. The IAT can provide clinicians with an idea about the extent of a patient's addictive Internet behaviors and can be used as a screening tool to suggest further assessment. It is also the first measure to be validated in English (Widyanto & McMurren, 2004); Italian (Ferraro, Caci, D'Amico, & Di Blasi, 2007); and French (Khazaal et al., 2008).

Another tool that can facilitate gathering more information to determine the course of treatment is having the significant other and/or other family member(s) complete a concerned person questionnaire (CPQ). The CPQ is similar to the detail of the biopsychosocial interview for the patient, but the CPQ can be completed by the concerned persons and not necessarily in an interview format. It is not to be used as a validated diagnostic tool, but instead contains a series of questions that concerned persons in a patient's life complete in order to provide their perspective of how the addiction has affected the patient's life. It also offers the therapist insight into how this disease is affecting the family member(s) or other concerned persons.

This information can be useful in breaking through the initial denial that a patient may be experiencing when entering treatment (Illinois Institute for Addiction Recovery, 2008).

Although these screening tools may appear to gather similar information and thus perhaps be redundant, they assist the therapist in getting a clear picture of the patient. An individual suffering from Internet addiction is often dealing with a significantly high level of denial about the negative impact that the behavior has had on his or her life. These tools allow the therapist to determine discrepancies within the self-report of the patient and to explore the impact the problematic Internet usage has had on the patient's life, which will allow the therapist to confront the patient and bring him or her to the reality of his or her disease.

Screening and assessment tools assist the clinician in determining the appropriate placement for the patient in treatment. The guidelines established by the American Society of Addiction Medicine (ASAM, 2001) can be useful in evaluating a patient's stability across six dimensions: acute intoxication/withdrawal potential, biomedical complications and conditions, emotional/behavioral/cognitive complications and conditions, readiness to change, relapse/continued use/continued problem potential, and recovery environment. Patients suffering from Internet addiction may be experiencing biomedical complications as a result of their excessive Internet use and lack of attention to medical issues, but they are almost always experiencing problems with respect to emotional, behavioral, or cognitive complications, readiness to change, relapse potential, and recovery environment. Placement in an inpatient or partial hospitalization program allows for an integrated treatment team approach in which both biomedical and psychiatric concerns are addressed, as well as providing a highly structured environment for the individual to learn about addiction and begin to progress through the stages of change.

INPATIENT/RESIDENTIAL TREATMENT

Within the first 72 hours of treatment, the client will be given the initial assignment to define what abstinence from the addiction means and to engage in a dialogue about his or her definition of abstinence from problematic behaviors related to the Internet/computer. Typically, this definition becomes more in-depth as the patient progresses through treatment, starts to receive education about the disease of addiction, and becomes more willing to look at the impact of Internet/computer overuse in his or her life.

Treating Internet and computer addiction is explained within the first day of treatment along with the 12-step concept and Third Tradition of Alcoholics Anonymous. All patients are expected to abstain from alcohol, drugs, and other addictive behaviors while in treatment. The client is given a copy of the *Emotions Anonymous* book, as well as copies of the Alcoholics Anonymous (AA) and Narcotics Anonymous (NA) texts to provide the origin and background of the 12-step philosophy. Other assignments include beginning with Step 1 to explore the patient's concept of powerlessness and unmanageability related to his or her Internet/computer use, assignments regarding denial, and the patient's feelings about beginning the recovery process. These are then completed and reviewed with the counselor by the end of the first week. The patient also needs to be involved in other group therapy related to the addiction, as well as be involved within the overall milieu of the unit (including, but not limited to, education on various types of addiction, not just Internet/computer addiction).

A rehabilitation meeting for the development of a master treatment plan is scheduled within seven days of admission. During this meeting, treatment team members (i.e., counselors, clinical coordinator, nurse, medical director, patient financial service representative, and possible consulting physicians) review diagnosis and discuss pertinent information gathered from the patient during the initial assessment, nursing assessment, and biopsychosocial interview, and information from collateral sources. At this meeting, a master treatment plan is developed that outlines goals, objectives, and methods the patient is to complete for preparation for outpatient services. This master treatment plan is reviewed with the patient within 24 hours of the team meeting.

In addition to the standard counselor-led group therapy sessions, persons suffering from Internet addiction attend groups specifically for this process addiction. This allows time for specific discussions related to their addiction. They will attend the Internet/computer addiction process addiction groups twice a week and work on the unique challenges they face with having an Internet addiction. Specific issues discussed could focus on how the patients' relationships at home, work, school, and socially have been negatively impacted by their addiction, as well as placing specific focus on their isolative behaviors.

There is also a focus on discussing the patient's perceived need for Internet/computer use, as well as barriers to be put in place when Internet/computer use is absolutely necessary (e.g., at work). Once per week, the client attends a more general process addiction group therapy session, which includes clients with any of the process addictions (food, sex, gambling, shopping/spending, Internet/computers/video games). In this group, they discuss how their process addiction has affected them during the past week, they provide one another with support, they confront each other's unhealthy behaviors and rationalizations for engaging in addictive behaviors, and they process feelings related to the difficulty of making changes. While persons suffering from Internet addiction spend the majority of their time in treatment groups comprised of individuals with all types of addictions (both chemical and process), it is important that individuals suffering from process addictions be provided with a group in which they are able to discuss the unique challenges posed by these addictions and the difficulties they experience in order to determine what abstinence and relapse means for their recovery. Patients who have co-occurring addictions and mental health diagnoses also attend a dual-diagnosis group once a week. Depression and anxiety appear to be the most common mental health diagnoses present in those treated with Internet addiction; 76% had some type of depression diagnosis and 24% had an anxiety disorder (Scherer, 2009). As with all other addictions, those suffering from Internet addiction experience significant negative consequences in their lives. Some common consequences are the following:

- Financial debt related to the cost of monthly video gaming services, as well as cost of equipment (special headset/microphones, handset controllers, games, computers, speakers, high-speed processors, modems, high-definition monitor and video system).
- Missed work, school (fired, suspended, expelled from school).
- Suicidal ideations/attempts/completions.
- Lack of meaningful interpersonal relationships.
- Social awkwardness.
- Malnourishment.
- Poor hygiene.
- Family discord.
- Lack of spirituality or emotional health.
- Failure to fulfill personal obligations or responsibilities.

THERAPY CONSIDERATIONS WITH INTERNET ADDICTION

Throughout the treatment process, there are many special considerations a therapist must be aware of when working with individuals suffering from Internet addiction. Although many similarities exist between those with chemical addictions and process addictions, some of the various personality characteristics of those suffering from Internet addiction may pose unique obstacles to the therapy process. This section discusses the group therapy process, as well as the role of the family and support system. As with most treatment programs, a significant emphasis is placed on relapse prevention and the development of a stable discharge and follow-up plan. The use of relapse prevention techniques and tools along with the role of ongoing Emotions Anonymous (EA) and other 12-step meetings and outpatient follow-up are addressed here as well.

As with most addiction and mental health treatment programs, group therapy is the preferred modality. The process of group therapy provides the structure needed to develop the therapeutic alliance that is crucial when working with those suffering from Internet addiction. Many of these individuals have become accustomed to isolating and restricting their social contact to the online, virtual world. Group therapy allows the patient the opportunity to begin engaging in healthy interactions, including giving and receiving honest feedback. While issues of shame, guilt, and denial tend to be universal for people with addictions, those suffering from Internet addiction appear to have significantly higher levels of denial and rationalization for their behaviors and are often supported in these beliefs by others in their lives who do not fully understand how Internet addiction fits into the disease concept of addiction.

Due to the nature of Internet addiction, there are often few physical signs compared to chemical use. As a result, the individual may be well into the pathological phase of Internet misuse before others become aware of the problem. For those suffering from Internet addiction, isolation is often their greatest ally during their active addiction. One of the primary tasks during therapy is to address the escape component and what function it serves for the individual. In doing so, one of the therapist's primary techniques is to link the individual suffering from Internet addiction with other members of the therapy group. This is important due to the isolative nature of Internet addictions. As the individuals are able to draw similarities between themselves and other group members, this sense of isolation and shame will begin to lessen.

The makeup of the therapy group is also of particular concern. In many treatment settings, the groups are mixed between various addictions, including chemical, sex, compulsive gambling, and Internet, to identify a few. The makeup of the group will steer the therapist in selecting various interventions and will also impact the group process (Yalom, 1995). One of the key techniques used to address this phenomenon is through cross-addiction education (i.e., addressing with the entire treatment milieu the realities of various addictive behaviors). This will expand the realm of understanding for group members and provide fewer loopholes for the individual suffering from Internet addiction to exploit in therapy. As with any individual life change, resistance, defensiveness, and apprehension are a normal part of the process (Yalom). At the outset of the treatment process, many patients will struggle with these various issues, as would any other individual with an addiction.

When discussing the role of the family/support system, there are some key issues to keep in mind. During the group therapy process, specific attention should be paid to addressing cognitive distortions. Consistency on the part of the treatment team and support system is central to help the individual confront and avoid continued thought distortions. Patients exhibit changes in mood and disposition over the course of treatment. Initially, many of these patients present as intelligent, socially awkward, superior, usually introverted, solitary, and largely in denial about their addictive behaviors. Some patients may present as extroverted; however, this comes off as exaggerated, appearing to overcompensate for a lack of social confidence. Many of these patients use their intelligence as a defense, attempting to utilize technical knowledge as a defocus or reason why they may not have a particular problem. Others may use it as backing for a sense of arrogant superiority and keep others from getting too close to them emotionally. For these patients, prior to coming into treatment the Internet had become their social environment. They could be anyone and act any way that they wanted to without ever being truly seen. They protected themselves from experiencing true rejection. Being forced to deal with live, flesh-and-blood fellow humans can elicit anxiety that can manifest as hostility or isolation.

Throughout treatment, anxiety tends to slowly dissipate, thus relieving social awkwardness, allowing the patient to become closer to peers and significant others. Patients who progress in this manner actively work at taking risks during group settings to share their stories and feelings and hear feedback from others. Coaching from the primary counselor is often required early in treatment to encourage the patient to take these risks. Patients who continue to challenge themselves to work through the uncomfortable feelings associated with socialization eventually are able to establish meaningful relationships in both personal and work/school environments.

RELAPSE PREVENTION

Relapse prevention planning, as with all addictions, begins from the first day when the individual enters treatment. The relapse prevention process is a well-defined series of steps the individual can take to reduce the risk of returning to active addiction. The relapse prevention process can take on different roles and variations depending on the individual's level of care. While patients are in an inpatient modality, relapse prevention is a preparatory process to aid the patients once they enter into an outpatient setting. During the inpatient phase, plans are made to develop support networks, identify 12-step meetings, and list possible relapse triggers and potential warning signs that they may be headed toward a relapse. Once the patient enters into the outpatient setting, the focus changes into practical application of relapse prevention tools and techniques. Here the individual recovering from Internet addiction will begin to utilize the information provided during the more intense phases of treatment. For patients who do not enter into an inpatient program, the educational and planning process is similar to the inpatient setting. Clients in the outpatient setting will need heavy involvement with 12-step meetings such as EA and regular, intense relapse prevention groups. One of the treatment planning goals for the therapist to consider is the implementation of EA meeting attendance and obtaining an EA sponsor early in the treatment process. As discussed earlier in the chapter, 12-step involvement is a vital part of each patient's social support and relapse prevention network.

While working on relapse prevention assignments, patients are challenged to identify specific triggers for engagement in addictive behaviors as well as identifying warning signs that may signal impending relapse. As a component of relapse prevention, an Internet addiction recovery plan will be completed. The patient will define what sobriety from his or her addiction looks like. Abstinence and sobriety from chemical addiction are very simply defined—don't drink or use. However, the definition of abstinence and sobriety for someone suffering from a process addiction can be trickier due to the nature of the "drug." Patients utilize the education they have received, as well as their peers in creating a specific definition, which may be altered over time. They also define what relapse looks like in terms of attitudes and behaviors related to Internet/computer use, as well as what constitutes a full-blown relapse episode. A relapse can be different for different people. For one person, touching a computer button may be a relapse, but for another a relapse may be more related to playing video games or visiting an Internet site.

During the final week of treatment, it is important for the patient and significant others to discuss with the counselor the importance or need of a computer or Internet access in the home. Although computers have become a major part of everyday life, patients are challenged to distinguish between wants and needs for their computer use. Input from family and employer is strongly encouraged, as patients will significantly rationalize and justify the need for Internet/computer use. We have found family and employers to be supportive of making accommodations to aid in patients' abstinence and recovery. Employers have been known to add monitoring software or limit e-mail access to intramail in order to get rid of Internet access completely from their computers at work. If it is determined that computer access is not needed, the family is recommended to have the access disconnected prior to patient discharge. Additionally, it is recommended that all related paraphernalia (i.e., video games, equipment, computers, modems) be removed from the home prior to patient discharge. This would be akin to removing all liquor from the home of a recovering alcoholic. It is important to give the patient an opportunity to process feelings of grief and loss regarding the removal of these items and Internet access. If it is determined that the computer or Internet access is still needed in the home (i.e., for family or children's use), it is important to discuss and establish appropriate security measures, creating barriers to Internet/computer access. It would be recommended that the family put passwords on all computers or place them in a locked room or cabinet to which the patient does not have access. It would be advisable that all of these measures be done prior to the patient's return home.

For teenagers or adults enrolled in school settings, it can be quite difficult to discuss removing the computer and Internet access completely from the home, as the majority of teenagers and 20-year-olds are still in school, which often requires Internet research and computer-generated assignments. However, even college professors have allowed recovering Internet/computer addicts to either handwrite or use a typewriter for papers. The library remains a great resource for research.

It is possible for many individuals recovering from Internet/computer addiction to reintegrate Internet/computer use back into their lives. It is important to begin discussing the concept of reintegration during family conferences and relapse prevention planning, and to continue during aftercare groups. By reviewing the problematic Internet/computer behaviors and identifying relapse triggers, the patient and the family can be aware of what healthy Internet/computer use will look like for that individual. Patients can identify why they need, or want, to use the Internet/computer (i.e., to e-mail an old friend or look up research online), and establish a time limit for this activity. They would be encouraged to discuss these plans with family members, with their counselor, and during aftercare groups in order to remain accountable. They can also process feelings about their Internet/computer use and receive feedback.

As with all addictive behaviors, the importance of continued follow-up is crucial to long-term success. Once primary treatment has been completed, ongoing continuing care groups are strongly encouraged to provide a longer-term support mechanism for the client and his or her support network. This continuing care may consist of many different components, including but not limited to psychiatric, medical, pastoral, financial, psychotherapeutic, and EA components. The exact combination of modalities should be developed prior to starting the continuing care program. In the final week of treatment, the client is given an assignment to create a continuing recovery plan, which addresses specific steps a patient will follow to promote his or her recovery. The counselor will also be arranging continuing care services with a provider in the patient's home area whenever possible. This may be difficult, as Internet addiction services are extremely limited. Quite frequently, individuals suffering from Internet addiction must travel a long distance to find someone who can provide professional assistance in their recovery. If there is no professional counselor who specializes in Internet addiction or impulse control disorders in the area, clients are referred to a 12-step-based addiction treatment center that is willing to accommodate the individual's need for ongoing counseling and support. As with all forms of therapy, regular reviews of the treatment plan are useful to determine whether current needs are being met or if new issues have arisen.

CONCLUSIONS

Each day new advances in technology are fostering a reliance on the Internet and computers in order to stay connected. Just as society has seen the development and impact of chemical addiction, so too are we just beginning to understand the problems and damage caused by compulsive and problematic Internet/computer usage. As knowledge and understanding of problematic Internet usage increase, so will our ability to provide effective treatment for those who develop Internet addictions. Clearly, we as professionals are in our infancy when it comes to addressing and treating individuals suffering from Internet addiction, as we were decades ago with chemical addiction. The possibilities for improved treatment options are rapidly increasing with new discoveries in neurobiology, pharmacology, and psychotherapy. For these reasons, future research on pathological Internet usage and effective treatment modalities is crucial for the behavioral health field.

The ability for individuals to seek help and access treatment providers has continued to progress with more attention being drawn to Internet addiction. As professionals, we are facing an uphill battle in educating the individual, government, and society to the dangers of compulsive Internet/computer use. However, we have begun and will continue to climb the hill until all those seeking assistance for this problem have found the help they need.

REFERENCES

American Psychiatric Association. (2000). *Diagnostic and statistical manual of mental disorders* (4th ed., text rev.). Washington, DC: Author.

American Society of Addiction Medicine. (2001). *Patient placement criteria* (2nd ed., rev.). Retrieved from www.asam.org/

Block, J. J. (2008). Issues for *DSM-V*: Internet addiction. *American Journal of Psychiatry, 165*, 1–2.

Brunet, P., & Schmidt, L. (2008). Are shy adults really bolder online? It depends on the context. *CyberPsychology & Behavior, 11*(6), 707–709.

Emotions Anonymous Fellowship. (2007). *Emotions Anonymous* (Rev. ed.). St. Paul: EA International.

Fallows, D. (2005). How men and women use the Internet. *Pew Internet and American Life Project.* Retrieved April 28, 2009, from http://www.pewinternet.org/Reports/2005/

Ferraro, G., Caci, B., D'Amico, A., & Di Blasi. M. (2007). Internet addiction disorder: An Italian study. *CyberPsychology & Behavior, 10*(2), 170–175.

Greenfield, D. N. (1999). Virtual addiction test. Retrieved from http://www.virtual-addiction.com/pages/a_iat.htm

Ha, J., Kim, S., Bae, S., Bae, S., Kim, H., Sim, M., Lyoo, I., & Cho, S. (2007). Depression and Internet addiction in adolescents. *Psychopathology, 40*, 424–430.

Harris Interactive, Inc. (2005). $178 billion in employee productivity lost in the U.S. annually due to Internet misuse, reports Websense, Inc. Worldwide Internet Usage and Commerce 2004–2007. Retrieved from http://www.gss.co.uk/news/article/2105/

Illinois Institute for Addiction Recovery. (2008). [Concerned person questionnaire, rev.]. Unpublished survey.

Khazaal, Y., Billieux, J., Thorens, G., Khan, R. Louati, Y., Scarlatti, E., et al. (2008). French validation of the Internet Addiction Test. *CyberPsychology & Behavior, 11*(6), 703–706.

Mottram, A., & Fleming, M. (2009). Extraversion, impulsivity, and online group membership as predictors of problematic Internet usage. *CyberPsychology & Behavior, 12*(3), 319–320.

Scherer, P. (2009). [Survey of individuals treated at the IIAR for Internet addiction]. Unpublished raw data.

Smahel, D., Blinka, L., & Ledabyl, O. (2008). Playing MMORPGs: Connections between addiction and identifying with a character. *CyberPsychology & Behavior, 11*(6), 715–718.

Shek, Tang, & Lo (2009). Evaluation of an Internet addiction treatment program for Chinese adolescents in Hong Kong. *Adolescence*, Summer 2009.

Widyanto, L., & McMurren, M. (2004). The psychometric properties of the Internet Addiction Test. *CyberPsychology & Behavior*, *7*(4), 445–453.

Yalom, Irvin D. (1995). *The theory and practice of group psychotherapy* (4th ed.). New York: Basic Books.

Young, K. (2006). Internet addiction test. Center for Internet Addiction Recovery. Retrieved from http://www.netaddiction.com/

Young, K., & Rodgers, R. (1998). The relationship between depression and Internet addiction. *CyberPsychology & Behavior*, *1*, 25–28.

Zhang, L., Amos, C., & McDowell, W. (2008). A comparative study of Internet addiction between the United States and China. *CyberPsychology & Behavior*, *11*(6): 727–729.

CHAPTER 13

Toward the Prevention of Adolescent Internet Addiction

JUNG-HYE KWON

I NTERNET ADDICTION (IA) is one of the most serious public health problems in Korea. The challenge confronting the nation has been to develop cost-effective strategies to intervene in and prevent IA, especially with regard to adolescents who have been exposed to the Internet from their earliest years. Although there are very few studies on the prevention of IA, it can never be too early to discuss this issue. This chapter presents the clinical features of IA and data on the prevalence of adolescent IA, followed by conceptual models of IA, and finally current prevention efforts and future directions.

INTERNET ADDICTION IN ADOLESCENTS

Early studies utilized case studies to identify Internet addiction (e.g., Black, Belsare, & Schlosser, 1999; Griffiths, 2000; Leon & Rotunda, 2000; Song, Kim, Koo, & Kwon, 2001; Young, 1996; Yu & Zhao, 2004). Although there was no agreed-upon definition of IA, the case descriptions were remarkably similar. Individuals with IA commonly reported a compelling need to devote significant amounts of time to checking e-mail, playing games, participating in online chat rooms, or surfing the Web, even though these activities caused them serious academic and/or work failures, disruptions in daily routines, and family and other interpersonal problems.

The Internet addicts identified by the previous studies were mostly adults and college students. Recently, as the Internet has become an integral part of adolescents' daily lives for both academic and recreational purposes, their excessive Internet use has become a growing concern for parents, mental health professionals, educators, and policy makers. The clinical characteristics of adolescent addiction to the Internet are quite similar to those presented by adults. The following is from the case of a 16-year-old male high school student, who was self-referred for online counseling.

> Ever since I have become addicted to [StarC], my studies have taken a backseat in my life and naturally my grades have plummeted. Although my friends and family have shown concern, I cannot seem to break free from my obsession with the game and I play all night most nights. . . . Even when I sleep I think about the game, and sometimes I dream that I am a fighter unit in the game. . . . I want to become free from this obsession but I just can't (I usually sit in front of the computer nine hours a day and, on numerous occasions, even 24 hours a day . . .).
>
> I first started using computers during my first year in middle school and started playing computer games, in part due to peer pressure, at that time. In the beginning, I played computer games two to three hours a day, but by the time I got into high school, I sat in front of the computer seven to eight hours a day. If I did not spend at least that much time playing computer games, I could not concentrate on my studies, because my head would be filled with game scenes.

This phenomenon of excessive use has been labeled Internet addiction disorder (Goldberg, 1996), pathological Internet use (Young, 1998), and problematic Internet use (Shapira et al., 2003), among others. Although clinical case studies have converged to suggest the existence of IA, there has been much controversy and disagreement among researchers over the nature of the construct. Many attempts have been made to define it and construct its diagnostic criteria (see Table 13.1). Griffiths (1996) has argued that many excessive users are not Internet addicts and has proposed that six characteristic symptoms are necessary to define a behavior as functionally addictive: salience, mood modification, tolerance, withdrawal, conflict, and relapse. One of the most commonly used criteria is the one used by Young (1998), who modified the diagnostic criteria for pathological gambling in *DSM-IV* to construct diagnostic criteria of pathological Internet use. More recently, Shapira and his colleagues conceptualized problematic Internet use as an impulse control disorder and proposed rather broad diagnostic criteria (Shapira et al., 2003).

Ko and his colleagues made another attempt at formulating a set of diagnostic criteria for IA (Ko, Chen, Chen, & Yen, 2005). Although the definitions and terminology of IA vary among researchers, all variants share the following four features with regard to describing IA: (1) compulsive use, (2) tolerance, (3) withdrawal, and (4) negative consequences (Block, 2008).

Compulsive Internet use refers to the uncontrollable nature of the addict's increasing amount of time spent online. It is often accompanied by a loss of the sense of time passing or a neglect of basic drives ("He does not get out of his computer room even for bathing and meals," "He frequently sits up all through the night," etc.). Tolerance refers to the need to spend increasing amounts of time on the Internet to achieve the same level of excitement or

Table 13.1

Diagnostic Criteria for Internet Addiction as Proposed by Researchers

Researcher	Terminology	Diagnostic Concept	Diagnostic Criteria
Goldberg (1996)	Internet addiction disorder	Substance use disorder	Persistent desire, tolerance, withdrawal, negative consequences
Young (1996)	Pathological Internet use	Impulse control disorder	Preoccupation; unsuccessful efforts to control; persistent desire; tolerance; withdrawal; staying online longer than intended; using the Internet as a way of escaping from problems; lying to conceal Internet involvement; risk of loss of a significant relationship, a job, or an educational or career opportunity
Griffiths (1996)	Internet behavior dependence	Substance use disorder	Salience, mood modification, tolerance, withdrawal, conflict, relapse
Shapira et al. (2003)	Problematic Internet use	Impulse control disorder	Preoccupation, clinically significant distress or functional impairment
Ko et al. (2005)	Internet addiction	Impulse control disorder, behavioral addiction	Preoccupation; recurrent failure to resist impulse; use of Internet longer than intended; tolerance; withdrawal; persistent desire and/or unsuccessful attempts to cut down Internet use; excessive time spent; excessive effort to obtain access to Internet; continued heavy Internet use despite knowledge of having a persistent or recurrent physical or psychological problem; functional impairment

satisfaction that the addict experienced previously (e.g., "In the early days of her computer gaming, she needed only one to two hours to feel satisfied. Now, she plays the game for more than five to six hours at a time, once she begins."). Withdrawal refers to the addict's feelings of anger, tension, irritability, and/or depression when the computer is inaccessible. Some individuals tap their fingers in a manner reminiscent of keyboarding when there is no computer and ruminate about things they have done on the Internet. Negative consequences include alienation from or arguments with family and friends, neglect of work or personal obligations, low achievement, reduction in physical activity, fatigue, and poor health.

A recent approach viewing addiction problems from a syndromal perspective is perhaps worth noting (Shaffer et al., 2004). Shaffer and his colleagues proposed that each outwardly unique addiction disorder, such as alcohol dependence or pathological gambling, should be conceived of as a distinctive expression of one underlying addiction syndrome. With this broader conceptualization, IA can be understood as a new expression of the addiction syndrome, sharing common manifestations (e.g., tolerance and withdrawal) and sequelae with other addictive disorders. At this early stage of research on IA, it does not seem feasible to test whether IA is truly one expression of the addiction syndrome. However, conceptualizing IA as such provides a useful perspective for understanding the IA phenomenon and developing its treatment and prevention. For example, the high comorbidity rate observed in individuals with IA is often pointed out as evidence against viewing IA as a distinct disorder (Black, Belsare, & Schlosser, 1999). This feature is often observed in both chemical and behavioral addictions (Kessler et al., 1996).

It has also been reported that IA is resistant to treatment and has high relapse rates (Block, 2008). The high relapse rates of alcohol and drug addiction are well documented. For example, about 80% to 90% of individuals entering addiction recovery relapse during the first year after treatment (Marlatt, Baer, Donovan, & Kivlahan, 1988).

From the syndromal perspective, the most effective treatments are multimodal approaches that include both object-specific and addiction-general treatments. In fact, multicomponent preventive intervention has been demonstrated to be very effective for the preclusion of cigarette smoking (Botvin & Eng, 1982), which may have direct implications in the search for an effective treatment and prevention for IA.

PREVALENCE OF IA FOR ADOLESCENTS

This section briefly presents findings from the Korean national survey that used the self-report Korean-Internet Addiction Scale (K-IA) (Kim, Park, Kim, & Lee, 2002), and examines the prevalence of adolescent IA. In 2008, the survey sampled 5,500 people (2,683 youths aged 9 to 19 and 2,817 adults aged 20 to 39) using a stratified sampling method. The Korean-Internet Addiction Scale—Adolescent (K-IA-A), which is composed of 40 items on a four-point Likert scale, has seven subscales, as follows: disturbance of adaptive functioning (nine items), disturbance of reality testing (three items), positive expectance toward the Internet (six items), withdrawal (six items), virtual interpersonal relationships (five items), deviant behaviors (six items), and tolerance (five items). The survey identified high-risk adolescents as those having a total score >94 or having scores on three subscales as follows: disturbance of adaptive functioning >21, withdrawal >16, and tolerance >15. The survey

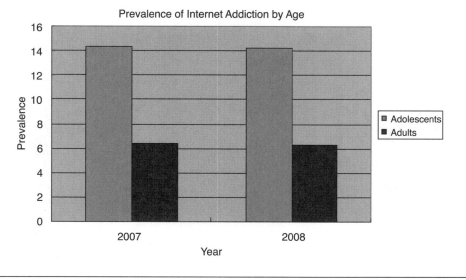

Figure 13.1 Percentages of Internet Addiction Among Adults and Adolescents

also identified adolescents at risk of IA (total score >82 or disturbance of adaptive functioning >18, withdrawal >14, and tolerance >13).

The percentage of high-risk adolescents was 2.3%, compared to 1.3% for adults. At-risk adolescents were estimated to be 12.0%, compared to 5.0% for adults (Korean Agency for Digital Opportunity and Promotion, 2008). See Figure 13.1. When the prevalence rate (high-risk and at-risk group combined) was examined according to age, the prevalence rate was highest among ages 16 to 19 (15.9%). The group with the next highest rate was ages 13 to 15 (15.0%), and the group with the lowest rate was ages 35 to 39 (4.8%). There was a gender difference in the percentages of high-risk and at-risk adolescents. The survey estimated that 3.3% of the boys and 1.1% of the girls were in the high-risk category and 13.6% of the boys and 10.4% of the girls were in the at-risk category. The combined percentage of high-risk and at-risk adolescents from two-parent households was 13.9%, while the corresponding percentage of those from single-parent households was 22.3%.

The survey examined which Internet activity on the Internet the high-risk, at-risk, and normal individuals most frequently engaged in. The information-searching activity frequency was similar among the high-risk (68.8%), at-risk (75.7%), and normal (79.8%) groups. However, frequency of the gaming differed greatly among high-risk (61.5%), at-risk (64.5%), and normal (45.3%) groups. This finding indicated that individuals using the Internet for gaming were at greater risk for developing Internet addiction. When the major activities of adolescents and adults were considered separately, results showed that high-risk adolescents participated in gaming (53.5%) much more often than the normal adolescents did (28.0%). By contrast, high-risk adults' activities

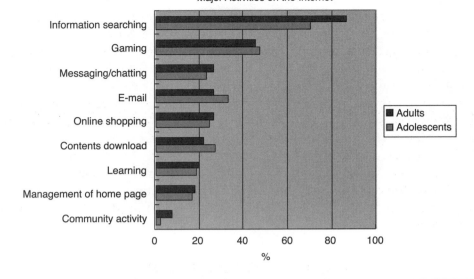

Figure 13.2   Major Internet Activities

included movies, music, and hobbies (58.8%) more often than did the normal adults' activities (28.5%). See Figure 13.2.

CHARACTERISTICS OF HIGH-RISK ADOLESCENTS

Numerous studies have examined the personality traits of individuals who were considered dependent on the Internet, mostly using college students or adult samples. The findings of the previous studies seem to suggest that specific personality traits may predispose individuals to develop IA. Characteristics frequently associated with IA have been identified as depressed mood, impulsivity, sensation-seeking, low self-esteem, shyness, and reduced attentiveness (Ha et al., 2006; Kim et al., 2006; Lee & Kwon, 2000; Lin & Tsai, 2002; Ryu, Choi, Seo, & Nam, 2004). It is also noteworthy that psychiatric comorbidity is common, particularly mood, anxiety, attention-deficit/hyperactivity disorder (ADHD), and substance use disorders (Black, Belsare, & Schlosser, 1999; Ha et al., 2006; Ko, Yen, Chen, Chen, & Yen, 2008).

Depression is one of the vulnerability factors consistently demonstrated in previous studies. Kraut and his colleagues (1998), using a community adult sample, demonstrated that excessive Internet use led to depression even when previous depression scores were controlled for. Such individuals tend to withdraw from interpersonal relations, show reduced amounts of communication with household and family members, and feel lonely (Kraut et al., 1998). Kwon (2005) examined temporal changes in adolescent Internet game addiction and related variables using a prospective design. The study assessed a total of 1,279 middle school students twice, five months apart, on measures of Internet game addiction, self-escape tendency, negative affect, peer relationships, relationships with parents, and other variables. The multiple regression analysis showed that the first assessment of Internet game addiction, self-escape tendency and negative affect, were predictive of Internet game addiction several months later. None of the relationship variables from the first assessment were able to predict Internet game addiction as of the second assessment.

Although previous studies shed some light on the characteristics of high-risk adolescents, they should be interpreted with caution due to common methodological weaknesses such as small sample size, lack of validated addiction criteria, and use of low cutoff scores. As most of the studies have a cross-sectional design, it is also difficult to determine whether those characteristics are the risk factors or the negative consequences of excessive Internet use. More empirical data is definitely needed to aid in identifying high-risk adolescents.

THE CONCEPTUAL MODEL OF INTERNET ADDICTION

Effective prevention requires a conceptual model that connects risk factors, mediating processes, and maladaptive behaviors. Most of the research on IA appears to lack a theoretical basis, despite the number of studies conducted in the field. Davis (2001) proposed a model of the etiology of IA[1], using the cognitive-behavioral approach The main assumption of the model was that IA resulted from problematic cognitions coupled with behaviors that maintain maladaptive responses. This chapter reviews the cognitive-behavioral approach and also briefly considers another model of IA, based on Baumeister's (1990) escape from self theory (Kwon, Chung, & Lee, 2009).

COGNITIVE-BEHAVIORAL MODEL

Using a diathesis-stress model, Davis (2001) proposed that the distal cause of IA was the underlying psychopathology (e.g., depression, social anxiety, substance dependence), and the stressor was the introduction of the Internet, suggesting that underlying psychopathology did not in itself result in symptoms of IA but were a necessary element in its etiology. He claimed a key factor in experiencing the Internet and associated new technology is the reinforcement an individual receives from the event. He also suggested that stimuli, such as the sound of a computer connecting with an online service or the tactile sensation of typing on a keyboard, could result in a conditioned response. Such secondary reinforcers could act as situational cues contributing to the development and maintenance of IA. It seems reasonable to assume that the presence of some psychopathology places people at increased risk for

---

[1]Davis (2001) used the term *Pathological Internet Use* (PIU), but PIU is referred to here as IA, to maintain consistent terminology.

developing IA. However, more research is needed to identify psychopathology associated with IA. Ko and his colleagues (2008) demonstrated that social phobia did not predict IA, controlling for depressive disorders and adult ADHD. Furthermore, the distal cause of IA needs to be expanded to include neurobiological and psychosocial antecedents to advance his model.

Davis (2001) assumed that the most central factor of the cognitive-behavioral model of IA was the presence of maladaptive cognitions. He classified maladaptive cognitions into two subtypes–thoughts about the self and thoughts about the world—which he viewed as sufficient proximal causes for IA. He further assumed that cognitive distortions such as rumination, self-doubt, low self-efficacy, and negative self-appraisal tended to contribute to, intensify, or maintain IA.

Although many important aspects of the model remain untested, the cognitive-behavioral model proposed by Davis seems to provide a useful framework for developing intervention and prevention programs. Davis suggested that cognitive restructuring should be an essential therapeutic component for intervention in and prevention of IA. The behavioral component of cognitive behavioral therapy (CBT) for IA would include keeping a record of Internet use, thought listing exercises, and exposure therapy (Davis, 2001).

ESCAPE FROM SELF THEORY

Like other addictive problems, IA can be placed somewhere on a continuum of self-destructive behaviors and thus understood as an attempt to eliminate self-estrangement and the accompanying negative mood state. It has often been assumed that the Internet may serve the purpose of an escape from real-life difficulties (Armstrong, Phillips, & Saling, 2000; Young, 1998). However, the escape hypothesis has been neither elaborated nor empirically tested. Kwon, Chung, and Lee (2009) tried to understand the process of escape using Baumeister's escape from self theory (1990).

The steps that Baumeister suggested are probably involved in escaping from the self are as follows. First, individuals are faced with a reality that does not meet their high expectations, such as failures, setbacks, or other disappointing results. When current difficulties are attributed to the self, the individual becomes acutely aware of himself or herself as inadequate, incompetent, unattractive, or guilty. Second, a negative affect, such as depression, anxiety, or suicidal guilt, arises from the unfavorable comparison of the self with self-standards. Third, the person responds to this uncomfortable state by trying to escape from meaningful thoughts into a relatively numb state of cognitive deconstruction. The term *cognitive deconstruction* is defined as a mental state characterized by present-oriented time perspective, denial of the future, absence of distal goals, and very concrete thinking. Finally, the consequences of this deconstructed mental state may contribute to an increased willingness to attempt suicide. In other words, suicide emerges as an escalation of the

Figure 13.3 Escape from Self Model of Internet Addiction

person's wish to escape from meaningful awareness of current life problems and their implications about the self.

Previous studies demonstrated that a tendency to escape from the self could be a major factor in accounting for a diverse range of behavioral problems among adolescents, such as "huffing" (the use of inhalants), drinking, running away, and impulsive suicide (Lee, 2000; Shin, 1992). As with other addictive problems, IA can be regarded as belonging to self-destructive behaviors in a broad sense. Kwon, Chung, & Lee (2009) demonstrated the validity of Baumeister's escape theory with regard to IA. They constructed and tested a path model, as illustrated in Figure 13.3, using structural equation modeling (SEM) on the observed variables. The fit indexes of the model were good, and all the path coefficients were significant, supporting the validity of the model.

This finding implied that escaping from the self could be a process leading to IA. When individuals suffer from real/ideal self discrepancy, they evaluate themselves as incompetent, unworthy, and inadequate. As a result, these persons become depressed, anxious, or defeated. At this point, such individuals can choose either to struggle to solve the problem or to attempt an escape from painful reality. When the Internet is adopted as a way to escape from oneself and is repeatedly visited, the individual's false sense of power, achievement, and connection, obtained through Internet activities, deepens, which will escalate the person's indulgence in the Internet. Although it should be recognized that the escape from self model presents only one possible path leading to IA, the present findings have important implications for the treatment and prevention of IA for both adults and adolescents. Implications for adolescents are highlighted here. First, adolescents who are afflicted with negative self-evaluation and negative mood could be susceptible to IA, especially when parents focus only on academic success and do not provide adequate supervision. Second, intervention programs should target not just changes in Internet use but also changes in the adolescent's behavioral and cognitive tendency to escape from the self. Finally, implementing programs that are geared toward improving adolescents' problem-solving and coping skills may be a promising avenue for effective prevention.

PREVENTION: THE PRESENT AND THE FUTURE

Using data from 2008, the Korean government estimates that approximately 168,000 Korean adolescents (2.3% of young people aged 9 to 19) suffer from IA and require treatment. Surveys done in many countries have also shown that IA has become an increasing mental health problem among adolescents

(Johansson & Götestam, 2004; Liu & Potenza, 2007; Siomos, Dafouli, Braimiotis, Mouzas, & Angelopoulos, 2008). Until now, many clinicians working in this field have struggled to find ways to treat IA effectively. It seems quite reasonable that there has been a great deal of emphasis on treating those with IA. However, there are urgent needs that we should place a high priority on developing prevention programs. First, most efforts to treat IA have been only partially successful. The first stage, motivating individuals with IA to seek treatment, is very hard to achieve since they tend to deny their problems. Unless they are referred by parents or teachers to participate in the treatment program, they seldom seek professional help on their own or show up for their appointments. Second, due to the prevalence of this problem, even the best program to treat IA can accommodate only a small fraction of those suffering from it. It has been noted that the number of people needing services continues to grow, while resources for providing such services have not been expanded. Third, once IA has evolved into a debilitating form, it is not only resistant to successful treatment but also has a high relapse rate. To make things worse, individuals entering recovery from IA are exposed to the Internet all the time, everywhere. It is an enormous challenge for them to maintain their therapeutic gains. Prevention is therefore an important option for solving this problem.

For these reasons, there appears to be some consensus that prevention is the preferred choice among approaches for dealing with excessive Internet use. Clinicians, educators, and policy makers all seem to agree that treatment strategies for tackling IA need to be complemented by preventive strategies that address risk factors before the addiction evolves into a debilitating form. Although the rising need for prevention is not debatable, no agreement has been reached regarding when, how, and to whom to direct preventive efforts.

CURRENT PREVENTION APPROACHES

A number of studies have highlighted the danger that excessive Internet use may pose to students as a population group (Widyanto & Griffiths, 2006; Yang, 2001). This population is deemed to be vulnerable and at risk given the accessibility of the Internet and the flexibility of their schedules. Any practitioners who have worked with severe IA have argued strongly for early identification and prevention. Given the urgent need, the simplest and easiest approach, a knowledge-based educational approach, has so far been preferred and implemented, and it has been partially successful in reducing the prevalence of IA. However, this approach's long-term effect remains to be documented, and major gaps remain between what the prevention programs should aim for and state-of-the-art practices.

PROVIDING KNOWLEDGE AND INFORMATION

Current approaches to the prevention of IA have relied heavily on the provision of factual information concerning the adverse consequences of excessive

Internet use. As a basic step to promote prevention, educators invite experts to give presentations to students, which usually include factual information on IA, and provide some advice about how to control Internet use. This knowledge-based educational approach has been based on the assumption that youngsters become addicted to the Internet because they lack knowledge of its negative consequences. Such an approach had a certain intuitive and logical appeal, especially in the days when IA was a new phenomenon. However, merely providing information about the extreme negative consequences of excessive Internet use is, by itself, of marginal value as a prevention strategy.

This does not mean that such information and knowledge cannot play an important role in IA prevention. To the contrary, some knowledge may be a useful component of IA prevention programs. For example, most youngsters typically underestimate their level of dependence on the Internet and normalize it as a temporary indulgence that they can grow out of anytime they want to. Certain anecdotal information, with vivid details, appeals to youngsters and is helpful in correcting misperceptions and myths about IA. It is important that the information and knowledge included in prevention programs is selected for meeting the needs of the target population. The vehicle for providing the information and knowledge is also critical. The younger generation is more attentive and responsive when new information is delivered through up-to-date audiovisual media than via old-style PowerPoint slides.

IDENTIFICATION OF HIGH-RISK ADOLESCENTS

The rate of IA for adolescents (ages 9 to 16) is twice that for adults (over 16). There are many reasons why adolescents are more susceptible to IA. First, and most important, they lack the cognitive and emotional abilities necessary to control themselves. It is likely that frontal cortex and other neurobiological systems responsible for executive control and emotional regulation are not fully developed. More research is needed in this area to determine the neurobiological basis of IA. Second, adolescents are more involved in Internet games than are any other age groups. Internet gaming can be very reinforcing to youngsters because of their interactivity and the sense of belongingness, competence, and power they provide. Online gaming can also be rewarding because of the inherent value of the stimulation and amusement they offer.

Those who use the Internet for gaming have been shown to be at greater risk for developing IA, as demonstrated by survey findings. Indeed, the rate of gaming differed greatly among high-risk (61.5%), potential-risk (64.5%), and normal (45.3%) adolescents. This finding was more pronounced among adolescents than among adults. The high-risk adolescent group engaged in online gaming at twice the rate of normal adolescents (53.5% versus 28.0%). Another factor that may play some role in inducing adolescents in Korea and other Asian countries to utilize the Internet is their stressful lives, with its high academic pressure. Typical school days of adolescents are mostly confined to academic activities, without many extracurricular activities, because college entrance examinations are very competitive. The Internet is therefore a major outlet for youngsters who are stressed out due to academic pressures.

For these reasons, adolescents are the main target group of prevention efforts. Unfortunately, very few longitudinal studies are available to aid in the identification of high-risk adolescents. Currently, as a quick method for identifying high-risk adolescents, a self-report questionnaire assessing IA is administered to students at the beginning of the academic year, and those who score high are either referred to counseling or monitored by teachers. Although there is a high probability that adolescents with high scores on such a measure of IA are likely to develop IA, this approach is not without caveats. First, some youths do not want to disclose the fact that they use the Internet excessively and do not answer the questionnaire honestly. Therefore, too much reliance on self-report measures may fail to identify "fake good" compulsive Internet users. Second, the basic question of who are high-risk adolescents needs to be addressed. A high-risk group, in the true sense, consists of those who do not show problem behaviors yet but are likely to develop dysfunctional behavior later. The current method, administering a questionnaire assessing IA, is limited in its ability to identify high-risk adolescents unless they develop an early form of one or more dysfunctional behaviors. There is a need for more empirical data, indicating who the high-risk adolescents truly are. For example, there is data showing that the prevalence of IA among youngsters from single-parent households is higher than for youngsters from two-parent households. It is not yet clear whether growing up in a single-parent family constitutes a risk factor or the lack of parental supervision associated with single-parent households is the risk factor.

PREVENTION PROGRAMS

The current prevention approaches include a mixture of behavioral and cognitive strategies designed to change Internet use patterns and enhance self-control. A cognitive-behavioral group program is often used to reduce youngsters' heavy and compulsive use of the Internet. One example is the Self-Management Training (SMT) developed by Kwon and Kwon (2002).

The main objectives of the SMT program are as follows: (1) to provide youngsters with accurate information concerning the prevalence of IA, its progress pattern, and related factors; (2) to encourage them to self-monitor their use of the Internet and identify environmental and psychological antecedents for engaging with the Internet for a longer period than they intended; (3) to promote behavior changes related to Internet use, such as setting rules regarding Internet use, reducing Internet time step-by-step, planning other activities in advance, and getting support from others; and (4) to teach youngsters how to cope with stress and increase other pleasurable or mastery activities. This program consists of six weekly 90-minute sessions, administered to groups consisting of seven to nine students. This psychoeducational program puts greater emphasis on self-directed behavior changes with regard to Internet use than on enhancing personal and social competence. To examine its efficacy, a randomized control trial was conducted, and preprogram, postprogram, and three-month follow-up assessments were administered. The SMT program was shown to be effective in reducing time on the Internet and enhancing self-control but less effective at decreasing the severity of Internet addiction. Lee (2001) developed a similar but improved program that included parent training and cognitive restructuring. This nine-session game-control program (GCP) was reported to be effective in reducing both time spent online and the severity of IA (see Table 13.2).

Table 13.2

Overview of Treatment Sessions of the Game-Control Program

Session	Objectives and Content
Sessions 1–2	Provide orientation and teach self-monitoring. • Provide a full description of the program. • Explore short-term and long-term effects of heavy Internet use. • Teach how to keep daily records of Internet use. • Write a self-contract limiting the Internet use.
Parent session 1	Provide information about Internet addiction. Teach how to cope with the child's Internet use.
Sessions 3–5	Encourage to write daily records and teach time management. • Identify antecedents of staying online longer than intended. • Determine self-rewards for staying online only as planned. • Search for alternative pleasure activities. Identify negative thoughts and teach how to change them. • Label cognitive errors. • Change self-defeating thoughts with self-enhancing thoughts. Encourage to set up long-term goals and develop steps to fulfill them. • Share each participant's life dream. • Discuss how to improve self-image.
Sessions 6–7	Identify major stressors and teach coping strategies. • Understand relationship between stress and Internet use. • Demonstrate and practice relaxation techniques. • Teach active coping strategies. Resolve interpersonal conflicts. • Teach communication skills. • Teach how to initiate and keep social contacts. • Teach how to be assertive.
Sessions 8–9	Review and consolidate what has been achieved through the program. Prepare for future challenges.
Parent session 2	Discuss what has been changed and what remains to be changed. Develop strategies to cope with remaining problems.

Based on these programs, preventive strategies using cognitive-behavioral techniques are now widely used. The Korean Agency for Digital Opportunity and Promotion (KADO) published a guide booklet for teachers on preventing IA. The DREAM approach is as follows. (1) In the first step, the Danger assessment, problematic Internet behaviors and school adjustment are assessed. (2) In the next step, Return, students are motivated to return to the normal use of the Internet. To facilitate this, teachers help students evaluate the benefits and costs of excessive Internet use and provide incentives for change. (3) In the Evaluation step, students receive a systematic evaluation on psychosocial factors such as mood, self-esteem, interpersonal relationships, and family environment. (4) In the Appreciation step, the student's strengths and assets are appreciated and utilized to facilitate self-directed behavior changes. (5) In the final step, Miracle, students take concrete actions to fulfill their short-term and long-term goals. Students are encouraged to perceive even a small change as a miracle. The efficacy of this approach has not been examined yet. Some other techniques, such as Internet holidays and weekend camps, are also in use but lack empirical data on their efficacy.

IMPLEMENTATION

As stated earlier, the typical school-based prevention approach includes a universal one- to two-hour, schoolwide, knowledge-enhancing educational presentation on the subject combined with a 10- to 12-session brief intervention for high-risk individuals. As prevention programs, these current school practices are far from ideal in scope, intensity, and duration. Many environmental realities in schools limit the possibilities for administering a comprehensive program that teaches important information, skills, and positive attitudes and focuses on the promotion of healthy Internet use and well-being. For students who intend to enter competitive universities, Korean schools put the highest priority on building academic competence. Therefore, programs that promote personal and social competencies receive only superficial attention from students, parents, teachers, and school administrators. Quite naturally, students are not enthusiastic about staying longer at school to participate in additional programs. In addition, teachers don't have adequate support when implementing prevention programs. Given the achievement-oriented zeitgeist, it is often pointed out that there is not enough time during the school day and year to accommodate longer and broader prevention programs. Therefore, without systems-level supports, comprehensive programs have little chance of being integrated into the current school curriculum.

GOVERNMENT FUNDING AND SUPPORT

In a country where there is a dearth of mental health resources, the big challenge in prevention is to secure funding and other resources. The Korean government is keenly aware of the heavy human and social costs of IA, especially for adolescents, the most vulnerable population. Until now, government funding has been focused on setting up counseling centers and training counselors to meet the high demand for IA intervention. Since the first special clinic (the Center for Internet Addiction Prevention & Counseling [IAPC]) geared to provide counseling for IA was established in 2002, more than 80 affiliated counseling centers have begun offering counseling to youngsters with IA. The IAPC has offered an IA counselor training program for teachers, counselors, and other mental health professionals since 2002. The program consists of 40-hour courses presenting basic knowledge about IA, rapport-building techniques for use with adolescents, and other relevant counseling techniques, mostly cognitive-behavioral. About 1,000 counselors have completed the courses and received IA counselors' certificates. These government-supported centers and trained counselors could play a pivotal role in providing preventive programs along with intervention programs. However, to develop a strong scientific basis for future preventive programming efforts, more funding needs to be secured for research to advance the quality of IA prevention programs and to stimulate investigation of IA.

FUTURE DIRECTIONS IN PREVENTION

In response to the urgent need to reduce the high rate of IA among adolescents, preventive interventions have been hastily designed and administered on a small scale in Korea. Current prevention programs are mostly narrow-band, targeting primarily adolescents who already present some features of IA. They aim to provide information and knowledge, encourage self-monitoring of Internet use, facilitate behavior changes, and enhance self-control. These preventive programs have demonstrated some short-term effects, but there have been no systematic, controlled, longitudinal field studies to evaluate the long-term effects. The difficult initial steps toward IA prevention have been taken, but there is a long way to go before effective prevention programs will be developed. Legislation should also be seriously considered to prohibit children from using the Internet for long hours. This section discusses some considerations for guiding the development and implementation of prevention programs.

PREVENTION ADDRESSING FUNDAMENTAL CAUSAL PROCESSES

Current prevention programs target the high-risk adolescents who spend more than three to four hours daily on the Internet. The primary goal of this intervention is therefore for the adolescents to reduce their time on the Internet and develop alternative leisure activities. These programs use behavioral and cognitive techniques to change the contingency of Internet use, correct misperceptions and exaggerated expectations, and encourage other extracurricular activities. Given the brevity of such preventive interventions, these strategies are well targeted and produce short-term benefits. However, they should not be considered sufficient for reducing IA, since they deal with only proximal and Internet-specific IA risk factors. All addictive problems have a high relapse rate, and IA is no exception. To have an enduring impact and prevent relapse, IA prevention programs should address fundamental causal processes. The syndromal conceptualization of addiction suggests that an effective treatment of addiction should address general addiction vulnerabilities. Previous research on school-based prevention programs also implies that a comprehensive program dealing with general vulnerabilities has greater potential than discrete, ad hoc, short-term interventions do (Weissberg & Elias, 1993). It would be not only desirable but also cost-effective, from a long-term perspective, for IA prevention programs to enhance youngsters' personal and social competence, so that they develop a subjective sense of role fulfillment and social effectiveness as they deal with daily tasks, responsibilities, and challenges.

NEED FOR BROADER MULTIMODAL PROGRAMS

There is a growing consensus that a broad-based approach to prevention is needed to address risk factors that are common to many youth problems (DeFriese, Crossland, MacPhail-Wilcox, & Sowers, 1990; Elias & Weissberg, 1989; Weissberg, Caplan, & Harwood, 1991). The literature supports this consensus, indicating that high-risk problem behaviors such as substance abuse, delinquency, and dropping out of school co-occur (Jessor, 1993) and that common risk and protective factors contribute to the development of these behaviors (Dryfoos, 1990). Previous studies have demonstrated that a tendency to escape from the self is a common risk factor underlying many youth problems (Lee, 2000; Shin, 1992). It has also been demonstrated that Internet addiction is significantly correlated with depression and suicidal ideation among South Korean high school students (Ryu, Choi, Seo, & Nam, 2004).

These findings converge to suggest that a broad-based approach dealing with risk factors underlying not only IA but also other related youth problems is more promising than are narrow-based approaches focusing on just one outcome. In this vein, life skills training (LST), the multicomponent preventive intervention shown to be effective in the prevention of cigarette smoking (Botvin & Tortu, 1988), is a good IA prevention model. Broader-based substance abuse prevention programs like LST are successful because they not only provide youngsters with skills for resisting social pressure to use tobacco, alcohol, and other drugs, but they also enhance personal and social competence. Such programs, enabling youngsters to cope effectively with life demands and challenges, can prevent youngsters from seeking escape from the self and the offline environment and are likely to be successful in IA prevention.

NEED FOR PREVENTION PROGRAMS TARGETING YOUNGER AGE GROUPS

It is widely agreed that early identification is crucial for successful IA treatment (Kim, 2001). People are starting to use the Internet at younger and younger ages, in Korea and other countries. The most recent survey of fourth graders by the Korean Ministry of Health and Welfare estimated that 2% of all fourth graders were high-risk and required treatment or basic counseling (Korean Ministry of Health and Welfare, 2009). To make things worse, elementary school children's most frequent Internet activity is gaming, which is known to have the greatest addiction-causing potential of all Internet activities (Ko et al., 2005; Yang, 2001). Considering that children in elementary school have a limited capacity for self-control, it is very likely that early exposure to Internet gaming increases their risk of addiction. It increases especially when both parents go to work and the children are left unsupervised. The highest-risk group of preadolescents may be those who spend long hours on Internet gaming without parental supervision. When children reach adolescence, risk factors are likely to become more varied and complicated. For example, during the early adolescent years, particularly those marking the transition to middle or junior high school, adolescents who have difficulty adjusting to a new school environment may indulge in Internet use in an attempt to cope with depressed mood or tension. Therefore, it is crucial to identify risk factors of specific developmental periods and tailor prevention programs to address specific risk factors of each age group.

SIGNIFICANT DURATION AND DOSAGE

Currently, most schools adopt very brief prevention programs lasting eight to 12 sessions. It is argued that schools cannot devote their limited resources to longer and more intensive programs. However, research findings converge to suggest that preventive intervention needs to be of significant duration and intensity to show an effect (Weissberg & Elias, 1993). For example, Bangert-Drowns's (1988) meta-analysis examining the effects of school-based substance abuse education demonstrated that "substance abuse education has, for the most part, failed to achieve its primary goal, the prevention of drug and alcohol abuse" (p. 260). Of 33 programs he reviewed, 29 lasted less than 10 weeks. Brief duration and low dosage were regarded as two of the primary reasons for negative outcomes. Reviews on the findings of health-focused, school-based prevention programs also showed that 40 to 50 hours were needed to produce stable behavioral effects (Connell, Turner, & Mason, 1985). Brief (i.e., less than one year) programs can produce short-term behavioral gains, but it is unrealistic to expect them to have an enduring impact. Overall, there is a growing body of literature suggesting that multiple years of intervention produce larger and more lasting benefits than a single year does (Connell, Turner, & Mason, 1985; Hawkins, Catalano, & Miller, 1992).

Although research findings highlight the direction that prevention programs should follow, development and implementation of programs with significant duration and intensity require the serious commitment and support of policy makers, school administrators, and researchers.

PARENT TRAINING AND UTILIZATION OF VOLUNTEERS

Given the schools' limited resources, the integration of school-based programs with parent training and volunteers' ongoing support is crucial for achieving long-lasting effects. Most adolescents use the Internet at home. Therefore, parental supervision based on caring, mutual relationships is of critical importance. The goal of parent training is to teach communication and conflict resolution skills and provide support for parents' efforts to deal effectively with adolescent offspring. Parents need these skills to negotiate Internet hours, monitor adolescents' activities without hurting their privacy, and encourage offline extracurricular activities. Volunteers can also play a critical role in educating youngsters to use the Internet in constructive ways. Within the prevention literature, strong arguments have been made for the use of non-professional change agents, based on effectiveness and cost considerations. Undergraduate student volunteers can be excellent change agents for many reasons. First, they are developmentally close to the adolescents. Second, they may have had many personal experiences with Internet use. Third, they can be role models in many areas other than Internet use. Therefore, parents and college student volunteers are important resources for IA prevention.

NEED FOR EMPIRICAL RESEARCH

Every aspect of prevention should be based on empirical research. Coi and his colleagues (1993) concluded that "nowhere in the mental health enterprise is the interplay between science and practice more crucial than in the domain of prevention." When it comes to improving IA prevention, lack of empirical data is the biggest obstacle. First, researchers need to specify the fundamental causal processes that prevention should address. Second, more empirical data is needed to aid in identifying high-risk individuals. Third, once prevention programs are developed and administered, their effects should be carefully evaluated. The responsibility for evaluating the outcomes of such programs rests mostly on the shoulders of researchers using appropriate samples, measures, and designs. However, good research on prevention cannot be performed in the lab. Conducting such research requires sustained collaboration among researchers, educators, and fund providers, and the findings could provide instructive leads about ways to conceptualize, design, and implement prevention programs.

REFERENCES

Armstrong, L., Phillips, J. G., & Saling, L. L. (2000). Potential determinants of heavier Internet usage. *International Journal of Human-Computer Studies, 53*, 537–550.

Bangert-Drowns, R. L. (1988). The effects of school-based substance abuse education: A meta-analysis. *Journal of Drug Education, 18*, 243–264.

Baumeister, R. F. (1990). Suicide as escape from self. *Psychological Review*, 90–113.

Black, D., Belsare, G., & Schlosser, S. (1999). Clinical features, psychiatric comorbidity, and health-related quality of life in persons reporting compulsive computer use behavior. *Journal of Clinical Psychiatry, 60,* 839–843.

Block, J. J. (2008). Issues for *DSM-V*: Internet addiction. *American Journal of Psychiatry, 165,* 306–307.

Botvin, G., & Eng, A. (1982). The efficacy of a multicomponent approach to the prevention of cigarette smoking. *Preventive Medicine, 11,* 199–211.

Botvin, G., & Tortu, S. (1988). Preventing adolescent substance abuse through life skills training. In R. H. Price, E. L. Cowen, R. P. Lorion, & J. Ramos-McKay (Eds.), *14 ounces of prevention: A casebook for practitioners* (pp. 98–110). Washington, DC: American Psychological Association.

Coi, J. D., Watt, N. F., West, S. G., Hawkins, D., Asarnow, J. R., Markman, H. J., Ramey, S. L., Shure, M. B., & Long, B. (1993). The science of prevention: A conceptual framework and some directions for a national research program. *American Psychologist, 48,* 1013–1022.

Connell, D. B., Turner, R. P., & Mason, E. F. (1985). Summary of the findings of the school health education evaluation: Health promotion effectiveness, implementation, and costs. *Journal of School Health, 55,* 316–323.

Davis, R. (2001). A cognitive-behavioral model of pathological Internet use. *Computers in Human Behavior, 17,* 187–195.

DeFriese, G. H., Crossland, C. L., MacPhail-Wilcox, B., & Sowers, J. G. (1990). Implementing comprehensive school health programs: Prospects for change in American schools. *Journal of School Health, 60,* 182–187.

Dryfoos, J. G. (1990). *Adolescents at risk: Prevalence and prevention.* New York: Oxford University Press.

Elias, M. J., & Weissberg, R. P. (1989). School-based social competence promotion as a primary prevention strategy: A tale of two projects. *Prevention in Human Services, 7,* 177–200.

Goldberg, I. (1996). Internet addiction disorder. Retrieved March 11, 2002, from http://www.cog.brown.edu/brochures/people/duchon/humor/Internet.addiction.html

Griffiths, M. D. (1996). Behavioral addictions: An issue for everybody? *Journal of Workplace Learning, 8,* 19–25.

Griffiths, M. D. (2000). Does Internet and computer "addiction" exist? Some case study evidence. *CyberPsychology & Behavior, 3,* 211–218.

Ha, J. H., Yoo, H. J., Cho, I. H., Chin, B., Shin, D., & Kim, J. H. (2006). Psychiatric comorbidity assessed in Korean children and adolescents who screen positive for Internet addiction. *Journal of Clinical Psychiatry, 67,* 821–826.

Hawkins, J. D., Catalano, R. F., & Miller, J. Y. (1992). Risk and protective factors for alcohol and other drug problems in adolescence and early adulthood: Implications for substance abuse prevention, *Psychological Bulletin, 112,* 64–105.

Jessor, R. (1993). Successful adolescent development among youth in high-risk settings. *American Psychologist, 48,* 117–126.

Johansson, A., & Götestam, K. G. (2004). Internet addiction: Characteristics of a questionnaire and prevalence in Norwegian youth (12–18 years). *Scandinavian Journal of Psychology, 45,* 223–229.

Kessler, R. C., Nelson, C. B., McGonagle, K. A., Edlund, M. J., Frank, R. G., & Leaf, P. J. (1996). The epidemiology of co-occurring addictive and mental disorders: Implications for prevention and service utilization. *American Journal of Orthopsychiatry*, *66*, 17–31.

Kim, C. T., Park, C. K., Kim, D. I., & Lee, S. J. (2002). *Korean Internet Addiction Scale and preventive counseling program*. Seoul: Korean Agency for Digital Opportunity and Promotion.

Kim, H. S. (2001). Internet addiction treatment: The faster, the better. *Publication Ethics*, *276*, 12–15.

Kim, K. H., Ryu, E. J., Chon, M. Y., Yeun, E. J., Choi, S. Y., & Seo, J. S. (2006). Internet addiction in Korean adolescents and its relation to depression and suicidal ideation: A questionnaire survey. *International Journal of Nursing Studies*, *43*, 185–192.

Ko, C.-H., Chen, C.-C., Chen, S.-H., & Yen, C.-F. (2005). Proposed diagnostic criteria of Internet addiction for adolescents. *Journal of Nervous and Mental Disease*, *193*, 728–733.

Ko, C.-H., Yen, J.-Y., Chen, C.-S., Chen, C.-C., & Yen, C.-F. (2008). Psychiatric comorbidity of Internet addiction in college students: An interview study. *CNS Spectrums*, *13*, 147–153.

Korean Agency for Digital Opportunity and Promotion. (2008). *2008 report of the Internet Addiction Survey*. Seoul: Author.

Korean Ministry of Health and Welfare. (2009). *Report of the Internet Addiction Survey*. Seoul: Author.

Kraut, R., Patterson, M., Lundmark, V., Kiesler, S., Mukopadhyay, T., & Scherlis, W. (1998). Internet paradox: A social technology that reduces social involvement and psychological well-being? *American Psychologist*, *53*, 1017–1031.

Kwon, H. K., & Kwon, J. H. (2002). The effect of the cognitive-behavioral group therapy for high-risk students of Internet addiction. *Korean Journal of Clinical Psychology*, *21*, 503–514.

Kwon, J. H. (2005). The Internet game addiction of adolescents: Temporal changes and related psychological variables. *Korean Journal of Clinical Psychology*, *24*, 267–280.

Kwon, J. H., Chung, C. S., & Lee, J. (2009). The effects of escape from self and interpersonal relationship on the pathological use of Internet games. *Community Mental Health Journal*. doi:10.1007/s10597-009-9236-1

Lee, H. C. (2001). A study on developing the Internet game addiction diagnostic scale and the effectiveness of cognitive-behavioral therapy for Internet game addiction (Doctoral dissertation, Korea University, Seoul).

Lee, S. Y., & Kwon, J. H. (2000). Effects of Internet game addiction on problem-solving and communication abilities. *Korean Journal of Clinical Psychology*, *20*, 67–80.

Lee, Y. K. (2000). Psychological characteristics of drug abusing adolescents (Master's thesis, Korea University, Seoul).

Leon, D., & Rotunda, R. (2000). Contrasting case studies of frequent Internet use: Is it pathological or adaptive? *Journal of College Student Psychotherapy*, *14*, 9–17.

Lin, S. J., & Tsai, C. C. (2002). Sensation seeking and Internet dependence of Taiwanese high school adolescents. *Computers in Human Behavior*, *18*, 411–426.

Liu, T., & Potenza, M. N. (2007). Problematic Internet use: Clinical implications. *CNS Spectrums, 12,* 453–466.

Marlatt, G. A., Baer, J. S., Donovan, D. M., & Kivlahan, D. R. (1988). Addictive behaviors: Etiology and treatment. *Annual Review of Psychology, 39,* 223–252.

Ryu, E., Choi, K. S., Seo, J. S., & Nam, B. W. (2004). The relationships of Internet addiction, depression, and suicidal ideation in adolescents. *Journal of Korean Academy of Nursing, 34,* 102–110.

Shaffer, H. J., LaPlante, D. A., LaBrie, R. A., Kidman, R. C., Donato, A. N., & Stanton, M. V. (2004). Toward a syndrome model of addiction: Multiple expressions, common etiology. *Harvard Review of Psychiatry, 12,* 367–374.

Shapira, N. A., Lessig, M. C., Goldsmith, T. D., Szabo, S., Lazoritz, M., Gold, M. S., & Stein, D. J. (2003). Problematic Internet use: Proposed classification and diagnostic criteria. *Depression & Anxiety, 17,* 207–216.

Shin, M. S. (1992). An empirical study on the mechanism of suicide: Validity test of the escape from self scale (Doctoral dissertation, Yonsei University, Seoul, South Korea).

Siomos, K. E., Dafouli, E. D., Braimiotis, D. A., Mouzas, O. D., & Angelopoulos, N. V. (2008). Internet addiction among Greek adolescent students. *CyberPsychology & Behavior, 11,* 653–657.

Song, B. J., Kim, S. H., Koo, H. J., & Kwon, J. H. (2001). Effects of Internet addiction on daily functioning: Three case reports. *Psychological Testing & Counseling, 5,* 325–333.

Weissberg, R. P., Caplan, M., & Harwood, R. L. (1991). Promoting competent young people in competence-enhancing environments: A systems-based perspective on primary prevention. *Journal of Consulting & Clinical Psychology, 59,* 830–841.

Weissberg, R. P., & Elias, M. J. (1993). Enhancing young people's social competence and health behavior: An important challenge for educators, scientists, policymakers, and funders. *Applied & Preventive Psychology, 2,* 179–190.

Widyanto, L., & Griffiths, M. (2006). Internet addiction: A critical review. *International Journal of Mental Health and Addiction, 4,* 31–51.

Yang, C. K. (2001). Sociopsychiatric characteristics of adolescents who use computers to excess. *Acta Psychiatrica Scandinavica, 104,* 217–222.

Young, K. (1996). Addictive use of the Internet: A case that breaks the stereotype. Psychology of computer use: XL. *Psychological Reports, 79,* 899–902.

Young, K. (1998). Internet addiction: The emergence of a new clinical disorder. *CyberPsychology & Behavior, 3,* 237–244.

Yu, Z. F., & Zhao, Z. (2004). A report on treating Internet addiction disorder with cognitive behavior therapy. *International Journal of Psychology, 39,* 407.

CHAPTER 14

Systemic Dynamics with Adolescents Addicted to the Internet

FRANZ EIDENBENZ

A s HAS happened so often in the history of humankind, a new advance in communication technology is now leading to shifts in social and economic paradigms. Ultimately, we see that the Internet opens a whole new ways of looking at the world. Nowadays, the time we have for learning how to make beneficial use of information and communication technology (ICT) is limited. ICT is advancing at an unprecedented pace. Our day-to-day reality has been fundamentally changed over the past decade by new communication capabilities and the flood of information they have unleashed. The Internet generation faces a situation totally different from what their parents have faced. The dynamic rate of change allows no role models anymore, no points of reference. Parents and educators can no longer ask each other: Now how did we handle that? They are familiar with other risks on the road to adulthood but often lack personal experience with cyberspace. They are the first generation challenged to set limits for their children in an area in which the children know more than they do. They should not be daunted by this new situation. They can still draw on their life experiences to set limits. Access to the Internet and cell phones makes young people and children more independent from the adult world, but this independence entails risks as well as opportunities.

ADDICTION AND SYSTEMIC THERAPY

Addiction research shows that family influences play a significant role as risk factors for substance abuse and dependence disorders in youth (Andrews, Hops, Ary, Tildesley, & Harris, 1993; Barker & Hung, 2006; Brook et al.,

1998; Loeber, 1990; Sajida, Hamid, & Syed, 2008; Yen, Yen, Chen, Chen, & Ko, 2007).

Substance abuse in young people is associated with family conflicts, especially with a lack of family communication and a family's inability to resolve problems and conflicts. Psychological problems and a malfunctioning family are crucial risk factors in promoting dependence behavior in young adults (Sajida, Hamid, & Syed, 2008). Kuperman et al. (2001) described and covered in their study the following risk factors for the development of alcohol dependence at a young age: negative parent-child interaction, difficulties with school and human interaction, and early experiences experimenting with different substances (Kuperman et al., 2001).

Liddle and his team reported on protective factors that reduce the probability of developing substance dependence. They include, among others, good academic performance and general family skills (Liddle et al., 2001). Resnick et al. (1997) reported in their research on a number of important protective factors that promote the healthy, nurturing development of young people. Young people feeling close to their parents, perceiving them as caring and having a positive relationship with them, is one influence that has proven positive for development. Others are parents having high academic expectations of children and parental presence and interest in young people and their lives.

These findings are considered highly relevant. After all, a young person's family environment and in particular the perceived family support, the parents' methods and attitudes, as well as the parent-child relationship have all been described in research as not only protective factors for preventing drug dependence but as predictors for the success of therapy in dependence treatment (Brown, Myers, Mott, & Vik, 1994).

These results strongly suggest that the family environment should be included in the treatment of young people for dependencies. Schweitzer and Schlippe (2007) presented systemic approaches as their therapy of choice for young people with addiction problems, noting the close but often ambivalent relationships many addictive clients have with their parents. Numerous studies have shown that planned and continual work with families, as opposed to their occasional inclusion, is efficient and effective especially with adolescents (Sydowe, Beher, Schweitzer, & Retzlaff, 2006). In various studies, Liddle and his team (Liddle, 2004a; Liddle et al., 2001) showed and proved the efficiency of multidimensional family therapy (MDFT). This form of therapy proved effective in reducing substance abuse and in promoting pro-social behavior, improved academic performance, and better functioning family life. Family-oriented interventions have the maximum effect in the treatment of addictive young people, so many are calling for their more frequent use. When compared to cognitive behavioral therapy (CBT), MDFT has proven the more lasting treatment method (Liddle, Dakof, Turner, Henderson, & Greenbaum, 2008).

In a meta-analysis of 47 randomized controlled trials, the effectiveness of systemic family therapy was demonstrated for young people with substance disorders and psychiatric comorbidities, and its effect remained stable over longer catamnestic periods (Sydowe, Beher, Schweitzer & Retzlaff, 2006).

In connection with the treatment of online addiction, Barth and his team (2009) mentioned that parents are becoming a focal point of therapeutic interest. Multiple interventions are undertaken to strengthen parental monitoring. The intent is to focus on the young person's problematic behavior as well as to examine its role in family dynamics.

In their study, Yen and his team compared substance-linked addictions with online dependency. They showed that Internet addiction and substance dependencies among young adults occur in connection with the same negative family factors (Yen, Cheng, Chen, Chen, & Chih, 2007). This fact suggests that systemic therapy is effective for online addiction and for substance-linked addictions and can achieve comparable effects. More precise research is needed in this area, however. Given the existing and increasing need for treatment, the field cannot afford to wait for scientific proof of this effectiveness. The object at present must be to gather experience from actual clinical practice to develop treatment approaches and then evaluate them scientifically.

ONLINE COMMUNICATION

The Internet and the applications associated with it are virtual spaces that can be viewed as separate worlds where different conditions and rules of social interaction apply. Knowledge of these conditions and rules is essential to the understanding and treatment of online addicts.

Face-to-face or offline communication is more personal and identities are defined. Making contact is complex and involves anxiety; separation is sometimes difficult. The perception of self and others is complex and all five senses are involved. That means that in general offline communication is more sensual and connected with physical experiences (Eidenbenz, 2004).

Screen-to-screen or online communication creates the possibility of anonymity or a selectable identity. People "feel less restrained and express themselves more openly" (Suler, 2004). Suler calls this phenomenon the online disinhibition effect.

Establishing contact and separation is easier and free of anxiety. Projections in how we imagine our communication or game partners are more intense and the perception is less sensory and physical than in face-to-face communication. In the online world, people just behave differently: "When people have the opportunity to separate their actions online from their in-person lifestyle and identity, they feel less vulnerable about self-disclosing and acting out" (Suler, 2004).

Playing with and developing virtual identities accommodate the search for personal identity so typical of adolescence. The chance of donning a mask also has a certain fascination for adults. Anonymous figures on the Internet are generally younger, better looking, smarter, and also wealthier than in reality. It is quite tempting to be all that, at least for a while. The problem begins when you look in the mirror and can no longer accept yourself the way you are, preferring instead to immerse yourself in a virtual world. The inability to accept yourself or reality can lead to compensatory usage (Eidenbenz, 2008), as is often the case with addicts.

Repeated experiences in virtual worlds leave tracks in the brain and result in priming effects. Future action follows these tracks if pleasant stimuli are associated with them (Spitzer, 2005). Virtual worlds can unleash the kind of intense emotional reactions associated with a release of dopamine. Young people are particularly vulnerable to these reactions, as the adolescent's frontal cortex, the part of the brain responsible for self-discipline and self-control, is not yet fully mature (Jäncke, 2008; Small & Vorgan, 2008).

If sufficiently clear structures and limits are put in place by the parents, a young person can make complementary uses of the Internet that can expand or enrich real life.

ROLE DIFFUSION AND ROLE DIVERGENCE

The photojournalist Robbie Cooper photographed people with their screen characters, also known as avatars (Cooper, 2007).

The first picture (Figure 14.1) shows a boy who spends 55 hours a week playing the online role-play game EverQuest. He says: *"I just want to win*

Figure 14.1   (*Photograph by Robbie Cooper.*)

Figure 14.2   *(Photograph by Robbie Cooper.)*

respect from people in the game, to be somebody in the EverQuest world. But it cost me. Everything else in my life started to suffer—my social life, my schoolwork, even my health" (Cooper, 2007). Judging from this huge investment of time, he is obviously making compensatory use of the game.

The young man in the second pair of photos, Figure 14.2, devotes even more time to weekly gaming in Star Wars Galaxy, 80 hours a week. In this instance, a handicap excludes other leisure-time activities, so the virtual world enriches the boy's life without replacing other activities: *"Online you get to know a person behind the keyboard before you know the physical person. The Internet eliminates how you look in real life, so you get to know a person by their mind and personality"* (Cooper, 2007).

This is a case of complementary usage and does not constitute addictive behavior.

The very idea of Internet addiction is still a bone of contention today. Addiction, it is argued, arises from behavioral patterns, not from the medium itself. Grohol (1999) and Kratzer (2006) stated that the Internet is not the cause of the disorder, noting that the disorder is an expression and symptom of hidden personality problems or primary disorders, such as depression. Hahn and Jerusalem (2001), however, argued quite correctly that the applied criteria are normative descriptive characteristics from phenomenology and not etiological characteristics, as is the case with alcohol dependency.

Instead of *Internet addiction*, the Swiss Addiction Professionals Association (2008) recommends the term *online addiction*, because it expresses a pivotal aspect of the fascination as well as the addiction involved. You could say that *online* means being connected with a worldwide network in the here and now, having your finger on the pulse of the times, being linked to current information or to other people.

Online addiction will be used to refer to a spectrum of excessive behaviors and impulse control problems based on known addiction criteria, as cited by Kimberly Young (1998) and by Hahn und Jerusalem (2001), two researchers at Humboldt University in Berlin.

ADDICTION AND COMMUNICATION

The communicative aspect plays an important role for many online addicts. They often communicate by keyboard or with earphones and microphones, not only in chats and communication systems but also in online computer games. The medium appears to be more appealing when other individuals are active online behind the monitors as opposed to having an electronically controlled partner on the other end. Games and other types of usage in real time appear to have greater potential for being addictive. Young (1998) said that gaming addicts have been found to have a ratio of online to offline play time that is extraordinarily high compared with other users (Rehbein, Kleimann, & Mössle, 2009).

The availability of a large circle of virtual contacts such as, for example, in Facebook and the alluring opportunity of regressing to an "ocean feeling" of the kind felt in connection with the Internet appear to satisfy a desire to be connected to other people (Bergmann & Hütter, 2006).

For affected individuals, the contacts they build up in virtual worlds successively replace the ties they have in real life (Petry, 2010). They are scarcely aware that they are simultaneously neglecting and losing social contacts in the real world. One possible hypothesis would be that a dependency on interactive media (i.e., online addiction) is linked to a desire for communication or is related to communication problems. This is one reason why building and encouraging real human contact and the conflicts associated with it is so crucial to the treatment of online addiction.

Understanding and treating online addiction entails more than a careful analysis of the new media, a subject to be covered in detail later. It also requires knowledge of substance-related addictive disorders, according to Schweitzer and Schlippe (2007). There are many parallels between these two forms of addiction, yet also many essential differences.

Aside from parallels that emerge from the joint diagnosis of addiction, the following similarities are worth noting and relevant to treatment:

- Motivation to change or seek treatment is minimal.
- Change is sought only after great pressure is applied.
- There is denial or trivialization of usage and its effects.

Aspects that differ from substance-related addictions include:

- Information and communication technologies are viewed as positive.
- There is high availability and inconspicuous usage.
- Costs are low and not based on usage (flat rates).
- There is a lack of knowledge about the risk of addiction and its potential harm.
- Abstinence from new media is possible only temporarily or not at all.

Besides these parallels to substance-related addictions, other aspects must be considered in the treatment. Based on their own research, Hahn and Jerusalem (2001) mentioned the risk of high expectations in the new media combined with minimally developed control of impulses to use the media. Availability and low costs will be even more widespread in the future, and living without an Internet connection is already becoming seemingly impossible.

Online addicts seem to have difficulty in using the new media in a self-controlled manner, especially the sector or area in which they are addicted.

TREATMENT

Different psychological treatment methods are suggested in the pertinent literature, but it is still impossible to give evidence-based therapy recommendations (Petersen, Weymann, Schelb, Thiel, & Thomasius, 2009).

Cognitive behavioral therapy (Schorr, 2009) is the approach most frequently mentioned. Stress-coping strategies and training in social and communication skills were two other methods described as helpful, as were family therapy activities. In addition to cognitive-behavioral individual therapy, group therapeutic approaches such as the ones developed by Orzack et al. (2006), Wölfling and Müller (2008), and Schuler, Vogelgesang, and Petry (2009) are also used. The advantage of the latter approaches is that clients interact within a group and real communication occurs. The group is a source of support, and clients have a chance to learn from the experiences of fellow group members. The same would theoretically apply to self-help groups. After repeated attempts to form a group in Zurich, we realized that addicts would not keep appointments without multiple reminders or pressure from the outside. They remained at home instead, unable to tear themselves away from their monitors.

Many approaches have mentioned that the inclusion of the family in the therapy of adolescents is helpful and useful (Young, 2007), but very little has been published thus far on the use of systemic therapy in treating online addiction. Barth et al. (2009) noted that parents and families are becoming the center of therapeutic interest to offset maturity deficits, emotional control, and a lack of control over actions.

Fondation Phénix (Nielsen & Croquette-Krokar, 2008) in the Swiss canton of Geneva offers family therapy to online addicts as one of its services. It considers family sessions important for working through issues that give rise to conflicts and for supporting parenting skills and promoting a healthy emotional climate.

Young (1999), too, recommended family therapy as a way of promoting communication skills and preventing recriminations. Grüsser and Thalemann (2006) pointed out a further aspect in support of family therapy, namely the family as an important factor in the origin and continuation of dependencies.

Systemic therapy gives due consideration to the client's social environment and incorporates it directly into the treatment. This approach helps the client to establish an emotional point of reference and to rebuild contacts. Systemic techniques such as questions on reality constructs or circular questioning (Schweitzer & Schlippe, 2007) also aid clients in clarifying their own self-images and the way they are perceived by others. Families should be included in treatment strategies. In their study about family factors, Yen, Yen, Chen, Chen, & Ko (2007) noted that "a family-based preventive approach for Internet addiction and substance abuse should be introduced for adolescents with negative family factors."

CENTER FOR BEHAVIORAL ADDICTION: CLINICAL EXPERIENCES

The outpatient clinic Open Door for Zurich received its first inquiries about online addiction from addicts and their family members 10 years ago. In the year 2000 the clinic organized an international conference: "Online Between Fascination and Addiction"; Professor Kimberly Young and Professor Mathias Jerusalem were among the speakers. And 2001 research together with the Humboldt University, Berlin (Eidenbenz & Jerusalem, 2001), made clear that online addiction in Switzerland is an existing problem.

Today, the successor center for behavioral addiction is specialized in treatments of online and game addiction. People from far and wide go there seeking advice. Since 2005 the center has treated between 25 and 40 cases a year with 150 to 200 sessions. The main people seeking help are parents of boys or young men aged 13 to 25 who feel utterly helpless in dealing with their offsprings' excessive computer usage. Cases of young females have been quite rare thus far. We seldom see adults on cybersexual affairs, problematic consumption of pornography, and so on.

The Center (Center for Behavioural Addiction, 2009) is known for this subject matter, so the people contacting it have classified their problems based on self-assessments. The following symptoms are described in the application:

- Decline in performance (school, work)
- Disinterest in social environment
- Decline in offline leisure interests
- Fatigue (chronic lack of sleep)
- Aggressiveness, nervousness if online usage is hindered

The main group of young online addicts has a basic problem with motivation. That is one central reason why families are integrated into the treatment in the vast majority of cases. The parents seeking advice come from all social classes, from physicians to blue-collar workers. A striking number of them are associated with the information technology (IT) industry.

THE CLIENT'S ENVIRONMENT AS A RESOURCE

Clients' failure to acknowledge their illness and their lack of motivation pose serious obstacles to treatment. The further advanced the addiction is, the more difficult it is to influence the client. Young people in particular live in the here and now and are looking for exciting, stimulating experiences. They have trouble judging the long-term impact of their actions on their future prospects (Jäncke, 2007). That is why young people belonging to the risk group of online addicts (cf. Eidenbenz, 2001, 2004; Hahn & Jerusalem, 2001) have to rely on reactions from people in their everyday lives. This assumes of course that parents are willing to set limits, where necessary. In many cases, parents are overwhelmed by this task, especially if they have diverging opinions or have fallen out with each other. This can be especially true of parents who are separated.

If teachers, employers, and other individuals important to clients in their everyday lives can detect early signs of a problem, there is a much better chance of responding or initiating treatment on time. Therefore, different tests exist on the Internet to give clients and the people in their everyday lives an idea about the risks of being addicted. The test developed in 2006 gives clients a direct idea about the risk of being addicted (Eidenbenz, 2006). There is also a need for information material understandable to those in the client's everyday life; of course, prevention work is included, too (Eidenbenz, 2008).

In addition to personal factors and environmental influences, Internet usage itself or, in this case, gaming is a central factor and must be covered in the treatment. For this reason the findings from a recent representative study dealing with the risks of computer games is presented here in more detail. In this study in Germany involving a random sample of young people ($n = 44,129$) (Rehbein, Kleimann, & Mössle, 2009), it was found that 3 percent of boys displayed addictive gaming behavior; a further 4.7 percent were classified as being at risk; in other words, 7.7 percent were either addicted or at risk. Only 0.5 percent of girls were found to be at risk and 0.3 percent to be addicted. These figures show how minuscule the chances are of an addicted World of Warcraft (WoW) gamer getting to know a girl in his free time.

Online addicts and avid gamers have worse grades in school, even in physical education, which is a sign of their lack of exercise. Addicts have a higher rate of absenteeism and a higher level of anxiety about school. On the scale developed by the authors to measure computer dependency, WoW was by far the game with the largest potential for addiction, followed by Guild

Wars, Warcraft, and Counterstrike. A total of 36 percent of the WoW users played for more than 4.5 hours a day.

Dysfunctional stress regulation, a factor proven in a longitudinal study in Berlin (Grüsser, Thalemann, Albrecht, & Thalemann, 2005), also goes a long way toward explaining this addiction. This term refers to a technique people use to escape from dealing with real-world problems or conflicts. Other key variables that were emphasized were the role of experiencing power and control, and gaming as the sole source of a sense of achievement. Young people less adept at empathizing and communicating with others in conflict situations also showed an increased risk. Being the target of serious violence from parents in childhood is a further risk factor. Another disconcerting finding is that 12.5 percent of all addicts answered "Yes, often" when asked if they had ever considered suicide as opposed to 2.4 percent of the normal group.

This picture coincides with our experience that eight out of 10 young gaming addicts are WoW players. Therefore this game will be explored in greater depth at this juncture.

Working with this type of Internet addiction requires a minimal understanding of online games. It is important for young people that the therapist shows an interest in the world (the virtual world) in which they spend so much of their free time. The therapist does not necessarily have to be well-versed in the various online role-plays, but it is important and helps to build trust if the professional can pose the right questions and use key terms such as *avatar* (the player's visual on-screen in-game, also known as character), *level* (levels of advancement achieved by the avatar), *raid* (battle), and so on.

This is the only way that a therapist can build up a differentiated picture of the client's virtual identity and its connections to and status within the online community. These questions might include the following: "What level do you play at? What kind of avatar do you have? Do you have multiple avatars? Are you in a guild or a clan? What status does the clan have and how many of you are there? How many raids do you do per week and when do you do them?"

The following interview was conducted with a client at the end of therapy and is included here to give the reader an insight into a young person's viewpoint. This example shows the crucial influence of environment on a client's willingness to submit to treatment.

Interview with Martin, 16 Years Old, Information Technology (IT) Apprentice

Interviewer: Martin, you live with your brother at your mother's and were addicted to WoW. How did your gaming career start?

Martin: I played Nintendo and Game Boy in preschool. When I was 8 we played on my father's computer. He is a computer specialist. I first got into 3-D online games when I was 12. Then my brother got me onto the strategy game Counterstrike and from there I started playing WoW about a year and a half ago.

Interviewer:	How did you find out about the game?
Martin:	I did a six-month introductory course in the IT department at a major bank. Half of my fellow trainees played WoW, some of them very intensively.
Interviewer:	And then?
Martin:	I got into the role-play quite quickly. First I would play an hour a day; then the time I'd spend increased rapidly. WoW is a game that drives you forward. You constantly set new goals, want better and better sets of armor and weapons, and then you play more and more frequently.
Interviewer:	How long were you playing during your most intensive period?
Martin:	That was six months ago. I gamed five to six hours each night after work. On weekends, I would get up at 1:00 in the afternoon and play until 1:00 or 2:00 at night.
Interviewer:	Didn't you ever have the feeling you were playing too much?
Martin:	No. I always compared myself to friends who were gaming even more than I was.
Interviewer:	Didn't anyone ever try to stop you?
Martin:	Of course. My mother tried all kinds of things. There were several times she hid my monitor, also my keyboard. We argued a lot about gaming; also because I didn't abide by her rules. She even wanted to take me to a psychiatrist, but I refused. That just sounded too weird.
Interviewer:	What triggered you to want to change your gaming behavior?
Martin:	I realized my friends had stopped asking me to go out with them. Add to that the big pressure my mother was applying all the time. She actually took away my PC for 14 days.
Interviewer:	How did you react to that?
Martin:	I was furious.
Interviewer:	Was it boring for you?
Martin:	I watched more TV, started to draw again, and read books.
Interviewer:	You two had a counseling session together. Why did you agree to it?
Martin:	Another thing was that my supervisor at work brought up my excessive gaming to me directly and pushed me to get counseling.
Interviewer:	Had your performance declined?
Martin:	No, but she knew I often overslept in the morning. Sometimes I would also call in sick when I did that. And my mother had talked to the supervisor.
Interviewer:	And today? Do you still play?
Martin:	Yes, but I have been able to cut down my gaming time with the rules we set during counseling. I abstain from gaming one day a week and play only until 10:00 at night.

At the start of therapy, therapists must create a stable setting that allows them to work through this issue until lasting and constructive progress can be made.

INITIAL SITUATION

As with other forms of addiction, parents, family, or partners suffer from the online addicts' excessive behavior whereas the addicts themselves scarcely acknowledge that they have a disorder. The classic initial situation is that a parent calls and complains about his or her son's excessive gaming behavior, but the son refuses to come in for therapy, claiming he has no problem. Here is the first core challenge: how to motivate the young man to come in for therapy. The initial situation should be exploited. The parents have a problem. They cannot cope with the situation and are highly motivated to take action. The therapy can get off to a good start if the parents can persuade their son to show up for an initial session. This is a decisive step toward restoring the parents' hierarchical position, which is often shifted in families struggling with addiction. It is also recommended that the parents talk with their son and make it clear that the problem can be resolved only in cooperation with him and any siblings he may have. The sense of solidarity in the system increases the chances of establishing a new equilibrium in the family without putting the whole blame on the young person.

Various authors (Petersen, Weymann, Schelb, Thiel, & Thomasius, 2009; Yen, Ko, Yen, Chen, Chung, & Chen, 2008) have pointed out comorbid disorders such as depression and associated low self-confidence, low drive, a desire for recognition, and attention-deficit/hyperactivity syndrome (ADHS), as well as substance-related disorders. Besides asking which underlying disorders play a role in the young person's online addiction, the therapist should consider other family members in the diagnosis (e.g., an overprotective mother and the interaction of the system as a whole).

Family members and possibly other individuals from the client's everyday life should participate at least in the initial sessions. Young addicts are more likely to agree to therapy if this approach is taken, especially if they see the prospect of their own issues being taken seriously or feel that the difficulties they are facing are understood by others.

It is also equally important to lay the groundwork for enabling the therapy to continue over an extended period of time. Without support and also pressure from parents and siblings, young people usually cannot muster motivation for any more than two to three sessions at most. Even if they want therapy, it is difficult for them to give their therapists priority over their virtual world and to keep appointments. Family sessions eliminate the problem of young addicts not showing up for appointments. Young people will participate even in extended therapies if they continue to feel pressure and solidarity from the system.

THERAPY PROCESS: PHASE MODEL

The systemic approach suggested here is solution and resource oriented and is adopted from Carole Gammer's model of phase-based family therapy (Gammer, 2008). The approach also integrates various elements of cognitive behavioral therapy, particularly Kanfer's self-management therapy (Kanfer, Reinercker, & Schmelzer, 2006). The therapy process is divided into four phases of therapy intended to represent an ideal course of treatment. The entire therapy process generally takes between six and 18 months.

START-UP PHASE (ONE TO THREE SESSIONS)

The goal in the start-up phase is to create a cooperative working relationship and to obtain information for conducting an individual and systemic analysis of the problem (diagnostics) and for forming hypotheses.

The first therapy session should ideally be attended by the entire family. After having everyone introduce themselves and establishing a respectful and open attitude within the group, the therapist asks all present about resources and about any immoderate behaviors—for example, the father working excessive hours.

This approach is a way of putting the problem in perspective (others in the family may also display tendencies toward addiction) and to take pressure off the addict. Then everyone is asked what they would like to change and what problems they would like to discuss as a family. To relieve the identified patient of further pressure, he should not be addressed first or last in this round. Normally he will not raise any issues at first, except a desire for fewer restrictions to be placed on his Internet access. Asked whether they are otherwise satisfied with their parents and have a large enough allowance and so forth, most young clients give their parents high ratings. The object is to have the gamer raise issues he would like to see changed in real life, particularly in connection with his parents. He should be given opportunities to express the problems that young people normally have with their parents. The therapist can be available as a mouthpiece and the ally of the client at this stage. Sometimes young people do not want to say anything at first, feeling that the only reason they are there is because their parents pressured them into coming. They should not be criticized for this. If a client remains silent, other family members can be asked to speculate on why he is not saying anything. In the first session, the young person should receive positive reinforcement by having his good traits also mentioned. The parents should be able to endure a certain amount of confrontation.

The client's addictive behavior is discussed in the course of the session. It is important for the therapist to show an interest in the client's behavior specifically as it relates to the game, focusing on triggering factors and mood-regulating aspects. When does the client play, in which situations, and what other leisure activities does he have? The role and function of the avatars in the group are also important, along with their identity—for example, set of armor and status. This information allows hypotheses to be formed on the function of the addictive behavior and on any deficits the client may have in real life.

The initial sessions often also serve as crisis interventions, in which conflicts are clarified and de-escalation options are discussed. Initial rules on computer usage are laid down, and the parents are encouraged to set clear limits. It is helpful if clients draw up a weekly schedule and record how long and how frequently they play and include other Internet activities in which they are involved. The act of recording and the way clients deal with this task, namely whether they can do it and if so, how they do it, provide more precise information for establishing further hypotheses. At the same time, the young clients should be encouraged to formulate their own issues outside gaming activities and to justify them effectively.

When forming hypotheses, the therapist should draw on the entire system to arrive at a systemic diagnosis. How clearly defined are the hierarchies within the family? In which situations do the parents prevail and how do they do so? Is there evidence of sibling cooperation? How does the system deal with conflict? The client's individual behavioral patterns should also be integrated in diagnostic deliberations (e.g., strategies for avoiding conflict and stress, impulsiveness, withdrawal tendencies, and traumatic events). The therapist should develop a strategy for working on pertinent issues in the phase that follows, and should explain this strategy in general terms to the family.

It is recommended that two to three sessions be suggested for the start-up phase, followed by an interim evaluation.

Changes in symptoms, even minor changes, should be achieved as early as the start-up phase. For example, the amount of Internet consumption should no longer be determined based on assumptions but recorded precisely in a log. A good approach is to cloak this log as a homework assignment. Most importantly, however, the family should come again with the client. Siblings and clients can give their opinions on that, but the parents should ultimately make the decision based on the therapist's suggestion. They should prevail over young people on this issue.

MOTIVATION PHASE (THREE TO FIVE SESSIONS)

The motivation phase focuses on understanding the obvious circumstances that cause and maintain addiction and on addressing related topics such as recognition, respect, and methods for dealing with conflict and stress (Wölfling, 2008). Parallel to these activities, the client should reduce his Internet usage and be required to build up a minimum of self-control.

Clients themselves have difficulty in admitting they have a problem. Admission is essential for making a change, and family members can help clients greatly in taking this step. Clients will not be willing to take further concrete action until they realize that excessive gaming has negative effects on their lives and that they no longer have control over their gaming behavior. It is important that family members take an approach toward the client that is firm in terms of the limits set on gaming but interested in terms of the content of the game. Speaking in the first person for themselves, family members should express how their son's or brother's addiction has affected them and which risks they see for the client and for relationships within the family.

It is important to find out exactly what fascinates the client about the game and how he could have comparably satisfying experiences in real life. The extent of gaming should then be reduced in stages, based on rules and goals jointly worked out by the client and family members. Both positive and negative consequences can be formulated in connection with implementing these rules and goals.

Everyone should work together to uncover the causes of the addictive behavior step-by-step. These causes could include, for example:

- *Lack of say:* Does the client or, for example, his sister have any say in what happens in the family, and if so, with regard to what?
- *Lack of respect:* Do the family members express respect and recognition toward each other?
- *No sense of achievement:* Does the client ever have a chance to be a hero in the family?

When the client actively criticizes the people and situations in his everyday life, for example his father, he has taken an important and necessary step toward showing a willingness to face conflict.

At the same time, the client must build up alternative recreational activities in his real life. Counselors and family members should all support this renewal of interest in the client and encourage him to act on it.

EXPLORATORY PHASE (THREE TO EIGHT SESSIONS)

This phase seeks to promote an in-depth exploration of the causes of online addiction as well as active discussions and respect within the family and alliances at parental and sibling level. Points of conflict with the parents and siblings are clarified and processed.

Deeper structural causes meant to be dealt with in this phase could be, for example, the client's conflict with his father, his inability to find closure on a family member's death, or his separation from one of the parents. Gamers often immerse themselves in virtual worlds to wage heroic fights because they have almost no say in their own families. Perhaps the father, frequently absent and working long hours, shows his son little respect, least of all for his hard-won victories in his virtual world. The boy never has a chance to take on a dominant male position. He should be supported in expressing anger and rage but also in talking about hurts from the present or even events that occurred years ago.

Both parents must participate when setting the rules for game usage to give a strong and consistent guideline to the client. When working through conflicts at this stage, however, the therapist should keep the other parent from actively participating or interrupting. This ensures a level playing field for a face-to-face encounter and a chance to solve personal conflicts with the father or mother. Resolving the conflict constructively is meant to serve as a model and to encourage the client to try out new behaviors and other roles in real life at home and elsewhere in the client's life.

This phase can also address the role played by other siblings who suffer from the psychological absence of their addicted brother but also want to show solidarity with him. Adequate attention is often not given to their own suppressed issues until the acute addiction problem has been resolved.

In this phase a client might be invited, usually in passing, to come alone the next time if he wants to. Siblings do not need to attend each session during this phase. Sometimes older siblings, for instance adult siblings, could be included for the first time in this phase.

STABILIZATION AND FINAL PHASE (ONE TO THREE SESSIONS)

The client will have reached a level at which a satisfactory change is possible when he effectively controls online times, for example, or takes up other recreational activities, improves his academic performance, deals more constructively with conflicts, and so on. At this stage, it is advisable to schedule further therapy sessions at longer intervals or to include at least one control session. This approach helps to prevent a relapse and can be used to stabilize new options within the family and to support further changes.

Even if the client and his family members have had several discussions and he has reduced his gaming, he may still differ greatly from the others in how he views these matters. The client may consider the objective already achieved, whereas his parents still think there is a need for further action. It is important at this stage to recognize the steps in these changes (e.g., stabilizing or improving school performance, the possibility of now having evening meals together, going to bed at a decent hour, or meeting up with friends). During this phase, the therapist should recap achievements retrospectively or prospectively and guide the family in defining further objectives.

In some cases, children rightly complain that their parents will never be satisfied. By the same token, parents are sometimes not fully content with what is achieved in therapy. It is therefore all the more important to stress and praise minor positive changes that do occur. We should be aware that this work involves addicts. When these types of issues are involved, people seldom are fully satisfied.

ABSTINENCE FROM GAMING

If clients do not succeed in controlling their excessive gaming, it may be necessary for them to stop gaming altogether. Complete abstinence from gaming or problematic uses, not from Internet use (Petersen et al., 2009), may be the only solution in severe cases and with certain games such as WoW, contrary to clinical experiences at the beginning of treatment. This cold turkey approach to game addiction entails certain risks. The client will undoubtedly display an extreme reaction (e.g., aggressive behavior breaking through, depressive withdrawal, or, at the very least, a loss of motivation). Parents sometimes try this experiment themselves. After an escalation, many of them vow to never take this drastic step again.

But parents have to know how to respond at the latest when their son or someone else is endangered (e.g., by threats of violence, murder, or suicide). Before reaching this point, young addicts have already gone through a long period of their parents making threats, imposing restrictions, then caving in and letting them pursue their gaming activities again, and tend not to take them seriously anymore. Recently asked about this fact, a young client said he thought there was only a 30% chance his parents would call the police or an emergency psychiatrist. He had certainly been right up to that point.

The therapist should talk with the parties involved about exactly how they want to handle this type of situation. The young person should be aware of the types of threats that would cause the parents to take action. Where appropriate, the parties could check in advance on where the client could be hospitalized if the situation began escalating dangerously. The therapist should give the family a phone number where he or she can be reached if cases like this arise, and should provide pertinent emergency numbers. In most cases, clients are not hospitalized. The point is to have the parents show that they are serious about the limits they set.

CASE EXAMPLE ON SYSTEMIC WORK

The parents of a 15-year-old high school student contacted the clinic about their son. He was spending over 30 hours a week playing the online game World of Warcraft, and had virtually stopped taking part in family life and family meals and was failing at school. They had had many arguments with him about gaming, and their attempt to cut his game playing time to two hours a day had been a miserable failure. At age 11, M. had begun saving his allowance to buy the individual components for a computer, which he then assembled himself. Up to that point, he had always been content and friendly.

The family agreed to come to the clinic with him and his sister, who was two years younger. In the first session, M. complained about not being understood, while his parents said the gaming was having a devastating effect on them. I suggested that we continue the therapy with the entire family, and everyone agreed. The topic up to the third session was the aggressive arguments the client had with his parents, especially when they tried to restrict his gaming time. Once M. put his hands around his mother's throat when she tried to block his access to the Internet but did not actually choke her.

By their fourth session, the family was dealing somewhat more constructively with conflicts. The client was monitoring his gaming activities with lists he drew up himself and had reduced his gaming time by 10 hours a week. Both father and son had trouble controlling their own impulses, but everyone wanted to live together harmoniously as a close-knit family. In one session, the father and son drew a diagram of the emotions they felt during an argument, which showed a phase-shifted rhythm. The rest of the family commented on the diagram. This approach helped them to gain objectivity and an understanding of the dramatic moments in the argument.

Incidentally, M. had selected two roles in WoW: a healing monk on the one hand and an aggressive warrior on the other. This choice can be interpreted as an expression of how he wanted to develop emotionally.

And alongside his domineering father, it seemed impossible indeed for M. to achieve this situation in the real world, namely, being a heroic and victorious warrior as well as healer or, in other words, being recognized for his achievements while at the same time feeling backing, solidarity, and support in the family.

Various family problems were brought up in the course of the therapy. The son began to confront his father actively after he had been helped by the therapist to formulate his concerns more clearly and was able to overcome his withdrawal tendencies.

He performed better in school and often took part in family meals again. Everyone had made a contribution: The father stopped working such long hours at night, the mother put a Post-it on M.'s monitor 30 minutes before dinnertime, and M. shut off his PC by himself in time to make it to the meal.

M. noted in retrospect that he had defended the therapy in talks with friends because it also benefited him as part of the family, but especially because his own concerns were now taken seriously and he was no longer blamed for everything.

DISCUSSION AND OUTLOOK

The phase model presented in this chapter is not yet evaluated or standardized in a therapeutic manual. It should be considered as a contribution to the overall discussion and is meant to serve as a guideline for developing a therapeutic process.

However, existing literature makes the assumption plausible that the following factors are related with the development of an addicted online behavior: a client's lack of possibilities in everyday life to influence something directly, to gain a sense of achievement, and to work through conflicts.

The family is the core group that offers models on patterns of action and constructive methods of conflict resolution, or in some cases does not. Compassion, empathy, solidarity, and personal responsibility can be learned in the family and serve as models and resources for the client to make changes within the extended environment. Integrating the system into a treatment of online addiction therefore seems a reasonable and useful approach. As with other addiction therapies, perseverance and loving firmness on the part of therapists and family members are required to bring about changes. The goal is to build a culture that has greater knowledge and awareness of the opportunities and risks in dealing with the new media so that individuals are in a position to determine for themselves how they wish to use these media.

Commitment pays off, because therapeutic assistance can favor and enable constructive long-term development, especially in young people.

More research is needed in the future to assess the effectiveness of different treatment methods. What is now certain is that young people need committed individuals in their everyday lives, whether in the family, at school, or in their circle of friends and acquaintances. In the interest of prevention, the ultimate objective is to create an environment that offers appealing opportunities for challenges, encounters, and participation so that young people can be shaped by the incomparable uniqueness of genuinely experiencing real life with all of their senses.

REFERENCES

Andrews, J. A., Hops, H., Ary, D., Tildesley, E., & Harris, J. (1993). Parental influence on early adolescent substance use: Specific and nonspecific effects. *Journal of Early Adolescence, 13*(3), 285–310.

Barker, J. C., & Hung, G. (2006). Representations of family: A review of the alcohol and drug literature. *International Journal of Drug Policy 15*, 347–356.

Barth, G., Sieslack, S., Peukert, P., Kasmi, J. E., Schlipf, S., & Travers-Podmaniczky, G. (2009). Internet- und Computerspielsucht bei Jugendlichen, 41. Retrieved September 3, 2009, from http://www.rosenfluh.ch/images/stories/publikationen/Psychiatrie/2009-02/07_PSY_Spielsucht_2.09.pdf.

Bergmann, W., & Hütter, G. (2006). *Computersüchtig, Kinder im Sog der modernen Medien.* Düsseldorf, Germany: Walterverlag.

Brook, J. S., Brook, D. W., De La Rosa, M., Dunque, L. F., Rodriguez, F., et al. (1998). Pathways to marijuana use among adolescents: Cultural/ecological, family, peer, and personality influences. *Journal of the American Academy of Child and Adolescent Psychiatry, 37*(7), 759–766.

Brown, S. A., Myers, M. G., Mott, M. A., & Vik, P. W. (1994). Correlates of success following treatment for adolescent substance abuse. *Applied and Preventive Psychology, 3*, 61–73.

Cooper, R. (2007). *Alter ego: Avatars and their creators.* London: Cris Boot.

Eidenbenz, F. (2004). Online zwischen Faszination und Sucht. *Suchtmagazin, 30*(1), 3–12.

Eidenbenz, F. (2006). Online-Internet-Sucht-Test. Retrieved July 6, 2009, from http://suchtpraevention.sylon.net/angebote_suchtpraevention/selbsttests/selbsttests_i_f.html

Eidenbenz, F. (2008). Onlinesucht, Schweizerische Fachstelle für Alkohol und andere Drogenprobleme. Retrieved July 6, 2009, from http://www.sfa-ispa.ch/DocUpload/di_onlinesucht.pdf.

Eidenbenz, F., & Jerusalem, M. (2001). *Wissenschaftliche Studie zu konstruktivem vs. Problematischem Internetgebrauch in der Schweiz.* Retrieved October 10, 2009, from www.verhaltenssucht.ch

Center for Behavioural Addiction. (2009). *Zentrum für Verhaltenssucht.* Retrieved April 28, 2010, from www.verhaltenssucht.ch

Gammer, C. (2008). *The child's voice in family therapy.* New York: W.W. Norton.

Grohol, J. M. (1999). Internet addiction guide. *Mental Health Net.* Retrieved November 1, 1999, from http://psychcentral.com/netaddiction/

Grüsser, S., & Thalemann, R. (2006). *Verhaltenssucht, Diagnostik, Therapie, Forschung.* Bern, Switzerland: Huber.

Grüsser, S., Thalemann, R., Albrecht, U., & Thalemann, C. (2005). Exzessive Computernutzung im Kindesalter: Ergebnisse einer psychometrischen Erhebung. *Wiener Klinische Wochenschrift, 117,* 173–175.

Hahn, A., & Jerusalem, M. (2001). Internetsucht: Jugendliche gefangen im Netz. Retrieved July 6, 2009, from http://www.onlinesucht.de/internetsucht_preprint.pdf

Jäncke, L. (2007). *Denn sie können Nichts dafür,* University of Zürich, Department of Neuropsychology. Retrieved July 6, 2009, from http://www.psychologie.uzh.ch/fachrichtungen/neuropsy/Publicrelations/Vortraege/Kinder_Frontahirn_1Nov2007_reduced.pdf

Jäncke, L. (2008). Onlinesucht, Gesundheitsmagazin Puls. *Schweizer Fernsehen.* Retrieved February 18, 2008. www.sf.tv/sendungen/puls/merkblatt.php?docid=20080218-2

Kanfer, F., Reinercker, H., & Schmelzer, D. (2006). Selbst-management-Therapie. In *Lehrbuch für die klinische Praxis* (pp. 121–321). Heidelberg, Germany: Springer.

Kratzer, S. (2006). *Pathologische Internetnutzung eine Pilotstudie zum Störungsbild.* Lengerich, Germany: Pabst Science Publishers.

Kuperman, S., Schlosser, S. S., Kramer, J. R., Bucholz, K., Hesselbrock, V., Reich, T., et al. (2001). Risk domains associated with an adolescent alcohol dependence diagnosis. *Addiction, 96*(4), 629–636.

Liddle, H. A. (2004a). Family-based therapies for adolescent alcohol and drug use: Research contributions and future research needs. *Addiction, 99*(2), 76–92.

Liddle, H. A., Dakof, G. A., Parker, K., Diamond, G. S., Barett, K., & Tejeda, M. (2001). Multidimensional family therapy for adolescent drug abuse: Results of a randomized clinical trial. *American Journal of Drug and Alcohol Abuse, 27*(4), 651–688.

Liddle, H. A., Dakof, G. A., Turner, R. M., Henderson, C. E., & Greenbaum, P. E. (2008). Treating adolescent drug abuse: A randomized trial comparing multidimensional family therapy and cognitive behavior therapy. *Addiction, 103*(10), 1660–1670.

Loeber, R. (1990). Development and risk factors of juvenile antisocial behavior and delinquency. *Psychological Review, 10,* 1–41.

Nielsen, P., & Croquette-Krokar, M. (2008). Psychoscope 4. Retrieved July 6, 2009, from http://www.phenix.ch/IMG/pdf/article_psychoscope_final_cyberaddiction_a_l_adolescence_4_2008.pdf

Orzack, M., Voluse, A., Wolf, D., et al. (2006). An ongoing study of group treatment for men involved in problematic Internet-enabled sexual behavior. *CyberPsychology & Behavior, 9*(3), 348–360.

Petersen, K., Weymann, N. Schelb, Y., Thiel, R., & Thomasius, R. (2009). Pathologischer Internetgebrauch—Epidemiologie, Diagnostik, komorbide Störungen und Behandlungsansätze. *Fortschritte der Neurologie–Psychiatrie, 77*(5), 263–271.

Petry, J. (2010). *Dysfunktionaler und pathologischer PC- und Internet-Gebrauch.* Göttingen, Germany: Hofgrefe.

Rehbein, F., Kleimann, M., & Mössle, T. (2009). *Computerspielabhängigkeit im Kindes- und Jugendalter: Empirische Befunde zu Ursachen, Diagnostik und Komorbiditäten unter besonderer Berücksichtigung spielimmanenter Abhängigkeitsmerkmale.* Forschungsbericht Nr. 108, Kriminologisches Forschungsinstitut Niedersachsen e. V.

Resnick, M. D., Bearman, P. S., Blum, R. W., Bauman, K. E., Harris, K. M., Jones, J., Tabor, J., Beuhring, T., Sieving, R. E., Shew, M., Ireland, M., Bearinger, L. H. & Udry, J. R. (1997). Protecting adolescents from harm: Findings from the national longitudinal study on adolescent health. *The Journal of the American Medical Association, 278,* 823–831.

Sajida, A., Hamid, Z., & Syed, I. (2008). Psychological problems and family functioning as risk factors in addiction. *Journal of Ayub Medical College Abbottabad, 20*(3).

Schorr, A. (2009). *Jugendmedienforschung, Forschungsprogramme, Synopsen, Perspektiven, Neue Gefahren: Onlinesucht* (pp. 380–383). Wiesbaden, Germany: Verlag für Sozialwissenschaften.

Schuler, P., Vogelgesang, M., & Petry, J. (2009). Pathologischer PC/Internetgebrauch. *Psychotherapeut, 54,* 187–192.

Schweitzer, J., & Schlippe, A. (2007). *Lehrbuch der Systemischen Therapie, Therapie und Beratung II, Süchte: Von Kontrollversuchen zur Sehn-Sucht* (pp. 191–212). Göttingen, Germany: Vandenhoeck & Ruprecht.

Small, G., & Vorgan, G. (2008). *iBrain.* New York: Morrow/HarperCollins.

Spitzer, M. (2005). *Vorsicht Bildschirm! Elektronische Medien, Gehirnentwicklung, Gesundheit und Gesellschaft.* Stuttgart, Germany: Ernst Klett.

Suler, J. (2004). The online disinhibition effect. *CyberPsychology & Behavior, 7*(3), 321–326.

Swiss Addiction Professionals Association (2008), *Fachverband Sucht,* Retrieved April 28, 2010, from www.fachverbandsucht.ch

Sydowe, K., Beher, S., Schweitzer, J., & Retzlaff, R. (2006). Systemische Familientherapie bei Störungen des Kindes- und Jugendalters. *Psychotherapeut, 51,* 107–143.

Wölfling, K. (2008). Generation@—Jugend im Balanceakt zwischen Medienkompetenz und Computerspielsucht. *Sucht Magazin, 4*(8), 2–16.

Wölfling, K., & Müller, K. (2008). Phänomenologie, Forschung und erste therapeutische Implikationen zum Störungsbild Computerspielsucht. *Psychotherapeutenjournal*, 2.2008, 128–133.

Yen, J. Y., Ko, C. H., Yen, C. F. Chen, S. H., Chung, W. L. & Chen, C. C. (2008). Psychiatric symptoms in adolescents with Internet addiction: Comparison with substance use. *Psychiatry and Clinical Neurosciences, 62*: 9–16.

Yen, J. Y., Yen, C. F., Chen, C. C., Chen, S. H., & Ko, C. H. (2007). Family factors of Internet addiction and substance use experience in Taiwanese adolescents. *CyberPsychology & Behavior, 10*(3), 323–329.

Young, K. (1998). *Caught in the Net*. New York: John Wiley & Sons.

Young, K. (1999). Internet addiction: Symptoms, evaluation, and treatment. In L. VandeCreek & Jackson (Eds.), *Innovations in clinical practice: A source book* (Vol. 17). Sarasota, FL: Professional Resource Press. Retrieved October 10, 2009, from http://www.netaddiction.com/articles/symptoms.pdf

Young, K. (2007). Cognitive behavior therapy with Internet addicts: Treatment outcomes and implications. *CyberPsychology & Behavior, 10*(5), 671–679.

CHAPTER 15

Closing Thoughts and Future Implications

KIMBERLY S. YOUNG and CRISTIANO NABUCO DE ABREU

A S WE live in a world of growing dependence on technology, it is hard to tell the difference between necessity and addiction. There are times when it is necessary to use technology in ways that are meaningful and productive. Besides, we live in a phase of history in which knowledge is no longer passively absorbed by the individual; that is, nowadays we can act and interact with information in order to establish it as a new expression of our personal and social reality. This makes us eyewitnesses to one of the biggest changes in the history of science: the possibility to interact in real time with people and information. Although many are the descriptions of the Internet's impact in modern life, one of the biggest impacts that can be cited is the progressive change of the *mores* (from the Latin, customs) that regulate and govern human behavior. Less than two decades ago, no adolescent would have even considered the possibility of sharing with someone the experiences of his or her most recent sexual event, but nowadays details of such experiences are blogged so that a few million people may have access. Rather than bringing people near the information, the Internet is contributing to the creation of new forms of relationship (and existence), just to name one example. The concept of intimacy, therefore, is gaining more and more new dimensions. More than ever, then, the rules governing human relationships are being directly affected by virtual life. The good news is that we move forward with giant steps toward the future. The bad news is that we may not be very prepared to deal with them.

So, this book is not trying to focus on the negative aspects of Internet use or mobile technologies. Perhaps the new technologies are just a new stage of our personal vulnerabilities; therefore, the book is not trying to demonize technology. It is pointing out that there is a serious danger in the overreliance on technology to fulfill emotional, psychological, and social needs. Although many of the mental disorders being observed have existed for a long time—for example, Roman *vomitoria* (places used for vomiting after taking part in banquets) may have been an early manifestation of bulimia nervosa, or even some religious women of the Middle Ages who fasted to attain holiness (for instance, St. Catherine of Siena) may have actually been rehearsing the first acts of what would be considered in future to be anorexia nervosa—the Internet addiction and new technologies have never before been present. Therefore, their understanding and analysis are still under scrutiny by researchers and clinicians.

For instance, the BlackBerry is a must-have gadget. A lingo has sprung up around the devices, with heavy users calling themselves "CrackBerry addicts," referring to the highly addictive form of cocaine. The surreptitious glance downward, head bowed, to check for e-mail during a meeting is referred to as a "BlackBerry prayer."

While many users say owning a BlackBerry makes them more efficient, some researchers—and some spouses, as well—say the wireless devices offer their owners new ways to distract themselves, often annoying others in the process. The seemingly exponential growth of portable technology has sparked fears that people are becoming addicted or swamped by gadgets and their uses. One major consequence of this phenomenon is that the line between work and private life is much more blurred, now that e-mail and cell phones provide a 24-hour link between employers and staff. That is, the former private life has lost its total intimacy. Furthermore, experts believe that even the decision-making process of the average person can be adversely affected. However, others think that the bombardment of various communications can enhance the brain's ability to process information.

Researchers have become concerned about the addictive nature of handheld devices and the effect on decision-making processes. They fear that individuals lose spatial judgment while using them, so instead of walking through the door you walk into it. You are more prone to have a car accident if you drive. Because of this danger, many states have initiated laws to stop people from texting while driving. The reality is that with such portable technology, you take it with you anywhere, and like with any other addiction, the more time people spend using their technology the less time they spend in socializing or in family time.

Some people have become concerned about "interruption overload" and "continuous partial attention" associated with BlackBerry use. Our ability to multitask prevents us from being fully present at the task at hand. Being forced to divert attention to interrupting messages can cause memory loss and decreased memory accuracy, besides contributing to a state of emotional anesthesia or emotional numbing. The technology makes it difficult to make decisions because of this mental parsing of our brains' attention and memory.

It is easy to dismiss an addiction to mobile technologies as harmless. We live in a world that strongly encourages mobile phone use, especially among teenagers. However, new studies have found that mobile phone addicts can be seriously affected at the psychological level but, as they don't show any physical symptoms, their dependency goes unnoticed to others, contrary to what is noticed in the abusive use of alcohol or other substances. About 40 percent of young adults admit using their mobiles for more than four hours a day. Most of them say they spend "several hours a day" on their phones. Many are "deeply upset" if they miss calls or messages, and some of them say they think they hear the phone's ring tone when in fact they have not received any call. Generally, mobile addicts tend to neglect important activities (job or studies), drift away from friends and close family, deny the problem, and think about their mobile constantly when they do not have it with them. Most mobile addicts are people with low self-esteem, who have problems with developing social relationships and feel the urge to be constantly connected and in contact with others. They can become totally upset when deprived of their mobile phones, and switching off their phones causes them anxiety, irritability, sleep disorders or sleeplessness, and even shivering and digestive problems. It is common for owners to "humanize" these devices with names and also attribute feelings of safety and support to them.

To disengage from technology dependency, in whatever form it takes—be it to Facebook, texting, playing role-playing games, viewing online pornography, or checking e-mail—the core of recovery must be to understand new ways to relate to others.

We have seen a theme throughout this book that technology has facilitated new ways of obtaining information and connecting with others. For those who suffer from depression, anxiety, social phobia, or Asperger's syndrome, online connections provide those individuals new ways of developing and continuing relationships. Social media such as Facebook and MySpace model how connections are formed in the real world and provide that information through a set of applications that allow people to share information, photos, or videos of events. Instead of trying to build a community, social networking is trying to make new connections. Certainly, for those who have trouble connecting in the real world, online communication is an alternative medium to build connections. This is important. Throughout the book, we have seen in various chapters how interactivity through online communication and applications has been a major source of addictive behavior. Children and adolescents have engaged in multiuser role-playing games to the point of excess. Adults have engaged in virtual communities such as Second Life to the point of excess. These are a few examples illustrated through the text. This shows that the interactivity of online applications is most compelling.

Yet, too much dependence on technology also creates new social problems as people become socially withdrawn, disliking real-life meetings, avoiding working in collaborative teams, and fearing face-to-face contact, while preferring only online communication. Perhaps this explains why the social networks have increased exponentially in recent years. It is possible that these spaces make people feel more heard or they can more easily express their personal difficulties and anxieties. Therefore, the virtual life connects people on one hand and separates them on the other.

We can see how the Internet has changed the way we live. We can do research, book hotels, make airline reservations, shop, instantly keep in touch with family and friends, and make new friends and connections. It is difficult to differentiate healthy from unhealthy Internet use because of its utility as a productive tool. We have examined much of the latest research that focuses on the most problematic areas of Internet use—those areas being interactive applications such as online role-playing games, sexual chat rooms or interactive porn sites, or multi-user Internet gambling sites—to help therapists understand the most common reasons individuals may be seeking treatment. These provide theoretical concepts to guide the evaluation process and treatment planning.

The book examines several treatment strategies that vary depending on the client's age, presenting problem, and individual situation. This type of specificity is highly relevant when treating a person who suffers from Internet addiction. In clinical practice, a 16-year-old who is addicted to multiuser role-playing games may need a different treatment approach than a 50-year-old man who is addicted to Internet porn. These variables have been fleshed out and elaborated upon throughout the book, enabling therapists to use it as a reference guide as they encounter clients with a wide variety of Internet-related issues and concerns. Even if a client presents with depression or anxiety, when the Internet plays a factor in these other psychiatric conditions, therapists will be able to utilize this information to facilitate treatment planning.

Like many addictions, treatment is often necessary to fully recover from Internet addiction. Sometimes it is not enough to simply go cold turkey. Having a professional to talk with enables clients to explore deeper issues that led to the maladaptive or unhealthy online behavior. The technology and the Internet may be symptoms of other problems a client is experiencing. Therapists need to help clients address these problems, identify new goals, and learn new behaviors and/or responses while we, as clinicians, still learn how to better assess and treat the impacts of the overuse. Although we are seriously committed as professionals, our knowledge is still embryonic. Therapists ultimately must help clients understand why they use technology and whether it is a way of avoiding or escaping from a real problem.

Therapists vary greatly depending on the level of training, the type of education and experience they have had, and the amount of knowledge that they have about the Internet and technology. It is not unusual to find professionals who claim to be totally ignorant regarding these new pathologies, though specialized and trained professionals in this area are slowly emerging. Therefore, this book provides a comprehensive examination of Internet addiction, technology addiction, and the overall impact technology has on human behavior. The information contained in the book helps therapists learn and appreciate the role of technology in the client's life. It also opens an important discussion about how technology can have a profound emotional and psychological impact.

We see that the Internet is not a benign tool but technology. Its misuse has consequences that may need clinical intervention. We also see that in extreme cases, residential care may need to be considered. Interestingly, addicts from all walks of life falsely assume that just stopping the behavior is enough to say, "I am recovered." There is much more to full recovery than simply refraining from the Internet. Complete recovery means addressing the underlying issues that led up to the behavior and resolving them in a healthy manner; otherwise, relapse is likely to occur. This book describes how compulsive online use often stems from other emotional or situational problems such as depression, attention deficit/hyperactivity disorder, anxiety, stress, relationship troubles, school difficulties, impulse control problems, or substance abuse. While using the Internet offers a convenient distraction from these problems, it does very little to actually help clients cope with the underlying issues that led to the compulsive behavior.

As we write this, new inpatient treatment centers are opening around the world and in the United States, such as the Redmond, Washington, program, reStart. This is a 45-day inpatient facility completely devoted to Internet addiction recovery. Often addicts refuse treatment until they become deeply in debt, are about to lose (or have lost) their jobs, are facing legal charges, are threatened with divorce or separation, or are thinking about suicide. Once problems have become this severe, it is important to seek professional help for evaluation. Some addicts may require more or less time, so recommendations will be made following an initial assessment. In most cases, the treatment program or a residential care facility is specifically designed to fit the needs of the client, and most sessions focus on individual treatment, educational groups, and family therapy where appropriate to best manage and address the intense feelings surrounding the addiction.

The need to be online may be so powerful that treatment may require clients to go through a kind of detoxification program. In the same manner an alcoholic goes through a detox program to dry out, detox programs such as the Video Game Detox Center in the Netherlands have emerged to wean clients from excessive online use. While the concept of detoxification as part of the recovery from alcoholism is well understood, it is still a relatively new intervention applied to the Internet but one that must be explored in severe and intensive cases.

With the growing popularity of the Internet, increased awareness within the mental health field will help clinicians provide knowledgeable care and intervention for the Internet-addicted client. Since this is a new and often laughed-about addiction, individuals may be reluctant to seek out treatment, fearing that clinicians may not take their complaints seriously. Drug and alcohol rehabilitation centers, community mental health clinics, and clinicians in private practice should be aware of the negative ramifications of compulsive use of the Internet and recognize the signs, which may easily be masked by other comorbid conditions or by legitimate use of the Internet.

While this book provides one of the first comprehensive resources to empirically examine Internet addiction, the field is still quite new and further research should continue to investigate its impact, risk factors, and treatment effects. Areas for future research should also explore systematic comparisons with various treatment modalities such as cognitive therapy, behavior modification, psychoanalysis, gestalt therapy, interpersonal therapy, group counseling, or in vivo counseling within an online community to determine their therapeutic impact and efficacy for this new client population. Future studies should also investigate treatment differences among the various types of Internet abuse and through the different therapeutic modalities. Studies should examine whether treatment outcomes vary along each subtype. Methodologically, as many studies rely on self-reported data to gauge changes in online behavior, psychological health status, and social functioning, the results may be biased. Because client self-reports may be inaccurate, future studies should include the requirement that the reports be verified by relatives or friends close to the client and/or by periodic computer monitoring to ensure greater reliability of self-reported data. Finally, as the mental health field devotes more resources to recovery from Internet addiction, future studies should evaluate how specific treatment intervention impacts long-term recovery. We know that many forms of psychotherapy are shown to be effective in the short term, but not efficient in the long term. Traditionally, addiction treatment programs for alcoholism and drug abuse have offered patients a mix of treatment approaches. A promising new strategy involves matching patients to interventions specific to their needs. In this same manner, matching which types of Internet addiction respond best to which treatments can increase outcome effectiveness, and such treatment matching is likely to increase long-term recovery.

To pursue such effective recovery programs, continued research is needed to better understand the underlying motivations of Internet addiction. Future research should also focus on how psychiatric illnesses such as depression or obsessive-compulsive disorder play a role in the development of compulsive Internet use. Longitudinal studies may reveal how personality traits, family dynamics, cultural aspects, or interpersonal skills influence the way people utilize the Internet. Last, more outcome studies are needed to determine the efficacy of specialized therapy approaches to treat Internet addiction and to compare these outcomes against traditional recovery modalities. This is especially true for various client populations impacted by Internet addiction—children versus adults, for instance.

The main theme emphasized throughout the chapters in the book and in our final chapter is prevention. Prevention of Internet addiction is the key element. We can see how prevention has been well established in alcohol and drug dependency. We know that awareness helps in prevention of many medical disorders. We understand that prevention works. Prevention and awareness also play a significant role in Internet-related conditions. If we could institute more awareness programs for Internet addiction, people would not believe it is a harmless tool. As the various authors and contributors for this book have outlined, the Internet and technology in general have a potential impact. This certainly can be a positive impact, and again, our book is not meant to demonize the Internet and technology, but rather it takes the view that the establishment of responsible computing programs to help people understand the potential negative aspects will ameliorate the consequences.

It is our hope that this book will help clinicians facilitate their practices in this new and evolving field. Internet addiction has grown tremendously since first identified in 1996 at the American Psychological Association. It is a field with tremendous impact. Almost everyone all over the world utilizes the Internet for a wide variety of reasons. Still in its infancy, the Internet itself has had a tremendous impact. We have only begun to understand its full potential. The journey along the way has been incredible. The Internet has made life easier in many ways by its many applications. It has also made life more difficult through its potential for addiction. We can only hope that this new knowledge will spark more research to better understand the future of technology and how it will continue to influence our way of life.

Before concluding, we would like to thank all contributors to this book, from widely different countries, for helping with the team task of refining and improving the knowledge and therapies involved in the treatment of Internet addiction. We also thank John Wiley & Sons for believing in our project and for giving us all the necessary support.

Author Index

Subject Index

STUDY PACKAGE
CONTINUING EDUCATION
CREDIT INFORMATION

Internet Addiction: A Handbook and Guide to Evaluation and Treatment

Our goal is to provide you with current, accurate and practical information from the most experienced and knowledgeable speakers and authors.

Listed below are the continuing education credit(s) currently available for this self-study package. *Please note: Your state licensing board dictates whether self study is an acceptable form of continuing education. Please refer to your state rules and regulations.*

COUNSELORS: PESI, LLC is recognized by the National Board for Certified Counselors to offer continuing education for National Certified Counselors. Provider #: 5896. We adhere to NBCC Continuing Education Guidelines. This self-study package qualifies for **5.0** contact hours.

SOCIAL WORKERS: PESI, LLC, 1030, is approved as a provider for continuing education by the Association of Social Work Boards, 400 South Ridge Parkway, Suite B, Culpeper, VA 22701. www.aswb.org. Social workers should contact their regulatory board to determine course approval. Course Level: All Levels. Social Workers will receive **5.0** (Clinical) continuing education clock hours for completing this self-study package.

PSYCHOLOGISTS: PESI, LLC is approved by the American Psychological Association to sponsor continuing education for psychologists. PESI, LLC maintains responsibility for these materials and their content. PESI is offering these self- study materials for **5.0** hours of continuing education credit.

ADDICTION COUNSELORS: PESI, LLC is a Provider approved by NAADAC Approved Education Provider Program. Provider #: 366. This self-study package qualifies for **6.0** contact hours.

Procedures:

1. Review the material and read the book.

2. If seeking credit, complete the posttest/evaluation form:

   -Complete posttest/evaluation in entirety; including your email address to receive your certificate much faster versus by mail.

   -Upon completion, mail to the address listed on the form along with the CE fee stated on the test. Tests will not be processed without the CE fee included.

   -Completed posttests must be received 6 months from the date printed on the packing slip.

Your completed posttest/evaluation will be graded. If you receive a passing score (70% and above), you will be emailed/faxed/mailed a certificate of successful completion with earned continuing education credits. (Please write your email address on the posttest/evaluation form for fastest response) If you do not pass the posttest, you will be sent a letter indicating areas of deficiency, and another posttest to complete. The posttest must be resubmitted and receive a passing grade before credit can be awarded. We will allow you to re-take as many times as necessary to receive a certificate.

If you have any questions, please feel free to contact our customer service department at 1.800.844.8260.

PESI LLC
PO BOX 1000
Eau Claire, WI 54702-1000

PESI

Internet Addiction: A Handbook and Guide to Evaluation and Treatment

PO BOX 1000
Eau Claire, WI 54702
800-844-8260

Any persons interested in receiving credit may photocopy this form, complete and return with a payment of $20.00 per person CE fee. A certificate of successful completion will be sent to you. To receive your certificate sooner than two weeks, rush processing is available for a fee of $10. Please attach check or include credit card information below.

Mail to: PESI, PO Box 1000, Eau Claire, WI 54702 or fax to PESI (800) 554-9775 (both sides)

CE Fee: $20: (Rush processing fee: $10)   **Total to be charged** _____

Credit Card #: _____ **Exp Date:** _____ **V-Code*:** _____
(*MC/VISA/Discover: last 3-digit # on signature panel on back of card.) (*American Express: 4-digit # above account # on face of card.)

	LAST	FIRST	M.I.

Name (please print): _____ _____ _____

Address: _____ Daytime Phone: _____

City: _____ State: _____ Zip Code: _____

Signature: _____ Email: _____

Date Completed: _____ Actual time (# of hours) taken to complete this offering: _____hours

Program Objectives After completing this publication, I have been able to achieve these objectives:

1.Identify the criteria used to diagnose Internet addiction.	1. Yes No
2. Describe the etiology associated with developing Internet addiction	2. Yes No
3. Understand the prevalence rates associated with Internet addiction.	3. Yes No
4. Identify the social needs that Internet usage fulfills.	4. Yes No
5. Understand the issues surrounding online gambling and gaming addictions.	5. Yes No
6. Understand the issues surrounding cybersex addiction and compulsivity.	6. Yes No
7. Describe treatment techniques for adults suffering from Internet addiction.	7. Yes No
8. Describe ways of dealing with Internet infidelity among couples.	8. Yes No
9. Describe treatment techniques for adolescents suffering from Internet addiction.	9. Yes No
10. Describe prevention methods for Internet addiction for adolescents.	10.Yes No
11. Describe the Twelve-Step Recovery in inpatient settings for Internet addicts.	11.Yes No
12. Describe future trends in the technology addiction field.	12.Yes No

PESI LLC
PO BOX 1000
Eau Claire, WI 54702-1000

ZNT042735   CE Release Date: 8/04/2010

Participant Profile:
1. Job Title: _____ Employment setting: _____

1. By using _____ as a model, Young first developed an eight-item screening questionnaire to describe symptoms of compulsive online use.
a.   eating disorders
b.   sexual addiction
c.   Twelve-Step Recovery
d.   pathological gambling

2. An Internet addict's use of the computer is less about using it as an information tool and more about finding
a.   a recreational outlet for tension
b.   an effective way to communicate with friends
c.   a way to increase personal income
d.   a psychological escape to cope with life's problems

3. The Internet Addiction Impairment Index was developed to help therapists
a.   classify impairments levels
b.   facilitate third party reimbursement for treatment
c.   document progress in treatment
d.   prevent client relapse

4. Those who suffer from _____ may be at greater risk to develop problem Internet use.
a.   social anxiety
b.   depression
c.   loneliness
d.   all of the above

5. Among adolescent populations, _____ has been found to be one of the most addictive online applications.
a.   chat rooms
b.   multi-user role-playing games
c.   online commerce
d.   virtual casinos

6. Treatment for Internet addiction is similar to those methods used for _____ behaviors like pathological gambling or overeating.
a.   destructive
b.   compulsive
c.   psychological
d.   irrational

7. The primary goal of Internet addiction treatment is
a.   Internet abstinence
b.   Moderate Internet use
c.   Restoring personal self-confidence
d.   Avoiding loss of employment income

8. Regarding Internet infidelity, having ones needs met through _____ will adversely affect an ongoing long term face-to-face relationship.
a.   online porn
b.   chat rooms
c.   interactive gaming
d.   an online affair

9. According to treatment professionals, _____ is the most common model or approach used to understand and treat Internet addiction at this time.
a.   psychoanalysis
b.   object relations therapy
c.   insight therapy
d.   cognitivebehavioral therapy

10. _____ means investigating the underlying issues that led up to the behavior and resolving them in a healthy manner; otherwise, relapse is likely to occur.
a.   Complete recovery
b.   Initial evaluation
c.   Problem identification
d.   Marital counseling

PESI LLC
PO BOX 1000
Eau Claire, WI 54702-1000